Let Me Sell
You a Ferrari

Let Me Sell You a Ferrari

A Dealer's Memoir

Robert E. Guarino

McFarland & Company, Inc., Publishers
Jefferson, North Carolina

All photographs are from the author's collection unless otherwise indicated.

The stories in this book reflect the author's recollection of events. Some names, locations, and identifying characteristics have been changed to protect the privacy of those depicted.

Library of Congress Cataloguing-in-Publication Data

Names: Guarino, Robert E., author.
Title: Let me sell you a Ferrari : a dealer's memoir / Robert E. Guarino.
Description: Jefferson, North Carolina : McFarland & Company, Inc., Publishers, 2021 | Includes index.
Identifiers: LCCN 2021011954 | ISBN 9781476681221 (paperback : acid free paper) ∞
ISBN 9781476639697 (ebook)
Subjects: LCSH: Automobile dealers. | Ferrari automobile. | Automobile industry and trade. | Guarino, Robert E.
Classification: LCC HF5439.A8 G83 2021 | DDC 381/.45629222092 [B]—dc23
LC record available at https://lccn.loc.gov/2021011954

British Library cataloguing data are available

ISBN (print) 978-1-4766-8122-1
ISBN (ebook) 978-1-4766-3969-7

© 2021 Robert E. Guarino. All rights reserved

No part of this book may be reproduced or transmitted in any form or by any means, electronic or mechanical, including photocopying or recording, or by any information storage and retrieval system, without permission in writing from the publisher.

Front cover: (top) The author beside a Ferrari F40 outside the Autohaus, 1991; (bottom) a Ferrari 365 GTB/4 "Daytona" (Matthias Elbe); (background) a pen and ink drawing of the Autohaus (author's collection)

Printed in the United States of America

McFarland & Company, Inc., Publishers
Box 611, Jefferson, North Carolina 28640
www.mcfarlandpub.com

For my traveling partner,
Jack

Acknowledgments

I SHOULD START BY THANKING my wonderful family. Whatever I pursued, my parents were there to help and to support me although it was my brothers Jim, Richard, Doug and Gerry whose incessant car talk made me think of memorializing all these experiences and events.

Our all too infrequent get-togethers inevitably led to competitive stories almost always revolving around automobiles, and imported ones primarily. These tales went back even to the 1940s with brother Jim's 1940 Ford, and traversed the decades up until 2019 with brother Doug's exploits with his burning Aston Martin. What these discussions did for me was to bring back to memory how my brothers had impacted my adventures and accomplishments; to them I owe so very much.

I would also like to mention the people along the way that encouraged me to pursue my interest in automobiles and those who helped me attain my goals, such as Bill McNaughton, Jack Crusoe, Lindy Hansen and many automobile dealers who assisted a young and inexperienced salesman to learn about the business.

I also want to thank Bill Morgan for his assistance in understanding the author publisher relationship; Jack DePalma for his introduction to the vagaries of Hollywood and its complex scenes; to Ruedi Baggenstoss, our Swiss connection, that helped in finding the ways to those beautiful European roads and to Steve Wilson of McFarland for keeping me in the fast lane of indexing.

My business partner Fritz Muelhaupt and his wife Alice made much of this possible, and we were fortunate through the years to have an exceptional staff including Jim Theriault and Linda Nickerson, who created many of the stories I remember today.

Lastly the most thanks goes to my traveling partner Jack Leonard whose skill at navigation made sense of our many European trips and their destinations

His keen eye also helped review much of this manuscript and prevent me from racing ahead too quickly with stories that never would have made it into print.

And to him this book is dedicated.

Table of Contents

Preface — 1
Introduction — 3

1. Carless — 5
2. The Speedster — 14
3. Auto Engineering — 30
4. Off to the Races — 46
5. Autohaus — 59
6. Porscheless — 71
7. Automatico — 84
8. And Then There Were Two — 99
9. Sixes and Twelves — 109
10. No Gas for the Speedy — 121
11. The 308 — 135
12. The Boxer — 149
13. Snowbound — 161
14. Mondial — 176
15. Madame Ibarra — 185
16. Maranello — 197
17. The Red Machine — 211
18. Il Commendatore — 220
19. GTO — 231
20. Italy, Italy — 242
21. 200 MPH! — 253
22. Ciao, 328 — 266
23. The Blue Prince — 279
24. Mugello — 289

Epilogue — 296
Index — 299

Preface

THE INCREDIBLE DESIGNS, the sounds of V12 engines that have never been duplicated, the heritage of racing victories that stand alone in the automobile world; these are some of the thoughts that come to mind when someone—almost anyone—hears or sees the name Ferrari.

I was fortunate enough to be part of that world for some 30 years when I was a factory authorized dealer for Ferrari automobiles in the small coastal town of Cohasset, Massachusetts, some 20 miles southeast of Boston. Prior to that I had been a salesman at one of the leading imported car agencies in the northeast: Auto Engineering in Lexington, Massachusetts, who were dealers for not only Ferrari but also Mercedes-Benz, Porsche, Alfa Romeo, Maserati, Volvo, Aston Martin, BMW and Jaguar automobiles.

It was an education and training experience that far exceeded what I expected as a recent college graduate who couldn't settle on a direction and decided to try his hand at selling cars. And what cars they were—just about all the automobiles of the times that car enthusiasts recognized and esteemed.

This automotive autobiography is about my history of connections to automobiles and specifically to the Ferrari brand. It starts when I was 18 and my older brother Jim, after being stationed in Germany in the late 1950s, returned home to Milton, Massachusetts, with a Mercedes-Benz sedan which kindled my interest in foreign cars. As it turned out this enthusiasm was contagious as it was transferred to my three younger brothers, Dick, Gerry and Doug, who all worked at Autohaus at one time or another and shared my passion for foreign cars.

After working in Lexington for three years, I and Fritz Muelhaupt, one of the mechanics with whom I had become friendly, had the opportunity to start our own dealership, Autohaus. We became factory authorized dealers for Ferrari cars from 1967 until 1993 and the story mainly is about our involvement with the Ferrari factory, their cars, and the fascinating people who bought them and drove them and the often colorful events in the general operation of a Ferrari dealership.

But it wasn't only Ferraris, as over the years Autohaus was also an authorized dealer for Datsun/Nissan, BMW, Porsche, Rover and Alfa Romeo cars and we were intimately involved with every other imported car at one time or another in what has been called the "golden age" of sports cars.

The narrative concentrates, however, on the connection with the Ferrari factory (Ferrari SpA), their U.S. arm, Ferrari North America, and the people associated with them including Enzo Ferrari himself, his son Piero Lardi, Leonardo Fioravanti of Pininfarina and many others who worked for them in various capacities. I talk about the many exciting trips I took to Italy and to the factory in Maranello as a guest of Ferrari, their racing cars, and the opportunities I had to drive many of their automobiles on their famous—and challenging—race tracks.

My frequent traveling to Europe and back instilled in me a gradual understanding of what both cultures wanted and enjoyed automotively, and also gave me the ability to interact with our customers in a way that demonstrated both the American and European passion for cars and how that related to everyday driving.

The cars, the trips, the roads and the people made for a story that I thought I should tell. I hope readers will feel the exhilaration and sense the excitement that we encountered pretty much every day as Ferrari dealers. It was quite a ride.

Robert E. Guarino

Introduction

It was a fairly small room, nothing like the oversized office of Max Hoffman that I had seen in New Jersey, but rather a space that was defined not by its size, but by its ambiance and resident. There were black and white photos all over the walls, along with many trophies and plaques on bookcases and tables, and there, under a row of windows looking out to the factory courtyard, was Enzo Ferrari seated at his desk on which were stacked copies of his recently published book titled *Piloti, Che Genti*. I had seen him a few years before here in Maranello at a brief meeting of introduction he had given to us North American dealers, but had never met him personally.

By his side was Claudio Squazzini, the President of Ferrari North America, who would tell Ferrari, as he introduced each dealer, which dealership we represented and which city we were from, and with that Ferrari would open a copy of the book and sign it with his hallmark purple pen and then hand it to us while shaking our hand. There was nothing perfunctory about it as you could see how pleased he was to meet us all, and the dealers' faces showed their pleasure to meet Ferrari. When Fritz went up to receive his copy, Ferrari nodded and smiled to acknowledge that they had met before. It was quite a moment for Fritz, and for us all.

And then it was my turn, so as I approached the desk Claudio introduced me saying in Italian, "Here is Mr. Guarino, the dealer from Boston," and Enzo smiled, took a book from the stack, signed it and shook my hand, while giving me the book. All I said was *piacere* and *grazie* when receiving the book, but the emotion I felt was really unexpected. It was as though I had officially become part of his family and this was his way of personally welcoming me. I was somewhat overwhelmed as I went back to the side of his office where Fritz was standing. Over the years I had met a number of what you could call important automotive people and various well known entrepreneurs, politicians and even movie celebrities, but this was different. I don't think it was until that moment that I realized how much I revered him as an automobile revolutionary and I guess as an Italian one at that. Truly unforgettable.

But then, most of my encounters with Ferrari the automobile in all its iterations and Ferrari the factory and its manufacturing and distribution arms, and all the people associated with the brand, had been truly extraordinary. So how did I arrive at this magical moment in the automotive world? That is the story that I thought worth telling.

Hence these memories.

1

Carless

As a teenager, I often had cars on my mind, but not Ferraris. Sure, I knew about them as rarely seen and even more rarely purchased exotic cars, especially in eastern Massachusetts. But that changed when one summer day in 1958 after returning from sailing with my friend Barry's father, Ernie, we spotted in the parking lot of the Savin Hill Yacht Club a very foreign looking black coupe.

We couldn't figure out what it was from a distance, although the chrome wire wheels meant it was probably European, and as we got closer we realized it was a big car, but still unrecognizable. It wasn't until we could read the script on the trunk that we knew it was a Ferrari, the first one either of us had ever seen. We looked inside and saw the huge tachometer and speedometer and the purposeful shift lever. On the outside it was very beautiful but also plain, no fins or excess chrome here. Wow, that's what all that automotive press fuss was about, and their glowing accounts of seeing

1960 Ferrari 250GT Coupe, similar to the first one I ever saw (Thesupermat/Wikimedia Commons).

and driving Ferraris. We never did see the driver, but when I got home I started scouring my brother Jim's magazines and found which model it was—a 250GT coupe.

That was a rare sighting, we thought, and I wondered if I would ever get to see one again, or any Ferrari for that matter, or hear those magical 12-cylinder sounds that I read so much about. Doubtful. I never could have imagined in my nascent automotive brain that I would be driving and selling the same Ferrari 250GT coupe model some seven years in the future.

My appreciation of imported cars was through my older brother Jim, the authority on all things automotive. He was driving a 1955 Mercedes 220 sedan that he had bought in Germany while stationed with the U.S. Army in Heidelberg.

After two years in Germany that he had managed to save enough money to buy a used Mercedes-Benz so he and his cohorts would have "wheels" to drive around much of Europe and accumulate tales that only he can tell. But that car is not the one he returned home with because about a year later he had the opportunity to purchase the 1955 220 that had belonged to the owner of the *Heidelberg Zeitung*, the local newspaper, who had an even fancier Benz that had been chauffeur driven, which meant it had a curtain that could be raised and lowered to cover the rear window for added privacy. And that is the car that Jim brought back to the States in 1957.

My early driving experience was confined to the (very) occasional use of my Dad's 1955 Ford Fairlane standard shift, on which Jim taught me to drive, and which I got to drive only to run errands for Mom and even more rarely to go to church. Having quickly became very devout in the late 1950s when I realized that this girl I was seeing planned on attending every Catholic Mass during the month of May, I told my parents that it was the proper Catholic thing to do. So Carolyn and I would meet daily at St. Mary's and pray together—at least that was the story. Her father was a Chrysler dealer and every so often she would arrive driving a 1957 Imperial 4-door which I thought was the most beautiful design then on the road.

When Jim had returned from the Army our knowledge of imported cars had begun to change. We suddenly became foreign car experts, reading all we could in the few sports car magazines of the time, going to auto shows and gymkhanas. The most memorable ones were held by the MIT Sports Car Club which had Triumphs competing against MGs against Corvettes against 300SL Gullwings! It was exciting and hilarious at the same time seeing these cars designed for race tracks going around pylons instead as they leaned and accelerated in such a small venue with their drivers working the steering wheels as if they were driving tractors.

We started visiting automobile showrooms that had imported cars as Jim wanted to drive every different one he could find, often pretending he wanted to trade the Mercedes, which few dealers knew much about. So while they were assessing the "trade-in" value of this car, we would be able to drive one exotic car after another; Jaguars, Austin-Healeys, Sunbeams, Borgwards, Panhard Dynas, Citroëns, Porsches and many others.

As a result of these sporadic car tests I began to accumulate a knowledge of how these various cars really performed and handled and I was able to store away their different traits and recall them at will. To this day I can still remember the sight, the

Jim's 1955 Mercedes Benz 220 with Mom in front; Boston, 1959.

sounds and personalities of just about all of the vehicles I have ever driven—they have never left me. It was different than reading an analysis and "road test" that was recounted by the magazines of the day, some of which I agreed with, but many of which I didn't.

I had been bitten by the "foreign car bug," but had no car of my own as I had no money, no job and had just stopped attending Worcester Polytechnic Institute (WPI) after one semester of much harder than imagined engineering studies. So for now I would have to settle for the occasional drive in the 220.

That summer I was able to get a job working in an architect's office as a draftsman (the WPI experience helped a little) and was accepted by Northeastern University (NU)—somewhat reluctantly, as they had accepted me before I decided to go to WPI instead. Anyway, I was happy to be back in school and looked forward to their work study program where I could earn money to pay tuition and to save up for my own car—perhaps a nice used Jaguar XK 120! But it didn't work out that way, as the

Jim and Giulietta—his 1960 Alfa Romeo Giulietta Spyder Veloce, a car ahead of its time.

work program, while providing experience in your own field, didn't pay very much at all, so a car was way out of reach.

Meanwhile Jim finally traded the Mercedes and bought a true sports car—a white Alfa Romeo Giulietta Spyder Veloce that he purchased from Gaston Andrey Motors in Framingham. Now that was a car, with beautiful lines, smooth transmission, incredibly easy top to put up and down, and the coolest cigarette lighter to be found anywhere. Just behind the shift lever was an ashtray and inside that was a "hole" surrounded by a casing, into which you would put an unlit cigarette and then push down the casing, and then voila! your cigarette was lit. Never mind that you had to take your eyes off the road to accomplish this remarkable feat, and that soon the ashes would blow in your eyes when the top was down, which it mostly was, it was sooo cool.

But I didn't get to drive the Alfa much as Jim was always off somewhere chasing the ladies. I, still living at home, commuted to school with some friends who would pick me up in the morning and sometimes drive me home, or I would take the MTA and the bus which would get me back just fine. But I still had no transportation of my own until Jim decided to augment his motoring stable with a 5 hp 1958 Vespa 150. Suddenly we were on the Via Veneto in Roma, zooming around—no helmets, no belts, no protective clothing, but it didn't matter as the Vespa was slow and we mainly stayed on back roads, or the breakdown lane on the highway (safe, huh?). So after getting familiar with the Vespa, I asked Jim if I could use it sometimes when he was away in the Alfa, and he said yes with certain restrictions; no night driving, no trips to Northeastern with the bizarre Boston traffic, and no passengers, such as our younger brothers. I agreed to everything and for the first time at my carless 20 years of age, I had access to some wheels.

It was the summer of 1960 and it was a beautiful one. I was regularly using the Vespa to bop around while adhering to Jim's rules, even if I considered them unreasonable. Actually it was tough, for one of my best friends of the time was my cousin Elaine Biagi, who had spent some time in Italy and was familiar with the Vespa lifestyle. So occasionally I would take her for a ride and she would sit on the back "sidesaddle," just like the Italians in Rome. I can still hear her mother saying *stai composto* or compose yourself, as we left her driveway for a short ride. But the rides turned out to be not so short as we infringed on another of my brother's rules by deciding to go into Boston for a ride

Author on 1960 Vespa 150 with brother Doug. Couldn't give him a ride (rules).

on the Public Garden swan boats, what with this beautiful summer weather and all. So off we went, the two of us on the scooter with no helmets, no belts, no protective clothing, and driving to Boston in the breakdown lane of the recently finished Southeast Expressway. Someone was carrying rosary beads.

I fessed up to my brother—such a nice guy—and he didn't seem to mind that much; in fact he said if you're going to take trips like that you should take the Alfa. What?! The only thing I had to do was be careful and put gas in the car, and at 22 cents a gallon I could fill it up. So it was with that I got to drive the Alfa by myself—and sometimes with cousin Elaine.

It was so cool, but it all ended rather suddenly as the result of an error on my part. When going to Jamaica Plain one morning via Blue Hill Avenue and about to turn onto Morton Street, I spotted another Alfa spider, a red one, with a girl driving it coming towards me on the Avenue. As she passed, and as I was turning left, I grinned and waved at her—and expertly drove over the curb, blowing out the left rear tire on the Alfa. Yikes! The traffic stopped, I stopped, the girl in the other Alfa stopped—what a scene. As I nursed the car to a parking lot, the rest of the scene dissolved as if it hadn't occurred. But the tire was still flat and the driver of the other Alfa was there too. She couldn't have been nicer or more beautiful, and after I explained that it was my brother's car, she gave me instructions as to where the spare was, where the jack was and where it went, etc. The storybook scene ended as I was tightening the lug bolts on the wheel, when she disappeared, never to be seen again.

The ruined Pirelli Cinturato was $35, a week's pay. But I had to replace it as neither Jim nor I would have it any other way. So that was that. Back to no car, no Alfa, no Vespa—no life! But things would change again because unbeknownst to me, all these scooter rides and sports car rides had convinced Elaine that she needed a sports car too. So after persuading her father (rather easily I think) that she should have a new MGA roadster, she joined the sporty crowd with a new beige with red leather 1600 MGA. Was I happy—for her I mean.

It was up to me, of course, to teach her how to properly shift, stop and put this slow but beautifully handling car through its paces. Elaine was a very good student and in no time was causing me to tighten my seatbelt as we whizzed around the fantastic roads through the Blue Hills in Milton. It was actually in this car, on those Milton roads, that I really learned how to drive and to understand the dynamics of drifting and downshifting and to learn the techniques of double clutching so as to not beat the synchros, something that was not an issue in the Alfa. The underpowered MG was in fact the perfect sports car in which to learn those driving skills as the car was so forgiving.

Jim in his Alfa and I in cousin Elaine's 1960 MGA, ready to race.

Elaine was enrolled at a college in Boston and occasionally we would rendezvous and drive around the city in the MG with the top down. Too cool. I remember in October we had read about John F. Kennedy going to a Democratic rally for his presidential campaign to be held at Mechanics Hall on Commonwealth Avenue, so we decided to see if we could get a look at him in his well publicized motorcade before he got to the hall. It was mobbed.

We found a place to park the MG and walked along Commonwealth Avenue to get close to the hall and then it started to rain. We stood there waiting for his car along with what seemed thousands of others, when a sort of roar emanated from the throng and we could see his car approaching. I think it was a late model Lincoln convertible with the top down, and JFK was standing up waving to everyone. The car was going very slowly as it approached the entrance to the hall, and as it slowed he turned and looked at us—no, at Elaine, very definitely at Elaine, who had no hat on and was drenched as was everyone. He smiled at her then turned to the other side of the street as the car disappeared into the hall's entrance. It was unforgettable! We looked at each other and without her saying a word, I nodded my head and said "Yes, that did just happen!" And of course we never forgot that moment as we both felt that we had met JFK.

Although I was still living at home and commuting with my friends, things were about to change as I was thinking of pledging a fraternity, something I had also done at WPI and that probably contributed to my early exit. But this fraternity had a house that you could live in and commute with your "brothers" back and forth to school, and at night you could study together. What with all that camaraderie it was bound to be an educational experience in itself. So as I was meeting some other fellows who also were considering pledging I met one in particular with whom I hit it off right away.

I was walking down a corridor between classes at NU when I heard "Hey Mercedes." What, who? "Hey Mercedes," someone yelled again and this guy came up to me and said, "What model do you drive?" Well, Jim had bought two Mercedes three-pointed star patches that Mom had sewn onto these windbreakers that we wore on the Vespa rides, and I had mine on that day. That's how I met Stan Williams, who saw the rare and enigmatic symbol and called out. He was a real nice guy, destined to be one of my best friends.

As Stan and I became buddies, he was the one who created my sobriquet of "Reggie van Gearshift" when he found out that my initials were REG and that fitted in nicely with TV star Jackie Gleason's character Reggie van Gleason III. Stan commuted from Wellesley to school in a Volvo 122 but he also had an MGA fixed head coupe into which he was having a Volvo engine installed. Love those dependable Volvos. He too was a sports car fanatic. So we talked cars and girls and soon I introduced him to some of my friends who were thinking of pledging the fraternity. Although he didn't seem too keen on it to begin with, he soon agreed to pledge with us. So we pledged, and were hazed, in good spirits, and were finally accepted as brothers of a local fraternity, Sigma Phi Alpha, as part of a pledge group of 20 students.

It was shortly after becoming a brother that I was able to convince my father that living at the fraternity house would be a good environment for me. Board was

Mercedes-Benz logo, a seldom seen star in the 1950s.

only twenty dollars a week, including two meals a day! I agreed to work in his office on Saturday mornings for that small recompense and he finally agreed. Living at the house was what I expected except that the studying part was harder to do than I expected (I think *National Lampoon* made a movie about that) so I did a lot of that in the college's libraries. We studied, then worked, then studied more as Northeastern's co-op program did what it advertised and gave you an education plus a means to afford it. Living at the fraternity was exciting and instructive as there were students from all the years who helped with course choices and sometimes homework; and then there were the parties and also alumni.

The alumni association owned the house and so to supervise the premises and to handle financial matters, they would have regular meetings at the house and would interact with undergraduates on a fraternal level. It was elevating to see what some had accomplished with an NU education. The alumni also had annual banquets which active brothers were invited to, for a modest fee, and I decided to go to one with a group from my pledge class. It was held a very posh banquet hall in Brookline, and as I remember there were 60 or 70 people there who enjoyed a great meal (we thought) and a number of the usual speeches and award presentations. A good time for sure.

I was staying at home the weekend of the banquet and the next morning I felt sort of queasy. Was that an understatement! I soon became violently ill and couldn't even get out of bed. When Monday came around I couldn't get back to school, so in came our family physician who diagnosed some sort of stomach disorder. Maybe food poisoning! The next day a fraternity brother called to see where I was and when I told him that I had become ill, he said, "Oh, you too?" It turned out that about 30 of the banquet attendees had also become sick from food poisoning, as a result of a kitchen worker who was not only dishing up salads, but salmonella as well. I had contracted the most severe case, having probably eaten the most that night, and ended up missing over a month of classes.

When I returned there was a meeting with the dean, who thought I should probably repeat the semester as there was too much lost time. I disagreed and told him that I would double up on my studies, take makeup exams and do whatever else necessary to "catch up." I had already lost a year at WPI and Northeastern was a five year school, which meant that I was going to be a "six year man" (without a master's), and there was no way I wanted to be a "seven year man" if that term even existed. The dean finally agreed and so back I went to class, exhausted, emaciated and definitely educationless. Eventually I caught up with my classmates through hard work and some very accommodating instructors. Things were looking up but I couldn't imagine just how rosy events were going to become.

Fred Swartz had been in my pledge class and became a brother when I did. He was funny, talkative and a real sport and had a brother who was a newly minted attorney. At the request of some alumni his brother had looked into the liability of the banquet hall regarding the salmonella cases and had decided that a class action suit was in order. So no sooner had I returned to school than I was offered a settlement of $2,200 (less Fred's brother's cut, who, beginning with this case, became a world renowned product liability attorney) for all my pain and suffering. I wasn't sure if it was enough, but I took it anyway, immediately dreaming of my own first car!

With a net check to me of $1,300 there were so many choices; an XK120 or 140, my first choice; an MG or Triumph, I didn't think so; a late model American car like a Ford or DeSoto, no way; so many options, so little time, I thought. With the help of my older brother, my car crazy classmate Larry Gopen, and my fraternity brothers I scoured the newspapers and the used car lots. I came awfully close to buying a bugeye Austin-Healey Sprite (with no right front fender) which we test drove in a slushy storm with the top (was there one?) down, getting soaked in the experience; but no, too slow. Then I settled on a red with tan leather Jaguar XK140 roadster; it was fassst, handled well, and had a decent top and tires, and although my father was against it, I was all set. I put a small deposit on it and was arranging the insurance with Dad when I had a call from Stan, who had just seen a '55 Porsche Speedster for sale at an MG dealer in Wellesley. It had just been traded in the night before, Stan found out, and the dealer said if I took it right away before they fixed the door dent, I could have it for $1100. Whaaat! A Porsche for $1100 and a Speedster at that! So I bought it.

2

The Speedster

So it happened. At the age of 21 I had my first car, and it was a Porsche! Affectionately known as the "blue bathtub," it fit right in at the fraternity house where brothers had recently acquired an interesting array of cars: a '56 Austin-Healey 100, a Triumph TR3, a '62 Corvette convertible and finally Stan's MGA coupe with the Volvo engine (an MGV?). Quite a lineup, we thought. It wasn't long before there were daily races along the Jamaica Way between the Jamaica Pond rotary and the Fenway.

The Speedster was an incredible car, one of the three Porsche models of the mid-1950s, along with the Cabriolet and the Coupe, available at the time through the importer Max Hoffman. The Speedster, which weighed in at less than 1700 pounds, was the opposite of the Jaguar XK120 which was large, heavier, and had a front engine and a non-synchro gearbox. The Speedster was tiny, nimble, peppy and so easy to handle, assuming the roads were dry; if there was moisture on the pavement, then watch out! The rear weight bias made for touchy handling characteristics and if you went into a corner too fast you could find the rear end of the car leading you through the turn, or for that matter you could do a 360 or two before you finished the corner. Fortunately it had seat belts, the early quick unlatch aircraft type, to keep you in your seat. So it took well planned steering and wheel placement to keep the car in line, but otherwise there were not many cars that could follow you safely through a decreasing radius turn and stay on the road. I loved it but my fraternity brothers didn't appreciate it as I was often leading our races. And what races they were! Brother Bruce had an Austin-Healey 100-4 and we were known to be side by side going around those Jamaica Way esses; he was a good driver!

It wasn't unusual for some brother to ask if he could borrow another's car, but not many asked about using the Speedster. In addition to being tricky to drive, especially in the wet, it had such poor visibility (with the top up) that night drives were always dicey. Plus it had little heat and no defrosters—not that they didn't work, it just didn't come equipped with defrosters. So you had to have a good supply of rags, and in the winter you had to have an ice scraper or spray deicer for the inside, which could create a feeling of being an F1 driver. The windows were plastic side curtains that didn't open, so paying tolls, etc., meant opening the door, but it was all worth it.

One brother, Ernie, who was kind of a "wild child" and a close friend, really liked the Porsche, and its nickname the "Blue Bathtub." I had shown him once that you really didn't need a key to start the car as there was no locking steering and the ignition could be "jumped" just by putting a class ring behind the dashboard to complete

My 1955 Porsche 1500 Speedster—my first car, aka The Blue Bathtub; 1963, Milton, Massachusetts.

the circuit and start the car. That was a bad lesson to give to anyone. One Sunday I got up late after a party the night before, had some breakfast and went out to get my car. It was gone! Not far, but it was gone. Someone said, "Oh Bob, your car's around the other side of the house. Ernie just got back with it a few minutes ago." Oh no, was it ruined, damaged, upside down? I slowly went around the house and there was the car, top down but undamaged. But as I got closer I saw that a garden hose was hanging over the door pointing at the interior. What! And suddenly Ernie appeared from around the corner cursing because he couldn't get the spigot turned on where the hose was connected. Good grief, Ernie was going to make the car live up to its name of the "blue bathtub." Thankfully he never tried it again.

Northeastern had a sports car club to which Stan belonged, and it didn't take too much urging for me to join and participate in their events, the occasional autocrosses and shows where we could park our cars in the quadrangle and students could stop by and ask questions of us self-proclaimed experts. We also had an annual meeting of sorts where we would elect officers and have a speech or two by some professor or the like who might have an interesting history or anecdotes to tell. Well, in the fall of that year I read that the actor Peter Ustinov was in Boston where he was acting in a play, and in addition to being a world famous actor, he was well known for his love of sports cars—notably Aston Martins, one of which he drove. So it was decided that I should invite him to speak at our meeting—huh, me? But they all thought I could pull it off. Reasoning that there was just one place where a famous actor would stay in Boston, the Ritz Carlton, on the Public Garden, I called the hotel and asked for Mr. Ustinov's room—and they put me through! And who answered the phone but Peter Ustinov himself, his voice being unmistakable. So I introduced myself and told him how we were impressed with his acting, but more so with his choice of cars, and with that he chuckled, and then I invited him to speak at our club annual meeting. He was so gracious and thanked me for my kind words and for my automotive enthusiasm, but added that his schedule was full and he was departing Boston soon so he had to decline our kind invitation. What a gentleman!

And so college years continued as did the races, and the parties. One of our frequent weekend destinations was Lime Rock in Connecticut where the SCCA held races. Sometimes I would drive the Speedster or go with my brother in his Alfa and sometimes with Stan, who now had the "MGV" operating perfectly—well, most of the time. One weekend we had both cars going to Lime Rock Park via Thompson in a sort of caravan, Stan and I in the MG and my brother and his friend Vinnie, of Peugeot 403 fame, in Jim's Alfa. There were a couple of routes to get there from Boston but our favorite went down route 109 through the "M" towns of Medfield, Mendon, Millis and so on. There were a lot of curves with just a few straight stretches where you could pass, and eventually you came to Lake Chaubunagungamaug, aka Lake Webster, and then you were in Connecticut and close to Thompson Raceway. There often were quite a few other race enthusiasts on the same road, mostly in Sprites and Triumphs, and we kind of played cat and mouse with them but always ended up in front.

That particular caravan weekend, we were in great spirits with the Alfa behind us most of the time. When I checked the rear to see who else was there, I saw what looked like a Ford passing the car behind the Alfa. Huh? Then it passed Jim, and right on our tail was a '58 Ford with New Hampshire plates. It was big, and as Stan sped up to lose it, it kept right up with us. Huh? This was no ordinary Ford, and it was a wagon to boot! It was cornering flat and the driver obviously could handle the car, but Stan was staying ahead until the road straightened out and the wagon flashed by us, its V-8 roaring, and disappeared around a series of turns. What had just happened? As we were shaking our heads in disbelief we rounded a corner and found a narrow bridge with a man standing in the middle with his hands up, signaling us to stop. I could see the Ford just disappearing over the bridge and a line of cars behind the signaler, meaning the road must have been reduced to one lane at that point. But the speed of the MG trying to catch the Ford, and our marginal brakes, meant we weren't going to be able to stop before reaching the bridge. At the last moment Stan jerked the steering wheel to the left, sending the MG sideways with tires screeching, and as we slid sideways onto the bridge, the terrified signaling man jumped over the bridge rail and disappeared below. The MG came to an ungraceful stop, its left fender

The author, Stan, and Vinny with Stan's damaged MGA and Jim's Alfa at Lime Rock Park, 1961.

embedded in the wooden bridge rail, both of us in disbelief that we had stopped and were unhurt. But Stan knew how to drive, and to stop. People ran from their cars to help and Jim, who had witnessed the whole event, was in shock. The signal man, who turned out to be a part-time police officer, reappeared half wet and was still shaking but glad to be in one piece. And before it all settled in with him, we left as we could still drive the car, and off we went while thanking everyone that had offered to help. We never saw the Ford again, though we half expected to see him on the track in one of the races at Lime Rock.

Those were exciting races as we were all championing different cars; me the Porsche Carreras that were valiantly chasing and beating the Corvettes, Jim rooting for the Alfas and Stan urging on the MGs. Sometimes we were happy with the results, sometimes not, but we always had a great time with many stories to tell.

I talked a lot with some of my fraternity brothers about my brother's time in Germany, and so some of us decided that after we graduated we should go for a long tour of Europe. Stan and I along with two other brothers, Fred and my roommate at the house, Jack Shanahan, started to plan the trip, which of course would include visits to different factories including Porsche and Mercedes-Benz. A good friend of Stan's was a lovely girl whose father Ernest was a travel agent in Boston. He was Swiss and had an office on the top of the (old) John Hancock building, and he was going to make recommendations and arrange for passage on a ship. He was a real character, always joking, but had a good business sense and knew his way around Europe like I did around Jamaica Plain. As we got closer to graduation, the plan solidified, including the idea of renting a VW microbus as a roomy vehicle in which to travel and even sleep if need be. It was going to be slow, but we had to sacrifice something!

But then Stan got sick. He had endured a kidney problem for some time but remained hopeful that he could go, despite his physician recommending against a European trip. But he couldn't. It turned out that he needed occasional dialysis, so being away from the necessary medical equipment was impossible. We were all so disappointed, but then another brother, Carl Stone, offered to go with us so we wouldn't have to cancel the trip. The expenses were manageable when divided by four, but not by three.

It wasn't going to be the same without Stan, but he graciously vowed to write us via American Express with updates from home, and we promised to send him cards as we progressed on our trip. But to raise enough money for the trip, I would have to sell my Speedster. The Porsche had been a very reliable car, the only major problem having been a broken timing gear (they were plastic). It hurt to part with such a fantastic car, but I told myself I'd have another someday. When I put the car up for sale after graduation, I found it wasn't easy to sell, but finally around the middle of July a fellow from Gloucester called. After too much haggling he bought it for $800. It wasn't that bad, I thought, as I had only lost $300 over two years. So now I had the Speedster money and the small amount I had saved and was ready to follow in my brother Jim's footsteps.

The trip was pretty well planned out: New York to Southampton via Galway aboard the SS *Maasdam* of the Holland American line—and for $300 each, round trip! Then to London and Brussels where we would pick up the VW bus courtesy of Auto-Europe. It was fully insured and had German tourist plates on it. We had three months with unlimited mileage; all we had to do was put gas in it and check the oil, etc. It never let us down except for its struggles to get up the mountain roads with four guys and their luggage aboard. Lots of second gear use. In fact there was an article in a car magazine about that time titled "Through Europe in Second Gear" which we could have written ourselves.

The voyage on the ship was memorable, thanks to interesting people including a large group going to Galway who sang Irish ballads all the way over. We met Peggy and Harriet, two American girls whom we were to see again in numerous cities and who were great traveling companions. When we arrived in London, I had been designated the only one to handle the English traffic in a right hand drive car. In the roads we mingled with Jaguars, Cortinas, Rileys, Wolseleys, Daimlers and innumerable Austins and MGs. The only high performance cars we saw other than the Jaguars were a few rare Bristols and Aston Martins.

Our next destination was Brussels, where we found the Auto Europe facility and picked up our new Volkswagen Microbus. It was the perfect vehicle for the four of us, very spacious for its overall dimensions, but agonizingly slow. It really was the first minivan and it would take the American car manufacturers another decade to decide it was a saleable vehicle. Then on to Amsterdam where many people were smoking funny smelling cigarettes and where we learned about beer tasting at the different breweries with Tuborg having the strongest we ever tasted. Fine with us. We met up with Harriet and Peggy in the Danish capital while Fred disappeared for a few days with a Danish girl that he met at Tivoli gardens, and Jack did his own thing. Talk about free love!

Carl, Fred, the author, and Jack aboard SS *Maasdam*, 1963. The bottle was already empty.

Finally we were heading into Germany—that is, West Germany. The country was divided in two, East and West, and the west had three sections, English, French and American (U.S. troops are still there), with only three "corridors" through which you could travel from West Germany via East Germany and into Berlin. Coming from Denmark we of course chose the northern corridor, only to find out when we arrived at the Helmstadt checkpoint that it could only be used by military or official vehicles. How could that be? Nothing was mentioned on our maps or guidebooks—but the soldiers said that the rules were always changing and actually apologized for the problem as they told us we could use the central corridor which was around 100 miles south. Having no choice, we were turning around when one soldier ran up to us and said that there were two students who were hitchhiking and had made the same mistake as us and asked if we could give them a ride. Why not, we said, and with that we made friends with two fellows around our age, leading to the most memorable event in Germany.

Carl, Horst, Fred, and Wolfgang; Berlin Congress Hall, summer 1963.

They were coming from Bremen, where they were studying, and had only a few days for vacation. Carl spoke some German, Fred spoke some Yiddish and both of the students spoke some English, so communication was OK. Horst was from Berlin and Wolfgang was Austrian and had family friends in East Berlin whom they were going to visit. They asked if we might be interested in going to East Berlin, and since we had a car it would be a lot easier to get around. We had considered going there but heard horror stories about the East German police and how they treated Americans. Horst and Wolfgang assured us it shouldn't be a problem as we would be with them and we had a specific destination, namely Wolfgang's family friends.

So we agreed to go. The next day after settling into our modest hotel on Kurfusterdam, the six of us headed to Checkpoint Charlie, the main access point to East Berlin, which was by that time surrounded by a concrete wall. On the American side we had no problem, but once the gate was opened into the East Berlin side, four armed soldiers appeared to escort us into a room where we had to show our passports and give a reason why we wanted to enter. As they inspected us and our papers, I thought all would be fine, but then they started talking heatedly with Horst, the West Berliner. Great, I thought, what have we gotten into? Well, the rules had recently changed, again, and no longer were residents of West Berlin allowed to visit East Berlin. We couldn't understand why, but they probably didn't want unrest created by western dissidents that lived so close. The rest of us were allowed to pass through without even an inspection of the VW, which I thought was strange.

So we left our Berlin friend there—Horst knew how to get to his home—and the four of us plus our Austrian friend, Wolfgang, headed into the dark zone. It was like

Volkswagen Bus, 1963, somewhere in East Berlin long before the wall came down.

a scene from a war movie, buildings half destroyed, buildings and homes with bullet holes everywhere, and virtually no people in sight. Few vehicles were on the road except for military jeep type vehicles and an occasional car such as an East German Wartburg, Czech Tatra or Russian Lada, but not much else on the surprisingly wide avenues. We arrived at the house where the friends were eagerly awaiting us as Wolfgang had been able to contact them and tell them who was arriving and when. We were the first American civilians they had ever met, and they were so welcoming, offering us Russian champagne, which was very, very, good, and cheeses and meats. When we left after some hours visiting, they gave us some chocolate and Wolfgang whispered in my ear that if we had anything American, anything at all they, would be thrilled to have it. We only had a few things but I think we left them with some chewing gum, cigarettes and toothpaste. Although we were prepared to see the worst in East Berlin, the people we met changed our perspective and the visit was the most eye-opening of many experiences of our trip.

After a few days in Berlin we were on our way to Stuttgart, home of Porsche and Mercedes-Benz, and driving at last on a real stretch of autobahn that I had read so much about. Nicely surfaced, well banked, wide open and *no* speed limits—what every serious driver dreams about. But we weren't in my Porsche or Carl's Corvette, we were in the VW, and as much as it wanted to reach 85 on the straightaways, it just couldn't do it. But going downhill she was like a race car. We were being passed by just about everything, and those flashing lights that I thought were so cool on my brother's 220 began to annoy me no end, so that we spent most of the time in the right lane. Oh well, we were in Europe!

My International Driving Permit; a Massachusetts driver's license wasn't enough.

Before seeing Stuttgart we had to visit Heidelberg to pay homage to the town where my brother spent so much time and to visit Zum Seppls, the *gasthaus* where Jim had his own seat at a table. We found a hotel and then went directly to Seppls as they of course had food as well as beer. I found the manager and told him who my brother was, and he laughed and took me to a wall that was full of pictures of students, soldiers and their girls. He looked them over and then stopped, pointing at one that showed maybe ten guys sitting around a table with their *steifels* raised and said "Here is Jim"—and there he was! It had been six years so I guess he left his mark there, something I didn't think I could do in just one or two days. We did some touring, including a few more beer halls, and then visited the Castle, which was magnificent even in ruins. The next day we were gone and heading south to the factories and museums.

These factory visits were mandatory, especially the Porsche museum which was small but sensational. Seeing the originals, the racing cars including the Formula One model, raced by Dan Gurney, was exciting. Then there were the 356 series, including of course a 1500 Speedster in silver. My heart hung low. There we heard of a new model named the 901 that was to be introduced at the Frankfurt Auto Show in September—could we go there and see it? Maybe? Then to the Mercedes museum, which was much larger and highlighted many prewar cars, all significant and many beautiful including the new 230SL, which had replaced the anemic 190SL and the gorgeous 300SL, and which had yet to be seen in the States.

Then we drove into Switzerland where our travel agent friend had arranged a gratis meal at the Bahnhof Buffet in Zurich. Those Swiss could cook, even in a train station! This is where the VW showed its stuff on those two-lane mountain roads with no guard rails and steep dropoffs. Why, that would never be allowed in the States. Next we headed down to Italy, where I could speak some Italian and where the autostrade gave us a taste of Italian driving methods. There everyone was flashing their lights, whether they were in the right or left lane, in the country, in the city; what chaos. We loved it, though, as it proved the old adage (maybe we made it up): "If you can drive in Boston, you can drive anywhere." But where were the Ferraris or Maseratis? In Milano we saw Lancias and Alfa Romeos—always going full speed—and many, many Fiats, including quite a few prewar models which weren't going as fast. But no real supercars.

From there we visited Pisa and Rome and then headed back north, stopping at Via Reggio which had a beautiful beach but ferocious surf. We camped out overnight with a couple of us in the VW and the other two in their sleeping bags on the sand. No wonder I never became a camping aficionado.

After that we stopped in Rapallo to see my grandmother, Dalma, and her sister Ines, who was living in Italy at the time, and had dinner with them in an outdoor cafe where they had all the patrons moving around from their tables so that the six of us could eat together. It was an hysterically funny scene, as my grandmother couldn't see that well and her sister couldn't hear that well as they were ordering people around and moving chairs. I felt really at home there and didn't want to leave, so I said to myself that I would return.

Dalma was an unforgettable character. Putting aside that she was my grandmother, she had a colorful past including coming to Boston in the early 1900s from the village of Comacchio at the mouth of the Po River, then marrying a man from the same village, and having three children, two boys and my mother, Iris. She had a magnificent soprano voice that enabled her to gain a position in the San Francisco Opera Company and many other roles in performances around the country. As a child I remember her practicing at her home on Commonwealth Avenue with a pianist as an accompanist, singing the Habanera from *Carmen*. It is from her that I got my early appreciation of opera. Now she was living in Rapallo with her sister Ines, I think in an apartment that belonged to her brother Ives, as she had left the States after her husband passed away, but she would return a few years later.

After a few days we left Rapallo and then headed west along the coast through Monaco to Nice, stopping at St. Tropez. I think that was a destination because Brigitte Bardot had a house there and the sleepy town had been written up in magazines as an inexpensive and very lively seaside resort. Well it's still lively, but it isn't inexpensive anymore. It was there that I saw my first Ferrari in Europe. We got sort of lost going to the harbor, and as we entered a rotary a black California Spider was entering from another road. I was driving and gave way to the convertible, and the driver waved and smiled and disappeared. The image and the sound remain with me today. Was that Alain Delon, I later wondered. We found our way to Tahiti beach where the sand was warm and the water full of seaweed; it definitely wasn't Cape Cod. But then neither were the bathers as the women were topless and the men seemed to be

Zia Ines, Nona Dalma, the author and Fred—Rapallo 1963.

wearing skimpy underwear. But it was great. We walked along the beach and soon came upon a section where nobody was wearing anything, our first nudist beach. Fred and I joined in but we couldn't convince Jack and Carl to join us. Oh those uptight provincials from Boston.

We only stayed there for a few days and then headed along the Côte D'Azur towards Marseille, where Carl had to leave the group and head back to the U.S. via Paris and Le Havre to start his last year at NU. We put him on the train and said goodbye for now.

From there we drove into Spain, the VW never skipping a beat. It was in Madrid that we received our first letter from Stan. We had written cards to him as we progressed, but this was the first correspondence from him. It was waiting for us at the American Express office where there were often long lines of Americans, mostly students, waiting for letters from home (with cash in them). We always were thinking of Stan's health, but the letter was not about him; it was about one of our fraternity brothers, Jay, who had died from a brain hemorrhage at the age of 24. Incredibly sad. He was one of those guys that you figured would go far as he was smart, personable and handsome. He had recently married too.

Our next destination was Paris. Except for Italy and Stuttgart, this is what I wanted to see and experience most. My French was pretty good and I think Jack spoke a little. We found a small hotel off the Rue des Ecoles on the Left Bank and traveled both in the city and out to Versailles while we still had the VW. The car "scene" in Paris was interesting as in addition to the car showrooms on the Champs-Élysées,

Ferrari 250 California Spyder as seen in a factory brochure. I still remember its sound as it roared past us with the driver waving and smiling.

which had most of the major European manufacturers, there were many quasi-exotic Citroëns, Renaults, Peugeots and even Facel Vegas. One day I got stumped, however, in identifying a white car I saw parked on Rue Saint-Honoré. It was fairly large, for France, but it was definitely not American, or so I thought. It had nice lines with little overhang, and a very smartly dressed lady was just exiting it. As I got closer and was about to ask her what it was—good chance to practice my French—I saw the "S" emblem and realized it was a Studebaker! Turned out to be a new GT Hawk. It fit right in in Europe.

We had timed the Paris stay perfectly as the Paris Auto Show was in progress, and we had to go and see if the new Porsche model we heard about in Stuttgart would be there. And it was. There beside 356 models including the Carrera was the new 901 (later to be known as the 911) in yellow. What a change! Bigger, prettier, and from all accounts much faster, as it was a six cylinder. Finally something to chase the Mustangs and Corvettes with. We also saw the Facel Vega models, which I always thought were beautiful, and along with the Citroëns, the only decent looking French cars around. It was also the European introduction of the Chrysler Turbine which we had read about and wondered if this would revolutionize the auto industry. Another exciting surprise was the Ferrari 250LM that was having its world premiere—just beautiful. There were so many makes that we never saw—or would ever see—in the U.S. that it was a real automotive education that would be reinforced by all the brochures I was accumulating. It was a real highlight of Paris.

But our VW was due back in Brussels, and Jack was due back in the States as he had enlisted in Officers Training with the Army and couldn't be late for that. So off he went with our beloved microbus to Belgium and then to LeHavre to take the boat back to New York. So now it was just Fred and I. Our return tickets were open ended; that is, we didn't have a definite reservation, but could book a passage on a ship when we wanted, and when space was available. So we stayed at the Hôtel des Carmes, on the sixth floor—there was no elevator. There was a bath down on the third floor, but we did have at least a sink in the room—cold water only. But it was Paris in the fall, and it was beautiful, and we learned to love Muscadet, which you could buy for the equivalent of six cents a bottle if you brought your own bottle—so we had plenty of bottles. Still, we were running out of money, fast. So we became thriftier than we had been, and as luck would have it that autumn we met some girls from San Francisco who loved taking us out for meals, and then we met some girls from Boston that we knew, and they took us out for meals, and on and on. Fred got some money from his girl friend in Boston and I got some from my Uncle Chester in Milan and older brother Jim, who was now living in Ft. Lauderdale (he still is). So were able to stay on some more.

We stayed in Paris even longer and then I met up again with Peggy, the girl I had met aboard the SS *Maasdam* on the way over and again in Copenhagen. She and her brother John were staying in Paris for a few days before going to their grandmother's house in Normandy for a short visit, and she wanted me to come along and meet her family and enjoy the area. I was so tempted to go, but I didn't. I don't know if it was because I felt funny leaving Fred—who had absolutely no money, although I'm sure he wouldn't have minded—or because I didn't want to get more "involved," but for whatever reason, it didn't happen, and to this day I wonder what would have been the outcome.

After delaying as long as we could while accumulating more stories (and wine bottles) we decided to arrange the return passage. The *Maasdam* wasn't sailing at that

SS *Rotterdam*. I took this photograph in Nassau in 1989; she was still sailing.

time but there was the *Queen Elizabeth,* said the agent at the American Express office. Like the *Maasdam,* the *Queen* had three classes for passengers: First, Cabin, and Third (more accurately known as steerage). We had traveled Cabin Class on the way over, but on the *Queen* our transfer ticket would only allow us to book Third Class. We were thinking about that when the agent interrupted and suggested the Holland American SS *Rotterdam.* It was a new ship, two years old with just two classes—while the *Queen* was used as a troop ship during World War II and was getting a little tired, the *Rotterdam,* being newer, would have accommodations much nicer than Third Class on the *Queen.*

So, after those beautiful months in Paris, we said adieu to the Rue des Carmes and the Left Bank and headed back to New York, with only 50 francs between us. How could we buy beers on the boat? Dutch beers at that? How could we tip at the end? How could we make a call to have someone pick us up? But that would all come later; right now we were boarding the boat train for Le Havre. The *Rotterdam* was not a disappointment. It was modern and sleek and the crew was pleasant and efficient. We had made a really good decision as fortunately the beers were only 10 cents apiece and wine came with the meals (except breakfast). Fred found out there was a bridge tournament being held aboard, so he entered my name and surprisingly I won enough money to keep us in beers for the five days! So after a fun voyage, including a wild mid–November north Atlantic storm (we had to strap ourselves into the beds to keep from being thrown out) we arrived in New York.

We arrived in the morning after the fifth day at sea realizing that we weren't sure if some would be there to get us. So while I was waiting for my baggage and Fred for his in another place, I heard a familiar voice behind me asking, "How was the trip?" It was Stan. He was there to pick us up; after contacting our parents he volunteered to drive to New York. It was quite a reunion. All the way back to Boston we told him stories and he told us stories and told us about his health, which was going to require a kidney transplant. It was a new procedure and he was to be one of the very first to have that operation with a kidney donated by his mother.

Had I accumulated knowledge or what? Not only your basic European enlightenment, but a whole new encyclopedia of cars, models and driving. Although I had written Jim from Heidelberg I was disappointed that he was now living in Florida, having given up on Dad's insurance and real estate business, as I had so much to tell him about everything. But my three younger brothers were now getting the "bug" also and wanted to grill me about everything I saw, drove, and experienced. And of course Mom and Dad were thrilled to have me back. Really? Another mouth to feed? I was back in Milton with no money, no job, and once again: *no car.*

I had grown a beard of sorts (very Parisian), was smoking Gauloises (very, very Parisian) and was speaking much improved French with Mom. So for about a week I stayed at the house, decompressing, visiting friends and telling stories. But pretty much everything sobered up on November 23 when President Kennedy was assassinated. It was the only time I ever saw my father cry. Everyone was so sad. I knew I had to get "on the stick" and find a job and a car and a life back in the States. But what to do? Banking again, no. Work for Dad in insurance? I didn't think so, plus he really didn't have enough business to justify me. Go back and work for Al, the architect, that

I worked for off and on through high school and college? Yes. So, I called him, and he said sure he could use me, but just until the end of the year.

That was OK with me as by then I should have things sorted out—in my head—and saved enough for another car. But how was I going to get to work, which was about four miles away? I could have walked, but that didn't seem realistic; I could ride my old—and I mean old—bike, but in the cold, rain and snow. No. But what was that in the back yard? My 17-year-old brother Dick had picked up a '49 Oldsmobile 4 door that looked in reasonably good shape as he had been working on it while saving enough money to insure it. He was one of those mechanical—and electrical—geniuses that could figure out anything and everything that wasn't working. He was the only one of us brothers who had that gift. He said sure I could use

The author at home in Milton.

the car, all I had to do was insure it and get license plates. With what, I wondered. And then, both turning to Dad, we pleaded for help as he would have an extra car in the family, which he hadn't had since Jim went south, and it would help to get to work and contribute some "board." So Dad relented and we got minimum insurance and a set of plates for the Olds. After some repairs I did take the car to work, but only for a few months, as Al only needed me as a fill-in for another draftsman who would be returning for work in January.

Since I knew about the short time at Al's I was trying to think about another full-time job and decided that maybe I should try to sell cars. I certainly knew enough about most of them and I really liked driving them; what else was necessary to be successful? I decided Volkswagen would be the brand to sell. They were really coming along in the States and after the experience in Europe I knew they were well made (although slooowwww).

So I braved the Boston traffic one day with the Olds and went to a VW dealership in Brookline. The manager, Bill McNaughton, was a real nice guy who said it was an "interesting" profession, but they didn't need anyone at that time. But he added

Brother Dick and his 1949 Oldsmobile—my savior.

that he knew of a dealership in Lexington that "really needed to get someone else in there." I thought that was kind of a puzzling remark but he went on to say that the fellow who owned his VW dealership also owned the one in Lexington named Auto Engineering. I got the info from him and thanked him for his help, but then he said it wasn't a VW dealership but handled a number of different imported makes including Mercedes-Benz. Wow, I thought—I would love to sell Benzes.

All pumped up, I left there, went home and gave Auto Engineering a call. I spoke with the manager, Jack Crusoe, who said, "Sure let's talk, can you come up tomorrow?" I said yes, made an appointment, and hung up. It was after the call that I looked up A/E in the yellow pages to get the address and discovered that they not only sold Mercedes-Benz but also Jaguar, Volvo, Alfa Romeo, Maserati and Porsche!

Porsche!!

Oh my god, I couldn't believe it. I was going to get that job.

And I did.

3

Auto Engineering

Now I had to find a car. With Dad's help I went looking and found a private party in Quincy selling a 1956 black with red Ford Fairlane convertible for $100. I bought it and was back on the road again.

I met with Jack, the manager at Auto Engineering, the next day and liked him a lot. He asked me a few questions, and we talked about racing a bit. I told him that although I had been to Thompson Speedway and Lime Rock a number of times, I had always been on the outside looking in and he laughed at that. So he hired me.

I started work at Auto Engineering the first week of January 1964, just shy of my 24th birthday, clean shaven and eager to sell. Since I had only been there once and then in a state of nervousness I had only a vague memory of the layout of the dealership. So on that first day as I exited onto route 2A east off of 128 I was trying to reconstruct the way it looked. But I was soon there and remembered that it was a modest brick building in sort of an L shape on maybe an acre of land. There was a showroom that jutted out toward the street and the entire parking lot was fenced in. I soon knew why as the dealership not only sold what was advertised in the yellow pages but was also a dealer for Aston Martin and Ferrari. Whaaat ?? Let me get this straight, I thought; I'm going to be selling not only Porsche, but Mercedes-Benz, Alfa Romeo, Jaguar, Volvo, Maserati, Aston Martin and Ferrari! It was almost too much to digest, but here I was.

I parked the car out back amongst the mechanics'—today's technicians—cars and walked into the showroom to see Jack. Before I could get to his office I had to pass the two new cars that the showroom held that day; a white Mercedes-Benz 220SE convertible and a light blue-green metallic Ferrari 250GT Lusso. They were breathtaking, especially the Lusso—it was a piece of sculpture and a voluptuous one at that. How soon could I sell one, I thought, or even drive one?

In Jack's office hung a huge painting of someone racing a car, which I later learned was Walt Hangsen racing a D Type Jaguar that Auto Engineering had campaigned successfully in the 1950s. Jack raced an Alfa Giulietta himself, so there was a lot of Castrol flowing through the air here and I liked the smell of it.

Jack introduced me to the office manager, two clerks and the two salesmen, both named Ken. There was Ken (called Kenny) the Mercedes-Benz expert who talked a blue streak about all the safety qualities of the car, and there was the British Ken Fullerton (called Ken) with a slight accent and dressed in twill pants and a blue blazer. It was the only outfit he ever wore. Oh, the tie and shirt changed, but the rest was the

Auto Engineering, Lexington, Massachusetts, as seen in 2017. I took this photograph some 50 years after leaving Auto Engineering and was happy to see the name and the building still existed.

uniform for him; I liked it. He was jovial and friendly, but his eyes were always moving around, wanting to see what was going on, but really focusing on the driveways to see if any potential customer might be arriving. He was the best at that and I learned his techniques without him ever teaching me any. Later that day I met the service and parts department personnel, all very nice and very, very busy.

I decided to do all the learning I could those first few weeks, not only about the vehicles we sold, but also about the way a salesman was supposed to handle customers. The two Kens were quite different; both were highly attentive but the British Ken soon had people laughing and driving a car, while Kenny would steer the customer to a Mercedes to educate them on the benefits of that impressive line of cars. I liked Ken's approach better, but his familiarity with the clients was an acquired professional manner that was not easily imitated. It had obviously taken him years to refine his technique and I was just a kid with no sales background. So I sort of did my own thing on the occasions when I got to talk with someone in those early days. Most of the time I was learning how cars were traded, who appraised them and how to deliver the sold cars. I also had to drive the cars to be able to intelligently talk about them and show their respective qualities. This did not include, however, the Aston Martins and Ferraris—not until my second week when a tall man came in driving a beautiful Ferrari 250GTE in dark blue metallic with tan leather, obviously a new car. He was smoking a pipe and since I was at the showroom door when he arrived—where were the Kens?—I asked if I could help him and he replied "You must be Bob." He turned out to be the owner of the dealership, Lindy Hansen, also owner of the Brookline VW dealership and the distributor for both Volkswagen and Porsche for New England.

Lindy was a self made man who had started an automotive engineering company with John MacPhee and had operated one of the first Volkswagen sales outlets in the northeast. They pursued the franchise and eventually became the distributor for Volkswagen in the New England states except for Connecticut. It was an extremely successful company that followed the Volkswagen policy of single line dealerships with factory authorized building designs and that eventually awarded many franchises to loyal employees as a sort of bonus for their performance. Originally headquartered in Bedford, they subsequently built a distribution facility off route 128 in Waltham while retaining the Bedford location as an engineering shop that was renowned for its expertise in solving challenging automotive problems and for preparing racing cars.

Lindy was the nicest guy and made me feel comfortable right away. When he asked how I liked Auto Engineering, I'm sure I gushed about it, but he wanted to know what I knew and we talked for quite a while. He could tell I was excited about the cars and then asked if I had driven a Ferrari yet. When I said no he handed me the keys to his and said, "Be careful with it, it's my only car." I looked at him and he laughed. He showed me a few things about the dashboard, the auxiliary fuel pump and the shift pattern, and let me go. The sounds were what were the most immediately impressive, all the cylinders, all the valves, all the gears. The car itself was big; you sat high enough that it didn't seem so large, but it was, especially compared to a Porsche or the Mercedes SL series, as I was soon to find out when I drove my first Gullwing.

I was giddy, it was almost too much, so I carefully went around the still unfamiliar roads of Lexington, being very conservative, nothing over 5,000 RPM, but the tach had no redline … what was that about? I was actually driving a Ferrari—and a new one at that! It was easy to see the aura the vehicle created around the driver. Surging power, firm and responsive handling, and sounds that I had never heard that closely before. These were sensations I had never encountered and still are fresh in my memory even today. Did I dare floor it? Not now, I thought, that was for later, as I didn't want to overdo it and soon returned to the dealership. Holy smokes, I had just driven a Ferrari! As I parked the Ferrari back in the same spot, Lindy came outside from talking with Jack to see what I thought. Taking the pipe out of his mouth, he opened the car door and said "Emergency brake—did you disengage it?" The burning smell that I could now detect gave the answer. He wasn't angry but instilled an early lesson in driving cars you are not familiar with: always check the brakes! I later discovered that in a Ferrari, like a lot of high-performance cars, the emergency brake was by far the least useful or reliable mechanical device. I never made that mistake again. Lindy really revered the product as I remember him telling people not to put their hands on the paint as the oil from their hands might discolor the finish. And if he saw someone using the car's body or even the glass as some sort of writing surface base, he would say not to do that, and explain why. He was a mentor, at least for me.

I remember that when I was first considering a job selling cars, friends would kid me about the negative reputation of used car salesmen. I thought, however, that my passion for the automobiles would overcome any disapproval, at least as far as I was concerned. So what followed was a concerted effort on my part to allay any trepidation that friends or potential customers might have about trustworthiness and honesty. I was able to accomplish that to a certain degree by studying intensely the products I was selling, their good points—and bad if any—and relaying that to prospective purchasers.

Auto Engineering was a good training ground for that. Starting with Lindy Hansen, the owner, along with his partner John MacPhee, and right down through the management, service and parts departments and sales force, I perceived honesty. And they all followed through, including the service and parts department, with straightforward answers and truthful explanations of services performed and products described.

Maybe I was a little naive about these things, but future reflections made me believe I was correct in my analysis of Auto Engineering's mode of operation and resulting reputation, and I thought that if I ever had my own dealership, that is the way I would operate also.

That first day that I had arrived at Auto Engineering, in the corner of the fenced in lot was a red Mercedes-Benz 300SL Gullwing. It looked forlorn. It certainly wasn't being highlighted or showcased as the fine car that it was. It was just parked in amongst a group of older Mercedes-Benzes and Jaguars. When I asked Kenny about it, he told me it had been there for a year with the XKE and all. The Jaguar E-type had indeed replaced the 300SL in the public's mind—at least that segment of the public that could afford those cars—because it was newer, some thought prettier and definitely faster. Those three factors were important when someone was paying $6,000 or more for a performance car. In my mind, though, the 300SL Gullwing was still *the* car.

It being winter, there were few customers just walking into the showroom. Not long after I had started, though, a fellow came in driving an older Austin-Healey and asked if he could see the Gullwing. Ken wasn't there and Kenny was on the phone, so I welcomed him on a cold but clear day. I had sat in the SL numerous times, even started it, but hadn't driven it. The customer wanted to drive it, and remembering how my brother and I were always trying cars out for "the hell of it," I was skeptical of this guy's intentions. When I went in to get the keys, Kenny said he had seen that person before and thought he might be a real buyer, but he cautioned me about driving the Gullwing. "It's really tricky, sort of squirrelly," he said. "Don't go too fast." I said OK, started the car and moved it from its favorite corner so the customer could get in. That was a feat in itself as once you opened the upward moving door, you had to climb over the wide sill and kind of slide yourself in. The steering wheel was hinged so that you could fold it down to make the driver's entry easier, but not much. So off we went in this $5,000 red 1956 Mercedes-Benz. I had already learned to check the pedal arrangement before driving off as A/E sold so many different vehicles you had to be sure where you were putting your feet. It may sound basic, but once you started off you were often overwhelmed by the driving dynamics and didn't want to put the wrong foot on the wrong pedal.

The Gullwing had a great sound for a six cylinder car and after stuttering a bit at the start, the fuel injection cleaned itself out and we turned left on to 2A heading for the entrance ramp onto route 128. The shifting was easy, although the gear shift lever seemed spindly compared to the Ferrari and the latest Porsches. However, the throaty engine sound was encouraging, as I knew this was a fast car. I was learning quickly

Mercedes-Benz 300SL gullwing—my dream car of dream cars. The one I drove at Auto Engineering was comparable to the one pictured here but was red with red leather.

about the technical aspects of horsepower and torque and how they related "hands on" to driving a powerful car and this education was paying off in my ability to position the vehicle I was driving in the correct rpm range to maximize its performance, and this was demonstrable in the Gullwing.

Those ramps on and off 128 at 2A were great driving spots. It was a true cloverleaf, that is four ramps, two going off and two going on, depending on your destination. The one off 2A heading south on 128 was a decreasing radius turn that was a real test of the car's handling—and the driver's competence—so once you learned its line you could really enter fast and keep the car almost drifting until you merged onto 128. I had learned that from Ken, who was the best driver I had ever ridden with. Those Brits! Or was he Australian? I didn't know, but they all knew how to drive really, really well. He could take any car, foreign or American, and without even having driven it before go charging onto that exit ramp and within seconds know how it was going to respond. When a new car arrived or when he was testing a trade-in he would often beckon to me to come along and see how the car went. What an education for me! And Ken wasn't even trying to teach me. Or was he? He had a lovely wife and two daughters, and later I thought he might have seen me as a sort of apprentice to whom he wanted to impart skills. Or was that just foolish thinking?

As I entered the ramp heading south in the 300SL I decided not to use my newly learned handling skills and instead took it easy and the car just kind of sauntered through the turn. This car was sensational—why hadn't someone purchased it? It was very quick on 128, easily getting up to 90 before I let off the gas and took the next exit.

The customer had asked if he could try it, and I said yes, but before letting him take over I turned the car around so it was heading back to the dealership. You always had to first give the customer the correct direction. So with him driving we turned onto the entrance ramp to 2A and he was going too fast and before I could say anything he lost control—for a second—as the car swung frantically first left, then to the right, then straightened out. But that was enough; I was shaken but he was scared to death. He pulled the car over to the side, got out and asked me to drive back. I said OK.

He didn't buy the car. The trickiness of the handling, I learned from Karl, was due to the rear suspension design utilizing a high-pivot swing axle that if being driven too ambitiously by a novice would tuck in the rear wheels leading to unpredictable handling, and that could be a problem. So Mercedes had replaced that rear suspension setup in the 300SL roadster with a low-pivot axle resulting in a car that was much easier to drive at speed through the corners. Quite the improvement, I thought.

New customers were a scarcity that winter and the ones that did come in were usually people that either Kenny or Ken had already spoken to, so I spent my time learning and driving and learning. With so many lines of cars there was an enormous amount to take in, but I was pretty good at absorbing the facts as the cars were there for a hands-on education. I also spent a good amount of time in the service department—probably more than the manager Bob Edwards wanted me to—talking with the mechanics about this and that and trying not to get in their way. I remember Al Greene, who commuted from Rhode Island every day to work on the Ferraris and Maseratis, always smoking a cigar and always in a good mood; Karl Michaels, who took care of the Mercedes-Benzes with a true affection; and Paul Reitshamer, who loved the Porsches and liked to talk with me about the Speedster. Another Ken worked on the Jaguars, and he was always covered in oil. And then there was Fritz Muelhaupt, a Swiss, who was another MB man and was always joking, really a lot of fun, but at the same time so organized.

Jack seemed to like having me there although it wasn't until the last week in January that I sold my first car. It was a used Porsche convertible and the buyer was a fraternity brother, Dave. He was already driving a 356A coupe, having been bitten by the bug after my Speedster demos, and wanted a newer convertible. It was a great transaction as everyone came out feeling good about it—which became sort of my motto when selling. Jack had appraised the coupe for $600 which Dave thought was fair, and Dave got the convertible that he wanted. My first sale! Let's see, how many fraternity brothers did I have? And what was going to happen to the coupe he traded in? Could I get myself out of the '56 Ford Convertible and back into a Porsche?

Well, I did. It was an accomplishment considering I had so little money, but by coupling the trade-in value of the Ford and Jack's assistance with a modest loan, I was back in a Porsche again. It was a 1500 like the Speedster, and it had real roll-up windows and a defroster too. I was thrilled.

Back in the showroom, the Mercedes 220 convertible had been sold to a dealer in Florida and was replaced by a Jaguar XKE coupe in white with tan leather. So sexy. And the Lusso was still there and I thought probably would be for a while. Thirteen thousand dollars was a huge amount of money, but as I was told, who knew? One day in late January when Kenny was having a day off and Ken was out, probably at the gas station, a late model Ford Country Squire with New Hampshire plates drove in and out stepped a well dressed man in a suit and topcoat. I was on the phone when he came in the showroom and I saw he was circling the Ferrari. I went over to him and he asked if he could take a look inside the car. I opened it for him and he slid inside—and smiled as he sat there holding on to the wheel. The Lusso's steering wheel was very close to the slanted windshield and if you had big hands (or small) your knuckles would scrape the windshield as you turned the wheel! We talked about its design and performance and just generally about cars for an hour. He really seemed to like it—who didn't—and said he might be interested in buying it, but didn't really have to drive it. He added, "I'm sure it drives just fine." I got so excited and thought I should go get Jack to help me when suddenly Ken came in, saw my customer, and immediately went over to him and said, "Hello, John, I see you came back for another look at the Lusso." What? He was a customer of Ken's but didn't mention it! John turned to me and said thank you with a sort of apologetic look, and went off with Ken to his office where he bought the Ferrari. I always considered that my first Ferrari sale, even though Ken would have disagreed.

Even though that lesson left a bad taste, most of the lessons were very positive including always, and I mean always, getting a person's name and if possible phone number, even if they were asking about the availability of an outrageous sounding vehicle. Kenny had such a customer in February who came in wearing a plaid hunting jacket and matching cap in a Jeep with Maine plates on it. He was kind of a stocky fellow with a ruddy face and really looked like he had just come in from the deep woods hunting something.

The blue Lusso had been replaced fairly quickly with a red one, a much more appropriate color, I thought. The Maine man wanted to see the car and Kenny was showing it to him going into a lot of technical detail, which I think was more interesting to me than the customer. The customer suddenly got out of the car and asked Kenny if he had a green metallic Ferrari 330 America (the recent replacement for the 250GTE) that he could see. Kenny winced, and said no, that was a new model and was going to be very rare and hard to get especially in that color, it would have to be specially ordered and no one, and he meant no one, knew how long that would take. So Kenny added, let's talk some more about the Lusso. But the customer didn't want to hear any more, and very politely thanked Kenny and walked out the door, got into his car and drove away. Kenny started cursing himself for not getting the customer's name. All he knew was that he seemed to have come from Maine. Jack came out of his office and rather than berating Kenny, said he should have learned that lesson years ago. I thought to myself if that had been Ken's customer, he would have left in the red Lusso.

As I remember, the next week was Washington's Birthday holiday and many Boston area dealers had special promotions and sales, but we didn't. People would come in nevertheless to see what we might have had on sale, and I think Volvo did have some sort of promotion. But it was busy, and I remember both Kens were out on test drives or other business when this beautiful green (always my favorite color) Ferrari drove in—with Maine plates on it! I thought it was a 250GTE and it was pretty.

So who got out of it but Kenny's customer from Maine! It looked like he had bought a Ferrari after all. I went out to see it, and him, and when I walked around the back of the car I could see it was a new 330 America. How could that be? Just last week it seemed an impossible request and now the customer was driving one. When I asked, the man told me he had just driven it up from Chinetti Motors in Greenwich, Connecticut (the East Coast distributor for Ferrari cars in the U.S. and a retail dealership as well). He said the car ran beautifully but he wanted to have the oil changed because it already had 300 miles on it. Thinking that he wanted to have it done in our shop while he waited (without an appointment), I said, "So you decided on that rather than the Lusso?" He said no, he still wanted the Lusso and wanted to leave the 330 here for the oil change and drive the Lusso away today. He wanted *both* Ferraris? Yes, that's what he meant. And with that, Kenny arrived back in the showroom. He looked similarly confused after hearing the story, but was thrilled.

And so I learned about Luigi Chinetti Motors. Well, I knew of them because we actually got all our Ferraris through them, which at the time was just the 250GTE and the Lusso, although the 330 America would soon arrive too, as we just saw.

That was my introduction to the multiple car purchaser. Sometimes they would buy more than one car at the same time, and sometimes they would buy multiple cars in a relatively short period of time, such as a month. Yes, there were some interesting car people out there.

Most of my sales those first few months were used cars, but I remember a hot summer day when a nicely dressed lady came in driving a Buick sedan. I don't know where anyone else was but I started speaking to her and she said she was interested in a Ferrari. That was rare, a woman, and an older one, probably in her 60s, and interested in a Ferrari. So I showed her a 330 America that now we had in our showroom, but she said she wanted a convertible, not a "sedan." But Ferrari wasn't making a "production" convertible then—they were introducing the 275GTS at that time but only in Europe—so the next best thing might be a sunroof. She knew about the Lusso and wanted to know if we could install a sunroof in the car as she loved the shape of it. So I said I would inquire for her and she said there was really no hurry—words that salespeople didn't like to hear—but she would appreciate what I could find out for her. So I took down Mrs. Dane's name and telephone number and told her I would contact within a day or two. When I asked Jack about it he said, "She wants to ruin a Lusso with a sunroof, crazy woman. Why doesn't she just buy a Mercedes-Benz 230SL instead?" That was Jack, always saying what he thought. He added that I should find out myself about the sunroof possibility, he wasn't going to do it. So I did. We had a subcontractor that could install either metal or fabric sunroofs in cars, doing an incredibly professional job, really factory quality, but when I showed him the car's photos and specs, he said the roof space was much too small to install one. It would only be able to open around 2–3 inches. Not good enough. Mrs. Dane was disappointed when I called here the next day to report what the sunroof people had said. I guess it was too much to hope that I was going to sell a Lusso, and to a lady at that.

Women were buying Jaguars and Mercedes and even Maseratis, but I didn't know of any that drove a Ferrari. She said she would think some more about what might be best for her, thanked me, and said goodbye. Well, I had her name and number at least; maybe a used Ferrari 250 Cabriolet might arrive in trade or something, or when were we going to get the 275GTS?

Two days later she reappeared and asked to look at a 230SL; had Jack called her? We had a beautiful beige coupe/roadster with beige leather, and after a short drive she fell in love with it. I liked it too, and with a sticker price of over $8,000 it was about our priciest car outside of the Italian ones. Mercedes were really the most solid feeling automobile, from the way the doors "thunked" to the quality of the interior materials they used, to the firm way they felt on the road, you always knew how the car was performing. They were exceptionally well made. So we sat down in my office, and she wrote out a check for the full price, smiled at me and said she would like to pick it up tomorrow. No problem, said I, and with that I sold my first 230SL. Ken wasn't around then, maybe on a short vacation or something, but when she came the next day, and was just driving away in her new car, he came up to me and said, "Was that Mrs. Dane leaving in a new 230SL?" I said yes, as he snorted, shrugged his shoulders, and walked away. We never talked about it again.

Shortly after that Ken did trade in a dark red '59 Ferrari 250GT coupe, and there I came face to face with the mystery model I had seen in Dorchester some seven years before. I could never have foreseen my automotive trajectory, but I sure was happy with the results so far. This Ferrari wouldn't have been of interest to Mrs. Dane as she really wanted a convertible, but I never saw one of those come in trade. The 250GT coupe sat in the used car lot well over a year until I sold it to a local man, Mr. French, for $4,000. Ken was not happy that I had sold it for that price, but he had gone on vacation to the Riviera and left those decisions up to the sales department, and we couldn't bear to see that car sit around any longer.

And so the excitement continued. Every day was a surprise as you never knew what interesting and exotic car might appear in the driveway to be appraised or even traded. Most of the nice trades were funneled into our used car list, and of course I had to drive them in order to talk intelligently (and exuberantly) about their characteristics. What an education!

That summer customers were sparse and most had already spoken to Kenny or Ken, so I continued to spend my time learning and driving and learning. I was systematically going through the new models of Mercedes-Benz, from the 190D diesel (or gas), which was slower than a VW, to the 220 series with the weird vertical speedometer (but very solid feeling, and a little quicker), to the 300 sedan, with the same body but more luxurious, and the 230SL, which was my favorite but a stark change from the now discontinued 190SL and 300SL roadsters. The 230SL had replaced not only the pretty but sluggish 190SL, but also the 300SL, which had an enviable reputation, but was no longer the best performer. Some Ferraris were faster but certainly weren't mainstream; it was Jaguar and Corvette that forced their extinction, I think.

Mercedes was really the money maker for the dealership. Although it was still way behind Cadillac and Lincoln in sales, it was making some inroads in the American market. There was a common theme to all these Benzes, though, and that was the feeling of quality and superb suspension along with the reliability and safety that was built into the cars. Safety was their hallmark, and it would be a number of years before American cars followed that road. Mercedes also had an overseas delivery program where the customer could order the car through A/E to their own specifications and have it delivered some place in Europe, either the factory or a city of their choice. Jaguar had a similar program as did Porsche, but Mercedes was the most popular at the time.

Mercedes had just introduced the 600 series, which I had just seen once in our yard, driven by an executive with Studebaker-Packard, which was the U.S. importer for Mercedes-Benz at the time. In their last throes the two American brands had taken over the import rights from Max Hoffman and were still making money by distributing these cars. The 600 sedan was large—there was also a Pullman model that was even larger, and both were powered by a big V-8 and were super luxurious inside. It had hydraulic power windows—like the old Fords—that were so fast you could lose a hand, or neck, if you weren't quick enough to get out of the way. I think these cars were later described as being "Dictator Chic."

And then there were the Porsches, which had changed substantially since my 1500 model. In 1964 there was the 356C and SC in both coupe and cabriolet forms and the rare Carrera 2. The C series had a more rigid feel and certainly more power, with the coupe starting around $4,200 while the Carrera was just under $8,000, quite a price spread. As much as I loved the Porsches they were not an easy sell. There were many attractive features including the inherent quality of a German automobile, the reliability factor for which they were well known, and the gearbox, considered by many as the best in the industry by far. The synchromesh, on all four gears,

1965 Porsche 356C factory brochure.

was so smooth it was described as "like running a hot knife through butter." Alfa and Mercedes had synchromesh first gears, but not Jaguar, not yet at least. For about the same money as the Porsche C you could get a Corvette with a V-8 and so much more power, or for not much more, a Jaguar XKE with a smooth straight six and those gorgeous lines. Both cars were much faster than the Porsches—even the Carrera—and objectively were more modern and beautiful. But Porsche had its followers, who loved the quirky way the car drove—as did I—and realized it was much more than a glorified VW. So I was able sell them, both used and new, and by the end of the year I had sold a fair number.

Sometime in the late summer we received the limited production fiberglass bodied Porsche 904GTS Carrera coupe. It was considerably lower than the 356C series, and the fact that it was painted black made it seem even smaller. I had seen the 901 in Europe, but didn't know about this model that was for racing primarily, but also for road use, a true dual purpose car. However, the fact that it was in our showroom probably meant it was going to be bought by a road driver not racer. But we couldn't sell it—even Ken was unsuccessful—so it was bought by a competitor in Rhode Island, Jake Kaplan Motors, which was a well known dealer in high performance cars. Interestingly, the 904 nomenclature changed to Carrera GTs because of the same issue that caused the 901 to be renamed as the 911 before coming to the U.S., as Peugeot claimed ownership of the three digit format with a "0" in the middle.

When it wasn't busy in sales I would hang around the service department, trying to stay away from the manager's eyes as he didn't like me bothering the mechanics, and trying to learn something mechanical about the various cars. Everyone liked talking with me, and I with them: Paul about Porsches and Fritz about everything, and Al about the high performance cars.

As I said, Al worked on the Ferraris, Maseratis and also Jack's race cars. Before I got there Jack had raced Jaguars including 120s, 140s and even a C-Type and most recently an Alfa Giulietta Spider very successfully in SCCA races. But now his car was for sale as he had bought a VW Formula Junior, an open wheel racer with a VW engine that had its own SCCA class.

As summer was coming to an end Ken delivered one of the last 250GTEs that we received. It was an ivory color with a tan interior, really nice looking, but I didn't know who it was for. The day of the delivery I saw a Lancia Flaminia drive in. It was a 3C coupe, black, and really nice looking. You saw some Lancias in the shop now and then, including Aurelias and even a four-door Flaminia with the rear window wipers. Too cool! But when the door of this nice coupe opened, out came a very old man, very slowly, followed by what I think was a Russian wolfhound, also old and moving slowly, and they both sort of hobbled into the showroom. The man was dressed very sportingly, with a cap, tweed jacket and cane, and the dog was about the same color and seemed to be walking the same way. They both seemed so ancient! The man asked for Ken, and you guessed it, he was taking delivery of the Ferrari. L. Francis Herreshoff of boating fame was taking our last 250, and we were getting the Lancia.

As it turns out I sold the Lancia. That car drove differently than others, starting with the transmission, which although smooth, had a remote sort of feel to it, as the car had a transaxle setup where the transmission was in the rear and also the clutch had a different type of friction point which really took getting used to. A few days after it was traded I had a call from a man inquiring for an unusual car that you wouldn't see coming the other way—how about a Lancia? Well, that man wasn't—a man, I mean. It was a Miss Caldwell, who had a very gravelly voice and an understanding temperament toward a young salesman who had said "yes sir." She came in a few days later and bought the Lancia, although I had to spend quite a bit of time with her as she had never driven a standard floor shift before, and I offered to teach her. Miss Caldwell was a musical impresario of considerable accomplishments who had started the Opera Company of Boston which brought opera back to Boston. We remained friends for many years and my grandmother Dalma was delighted to know that. As an aside, we had to replace the clutch within three months—but in fairness to her, it wasn't an easy transmission to operate, even for a self proclaimed expert like myself!

The Jaguars were apparently close to Auto Engineering's heart, as Walt Hangsen had raced a D Type for them and Jack had raced a Jaguar XK120. Jaguars were quite different from the German cars, with a sportier character, and were preferred by some customers because of their perceived elegance; with the beautiful wood dash and the folding tray tables recessed into the rear of the front seats (did anyone ever use those, I wondered?) they were indeed beautiful inside. The new 3.8S sedan with independent rear suspension was replacing the 3.8 sedan although we had them both at the same time. These sedans were much faster than the Benzes and were the car of choice for customers that wanted more performance and for some who simply would not buy German cars.

And then there was the XKE, which was in a class all by itself, and while essentially using the same 3.8 liter engine as the sedans, its design was breathtaking even three years after its introduction. All these (except the E type) were offered with automatic or a four-speed manual transmission, but amazingly, they had no synchromesh in first gear.

You could see a history of the brand as you walked around the dealership parking lot. Mark VIII and Mark IX sedans from the '50s and '60s, XK120s and XK140s of the same vintage, all with similar flowing lines with wood and leather interiors, and all with a small puddle or drop of oil under them. It was kind of a curse, but one that customers were willing to put up with so they could drive one. It wasn't only the oil drops, it was the electrical systems, cynically supplied by Lucas, affectionately known as the "Prince of Darkness" because of the all too common failure (somewhere) of the electrics especially at night. It became smart to carry a long wrench, or spanner, in order to bang the starter motor if it failed to turn over. But they were swell cars to drive, especially the early XK series. You could tell why they were so popular as they felt like a much smaller car than they were. One day a man came in that I had worked for in one of my work-study jobs at Northeastern. He ran a securities company and was very pleasant to work for so I remembered him well. We had traded a '61 XK150S roadster—an absolutely beautiful car and one of my favorite designs—which had the same engine as the early XKE. It was white with red and in perfect condition and he loved it. He bought it for his son, he said, but I wasn't sure I believed him.

The white XKE coupe that had been in the showroom for quite a while, which I thought was very presentable, just wasn't selling. People were buying more roadsters than coupes, and white wasn't too popular, some saying it was more a "girl's" color, and to prove that one day a man came in with his daughter to look at the car. She was swooning over it and he more or less said she should do what she wanted. What a dad! So I moved it from the showroom and took her for a drive. Not a long one, but enough that she could enjoy the power—and my driving expertise?—before I turned it around and let her drive it back. She could really handle the four-speed well and as we turned into the dealership I said, "Do you think your father would like to go for a ride also?" She looked at me and replied, "First of all he can't drive a standard shift, and second, he's not my father!" Oops! Another lesson for a 24-year-old boy from Milton. I never made that mistake again. But she bought the car (or her "Daddy" did).

Alfa was great too as we now had the faster Giulia models replacing the Giuliettas. Of course I was familiar with Alfas after my brother's Giulietta, and loved the driving position with the steering wheels at arm's length giving you more control. There were some rare models that you didn't see too often, including the six-cylinder 2000 and 2600 spiders and coupes and the Sprint Speciale, which was much better looking than it was to drive, kind of slow.

Even Volvo had a sports car, the P1800, which had a peculiar seating position but was really solid to drive, like the sedans but with two seats. And Auto Engineering had recently taken on the BMW line, another brand coming in through the importer Max Hoffman. The cars had a good driving reputation but couldn't have looked more stodgy, except for the earlier 507 of which there was one in the used car lot—with a Chevrolet V-8 engine in place of the BMW V-8.

The used cars were kept in an area set aside for trade-ins; actually there was more than one area for used cars, and where the 507 was parked could have been called waiting for the graveyard. In that lot were cars that had sat a long time and in which few had shown any interest, and it was easy to understand why. They were dinosaurs, sort of, cars that had lost their appeal and were more connected to pre–World War II design than the 1960s. Included were three or four Jaguar MK VIII and MK IX's along with a number of Mercedes 300 series four-doors, both sedans and convertibles, B and C class. All these cars were huge, ungainly, but built like tanks; in fact the joke

BMW 507 roadster with hardtop, a lovely design but with a feeble V8.

Ferrari 250GT Berlinetta Lusso. How could metal be this beautiful?

was that they were really left over World War II battle tanks that had been converted to road use. The sad part was that the cars never recovered from their place in the "graveyard lot" and the only time they ever moved was when the plows had to move the snow. They eventually disappeared, being sold to someone that I never observed.

Maserati was in kind of a transition period as we waited for the new Mistral model that looked absolutely beautiful. They were going to be available with two different six-cylinder engines and fuel injection, and when they did arrive I was one of the first to test drive one. It felt lighter than the 3500, but still had that chunky, solid feel that was a Maserati feature. What was missing from the lineup, however, were the V8s that had powered the Mexicos, Sebrings, and the 5000GT. We did have customers that brought them in for service so I got to see them—although not the 5000GT—and one Volkswagen dealer had an A6G2000 spyder that was sensational looking.

Then there was Aston Martin. James Bond had made the name a household word and the new DB5 was a big improvement over the DB4. There had also been a DB4GT model which was lighter and faster than the regular DB4, one of which I took in trade on a new Porsche 356C—quite a switch—after the driver got tired of maneuvering that huge car around in traffic. It was fast, but not like a Corvette. More than once the Aston from James Bond movies with all the gadgets came to visit us for a few days and we made a big newspaper splash about it; there was even a TV segment done in the showroom. I think there were four of them made, all with the fake accessories, and already they were really, really beat. There was also a DB4 shooting brake that was contemplated and the prototype was left at the dealership for a while so we could gauge the interest. There was none.

It was an incredible education in the best cars of the day, and for many days and years to come. I joined the Porsche Club of America and went to many of the events including rallies, gymkhanas and even ice racing; what fun. It was hard to compete

Posing with my 1960 Porsche 356B normal roadster—one of my favorites.

with my old 1500 with the strange handling, so I dreamt about a later model—but that was all until in late October that changed. I had loved the 356B roadster, which I thought was the logical successor to the Speedster, but it was only made for three years, 1960–62, so I sort of longed for one. We had a customer that drove a 1960 Normal model that was Smyrna green with beige, a really nice combo. The customer walked on crutches and had hand controls installed in the car which was unusual as of course it was a standard shift! But I guess he had his fill of the car because one day in October one of the mechanics told me that he had traded his car for a Saab, of all things, at a dealership in Watertown, and they were advertising it for sale. I needed some creative thinking fast.

I drove to Watertown and found the dealership had quite a different feel than Auto Engineering. It was a much more hectic atmosphere, although in an urban sense. Just what do you want to buy, how much money do you have and how soon do you want it—right now. No schmoozing, just action. It was OK, I guess, so I met a salesman and saw the car. They had removed the hand controls and I didn't drive it, saying I was sure it drove OK. The salesman looked at me strangely when I said that, and we talked about financing. There they were really creative. A few dollars down with the balance of the down payment in the form of a loan from HFC, and a conventional loan from a bank, and voila, I bought the roadster! It was always one of my favorites. But they wouldn't take the 356A in trade, so I had to sell it privately. To my surprise Jack said I could sell it through the dealership. It didn't take too long as I sold it myself and got $500 for it, not bad I thought.

I loved my roadster, but was getting tired of the commute between Milton and

Auto Engineering ashtray or candy dish showing an incredible lineup of cars; later they added BMW.

Lexington and decided to look for a (cheap) apartment in Lexington. What I found was a whole house that seemed awfully reasonable, so I rented it for a six month period and it was only when I was there for the second night that I was almost thrown out of bed by a roar that seemed to shake the whole house. I hadn't noticed the railroad tracks that went behind the house and were occasionally used. I wondered why the realtor hadn't mentioned that. But I had my own place and with "contemporary parents" furniture I was set up with just enough to run my own household.

4

Off to the Races

It was early January 1965 when we were told that our first 911—formerly 901—Porsche was on its way to us from the port in New Jersey, officially designated as a 1966 model as were all of the new 911s for the American market. So we waited, but it didn't come as expected. It was trapped in a dock strike where nothing was being shipped in or out. How frustrating! In early February it finally arrived, but without a clutch—that is, it had been burned out, probably by the dock workers hot-rodding around the docks in a brand new Togo Brown 911. We couldn't repair it because we didn't have the parts yet. Who would have expected to need a clutch so early? When we did receive the clutch parts everyone was anxious to drive it including myself. It was astonishing and still a Porsche because it was rear engined, but aside from that it was totally different. The response of the flat six cylinder engine was immediate and thrusty, and the sound was energetic and much lower than the fours. And the handling seemed much more controllable. We all loved it!

Business improved in 1965, thanks in part to an across the board *decrease* in Mercedes-Benz prices. The factory had taken over the U.S. distribution from Studebaker-Packard and the result was the elimination of their distributor's commission—commonly called in the industry a "license to steal"—and a consequent decrease in list price of around 20 percent. It was very unusual for car prices to go down, at least on the manufacturer's sticker, and the buying public quickly became aware of it, as of course did I. Truthfully I had been coveting a blue with tan leather 230SL, standard shift with both tops, that was in our inventory. Of course I loved my Porsche but there was something about the Mercedes that said "Bob, you should have me." Well the decrease in price coupled with a special employees' purchase plan at the dealership made it too hard to resist. You could buy a new car with a balloon note, so that for the first 11 months you would pay $50 per month, and the last payment would be the balance of the selling price. Naturally being a salesman you would be able to sell the car before that last payment was due as the employee price you paid for it along with the monthly reductions would make for an easy and profitable sale. So I bought it. And I loved it. Karl was happy to see me in a Mercedes rather than that noisy air-cooled Porsche while Paul was disappointed that I had given up on Porsche, at least for the time being. The 230 handled really well but certainly wasn't as fast as the new 911s that were now starting to arrive at the dealership in a significant number. But it was a convertible also, so it had many personalities and it was sooo solid. I thought the design was beautiful and would probably endure, which it certainly has.

4. Off to the Races

Brother Jim, just married, pulls away in his 1959 Porsche 356A coupe.

When I had had the car about a week, my brother Jim arrived with his wife Barbara and their new daughter Kristen. They had driven all the way from Florida to Milton in his 1959 Porsche 356A sunroof coupe! What a ride with his new family, but they all really enjoyed the trip (at least that's what he said) as there was plenty of room in the back for the baby and her gear plus the room in the front. He got fantastic mileage and never once got stopped for speeding (I'm sure Barbara put her foot down and didn't allow him to put his down too far). It was nice to finally meet her and she was as likable as she was beautiful—he had the beginning of a fine family. It turned out that she liked cars and was wowed by the 230SL which she wanted to sit in right away, saying that someday she would have one just like mine.

Not too long after I bought the Mercedes a major change occurred at Auto Engineering for which I had no prior knowledge. Lindy had sold the dealership to Ken and a silent partner, Gus, an airline pilot and Alfa driver. What a surprise! Ken said nothing would really change except that Jack would be leaving to take a position at Porsche Cars Northeast, Kenny was leaving the auto business to "pursue other interests" and there would be a new salesman starting, another Brit, who had worked for Crandall Hicks, an MG and Austin-Healey dealer in Wellesley. The new salesman, Dick Lloyd, was to become one of my best friends. I guess he was about 10 years older than I but acted even older. He had a real British air and an incredible sense of

Author, Jim's wife Barbara and Dad with my 1965 Mercedes Benz 230SL. Fine gearbox but not fast enough. The timeless design still looks good.

humor. I was always laughing at his comments and anecdotes, and of course he was a very good salesman. So for a while it was Dick and I, and sometimes Ken, in sales and it was quite a complementary group. Dick liked the races as did Ken, so we often went to Thompson, and even Lime Rock occasionally, where Ken would soon be racing himself. To make it more interesting we would convince Ken that driving down in this car or that from the inventory would increase its exposure to the sports minded public, and therefore increase the possibility of a sale. He thought that was a good idea so often we would have the latest Porsche or recently traded used car to drive to Connecticut.

Ken had traded a '60 Aston Martin DB4 coupe that looked a lot better than it was. It actually had been raced for a while—unsuccessfully I'm sure—by a man who was part of a husband and wife racing team. He raced the Aston and she an Alfa Sprint Speciale—another nonwinner I guess. The Aston had been in the used car inventory for quite a while, and like a lot of higher performance cars, the longer it sat around, the worse it got. It was therefore a perfect choice to exercise it by driving it to Thompson Race Track where you could park your car on this slope that looked down on the straightaway after the first few turns. So I was to drive the Aston and Dick was taking a brand new silver Porsche 912, the first one that we had received. Being a true Brit, Dick thought it would be appropriate to bring a picnic lunch and a proper bar setup for the event. So I got some sandwiches and stuff and he brought a bar setup with all the vodka tonic fixings and plenty of ice which we packed in the

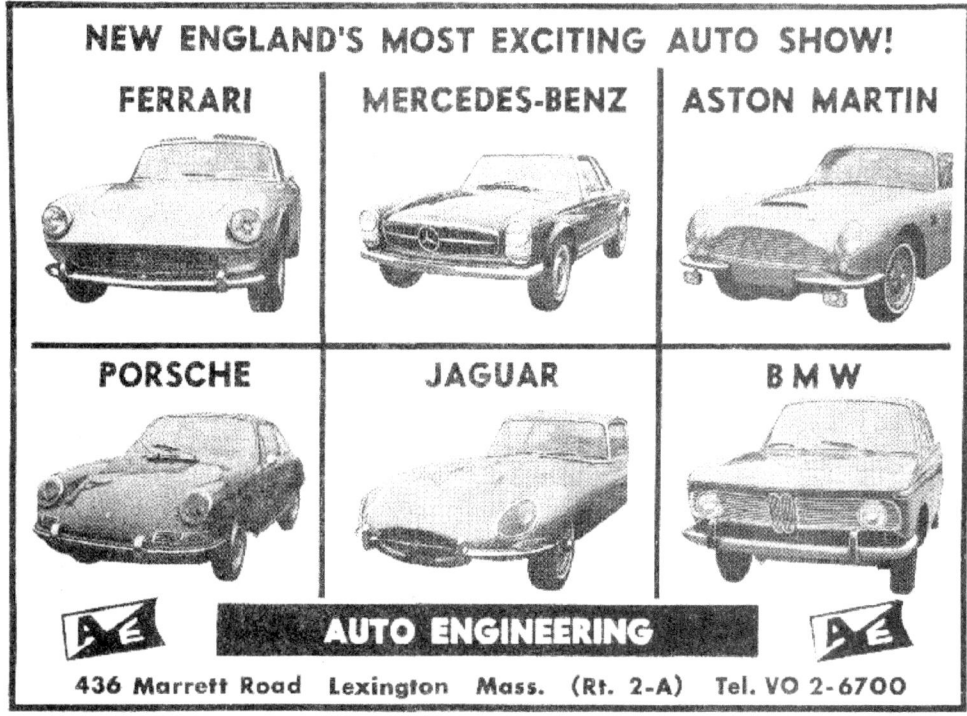

Auto Engineering advertisement in *Thompson Raceway Official Program*, October 1966.

accommodating trunk of the Aston. We rallied more than raced down the familiar roads—slowly passing over the bridge that Stan had memorialized—and arrived at the race track on a beautiful day. We found the perfect spot for the cars and immediately became hungry and thirsty.

I was also looking forward to seeing one of my fraternity brothers, Frank Grimaldi, who had been campaigning a Jaguar XK120 against the formidable Denise McCluggage and other C production cars. Frank and I often talked cars and for some reason he addressed me as Olivier Gendebien, the Formula One driver who was often called the greatest sports car driver of all time. Thanks, Frank, you must have tried to follow me on the Jamaicaway. We also were cheering on our favorites including the Porsche Carreras in B production that were showing the Corvettes how to take fast turns.

As the race went on we were accumulating quite a few admirers of both cars, and being gentlemen, we offered food and drink to those that we considered friendly. I know we left before the end of the race, probably after the spirits and food ran out, and headed back, this time on the Massachusetts turnpike where we decided to find out which car was faster. Well, the Aston was, but not for long, as after about twenty minutes of high speed driving it quit—just stopped running. I was able to nurse it over to the breakdown lane, with Dick behind me in the 912 with his flashers on. And there we left it. We had to send a tow truck down the next day to get it, but the repairs were not serious; a belt, I think, had broken. Better to have happened to one of us than a customer, we said. Dick eventually sold the car to a student at Harvard who

Frank Grimaldi and his Jaguar XK120 at Thompson Raceway, Thompson, Connecticut (*Thompson Raceway Official Program*, October 1966; Ken Fagan photograph).

thought it exciting that the car had been raced. He didn't have it for long, and finally traded it back in on a Jaguar. Oh those anglophiles!

I never did sell a new Aston although I took that DB4GT in trade. I guess I just wasn't English enough, but Dick and Ken certainly were. I remember Dick selling two DB6's, one to a local doctor, and at the same time selling a new Jaguar Mark X to his wife. They were going to be great service customers, I thought, and they were. The other DB6 he sold to a fellow that drove into the yard in a 427 Cobra, the first one any of us had seen. He told us he had just come into a sizeable inheritance and wanted to buy his dream car(s). He let us drive the Cobra and it was definitely hairy and scary, all raw power that was not easy to get to the ground. He had also bought his son a Cobra, a 289, that we never saw.

One of the Astons Ken sold was to a Mercedes owner who had bought his car from Ken and always circled the silver DB6 in the showroom whenever he visited the dealership, sort of romancing it. I remember Ken going up to the customer and saying, "Why don't you stop fooling around and just buy the bloody thing, you can afford it!" I was shocked at the forward way he said it but the customer just laughed and finally said, "OK I'll buy it," and he did. It would be quite a while before I could entice a customer to buy in that manner.

Ken decided the following year that he wanted to race a car in SCCA, just like Jack had, although he chose a 911 rather than an Alfa. The 911 was a complete departure for Porsche from the 356 series as it was the first six cylinder road car they had produced. It was fast, almost as fast as the XKE at least in acceleration, and it handled

Aston Martin DB4—bigger and stronger than Jaguar XKE but slow to get up to speed. We had several at Auto Engineering similar to the one pictured here (Michael Schafer/Wikimedia/Commons).

really well too. Ken had the advantage of a well equipped shop, available parts and mechanical expertise with Paul and others; he was sure to do well in his class. But he didn't. I don't think it was his fault, or Paul's either; it was just that the car wasn't competitive in its class. But he kept trying, and as he did it brought a lot of excitement to the dealership as many of us would go to the track to root for him.

That fall business was picking up as Mercedes was introducing the new 250 series and Jaguar now had the 3.8S sedan—one of which Dick bought—as well as the new Mark X, a really large car and beautifully appointed. Porsche's recently introduced the 912 was starting to arrive in greater numbers, although not all Porsche drivers were pleased with the design, preferring the 356 series mainly because of its size. Maserati had brought out the Mistral and we had a new coupe in the showroom, a magnificent Frua design that was also available in a spider form, though we never had one.

Ferrari had brought out the 330GT to replace both the 250 and 330 America. It was a little larger with an independent rear suspension and a really ugly nose with four headlights like a Ford Galaxie or something. Nobody liked the front end but everyone liked the way it drove—and sounded. But it was not selling well at all. Ferrari said they were going to change the nose, but in the meantime this was all that was available. Lindy was still the dealer we got the cars through as a sub-distributor for Chinetti, and he had two 330s over at his warehouse in Bedford, one a light metallic blue and the other a deep maroon, both with tan leather which complemented the exterior colors. I went to see them one day with Dick. I always like the lighter interiors as opposed to black or German gray, although red was nice too.

In early December a man who lived west of Boston called to inquire about the 330GT and asked if we had one he could see if he drove up. Although there was snow on the ground, the roads were clear, and in sales you found out early that if a customer

Paul, Ken, and Karl looking at Ken's Porsche 911, and Susie in Karl's 300SL at Bryar Motorsports Park in Loudon, New Hampshire, 1966.

Ken in his Porsche 911 with a checkered flag at Thompson Raceway, Thompson, Connecticut, 1966.

came in when the weather was bad, they were probably a buyer, and not just a looker. I said yes, we actually had two that we could show him. The next day a man drives in the dealership in a black 300SL roadster with a hardtop, gets out and is greeted by Dick who leads the man into the showroom and says to me that the gentleman talked with me yesterday. And so I met Dr. Riemer, a real gentleman who also had a home on Cape Cod. We drove over to see the 330GTs and when we arrived Ken was already in the warehouse looking at the Ferraris with a customer of his own. What?

There is a certain scenario that way too often occurs at dealerships, as I've observed before. That is, when you have cars that are difficult to sell, you can be sure that when you finally have a legitimate buyer, there will be someone else interested in the car at the same time. And so it was that day. But we had two 1966 330GTs to offer, and as long as both customers didn't want the same car it would be OK. And they didn't. Ken's man loved the light blue, and Dr. Riemer preferred the maroon, although he really would have liked black again. So after driving it and listening to those magnificent sounds, he bought the car, my first new Ferrari sale, and I think I was more excited than he. His 300SL was gorgeous, with a red interior and less than 7000 miles. We allowed him $6,500 for it as a trade-in toward the Ferrari, which was $14,200. He was happy, I was happy and Ken's customer who bought the 300SL shortly thereafter was also very happy.

Dick and I became good friends and the whole sales experience became much more gratifying in that, although we wanted to maximize our own sales, there was a sort of gentlemen's agreement that we wouldn't "hog" all the customers, but rather divide the customers between us and the new salesman, another Bob, an older man, quite debonair, who once sold Cadillacs in New York City.

Having an additional salesperson worked well and as business increased, so did my income, allowing me to start flying lessons at Bedford. Dick got me started on in and claimed it was "better than sex"! I don't think I agreed with him on that, but it certainly was exhilarating, and I managed to do my first solo flight about two months after starting. Dick was a real wit, always quoting some British playwright or author, and that worked well with the customers especially. There was something about a foreign (although still English) accent that went along with selling imported cars—it gave a feeling of confidence to the buyers, and a well deserved one at that. Dick, like myself, was a true believer in standard shift cars; how else could you jump start them if you didn't have gears to work with? I remember one young man who was looking at a Jaguar 3.8S—I think it was a graduation present from his folks—and was undecided about an automatic versus a standard. As Dick was slowly convincing him of the merits of a clutch pedal, he added, "Remember, it is better to have shifted and missed, than never to have shifted at all"! I could hardly contain myself from the next office where I was doing some paperwork. It was hysterical—and the customer bought a standard shift to boot. I wish I had a nickel for every time I've quoted that quip.

We still made some trips to the races and although the picnic lunches in the back of the Aston were a thing of the past, we still enjoyed the drives. Another time we went there in a used Jaguar XKE roadster with a removable hardtop, kind of a dull grey color with grey leather, that had been in inventory for quite a while. So in early September we decided to try our luck at Thompson, but no buyers were there.

Ferrari 330GT 2+2. This is like the one I sold in 1965. Though similar in feel to the 250 GT 2+2, it offered better handling and suspension. The four-headlight design did not last long.

I was able to use that car to confirm Jaguar's claim that XKEs could attain a top speed of at least 150 mph from the showroom floor—that is with no modifications. One night on a lightly traveled highway, despite the shaking steering wheel and woefully inadequate headlights, I was able to reach that magic mark. Astounding!

As 1966 began there was a general feeling of improving economy which resulted in increased sales and service business. I was still driving the 230SL but was quickly learning that it wasn't a Porsche in the snow or even the bad weather. I had put four snow tires on the 230 but it really didn't help very much. Convinced that it was time to go back to a Porsche, in March I picked out a grey with black 911 and was able to trade the Mercedes as Ken had a buyer who really liked the color combo and wanted a standard shift. So I was back in a Porsche, and what a car that was—totally different than the 230 and surely different than the old 356 series. It was so fast and handled so well that I was in love again with the rear engine masterpiece.

At the same time my friend Stan had started dating a beautiful young lady from Chicago who wanted to buy a used Porsche. So one day he brought Kitty in and they looked at a one-year-old 356C red coupe, and Stan suggested I take her for a test drive, which I did. She loved it, and after a few miles, I turned it around and said, "Why don't you drive?" She looked kind of puzzled about the shift pattern and I said it was easy as it drove just like a VW. It turned out Kitty had never driven a VW and had only driven a stick shift once before, but she did admirably, and bought the car. I think Stan was more pleased than she at her decision.

Shortly after that Stan and I decided to get an apartment together in Waltham

4. Off to the Races

My Auto Engineering business card.

in a new development that was close to both of our jobs. So we found a nice two bedroom unit and moved our meager belongings into a very modern apartment. Stan eventually had two separate kidney transplants, the first from his mother whom he thanked by saying "How often does a mother give life to a son twice?" and the second from his sister. He married Kitty and they had four lovely children and eventually settled in California where he bought a silver 308GTS that he loved. But his time was limited and he passed away in his mid-forties.

Things started to change dramatically as I heard through Fritz that there was a Mercedes-Volvo dealer for sale in Hingham. He was interested in buying the business and wanted to know if I would be interested in joining him as a partner. Me as a dealer in imported cars? It was very exciting to even contemplate but we certainly had to keep it quiet, and we did. As we were considering whether or not to attempt the purchase, I had a call from the manager of the largest Cadillac dealer in Boston, Peter Fuller Cadillac-Olds, who had heard about me (from whom I never knew) and about my enthusiasm and abilities in selling Porsches. He asked me to visit for a chat and I agreed to meet with him the next week. The Cadillac dealership was the premiere one not only in Boston but also New England, with a huge showroom dotted with oriental rugs and new and used Cadillacs, quite an incredible scene. I met with the general manager, Clifford, and his assistant and they explained to me that they were going to be awarded the Porsche franchise and were looking for someone to run it as general manager. It was a really enticing discussion, with their obvious interest in me as their prime candidate, maybe their only one. So after a lengthy discussion they made me an offer and I told them I'd respond within a week. What was I going to do? Try to start my own dealership with Fritz on the South Shore, or start up a new Porsche dealership in Boston and act as General Manager; this was not going to be an easy decision.

First, I had to investigate the plausibility of the Hingham dealership, which would need some dollars put in as a capital investment. I had managed to save some money but had no idea how much would be needed between the two of us. But it wasn't just the two of us as Lindy would be a third partner. What a difference that would make as his interest, and investment, would make it more feasible, plus his connections with banks and lines of credit would be invaluable. So the three of got together to work out some initial details and then decided to visit the dealership that was going up for sale in Hingham.

The man selling the dealership was also a VW dealer, so he and Lindy knew each other. The dealership was located in an old mill building in Hingham center, and was small in size but packed with interesting cars. They were selling Mercedes-Benz, Volvo and DKW, and although Mercedes was successful, and Volvo less so, DKW wasn't. That made the value of the dealership questionable, certainly in that location. The business was losing money and since they were renting their space, they really had no assets other than parts inventory and goodwill from the franchises. At this point it was really Lindy that was driving the conversation as he and his personal accountant soon told us that in fact the dealership had a negative net worth, and putting any money into the project would be a bad idea. We couldn't even be assured of obtaining the Mercedes and Volvo franchises as they were more interested in relocating closer to Route 3. With the building of no interest and the franchises essentially unavailable, what were we looking at? What were we doing?

Well, we found out that there was a dealership building in nearby Cohasset that was about to become available. Originally constructed as an American Motors facility, it was now being used by a Chevrolet dealer that was renting it while building a new larger facility in Cohasset, that was just being completed. That was nice but what were we going to sell, used cars? Showing his business acumen, Lindy said that we didn't need Mercedes-Benz and Volvo; we could start with a Porsche franchise (he was still the Porsche northeast distributor) and he liked this Japanese import that was just making inroads on the East Coast, Datsun, that he was pretty sure we could get a franchise for also, and as a sweetener, we could become a Ferrari dealer as well. Ferrari, Porsche and Datsun too! It made a lot of sense to Fritz and me, and although we would have liked to have Mercedes and Volvo as they were established brands and sold well, we were willing to follow Lindy's advice. And we did. So I called the Cadillac dealer and told him of my decision—I had explained about our interest in starting our own business—and while he was understanding, he was also disappointed.

We went to meet the owner of the property, who also owned the shopping center across Route 3A, which had a supermarket and a number of shops, many of which had a nice sort of upscale feel to them. I wasn't that familiar with Cohasset other than their well known "roller coaster road," aka Forest Avenue, that as teenagers we loved to drive at high speed, our stomachs starting to float as we raced down the undulating road which ended at a stop sign and then the ocean. Not everyone managed to stop at the sign so the road had quite a reputation for daredevil type driving. Anyway, it was a nice town and the dealership building was designed to harmonize with the shopping center, and with a lot of residences in the area, as it had a Cape Cod look, was constructed of brick and had only one floor. It was really attractive. The owner, a real down Mainer, had settled on the South Shore as he had worked in the shipyard in Hingham during World War II and had grown fond of the area. We liked him, and as it turned out, he liked us too. He told us also that some man with a British accent was also interested in the building, but Mr. Rice didn't like his approach at all and would prefer to do business with us instead. We didn't have to think too hard about who that person with the English accent was—it was Ken. He also knew about the Hingham dealership, and having an "in" with Mercedes-Benz, he probably would be able to put the franchise in that building. But we were able to secure a lease with Mr. Rice, and starting January 1, 1967, we were the proud owners of Autohaus, the first Porsche dealership on the South Shore. We had lengthy discussions about the name and I think it was Dick Lloyd who finally suggested Autohaus (pronounced Auto-house), the German word for car dealership. Fritz thought it was too commonly used to work, but it did.

So I had decided to leave Auto Engineering, one of the most respected and busiest import dealerships on the East Coast, for some adventuresome project with only a few years' experience in sales and no real experience in management. I was leaving the place of Ferraris, Maseratis, Aston Martins, Volvos, Mercedes-Benz, Jaguars and BMWs where I had built up a clientele that was both interesting and loyal, all for a possibility of some future success. What was I thinking?

I left A/E in early January after telling Ken of our plans—which he already knew about—and Fritz followed shortly thereafter, leaving his well paying job. We decided that I would handle the sales department and be general manager, and Fritz would be the service and parts manager, and Fritz's wife Alice would be the office manager, a job she presently had at a Saab dealership. But the underlying question was "How do you operate an automobile dealership?" Sure I knew how to sell cars and how to price trade-ins, and Fritz knew how to service cars and how to price repairs and parts costs, etc., but how did it all come together? And that's where Alice fit in.

Emigrating from Switzerland in the early 1950s and later becoming naturalized citizens, through Swiss connections in Massachusetts both Alice and Fritz had found employment with Gaston Andrey, another Swiss, who had a dealership in Framingham that sold SAABs, Morgans, and Alfas and had a racing arm that was very well respected. Fritz eventually became service manager there and worked on many of the competition cars that Gaston raced, including Ferraris and a Maserati Birdcage. Alice, who was also a racing fan (and still is), attended many of the races and became the office manager, a similar position to what she had held in Switzerland. But automobile dealerships were different than ordinary business offices because of the constant excitement that whirled around those places, and Alice was one of those people who really knew everything that was transpiring. Oh, not the details of various cars' performance specifications or the mechanical nuances, but she was aware of the personnel and most importantly the customers and how they were being handled and if they were paying their bills. All this expertise she brought to Autohaus, and although she didn't often voice her opinion on what was going on, she certainly had one. She would have made a very successful dealer on her own.

We were also to have immeasurable assistance from Lindy, both in the form of credit lines to purchase cars and an overall financial umbrella that was overseen by his personal accountant, Paul. It was going to work, we all thought. I never really questioned myself as to whether I could perform the roles that I would have, I just sort of knew I could. But I was to find out it was a long learning curve.

5

Autohaus

We officially opened Autohaus in Cohasset on Washington's Birthday in 1967. "Open House at Autohaus" was the way we advertised, and free sandwiches and beverages made for a well-attended opening day. With the help of friends and family we were able to put together an appealing showroom, office and service department, and with our inventory of new cars and a few used ones we were ready for business. The showroom held the fantastic silver Ferrari 330GT, a red Porsche 911 and a Datsun 411 wagon—something for everyone, we thought. We had a lot of foot traffic that day, and in fact the whole week, with much interest in what we were selling. People in town were excited about the new business with exotic vehicles that many had never seen before.

But what was this town of Cohasset about? It was a shore town that had transitioned from a fishing village to a summer destination for wealthy people starting in the late 19th century. Like the coastal towns of the North Shore of Boston it had a spectacular coastline, rocky in nature with beautiful vistas of the ocean and Massachusetts Bay. Many of the homes built at that time were sizeable and mostly either shingle style or Mediterranean stucco that reminded one of a semitropical locale.

However, following the Great Depression and World War II, these families either could no longer afford to maintain their houses or lost interest in that lifestyle with the change of generations, causing the houses to deteriorate or be sold for apartments or, unfortunately more often, to be torn down. That was the situation when we started Autohaus, but the town retained a certain cachet so that it was well known around metropolitan Boston, and therefore easily identifiable to the general public. It was a residential town with some tourism and most notably the South Shore Music Circus, a tent theater in the round that presented performances by world renowned artists and attracted thousands each year.

We had started Autohaus with a total investment of $18,000—$6,000 each from Fritz, Lindy and me. It's remarkable to think that we did it with so little money, but it was a different time; prices were certainly lower, and we had Lindy to cement our relationship with our bank. We had procured a line of credit—a floor plan, in dealership parlance—through Newton Waltham Bank and Trust, a bank that Lindy used, and used it to purchase the new cars: six new Porsches, mostly 912s but also a few 911s; eight Datsuns including sedans, wagons and one convertible; and one beautiful new two-headlight 330GT Ferrari in silver with red leather. They all were beautiful!

The Datsuns were interesting, if somewhat old fashioned. The sedans and

Autohaus opening lineup, February 1967. A Ferrari 330GT was in the showroom.

wagons were solidly built and featured a standard transmission with Porsche synchromesh, really smooth. The Porsches were coupes but there were pictures of a quasi convertible, the Targa, that was due out soon. And the Ferrari. We didn't have to pay for that as Lindy had left it with us "on the arm," so until we sold it there was no cost to us. Pretty nice. The used cars consisted of my grey 911, Alice's beautiful 190SL, Fritz's 220 and a few inexpensive domestic cars. The used cars we lined up along Route 3A

Autohaus Porsche-Ferrari ad, *Quincy Patriot Ledger*, February 1967.

under a string of bare light bulbs—very used car dealer—that gave some night illumination, while the new cars were up near the showroom and inside it.

When we opened Autohaus in 1967, the Auto Engineering–based philosophy of running a straightforwardly operating dealership was one of our underlying, if unspoken, tenets, and we followed that through the entire 30 years of operation. We were going to be a different type of dealership, not by advertising that philosophy, but by exhibiting it in every aspect of our operation not only through Fritz, Alice and me, but through our employees' behavior, and through the products and services we offered to the public.

We never transacted any business with the Hingham Mercedes-Benz dealer. For a while we tried obtaining the Mercedes-Benz franchise on our own, but were unsuccessful. After we declined to buy the Hingham operation, the owner closed it down, sending his inventory and parts back to the respective manufacturers. His staff, however, were looking for jobs and came to us right away. His ace mechanic, Jimmy Daugherty, was incredibly talented as Fritz recognized immediately. He was analytical, clean, and tidy; Fritz liked him a lot. Dave, a salesman, was a nice fellow with a customer following that was valuable. And Dan, the parts manager, would help set up our parts operation, a vital part of the business as so many parts, and so much money, went through that department.

Fritz knew how to assess mechanical problems, determine repair costs and handle employees. He had an innate ability to analyze technical problems, especially engines. In the time of carburetors there were not many mechanics who could ascertain their proper operation just by listening to them, but Fritz could. A Ferrari with

Porsches and BMWs at Autohaus, summer 1967.

six carburetors was a beautiful sight but it could be a nightmare to synchronize them without the assistance of a mechanical device. Somehow Fritz could just listen to them and know what adjustments needed to be done. I used to like just watching him work on these cars.

Fritz was no ordinary mechanic. He was like a musician who could play those carburetors into a concert of harmony and give a perfect performance. He had an interesting past that included being a service manager at a General Motors operation in Nigeria in the early 1950s. He had a rich bank of stories that he recounted in a Swiss accent, almost always with a humorous bent—not only about cars, but also about people in the many countries he had visited. As a teenager during World War II he lived in Switzerland and did not have to engage in any military action, although all Swiss had a mandatory time in the Army so he knew what had to be done if necessary. Through these positions and experiences he had developed a strong work ethic and didn't tolerate "sloughing off," which of course included mechanics in the Autohaus service department, but after work, in any kind of social occasion he was just one of the crew and wore an entirely different hat.

With our customers he was like a messiah that had been dropped into Cohasset and the South Shore to save them from their automotive maladies—and he did not disappoint them. Not only was he able to have their vehicles repaired properly but he

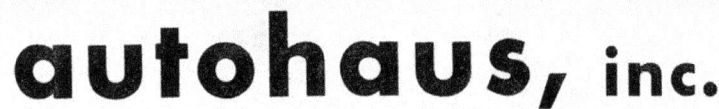

Authorized Sales and Service
For

PORSCHE

Ferrari

DATSUN

ROVER 2000

SERVICE ALSO AVAILABLE FOR MERCEDES BENZ-VOLVO-JAGUAR-TRIUMPH- etc.

OPEN 8 A.M. TO 8 P.M.

Cushing Plaza - Route 3A - Cohasset - 383-0095

Autohaus full line ad, *South Shore News*, 1967.

was their champion in any discussions with the various factories that had built their cars. So if they had a problem with a car that was out of factory warranty, and Fritz thought that the problem should never have occurred in the first place, he would say so to the factory service representative in no uncertain terms, and more often than not he would get the customer's repairs done at no cost to them—or to Autohaus.

In the early days our service department would be open on Saturday mornings and all sorts of people would drop in to have Fritz look at cars they were thinking of buying, or ask Fritz to listen to their engine, or have him take a short test drive with them to identify a strange sound; in short he was a one man band on those mornings. So not only did he create a devoted following, but he also brought in additional revenue which any small startup business needs. After a while the Saturday work log became too great and we reverted to Monday through Friday service appointments, but those Saturdays showed how devoted he was to his profession. Interestingly a lot of customers from Auto Engineering followed him—and myself—to our new business and stayed with us for many years. It was really gratifying.

It wasn't long after we opened that we had a visit from the district sales manager for Rover cars, who was looking for a dealership on the South Shore—actually Rover was looking for a dealership anywhere as they were not big sellers. There were two new models available, the 2000 and the 2000TC (twin carburetor) and some older 3 liter sedans. Alice and Fritz were familiar with the line, but I knew little about them other than having driven one at A/E. They handled well, and the TC model was a decent performer, but they had a weird feeling gearbox and were rather cramped. But Fritz liked them, and after running it by Lindy we decided to take on the line, with the stipulation that we wanted only the 2000 and 2000TC, not any of the older models.

It was interesting to observe what happened when we opened and advertised the lines we were selling and servicing. We certainly had people come in to inspect, and sometimes buy, the cars we were offering, but more frequently people would visit just to see the cars that had not been available in the area before. Then there were the older cars that came in for service that you never would have known were on the South Shore, including lots of 356 series Porsches, a few Datsuns, and quite a few older Rovers including Land Rovers, for which we were not a dealer but would service. Fritz wanted to service all imported cars, not just the ones we sold, so we had a "sandwich board" made advertising that "we service all imported makes," and it worked.

Soon we were servicing Mercedes, BMWs, Fiats (Fritz hated those), Borgwards, Jaguars, and even a Bentley R Type Continental Coupe. The Bentley driver was a woman whose late husband had driven it and she wanted to continue the tradition. She was a diminutive lady whose handwriting was the smallest and most elegant I had ever seen. But she was able to drive the Bentley Continental just fine, even though it was not an easy car to maneuver as it had a standard shift and no power steering and a long, long hood. It needed frequent service as she used it quite a bit. She was thrilled that we had arrived in Cohasset, and soon many other interesting drivers would come to meet Fritz. With his Swiss accent and his charm, people loved him, and never forgot him, even after they had long ago parted with their cars. It was continuously surprising to see the different cars that would show up at our doorstep and the various vehicles we would come upon in the area. That included a Ferrari 340 Mexico at an MG sales and repair shop in North Scituate run by Pres Gray. Pres had campaigned this yellow racer in hill climbs, and guessing from its appearance it did pretty well. What other exotic cars were lurking on the South Shore, we wondered.

Now we had four lines of cars which appealed to different buyers and we were therefore widening our customer base. The Porsche and Ferrari customers were already known to us, but the Datsun and Rover clients were very different. Datsun had a full line of vehicles including sedans, wagons, sports cars and trucks. They even had a four wheel drive vehicle, the Patrol. They were inexpensive, the truck being around $1600 and the cars starting around $1700, and being Japanese, they were expected to be cheaper than other imports. The quality was good with the bodies made of solid steel, not with recycled beer cans as people often thought. Their target market was the VW owner, but it was going to a long fight as VW was so well entrenched, mainly in the snow belt. But we were going to give it a go, and one of the salesman was soon driving one as a demo. Rovers were different again and I soon found out that the buyers were as quirky as the cars. But we sold a few of them and Alice was soon driving one as a demo. I still had the 911 which I really liked, so I continued to drive that.

One day in the middle of March, before we had been open even a month, two men arrived driving a BMW 2000CS, an early coupe model, that was the sportiest car BMW offered. They introduced themselves as Manny von Saucken and Fritz Zimmer. They represented Max Hoffman, the BMW importer at that time, and they were looking for a dealer in the area.

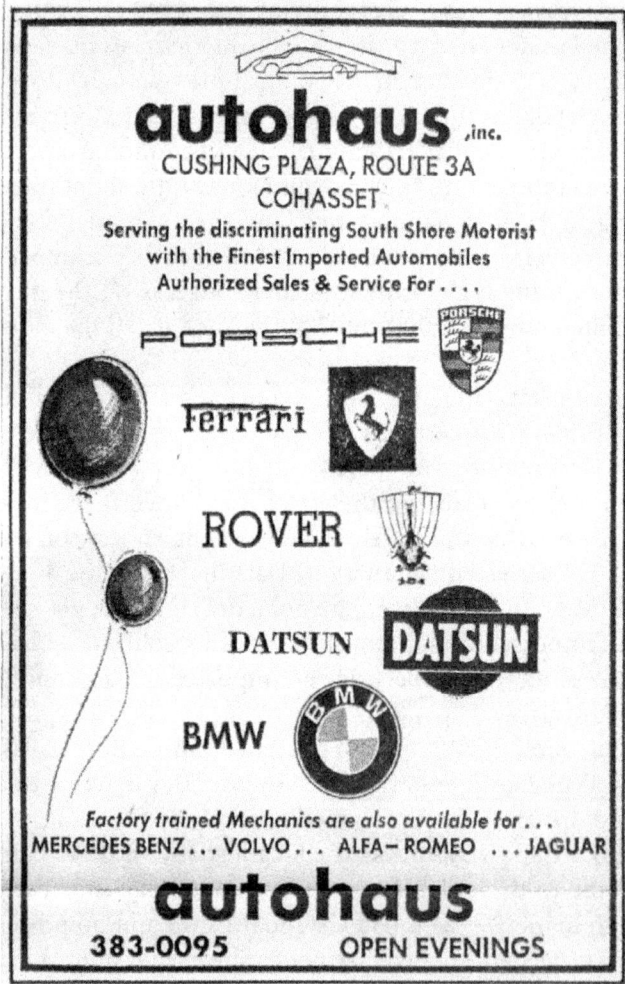

Autohaus ad, *Quincy Patriot Ledger*, October 1967. Now there were five lines of cars!

Interesting! Fritz and I certainly knew about the line of cars they offered and liked them despite their rather dowdy image. They were great to drive and had the German quality that we appreciated, but they were in no way competitive with Mercedes in popularity or name recognition. In fact they were more known for their motorcycles than their automobiles. They did tell us about a new 2 door sedan that was recently released and that would be more appealing to the public. We were excited about the line and after talking it over with Lindy—who also liked the brand—we decided to become a dealer. They offered various four door models from a basic 1600 to a high performance 2000TISA. The 2000CS coupe was being discontinued although we received one in Bristol Gray that we sold to a well known TV anchor from Quincy. In a few weeks we got our first truckload of BMWs and things were looking up.

I have to say something about "receiving a truckload" as there were few happenings at the dealership that were more consistently thrilling to me than the arrival of a car carrier with seven or eight brand new vehicles. Not that all trucks carried cars just for us, as sometimes we just received a partial load, which was still an occasion. I would watch the driver maneuver the truck so as to place the off/on ramps for easy unloading of the cars. The driver would have to pull levers moving levels up and down while unhitching chains and hooks that were keeping the cars secure. It was all exciting, to me at least, as they were each carefully backed off the truck and then parked in an assigned spot to be inspected. Every vehicle had to be checked carefully, for any damage or missing items such as a spare tire or tool kit, etc., had to be noted on the delivery receipt in order to make a claim against either the shipper or the car carrier. Damage was sometimes difficult to see because of surface dirt, bad weather (I hated rainy deliveries) or darkness.

Now we had five lines of cars, Porsche, Ferrari, Datsun, Rover and BMW, and every day things were getting more interesting, and more challenging. My practice of memorizing prices and specs really began to help and I tried to instill the same requirement with my salesmen. They never got to the same level although some tried more than others. We liked to sell pretty close to the list price and didn't do much discounting, figuring that someone from the area would prefer to do business locally as they were discovering the quality of our service—and sales. We made a habit of showing people our service department and introducing them to Fritz, with whom they would be talking after they bought a car.

I remember the first new Porsche we sold. It was a sand beige 912, purchased by a young man who lived in Connecticut but was on an assignment at the Fore River Shipyard in Quincy. The shipyard was busy in those days and was owned by General Dynamics, which was building various types of ships including nuclear powered submarines for the Navy. This fellow came in one evening in March driving a Pontiac of some sort and wanted to drive a 912, so Dave K. took him for a ride and he bought it. Good salesman, that Dave. We were excited as the first new Porsche delivery took place and then of course we had the used Pontiac, which we really didn't want to put in our front line of cars. So we put it in the back while deciding how and to whom we might sell it.

One of the first tests of our ability to trade unusual and therefore tricky to appraise vehicles involved the $14,900 Ferrari 330GT. That car created a lot of interest

The author with Alice and Fritz, winter 1967.

with just about every visitor to our showroom but drew no potential buyers. Ferrari at that time, although a known brand, did not enjoy the widespread attention or desirability that it would command in later decades, so it was not on everyone's wish list, even if they could afford it. So the interest that the car created was ephemeral—that is, until one day in June when a Rolls-Royce drove into the parking lot. I was the only person in the salesroom that day and when I spotted the car pulling in, of course I was interested in what the driver might be looking at.

The Rolls was a Silver Dawn, the predecessor to the Silver Cloud which I was familiar with at A/E. One of Ken's customers was a Mr. Newman whose acoustical engineering firm in Cambridge had conducted the famous test on which Ford based its advertising claim that "At 60 mph a Ford is quieter than a Rolls-Royce." Mr. Newman drove a Silver Cloud which I assumed was the one used in the testing—and having heard it run many times, I didn't think it was especially quiet, though at highway speed it may have been more so. The Dawn, however, I wasn't familiar with. It appearance was much like some of the pre–World War II designs.

When the well dressed grey-haired driver and the younger woman with him entered the showroom I said hello, introducing myself, although I never announced that I was the dealer at first meeting, not wanting customers to feel that I was making the final decision on any purchase offer. Telling me they lived in Cohasset, they gravitated to the Ferrari. They loved it, especially he, who it turns out was a liquor distributor who had retired to live on the South Shore, and then asked if they could drive it. Of course I said yes, but added that I would have to move a few cars as it was the rearmost car in the showroom. They said they could come back, but knowing you could never count on that to happen, I said it was no trouble to move the other three cars—all the time hoping that the Ferrari's battery was charged up. And it was.

There was nothing quite like the sound of a Ferrari 12-cylinder engine starting up (especially in an interior space), as it would turn over a few times before catching, arousing this almost palpable feeling of anticipation in the observers, and then whirrrr, it would fire up and the sound would descend to a lower pitch. It was always exciting. They both loved it as we drove along Jerusalem Road in Cohasset, along the coast, overlooked by the fantastic houses from the town's resort history of the late 19th and early 20th centuries.

When we returned to the dealership the man wanted to know if he could trade in his car and if so, how much we could allow for it. I was really on top of trade-in values as I not only used reference books but also had developed an innate feel for what they were worth, not only at a retail price, but also a wholesale price or what is in actuality the actual cash value (ACV). The ACV was the real value of a vehicle at the time it was traded in (while most dealers would adjust the value after 90 days in inventory, we did not) rather than the amount indicated on a sales contract as used car trade-in allowance.

To determine the Silver Dawn's value, we could inquire from other people who had more experience with that model or we could use our own sense to place a value on the car. We did the latter. They both thanked me for my attention and for the drive in the 330GT, which they enjoyed, but they left without making a deal. You really had to be cautious when showing a one-off car like this because too much pressure might result in no sale. It was also about desire for the car, not need, as people didn't really need a car like this. If you said that it's the only one around (think the man from Maine at A/E) or that someone else is also interested, you might be defeating your chances of a sale. So I asked them to please let me know if they had any other questions about the car (they didn't) or if they might like another drive in it (they wouldn't) and assured them I'd be happy to accommodate them, and with that they left the dealership. About a week later the man called and said he'd like to buy the car at the agreed upon price and take delivery that Saturday. Patience was the aid I used on that sale. And it worked. After he drove off in the Ferrari I had one less new car in inventory, but one more used one—and what a used one it was.

How and to whom was I going to sell this car? Advertise it, of course, and then sell it to a happy new buyer. But there weren't any, at least in the first few weeks I advertised the car, so I stopped the ad and the next day an older Ferrari that I had never seen before drove into the yard with Rhode Island dealer plates.

The driver and his associate were in fact new car dealers from Providence who handled several domestic makes but also loved dealing in imported cars, and the Silver Dawn was the sort of car that interested them. And so I met Charlie and Sid, two unforgettable characters. Charlie loved to trade cars; that is, he'd arrive with a car—such as the Ferrari that he assumed we would be interested in—and work to exchange it for a car that he assumed we didn't want—such as the Rolls-Royce. He actually performed a function that few, if any, other wholesalers were willing or able to do, and I liked his methods, keeping in mind of course that he was trying to make as much on a transaction as he could, as they often included transfers of cash, one way or the other.

It was important to sell cars to wholesalers who were middlemen that would buy from one dealer and sell to another, seldom selling to the retail public themselves and often selling the cars at auto auctions. On that first meeting Charlie and I exchanged cars; he ended up with the Dawn and we with a rare Ferrari 330 America with no exchange of cash. It was the ideal transaction. Although many of the deals we made weren't perfect, almost all were necessary in one way or another.

When Charlie arrived, almost always he would walk through the lot looking at the used cars we had recently, and not so recently, traded and then appear at my office saying he was interested in this car and that car and then another car and he would pay such and such an amount. He, like me, had these figures in his head and knew what he could pay. I rarely saw him refer to a wholesale book such as Galves to come up with a price, which almost every other wholesaler always did. And so it was with the Ferrari and the Rolls.

Now we had another Ferrari in inventory, albeit a pre-owned one, showing just how strange and unpredictable this business was going to be. Since we were still getting our Ferraris from Lindy we looked to him for a replacement and instead of another 330GT he provided us with a new 275GTB/4. What a car that was—12 cylinders, 4 cams, 6 carburetors, 5 speeds, and about the sexiest body on a contemporary car that there was. It was also silver but with black leather, the perfect combination. At that time not everybody wanted a Ferrari painted "arrest me red," many preferring a stealthier color, which silver definitely was. Of course it drove differently than the 330GT as this was a machine that could be raced, and raced it was including those campaigned at Le Mans in 1966. So it was more brutish, but easily maneuvered and extremely easy to drive even at low speeds. The front engine/rear transaxle setup made for excellent weight distribution which translated into almost perfect lines you could take through esses. It was beautiful to look at and sensational to drive. It enveloped you when you sat in it, communicating its capabilities viscerally; it was astounding!

Several customers expressed interest in the Ferrari, and for demonstration drives it was either Fritz or myself who showed the car's prowess to potential buyers. The car was fast and the suspension supple and rewarding as it absorbed the backroad bumps of Cohasset and Norwell. Many seldom used streets connected Route 3A to Route 3, and we knew them all. And after a few years the neighbors knew us and our vehicles well, as after a particularly spirited drive we would inevitably have a call from the police department—sometimes the chief himself—asking who was driving that damned foreign car so fast a few minutes ago. We would apologize for our customer's craziness, he would reply to "take it easy" and we would, for a while.

In fact this would be the final Ferrari that we would get from Lindy as it was the last that he could get from Chinetti, and one of the last Ferraris that Chinetti was able to get from the factory. Actually Chinetti continued to receive a limited number of new cars from Maranello that were classified as '67 models, including the 330GTS, 330GTC and 365 California, a real oddball four seat convertible. Impending changes in the U.S safety and emission laws which applied to any vehicle produced after January 1, 1968, would prevent Ferrari from importing and selling any noncompliant

Author's 1966 Porsche 911 (second from left) at Orange, Massachusetts, autocross. No hubcaps when racing.

vehicles. Since none of their vehicles came even close to conforming to the new laws, there were to be no new Ferraris for three years, we were told. As a result of these laws many European manufacturers stopped exporting vehicles to the U.S., and some never returned including Citroën.

It was a remarkable first year as we now had eight employees including Fritz, Alice and me, two salesmen, a parts manager, an assistant and a Porsche mechanic, T. Burke.

I still belonged to the Porsche Club of America since being at A/E and I liked to go to some of the events, mainly to have fun and maybe also to find new customers.

Autohaus rear oval sticker. Couldn't have been more succinct.

One of the best events was the autocross at the Orange Airport, which was closed to air traffic but open to car racing. These were timed events around a slalom course with cones and barriers to keep you on course. Well, it was harder than I imagined and although the 911 had more power than any of the 356 cars, it couldn't scoot around those pylons as quickly, so there were different classes meaning you competed against other 911s. I had sold a 911 to a dentist, Don, who was a kindred spirit and liked to drive fast, and we decided to form a short caravan and go to some of the Orange events. So my 911 got some workouts, but in those days buyers did not shy away from a performance car that was used in that way; in fact they liked the idea that the car was campaigned in some event or other, regardless of a victory.

I did sell my Porsche that summer of '67 to a local librarian, no less, and put myself in a Datsun Patrol—what a truck! To identify the Porsches as coming from Autohaus, we had a small plastic sticker affixed to the rear of the vehicle. It was easily removable without damaging the finish, and most people took them off.

6

Porscheless

WE CONTINUED TO HAVE CUSTOMERS who followed us from Auto Engineering and from Alice's Saab dealership days. One of those was an older man, Hugh, who drove a supercharged Jaguar XKE coupe, an unusual configuration. I didn't know if he wanted more performance or just wanted to say he had it; probably the former, although he was a very conservative driver and where he used the extra oomph I have no idea. He showed up at Autohaus in 1968 with a turbocharged Ferrari 275GTB4 cam that was a totally wild machine. I don't know who installed the turbo, probably Chinetti, but they did a respectable job. However, the car didn't like the turbo and was always developing problems which Fritz could only fix temporarily. At some point he stopped coming to us, and I heard he had sold the Ferrari and purchased another Jaguar. Strange! Another man we had known at A/E was at Harvard and came down to us and bought a rare BMW 1600 with the high performance Alpina package, which featured two very difficult to synchronize carburetors.

We were still buying our Ferrari parts from Chinetti so we kept in contact with them, actually with his son Coco, who was a car designer heading NART—the North American Racing Team, a Chinetti-sponsored racing team that campaigned at the Le Mans 24 hour race in 1967. We of course were following the rivalry between Ferrari and Ford at Le Mans and the competition that arose from bad feelings between Henry Ford II and Enzo Ferrari. Ford had made an arrangement to purchase Ferrari but Enzo backed out at the last minute, wanting to keep Ferrari as an Italian entity. Many of our customers, like ourselves, were racing enthusiasts who saw that Porsche was becoming a serious force in motorsports, coming in second at Le Mans while Ferrari didn't enter a factory car in 1968. The Ford GT40 was still dominating the event, but the Porsche-Ferrari competition had us conflicted as whom to cheer for.

We soon sold the Ferrari 275GTB4, but sadly had no new replacement for it. Despite all kinds of stories about Euro versions coming into the States, we never saw any—at least we thought we didn't until a wholesale dealer showed up with a used 1967 330GTS that he wanted to sell to us. It was red with black leather and even had a hardtop, and boy were we interested in that car. So he left it with us for a few days to check it out when suddenly the dealer reappeared saying the transaction was off as there were some issues with the car. I'll say. It turned out that the car had been produced in 1968 and therefore didn't have the necessary modifications to be sold in the States, and if we had purchased it we would have been out of luck. I think the government must have been following the car's whereabouts since its arrival in the

U.S. as they were aware it was in our facility and demanded that the wholesaler get it back. Whew!

So now we had no Ferraris to sell although we were hearing rumors of a replacement for the 275GTB that was going to be introduced that fall at the Paris Auto Show. We were keeping our fingers crossed. At the same time we recognized the importance of Porsche sales, along with the increasing interest in Datsuns; with BMW we weren't so sure, so our emphasis would have to be on what we had available to merchandise now and just hope for the future.

Autohaus became a very, very busy place as the combination of five lines of cars and the desire of the service department to accept all (most) makes made every day full of surprises and excitement. The daily drive from Milton to Cohasset (I had moved back to Mom and Dad's when I left A/E) was becoming difficult as I was spending so much time at the dealership. I had to get an apartment in the area, and I found one. One of our service customers, Parker Schofield, who drove a Land Rover 88 diesel—talk about slow—had an apartment for rent that was part of his house in Scituate on an island. I think Fritz had found out about it—and when I saw it, I loved it.

Now I could make it to work in just a few minutes and spend as much time as I wanted at the dealership—which was a lot. We were closed on Sundays, so I just worked six days a week while the service department was open Monday through Friday. They were very busy and with the multiple car lines we sold and with the "open door" policy for any imported make to come in for service work, the parts department was also too busy for just one man, so we hired an assistant who would also pick up parts at different depots so that service vehicles would be finished on time. It was then that we decided to use one of Datsun pickup trucks to transport parts, and to paint the logos of the cars that we sold on the truck. The doors were painted with Autohaus typeface and

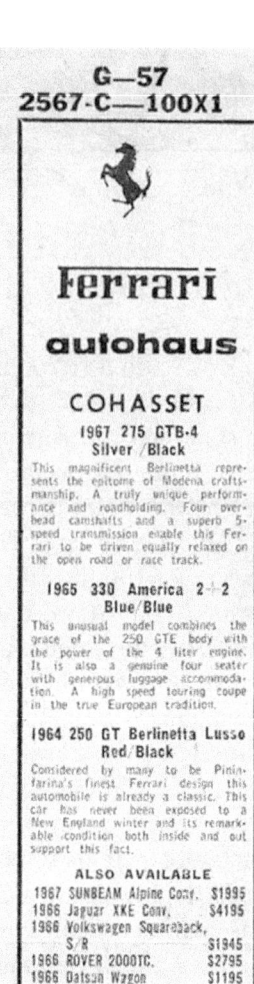

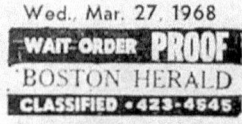

Ferrari ad, *Boston Herald*, March 1968. I always liked this ad.

Alice with new Porsche. The lime green 911 Targa was a hit!

the phone number and address (also on the tailgate). The truck looked great and served us well for over 250,000 miles before finally succumbing to New England rust.

But completing work on time became more difficult. The service department was so busy that Fritz had to hire more mechanics, but qualified people were difficult to find. Even though we had four mechanics at the time, Fritz had been trying to find someone with his "European work ethic," whatever that was. I guess he meant someone who was meticulously neat and had worked as an apprentice in a shop with tile floors under a master mechanic and therefore earned his stripes, so to say. That meant he was going to have to get someone from Europe, which really meant someone from Switzerland. So he advertised in the Swiss publication *Automobil Revue* and got a number of responses, including from a man named Ruedi who seemed well qualified. They wrote back and forth and Fritz's brother in Zurich went and interviewed him, reporting back that he was a good choice. That was step one. After reaching an agreement with Ruedi we had to get permission from the U.S. Department of Labor to allow him in to work here. That was step two. At that time the government wanted employers to hire Americans to do all their work and unless you couldn't find someone qualified they wouldn't consider allowing a foreigner a work visa. You had to advertise for a period of time for the position to be filled, and only after showing that no mechanics qualified to work on Ferraris, Porsches and BMWs were available could you present your case to the government. We did that, and finally got approval for Ruedi to work at Autohaus. And we were glad we did. He was a strong addition to the service department and got along well with everyone, even if they couldn't understand his broken English, but of course Alice and Fritz were happy to translate.

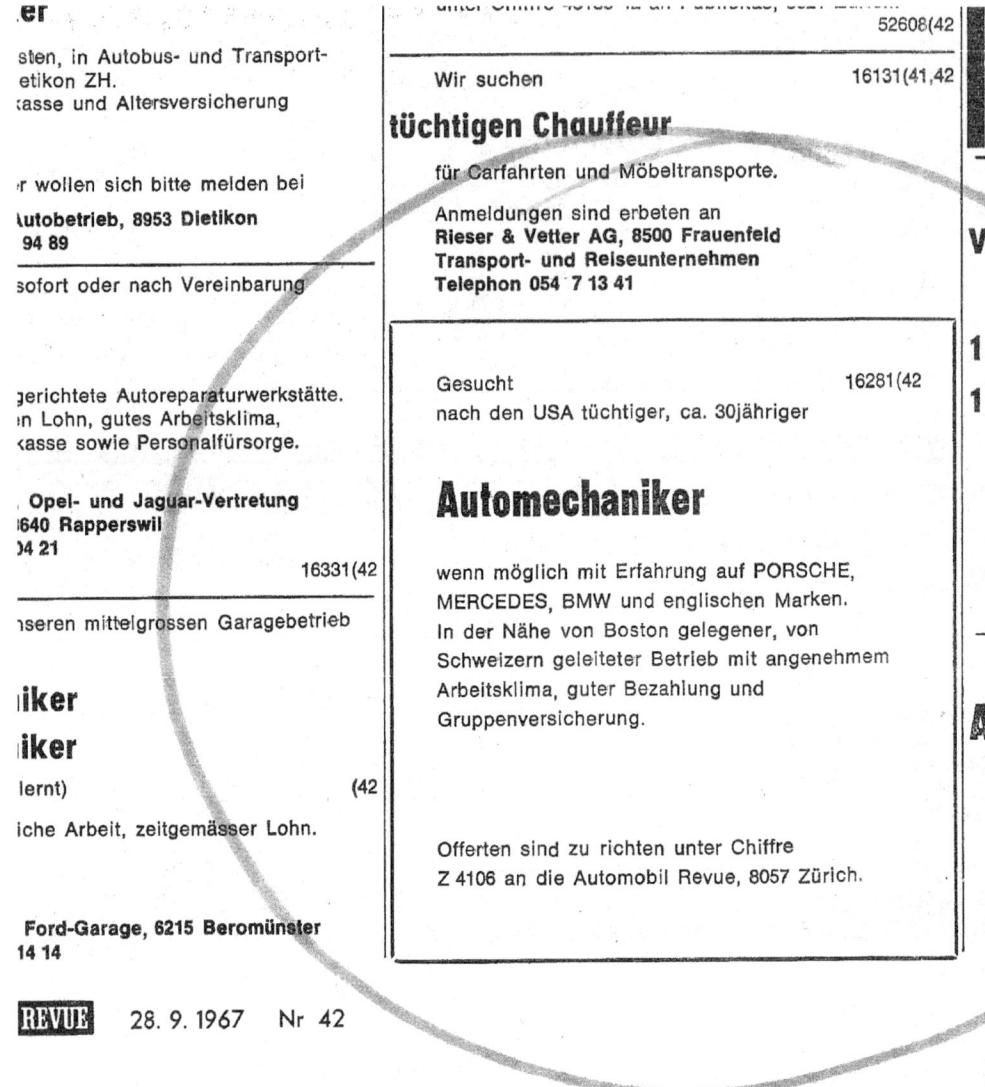

Our ad in the Swiss paper *Automobil Revue*, seeking a mechanic. It worked!

So by the end of our first year we had a total of 12 employees, and to thank them for their contributions we decided to have a Christmas party that would become a long tradition at Autohaus. We tried to have it at a nice place; the first year it was at the Red Lion Inn, a quaint local restaurant dating to before the Revolutionary War. It was also the time we gave out bonuses, and we gave one to every employee every year. Of course giving them out at the party increased attendance; in fact it was usually 100 percent. The next year we started a tradition at the Christmas party when we gave out the Autohaus Achievement Awards. Everyone received one of these satirically based tributes that I had a lot of fun creating and then handing out. The top award, the "Big Bertha Memorial Award" given out for the most egregious faux pas of the year, was sought after by all employees (or so they always said). That award was a framed black and white photograph of Big Bertha, a 1958 Bentley S1 that we had traded from Charlie, but that's another story.

In the late 1960s Porsche was really the only high performance foreign sports car being imported that was capable of competition of any merit. The 911 was an exciting car to drive with impressive acceleration and agile handling while the 912 handled even better but without the punch. Their competition included Mercedes, whose 250/280SL, though beautifully made, was a GT rather than a true sports car like its spectacular predecessor the 300SL, and the Jaguar XKE, which had become softer and also a GT. The same was true of Lamborghini, Maserati and even the Alfa Romeo 2600, which were all essentially GT cars, and of course Ferrari had disappeared from the U.S. market because of the new emission rules. Porsche's real competition was Corvette, which brought out a new body design for 1968 that was startling looking and proved to be very popular and very quick.

1958 Bentley "S"—"Big Bertha." Surprisingly sporty, but not a Continental "R" type.

Porsche for its 1968 lineup also did some modifications. They kept the 912 and 911 but deleted the 911S (because of emission regulations) and added the 911L. All the models were available in both coupe and, as in 1967, a targa configuration, the targa being a quasi convertible with a removable roof panel that could be stored in the forward trunk, while the rear window could be either fixed glass or plastic with a zipper and the option to fold it down.

The 911 L model would also be available with a $280 option, the Sportomatic transmission that was a semi-automatic transmission not unlike the Mercedes Hydrak and Saab Saxomat. It worked well enough, enabling the driver to still shift the car through four speeds but eliminating the tiresome—for some—clutch pedal. Now I was driving a Sportomatic as a demonstrator and was aware of its niceties but also the danger of forgetting that it was not a true standard shift as the extra wide brake pedal would remind the driver if their left foot tried to depress the clutch and hit the brake pedal in error. An experienced Porsche driver might encounter driving problems with this setup, as was demonstrated by a representative of Porsche of America at a new model introduction day at the Lime Rock, Connecticut, race track.

All the manufacturers had dealer meetings, some more than others, and some

Porsche Targa in a 1967 factory brochure photograph.

had them in more exotic locales than northwest Connecticut. But Porsche liked the dealers and their salesmen to enjoy a "hands on" experience; that is, being able to enjoy the car's performance not only on the road, but also on the race track. At Lime Rock we were all going to get an opportunity to drive the Sportomatic on the track, but before going out ourselves we were going to be treated to a demonstration of the car's abilities by watching a factory representative, the national service manager, Wolfgang (later a successful and much admired Porsche dealer in our area), go around the track and show its—and his—capabilities. We stood on the upper area of the course just before the downhill stretch that had a curve to the right, and as Wolfgang was heading to the turn and beginning to slow down, suddenly the car's brake lights came on and the car lurched to the left, then to the right and then unceremoniously rolled over onto its roof! As Wolfgang climbed out of the car, fortunately unhurt, I said to myself, "wide brake pedal!" And although we never heard what caused the rollover, many dealers would shy away from that model. The bottom line was that it's hard to break (no pun intended) old habits even for a short time. We were all sure that it took a long time for Wolfgang to recover from the embarrassment of that incident.

Buyers of some European cars had the option of taking delivery of their new cars in Europe through what was called the European (or Overseas) Delivery Plan. The customer would order the car to their specifications through a U.S. dealer, pay for it here while arranging insurance and return shipment, and decide where they wanted it delivered. Normally it was at the factory of the respective manufacturer but they could also arrange for delivery to numerous cities throughout Europe and also the Middle East. Rover had such a plan, as did BMW and Porsche, which all were very well organized. Prices of the cars were less than stateside and the savings were compounded by having no rental car fees abroad, which were much more expensive than here. We sold a few Porsches and Ferraris that way and also a few Rovers, but the BMW program proved most popular.

Meanwhile the sales staff was still having a difficult time remembering all the prices on all the cars, so I decided to print a price list that enumerated the different brands with their respective models and prices for same. The list also included some popular accessories so that we could give it to a customer (the salesmen would have it at hand) and they could take it home with them. All the prices were the list prices that appeared on the window stickers and if people wanted to negotiate on pricing that would be done on a blank piece of paper, not the price list, so that if they went to a competitive dealership they couldn't show them negotiated prices. Of course the customer might write their own fantasy discounted price on our list, but that didn't seem to worry us.

It was this summer that I met Dave Barrow, another Brit who was a real car guy. Were they all like that, I wondered? He loved to come in and gab about the latest and would occasionally buy an older American beast, as he called them, or sometimes a Datsun. A year or two later he joined us as a part-time salesman (he had a full-time engineering job) and did quite well—it was that damn British accent again! He was also a very good photographer and it was he who took the photos of "Big Bertha" that appeared at every

Porsche ad, *Boston Herald*, August 1968.

ROVER

2000 TC 4 door sedan	$4,198.00
2000 Automatic sedan	4,198.00

Ferrari

330 GT 2+2	$14,200.00
330 GTC coupe	14,200.00
330 GTS convertible	14,200.00
275 GTB-4 Berlinetta	15,500.00
365 California convertible	21,300.00

Ferrari prices are for 1967 models as 1968 cars have not been announced as of this printing.

All prices Port of Entry

SALES DEPARTMENT

8:00 a.m. - 9:00 p.m. Weekdays, March - October

8:00 a.m. - 8:00 p.m. Weekdays, November - February

8:00 a.m. - 5:30 p.m. Saturdays All Year

SERVICE DEPARTMENT

8:00 a.m. - 5:30 p.m. Weekdays All Year

8:00 a.m. - Noon Saturdays All Year

Service is available for all imported makes

autohaus

1968
PRICE LIST

Cushing Plaza, Route 3A

Cohasset, Massachusetts

617-383-0095

FEB. 1, 1968

	Coupe	Targa
912	$4,880.00	$5,380.00
911	6,220.00	6,620.00
911L	6,820.00	7,220.00

ACCESSORIES

Chrome Wheels	$110.00
Electric Sunroof	380.00
Fog Lights	44.00
Heated Rear Window	100.00
Tinted Glass	72.00
Wood Steering Wheel	60.00
5 Speed Transmission	80.00
Sportomatic Transmission	280.00

Additional Accessory List upon request.

PL 510

4 door sedan	$2,046.00
4 door sedan - automatic	2,211.00
station wagon	2,246.00
station wagon - automatic	2,411.00
SPL 311 convertible	2,841.00
SRL 311 convertible	3,073.00
L520 pickup truck	1,816.00

NOTE:

All manufacturers reserve the right to change prices at any time with no prior notice.

1600 2 door sedan	$2,597.00

ACCESSORIES

Radial Tires	$ 45.00
Sliding Roof	135.00
Tachometer	75.00
Air Horns	50.00
Power Brakes	45.00
Skai Upholstery	45.00

BMW 4 door sedan and coupe models are presently unavailable for 1968, but are expected for U.S. delivery mid 1968.

INSTALLED RADIOS for all makes

AM Motorola	$ 75.00
AM FM Motorola	125.00
AM Blaupunkt Vienna	125.00
AM FM Blaupunkt Frankfurt	175.00

Overseas delivery can be arranged for all automobiles listed in this pamphlet. Prices upon request.

Autohaus price list, 1968. Ferrari prices were for 1967 models as no 1968 models were imported.

Christmas party. He and his wife Elaine remain friends to this day. He had a friend, Jeff, that worked for Lucas and drove a Lotus Elite, a car that was even smaller than my old Speedster, and handled better. The three of us would gab for hours along with Fritz, after the shop was closed. It was fun and interesting as we could compare American vs. British customers and buying habits.

    As I mentioned, the General Dynamics Shipyard in Quincy was very busy constructing ships including LNG tankers and nuclear submarines, one of which, the USS *Sunfish*, SSN649, was nearing completion. When three of the officers aboard showed up one day in the showroom looking at Porsches, I guessed they wanted to reward themselves after the lengthy process of overseeing construction of such an astounding vessel. And I was right. Two of them wanted to buy new Porsche 912 Targas and the third a late model Porsche 356C Cabriolet—what a trio! Well, we had to order the 912s as it was January and we had none in inventory, which was OK with them, but the third officer, John, wanted something now and we could accommodate him as we had just traded a grey with black '65 356C Cabriolet with only 36,000 miles on it. He traded a '61 coupe and since he had a new girlfriend he was happy to have the convertible for the summer. When we received the Targas—one green and one silver—the submarine was almost ready to be launched, and since we had become friendly with the officers, they invited Fritz, Alice and me plus my friend Loring to the ceremony.

The christening ceremony was attended by all types of officers and politicians and the invited guests. After the ceremony we got to go aboard the USS *Sunfish* and to explore the cabins and different decks. It was the first and last time we ever got to board one of these remarkable and unforgettable vessels, and also just about the last time we would see our three officer friends as they were going to sea shortly after the launching. But before they went out for sea trials we had a visit from one more of the officers; in fact he was the commander of the ship, and he bought a new BMW 2002 from us. What a crew! Happily we frequently heard from Bill, and one year he sent us a Naval calendar with a picture of the *Sunfish* on the January page showing him quite visibly standing up in the conning tower. Maybe I should have gone into the Navy after all.

In the autumn the new Porsche models were introduced (not at Lime Rock Park) and they included the 912, 911T and the return of the 911S. The 911L had disappeared but the Sportomatic transmission continued in the 911T only. Into 1969 our Porsche sales continued to increase, and surprisingly for us we had many customers coming from Boston and points west. The Cadillac dealer that I had talked with a few years before had become a Porsche dealer and had the sales room in the same building as the Cadillacs. I guess buyers didn't feel comfortable with that arrangement, and often customers would tell us that they wanted to buy from someone who specialized in Porsches and imported cars. That was fine with me!

We were doing a lot of Porsche business as a result of advertising in the *Boston Globe* and *Boston Herald* almost every Sunday in their respective auto sections. The auto editor for the *Herald*, Cameron Dewar, was a real sports car fan—mainly English cars—who always had a nice writeup about new cars coming on the market and new dealers in the area.

All the Porsches that we were allocated from Porsche Cars Northeast were special orders; that is, we were told what cars we would get from a future month, usually four to five months hence, and which model and in what configuration, and we could select the exterior color, the interior and what accessories, if any. So January orders they were probably for June delivery, maybe May, and once the cars were ordered it was difficult to change the specifications.

Most customers didn't want to wait four or five months for a special order delivery and would take whatever color we had in inventory, or sometimes we would exchange cars with another dealer to obtain what they preferred—a "dealer swap."

These swaps were disliked by almost all the dealers but were a necessary evil. Occasionally customers did want cars exactly to their specifications, and for them Porsche had a very long list of options they could choose from, adding substantially to the price but personalizing the car to their taste. So every month we would order cars either for a customer or for inventory, and if for inventory we could create special color and equipment combinations that customers would not find elsewhere. Porsche had an extensive color selection, much broader than BMW, and more interior choices also, so we came up with what we thought were unusual and attractive combinations. And our customers must have agreed as we never had any vehicle on the lot for very long.

Jack Crusoe had left A/E when Lindy sold to Ken, but had been retained as the Regional Sales Manager for Porsche Cars Northeast. We thought at that time that we were really running smoothly and that 1969 would be the most profitable year so far, particularly with Porsche sales, until one day we had a visit from Jack Crusoe, our old friend and real Porschephile. He told us that he was going to retire as Porsche of America was preparing to absorb, or more accurately buy out, all the existing distributors such as Porsche Cars Northeast. We were definitely going to miss him; although Fritz had known him longer than I, Jack had been instrumental in getting me where I was. Porsche of America would now distribute cars from their central location in New Jersey starting with the 1969 model year, and we could only wonder what that might foretell.

I often wondered why some people came from such a distance to do business with us. It wasn't because of our aggressive (virtually nonexistent) discounting, so what was it? Sure, we had unusual colors and an interesting selection, but I think it was also a word of mouth reputation that developed without our realizing it or even trying to advertise. We became "the place" to buy a vehicle, perhaps because we were not only a new dealership, but a new type of dealership manifested by our selling philosophy that treated the customers honestly and reverently. In any case it was an exciting and rewarding experience as many of our customers became personal friends and many of our friends became customers.

Early in 1969 came the second Porsche revelation, that the new Porsche organization was going to start marketing the Audi brand through existing Porsche dealerships. Audi, whose front wheel drive sedans were sold just about everywhere except the U.S., wanted a ready-made network of existing dealers that knew how to market and sell and service German products to Americans. We wondered, did that mean we were going to have a sixth line of cars, now including Audi? No, said Jack, that's not what it meant. What this new arrangement was that we could continue to sell Porsches and become a dealer for Audis, but by agreeing to sell their products we would not be able to continue selling the other lines.

Whaaaat? Give up Datsun, BMW, Rover and Ferrari? And have only Porsche and the unknown Audi? Yes, that's what Jack was saying would be our choice. And even though Jack was losing his job, he still liked the idea as he thought Porsche was the best, and Audi was probably a good bet to become popular and profitable. Fritz and I, however, were speechless. This would all happen, Jack said, sometime in the fall before the 1970 models were to be introduced. Jack understood it would be a difficult decision for us to make and said an Audi representative traveling around to Porsche dealers to better explain themselves and would like to visit us soon. We contacted Lindy, who already knew the story and told us that it was up to us how to proceed. I don't think he was very pleased with the whole affair. So we agreed to meet with Karl, the Porsche factory representative, and the following week he arrived in a new Audi 100 sedan. We looked it over with the sales staff, finding it well appointed but very bland in appearance.

Fritz was familiar with the Audi line in Europe, and I had seen them there and read about their popularity in cold climates as they were all front wheel drive and performed well in the snow—sort of like a Saab, but German. Well, Karl was definitely German, and had just recently moved to the U.S. to oversee the administration of the new import line. He seemed nice enough, chatting with us and looking around our facility to see if it met his standards. I guess it did as he said they would be enthused to have us as one of their dealers. When we questioned him about their rationale for wanting exclusive Porsche and Audi dealerships, he pointed to the success of VW with its profitable program of having just one line of cars, and said with Porsche and Audi's two lines of cars, similar profits would emerge. But how well would the Audis sell, we asked. Karl replied that Americans would buy anything with the "made in Germany" label on it. Well, that wasn't enough for us, and we all agreed that to give up our other lines would be foolish, as they were well established with sales certainly greater than Porsche and the unknown Audi.

With that, Karl started speaking German with Fritz, leaving me out of the conversation. Fritz was going "ya, ya, ya" as he often did when listening, until suddenly he got up, saying he had to get back to the service department, and left our meeting. Karl thanked me for my time, said they would ask us soon for our decision and

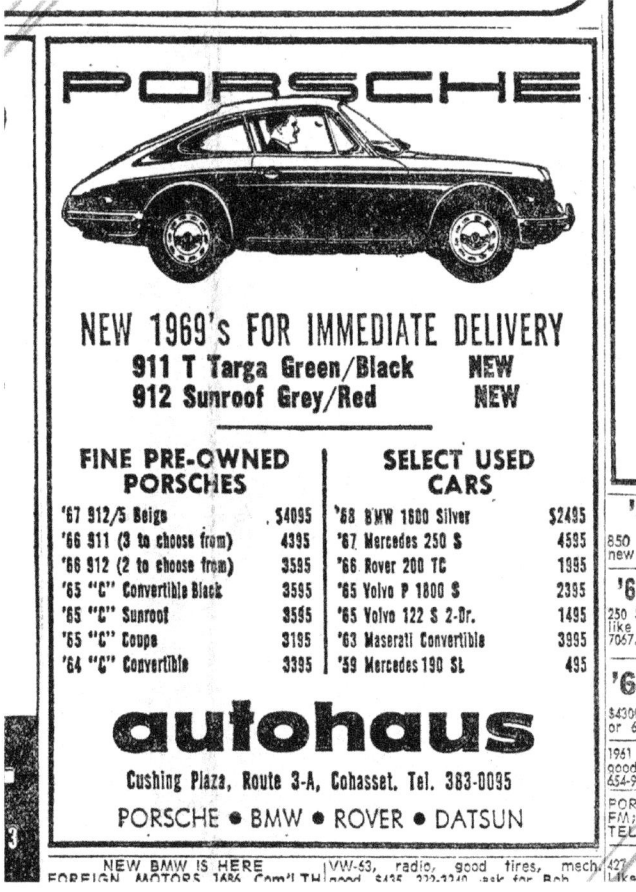

Porsche ad, *Boston Globe*, September 1969. One of our last Porsche new car advertisements.

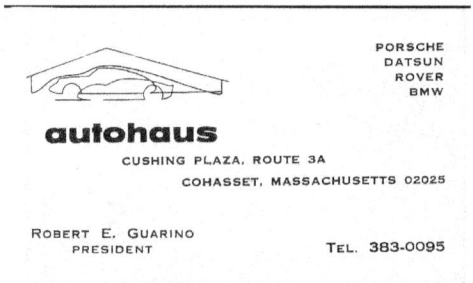 

Left: Autohaus business card, 1969—the last one with Porsche, but Ferrari is missing as the marque was on hiatus in the United States. *Right:* Autohaus business card, no longer listing Porsche.

then left the dealership. A few minutes later Fritz reappeared, looking furious, and asked if Karl had left. Then he told me what Karl had said after breaking into German when we had asked him how we could know that Audi would be successful. Karl had replied that "Americans were so stupid they would buy anything made in Germany, even a toilet seat that had nails sticking up on the seat." Wow. Of course Fritz had lived in Switzerland during World War II, and although Switzerland was neutral, a lot of German officers/soldiers lived there during that their time. I didn't know exactly his feelings about them, but assumed not many Swiss were fans of that regime. But it was the fact that Karl was insulting Americans that upset Fritz, who was an American citizen. It was in a way predictable that the Germans might be a bit haughty about their product, but to relate that story was a big mistake.

Brothers Doug, Dick, author, and Gerry with Dick's 1962 Porsche Super 90 dual grille roadster, Milton, Massachusetts, 1970.

This was a big decision. As much as we loved Porsche, when we looked toward the future there seemed more potential for sales and customers with our other lines rather than just selling Porsche and the unfamiliar Audi. So with the greatest reluctance, we gave up Porsche.

Of course we would continue to service Porsches and to sell used ones, but sadly that would be all. That was business and we had to move on. So we did. And although we were forced to move on, my brothers never did, as for many years thereafter they were driving Porsches—mostly roadsters with various engine configurations, and some coupes including a 912. They had been bitten by the "bug" as had I early on, and so it was that for many years, in fact even today, family gatherings inevitably include Porsche stories and sagas.

7

Automatico

ONE EVENT ON OUR FALL CALENDAR was the annual International Auto Show held at the Hynes Memorial Auditorium in Boston. Most of the manufacturers would display their products and would ask dealers to send salesmen in "to work the floor" during the ten days of the show, some ending up with what was called a "fluorescent pallor." It was kind of fun to see all the competition and speak with other salespeople about their cars, sizing up the new products. We had sent some salespeople to the 1968 show where both Datsun and BMW had product displays, and although we sold nothing at the show we did get some leads for future sales. This year, 1969, not only would BMW and Datsun be represented but also Ferrari.

I had received a call from Dick Fritz, the sales manager from Chinetti Motors, who said they were going to display a few used Ferraris, as no new ones were being imported, just to keep the name in front of the public. Like they really needed to do that, I thought. As in the past, the night before the show opened to the public, there was a "dealers' night" where importers, manufacturers and dealers (and

N.A.R.T. sticker for Luigi Chinetti's North American Racing Team.

special friends) would mingle in a festive atmosphere with hors d'oeuvres and wine to make everyone even happier. In the afternoon, I went to see what cars Chinetti was displaying and found that Dick had brought two very impressive cars from Connecticut—a 365GTB/4, or Daytona (a European version as the car was not yet available in the U.S.) and a race car that NART had campaigned. Dick, who was knowledgeable on most aspects of the Ferrari business, told me what the factory was thinking about the U.S. market. Since Ferrari was a small manufacturer—less than 1,000 cars a year—it was difficult and very costly on a per vehicle basis for them to comply with the recent safety and emission regulations. Dick's opinion was that we would not see any new models for at least a year or two; however, he did tell me that Chinetti was trying to get the factory to adapt one of their new four seat models, the 365GT2+2, to American specs and install an automatic transmission in it. Whaaat? An automatic Ferrari?

It's important to remember that Luigi Chinetti was a friend of Enzo Ferrari's from their association with Alfa Romeo before World War II, and then after the war when Chinetti drove for Ferrari, winning Le Mans in 1949 with a Ferrari Barchetta. Partly as a result of that, Chinetti landed the American distributorship rights for Ferrari automobiles. The factory also responded to special requests from Chinetti and would sometimes create special cars with one-off bodies for Chinetti's customers. Hence the request for the automatic 365GT. I kept a mental note of that as we knew a man from Cohasset who had inquired a couple of times about an automatic Ferrari, but we had told him the chances were slim. In truth, often people would ask us to let them know if we ever got a such and such car, as they might like to buy one; then, when we got such a car, they would say that they were no longer interested, or that they never were, or whatever. We never knew.

So, as I was talking with Dick I was surveying the rest of the displays, including Datsun, which was adjacent to us. As they were driving their cars in and arranging the display I saw a model in green that I didn't recognize. I didn't even think it was a Datsun as it was a coupe, and a very handsome one at that. But it was indeed a Datsun—the new and unannounced 240Z! I went over right away and couldn't believe my eyes. The car was beautiful and would be a true game changer for Datsun. No more dowdy image for them. And beyond the amazing exterior, it had a new six cylinder engine and a beautifully appointed interior which I sat in right away, getting a positive impression of the material quality and the dashboard design, which was reminiscent of the Ferrari Lusso with canted gauges sitting high on the dash. The Japanese had done their homework on this car. I think this was the American introduction of the car as I never had seen or even heard of it before.

This new Datsun introduced as a surprise 1970 model would shake the whole auto industry, especially the European sports car makers. It was to become probably the most sought after new imported car model since the end of World War II when new cars were so hard to get. At one point the waiting time for a 240Z would exceed two years. Just astounding!

It was just after the auto show, when Mr. Remick came by the showroom to give a ride to one his sons who was dropping off a BMW he had bought from us for service, that I told him of my conversation with Dick Fritz about the Ferrari automatic. His

Datsun 240Z, first factory brochure, 1970. This car stunned the automotive world and signaled the end of British domination of the sports car market. Still handsome today.

eyes lit up as he said, "Order me one—I'll take it." And he was serious. I showed him a picture of the 365GT2+2 from Fritz's Swiss journal and we talked about colors as we had some paint chips and leather samples from the 330GT model, and he got really excited. We didn't talk about price as I'm sure he had an idea of what it might be, and we didn't discuss delivery time—if Chinetti didn't know when, then we certainly didn't know when. But in any case he gave me an order for a metallic green car with green leather. Beautiful! The next day I called Chinetti and told Dick about our order and he said great, as they had just heard from the factory that they were going to manufacture just six of the 365GT2+2s with a General Motors Superturbine 400 transmission as that was the only automatic available that could handle the Ferrari engine's torque—or so they said. He would place our order, and we and our customer would wait.

Meanwhile back in BMW world, the large BMWs were getting popular and we were taking all sorts of different trades, making our used car inventory varied and interesting. One day a Mr. and Mrs. Alden drove in the lot and asked for me, much to the disappointment of the salesman who greeted them. Much of the time I would refer the customer back to the salesman, but occasionally they wanted only to talk/deal with me, and so it was this time. The Aldens were from Scituate, the next town, and I couldn't believe that I had never seen their car before as it certainly stood out: a pale yellow '59 Rolls-Royce Silver Cloud with a red leather interior, a distinctive combo that actually worked on the car. They had bought it in Boston but had picked it up at the factory in England, then toured the British Isles, in style I'd say. It was fully equipped including air conditioning, which most cars of that period did not have,

ROVER

2000 TC 4 door sedan $4,198.00
2000 Automatic sedan 4,198.00

SALES DEPARTMENT

8:00 a.m. - 9:00 p.m. Weekdays
April–October

8:00 a.m. - 8:00 p.m. Weekdays
November–April

8:00 a.m. - 5:30 p.m. Saturdays
All Year

SERVICE DEPARTMENT

8:00 a.m. - 5:30 p.m. Weekdays
All Year

8:00 a.m. - Noon Saturdays
All Year

*Service is available
for all imported makes.*

autorent

A new company formed to provide our customers with a convenient mode of transportation while their automobiles are being serviced.

Available is a new BMW 1600 and a Datsun 510, both at very nominal rates for short term rental.

Information on long term leasing is available upon request for all imported makes.

autohaus

1969
PRICE LIST

Cushing Plaza, Route 3A

Cohasset, Massachusetts

617-383-0095

February 1, 1969

	COUPE	TARGA
912	$5195.00	$5820.00
911T	5995.00	6520.00
911E	7195.00	7720.00
911S	7895.00	8420.00

Please add to the above prices $75.00 for preparation and $50.00 for Inland Freight.

ACCESSORIES

5 Speed Transmission .... $ 80.00
Sportomatic Transmission 290.00
Forged Alloy Wheels 343.00
Chrome Wheels 103.00
Leather Seats 162.00
Air Conditioning 660.00
Electric Sun Roof 408.00
Long Range Quartz Iodine Lights ... 82.00

Additional Accessory List Upon Request.

PL 510
2 door Sedan $1996.00
4 door Sedan 2046.00
4 door Sedan, Automatic 2226.00
4 door Station Wagon 2276.00
4 door Station Wagon
  Automatic 2456.00
SPL 311 Convertible 2841.00
SRL 311 Convertible 3171.00
L-521 Pickup Truck 1846.00

Please add $39.00 Inland Freight to the above prices.

RADIOS   Prices Include Installation
          Speaker and Antenna

BLAUPUNKT
AM Hamburg .... $ 85.00
AM–FM Montreal 125.00
AM–FM–SW Frankfurt 175.00
Snob 100 Tape Player 250.00

MOTOROLA
AM Pushbutton .... $ 75.00
AM–FM Manual 125.00
Stereo Tape Player 175.00

1600 2 door	$2727.00
2002 2 door	2982.00
2002 2 door automatic	3277.00
2000 4 door	4140.00
2000 4 door automatic	4435.00
2500 4 door	5284.00
2500 4 door automatic	5624.00
2800 4 door	6284.00
2800 4 door automatic	6624.00
2800 CS Coupe	7480.00
2800 CA Coupe automatic	7820.00

Please add $40.00 Inland Freight to the above prices.

ACCESSORIES

Skai Upholstery (1600, 2002) 45.00
              (2500, 2800) 70.00

Leather Upholstery 315.00
Sliding roof 135.00
Radial Tires 45.00

Autohaus 1969 price list. Last time with Porsches; still no resumption of Ferraris from Maranello. U.S. emission and safety standards were blocking the way.

and even sported an altimeter that was built into the wooden dashboard, providing continuing information on your altitude. How quaint!

They bought a BMW 2500 automatic, trading the yellow Rolls which became an instant attraction, though we expected it would not be very saleable. After much discussion we decided to change the color of the exterior by painting it dark green, Brewster green, a shade so dark that it looked black in most lights. But it was a big mistake. We learned that when you change the color of a car you not only change

Alice with 1962 Maserati 3500 GT convertible. The car had previously belonged to a woman from Winchester, Massachusetts, who later purchased a Dino 246GT from us.

its look, but its personality as well. The car had existed so far with its original paint and wanted to retain it, so changing it did not sit well with it. Anthropomorphism, you say—well, maybe, but not only did it take us forever to get the painting done at a body shop that we used regularly, but we were always finding little areas that would show some yellow. And it took forever to sell. If it wasn't the car's revenge it at least was very frustrating. We eventually sold it to one of our parts suppliers after he expressed a mild interest in it. That was a lesson for him as well.

  At that time BMW, like most manufacturers, suggested—no insisted—that you change the oil in a new car at 600 miles to remove any metal particles that might have accumulated from the early operation of the engine. Worse were the speed restrictions on the engine—rpm more precisely—that you were to observe during the "break-in period." Don't exceed 3000 rpm for the first 1000 miles, 4000 rpm for the first 2000 miles, etc., until at 5000 miles you could take the car to the redline, but not for sustained periods of time. Well, they should have seen Fritz test the cars. He was of the theory—as was I—that the faster you broke a car in, the faster it would be over its life, and he was right. There was nothing sadder than to see a beautifully maintained high performance car that had been "babied" and coddled so that when a subsequent owner tried to use its full potential, the car would develop major engine or drivetrain problems. As Alice said once in her beautiful Swiss accent after being stopped by the local police while driving a Ferrari, "I'm driving a fast car, why shouldn't I go fast!"

  It was in early 1970, after the loss of Porsche had really taken hold, that Lindy and we decided to part ways, while realizing that we never would be where we were without his participation. He had helped many, many friends and former employees start out in various auto related businesses and was known to relish getting things started, bowing out after seeing them heading toward initial success. So we arranged to purchase his shares and retire them, leaving Fritz and me as 50/50 partners—a perfect arrangement, except that now we would have to arrange our own line of credit with a new bank, as the one he had arranged for us to use wanted us to find someone new.

We set up a line of credit with the Rockland Trust Company, which had a branch right across the street from us. And that was when we started in earnest to arrange auto loans for our customers. It was another way to add profit to the sale, and the salesmen liked that it added to their commissions. The bank was small compared to Boston banks, but we liked the people and you could talk to anyone there if questions or problems arose.

It was about that same time that Mr. Rice, from whom we were renting the Autohaus property, approached us about buying the building and land from him. He said we had been reliable and on-time tenants, and because he wanted to see us succeed he set a reasonable price and took the mortgage at a low interest rate, making it easy for us to say yes to his offer. He had been a terrific landlord and a person we all liked very much. At the same time he offered the adjacent property to the restaurant chain that occupied it, and they also accepted his offer, having similar feelings about Mr. Rice. It was great to own the property ourselves, both from an appreciation perspective and because of the pride of ownership.

Despite the loss of Porsche our business increased as we concentrated more on BMW and Datsun, while Rover sales continued to stagnate and Ferrari existed only in the past and the future. We had a good staff going into 1970 and Alice had hired an office assistant, Linda Nickerson, who was young but very conscientious. Fritz had now five mechanics and in the sales department we had three salesmen plus myself. Quite a good group. Fritz and Alice decided to take a vacation to Europe to visit relatives and perhaps some factories if possible. Even had Ferrari had an overseas delivery program at that time, it would have been impossible to bring a car back to the U.S. So Fritz and Alice arranged for a new BMW 2800 coupe to be delivered at BMW headquarters in Munich. They ordered a dark blue, I think it was called Atlantic blue, with black leather, standard shift (of course) and American specifications. When they finished their trip they were going to leave the car in Zurich with Fritz's brother so that I could have use of it as I too was going to have a European vacation with a definite business side. I was going to Maranello to check on the "automatico"!

So in March Alice and Fritz left via Swissair for a spring return to the homeland and had a wonderful time. I hadn't met any of their relatives so I was looking forward to meeting Swiss in Switzerland. But my trip was going to be a little different because I was going to return by ship, from Algeciras, Spain, on the *SS Raffaello* of the Italian Line.

After a few days in Switzerland it was time to head for Italy in the BMW 2800CS. It was a really good looking car, and although it was seen on the roads in Switzerland, it was a rarity in Italy. Having driven this model extensively in the States, I was familiar with its capabilities, but I never had a chance to use its full potential until I got

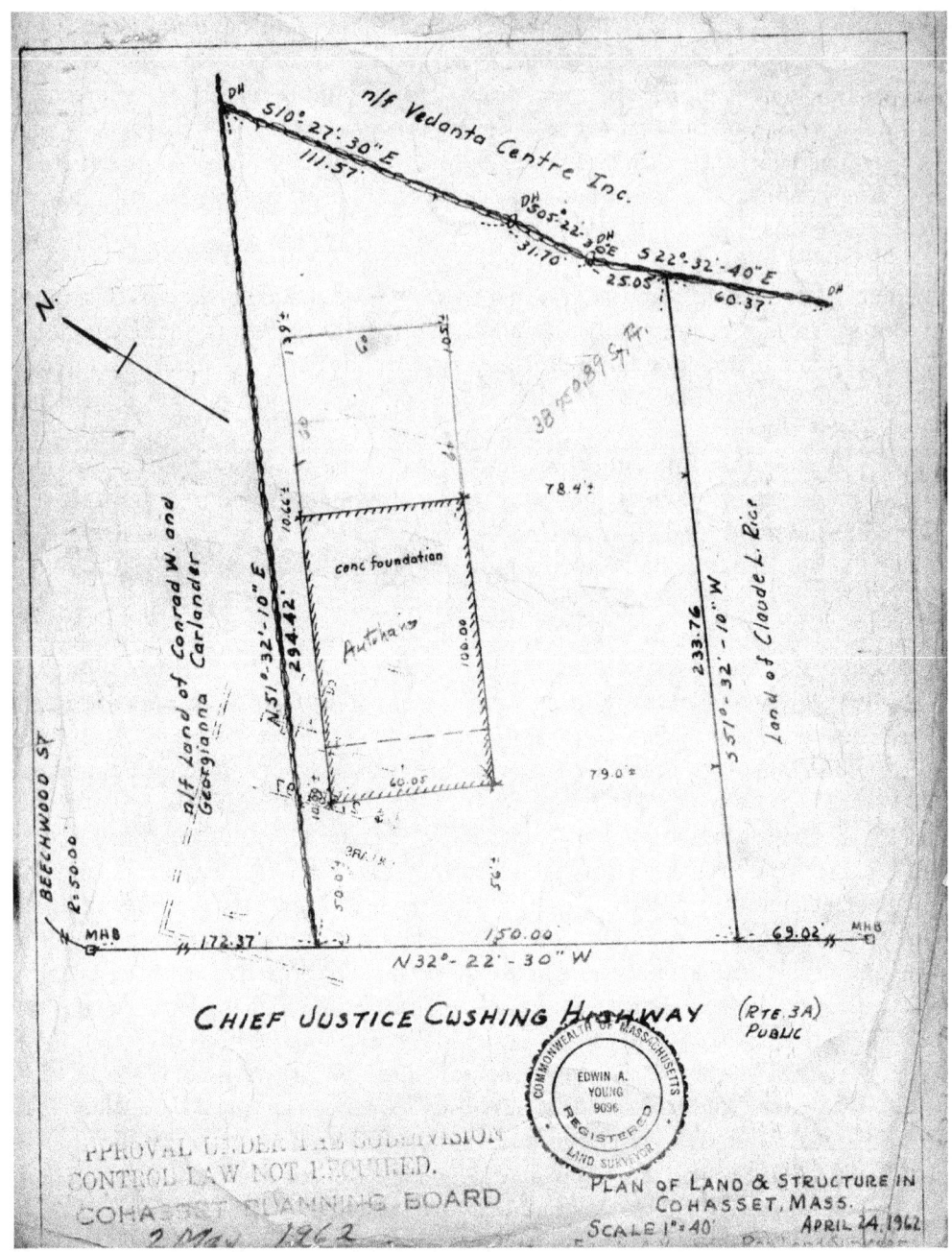

Autohaus property plot plan.

onto the autobahn leaving Zurich. It was fast. Very different than the old VW microbus, and it loved the left lane where the VW had seldom ventured. There might have been a speed limit in Switzerland at that time, but if so, nobody told me about it. As I started for Italy I was going to find at what speed it was most comfortable. That was around 120 mph!

The Europeans have slightly different ways of traveling fast, but most of them use their headlight flashers to advise slower cars that they are approaching at a higher speed. Some also leave their left directionals on the entire time they are passing cars, indicating their intention to keep passing and always on the left. It was astonishing to see slower vehicles just meld into the right lane as you approached them, something you certainly never saw in Massachusetts nor in most of the northeast states.

Wanting to go to the Ferrari factory first, I arrived in the morning after spending the night in Milano, from which it was a relatively short trip to Maranello, mostly driving on A1, the Milano to Roma autostrada where everyone was flying. The BMW loved that road, but still there was no sign of Ferraris. Well I was about to see all the Ferraris I wanted, or so I hoped as I arrived in Maranello and pulled up to the front entrance to the factory.

It was modest in appearance, all on one level, with the entrance guarded by a tall iron gate which was open. Inside the reception area two men asked if they could help me, and when I said I was dealer from Massachusetts they smiled and phoned someone. A man appeared shortly, a Mr. Albino, who was, as I recall, in charge of international marketing for Ferrari and was very cordial, inviting me back into his office, the walls of which were covered with photos of different models including the new 365GT2+2. It was almost overwhelming as I was expecting at any moment to see Il Commendatore himself, or at least get a glimpse of the inner workings of Ferrari. But aside from the entrance lobby and the corridor leading to his office I was to see little of the factory. It all seemed very casual and unstructured, but that was an initial impression that was to change over the years as I was to visit the factory many times. I could hear more than I could see, as the sounds of muffled—and not so muffled—engines emanated from somewhere in the building and from the street that was not that far away. Was I going to see a 365, maybe even the one being built for us, or maybe some of other models that we had heard were destined for the U.S.? I certainly hoped so!

Mr. Albino was very talkative, very animated, and interested in my opinions not about Ferrari models, but about what accessories they might be able to sell in the U.S. And by accessories they didn't mean ski racks or fog lights, but ladies' scarves and leather luggage, briefcases, etc. How strange, I thought. I was glad that his English was better than my Italian, so we talked for a while and finally I was able to ask him about our ordered 365 automatic. He said of course he knew about it as I think Chinetti had contacted him about my potential visit, and he excused himself and disappeared into another room. He returned a few minutes later carrying a huge book, a tome, that looked like it came out of some medieval monastery. He placed it on his desk, opened it and started looking through the pages, turning them carefully, one by one after moistening his fingers. I could see columns of what had to be serial numbers and names written across them in a sepia-like ink; it was wonderful to behold. He found what he was looking for and pointed out to me a line with Chinetti's name on it and following the line across I could see the words USA and the car's description, *including a serial number*. Well, I'll be, I thought to myself, there was the ordered "automatico" car, at least on paper, and an unforgettable paper at that. And when could we expect to receive the "automatic," I asked Mr. Albino. His response was "soon," which was better than hearing something even less definitive.

So I was happy to have confirmed the order, and to have found out that they were also producing a few 365GT2+2 standard shifts for the U.S.—interesting that we had never heard about that, I thought. Now I only wanted to get a tour of the factory, but unfortunately they were in the middle of a *sciopero* or strike. In Italy they frequently had work stoppages that were sudden and often short. They didn't seem to originate from a central union but rather from some manufacturer's work force on a spur of the moment basis. All too confusing, but it meant I couldn't take a tour today, although Mr. Albino assured me that he would enjoy doing that, so I would have to return another day.

Well, that was all fine and good, but here I was in Maranello at the Ferrari factory and I should at least get to see a Ferrari or two. As I was preparing to get into the BMW a pair of 365GTB/4 Daytona coupes—which were the first I had seen since Chinetti's display at the New England Auto Show last year—came out of the courtyard that was hidden behind one of the factory walls and roared up to the stop sign at the entrance gates. They really didn't stop but rather glided past the stop sign—like they do in Ft. Lauderdale—and took a left heading onto the road away from the factory, and as they did I could hear that 12 cylinder melody accompanied by the dual exhaust harmony that belonged to Ferrari and only Ferrari. It looked like they were going to road test the cars as I knew that every new Ferrari was tested on the road before final delivery. These two Daytonas looked like they were going to get a real wringing out as they screamed down the highway while the sounds set me a-tingling, and still do today. Darn that strike, as I was now so eager to see inside those brick walls.

I had other places to go and had to make sure I was on time for the *Raffaello*'s sailing, so I departed Maranello knowing that I would return another day. Now I was heading to Torino on the autostrada where there definitely was no speed limit and where I was not going to be the fastest as I was sometimes overtaken by big Mercedes sedans, Porsche 911s, the occasional Maserati, and as they passed I would resume my place in the left lane with lights flashing, flashing, flashing and directionals blinking, blinking, blinking, it was almost hypnotic. I loved it. Arriving in short order for a family visit, I was excited to see them all including new cousins that I had only heard of. Torino is a beautiful city with the Alps acting as a backdrop that appears and then vanishes according to the weather; just magnificent. I stayed with Ines, my grandmother's sister whom I had met in Rapallo, and her daughter Florence, neither of whom spoke English. Then there was Aldo, another son, who had five sons, just like my family. There was lots of laughing and lots of food, as you can imagine. It was a great time and I promised to return on my next European visit. They were all very impressed with the BMW, and although BMWs in general were seen in Italy, the 2800 coupe was indeed a rarity, so I took them for rides and offered the oldest son an opportunity to drive the car, but he demurred, saying if he damaged it he would forever be heartbroken. Those Italians, always so poetic.

From Torino I went to St. Tropez, following my route of seven years ago—and where you always saw the latest in high performance cars. Then after resting there a few days I traveled along the south coast of France to Perpignan near the Spanish border.

7. Automatico

After just one night in Barcelona I was on my way to Madrid on what were still secondary type roads. The only autopista at that time was north of Barcelona and the rest of my route was made up of two lane and seldom divided four lane roads. But they didn't inhibit the BMW as we traveled across the plains that I remembered well from my last visit. The cars, mostly Spanish made Seats, were greatly outnumbered by the slow moving trucks, and no one seemed to be in much of a hurry to get anywhere, except me.

The next day was the Grand Prix at the Jarama circuit, which, like everything else in Spain, starts late. I arrived too early, but enjoyed the practice laps and meeting some people. When the race finally ended the winner was Jackie Stewart driving a March Ford. I had been rooting for Ferrari's lone entry, Jackie Ickx, who unfortunately retired in lap seven due to an accident. He was a really good driver, but just had bad luck that day. Interestingly I was to meet his sister at a dinner in Vermont many years later where she told me that she had been at that race also.

Next I headed to Algeciras with a stop in Torremelinos. The roads south were almost all two lanes and almost all winding, through small villages and past ancient olive trees; it was a beautiful drive but I was going too fast to take it all in. When I arrived at the hotel in Torremelinos and told the desk that I had just driven down from Madrid they asked how long it had taken, and when I said less than eight hours they looked astonished and said that I had broken the record for that trip.

I had to catch the ship, which normally would have stopped in Gibraltar. Because of a diplomatic incident the border between Spain and Gibraltar was closed, so Algeciras was the alternative. But upon arriving at the hotel Reina Cristiana, which had mostly passengers for the ship staying there, I discovered the *Raffaello* was too large to dock in the harbor, so passengers would take a launch from the pier to the ship in order to embark. Well that I understood, but what about my car? Was that supposed to go on a launch also? Well no, there was some other way they were going to transport it, I was assured by a representative of the Italian Line that had a desk at the hotel. Whew!

Around 8:00 we decided to eat for there was still no news, and by midnight most people had gone to bed assuming we would be boarding the next morning, if the ship ever arrived at all. But at 2:30 in the morning there was a knock at everyone's door advising us that the ship had arrived and that we were to board immediately, and it was OK to leave on your nightclothes as when you boarded the ship you would be taken right to your stateroom to continue your night's rest. Sure. This was unbelievable, but so Italian. So the scene was 30 passengers dressed in pajamas and robes and whatever, loaded into a couple of launches that were leisurely making their way to the *Raffaello* that was brightly lit so that we wouldn't miss it. I wish I hadn't stowed my camera away. And as we were lurching along heading to the ship we passed what can only be described as a raft—a raft that was carrying the BMW—and a raft that looked like Tom Sawyer's doing—and it was bobbing up and down on its way with us. For some reason I felt reassured and as we approached the ship I heard one of the other passengers saying "you know the problem with these Italians is that they are still using Christopher Columbus's compass," and with that there was laughter heard all the way back to the hotel.

Spanish Grand Prix Program, 1970. The race was held at Jarama Circuit near Madrid.

It was tough adjusting after that long a voyage, and to compound that, when I got in the BMW I thought I was still driving in Europe. I arrived back at the dealership after a frustrating drive through Connecticut as the thrill of autobahns and autostrade was still in my brain and the 2800 also was behaving like a thoroughbred that was being held back by the reins of speed limits. When I got to Autohaus I

SS *Rafaello* passenger list, April 1970.

discovered all had gone fine in my absence—did I really need to come back so soon, I asked myself. But that was too much time to stay away from the business, as you get out of the groove and people are always referring to recent events that you know little or nothing about. It wasn't the best feeling so I said I wouldn't stay away that long again.

So who was waiting for me in the showroom when I returned but Mr. Remick, anxious for the latest news about his 365. I had written him a card from Italy telling him of my factory visit, and he wanted to hear all about it; so I told him that it was in fact going to be built and that we might see it later on that summer. That was fine with him, and as events happen with all things Italian, the car arrived at Chinetti's two weeks later as they transported it air freight. So predictable! I had a call from Dick Fritz telling me of its arrival, and all was fine except that the car was the wrong color— grey with black leather instead of green with green leather. A likely story, I thought, as probably one of Dick's customers liked the green better and got it. But that was the way of things, and at least we were receiving the car. When I told Mr. Remick about the color change he said he didn't care either.

I decided to go to Greenwich myself and drive the car back as I had never been to Chinetti's before. I suggested that Mr. Remick go too but he wasn't interested. So I went alone, taking the train to Greenwich and then a cab to Putnam Avenue. We liked to drive cars back to the dealership rather than have them transported—and that was before the ramp trucks had become popular. When we drove them we could see if there were any quirks or problems with that particular vehicle and if so have them corrected before delivery to the customer, plus it was a lot less expensive than having them trucked.

Chinetti's was an older building with a decent size showroom, a little bigger than ours, in the middle of which was a three-seater Ferrari in white. As I remember it was a 365P that the factory had specially made as a prototype that never went into production. The steering wheel was in the center with a passenger seat on either side.

ASA 1000 Spyder factory brochure. A beautiful but brief existence.

Ferrari 365 GT 2+2 window sticker: $22,750 including automatic transmission. Driving the car, whether with automatic or standard transmission, was a heart pounding experience.

Too weird, but the coachwork was beautiful. One other car that I saw there was an ASA 1000 Coupe that I had read about but never seen. The engine was reportedly made by Ferrari so there was much talk about an entry level Ferrari (read cheaper) being imported and also rumors of a spyder version ... we'll see, I thought.

So I met Luigi Chinetti and his sales manager Ivo and of course Chinetti's son, Coco too. Dick Fritz showed me around the service department, which was full of cars being serviced and waiting to be serviced, and just waiting. It was an astonishing collection of cars that I wish I could remember better, but amongst them was Mr. Remick's car looking beautiful.

Generally the dealership was in a state of controlled chaos with people running around, many speaking in Italian. There was a lot of energy there. I didn't bother to ask about the green car, but we did talk about other U.S. models and I was told that we should expect U.S. versions sometime in '71 and that should include the Daytona and also a Dino model that would be a V6 and mid-engine. A Dino, so that's the car I saw briefly outside of Maranello. I should have guessed as I'd seen pictures of the 206 in Fritz's Swiss magazine and had read about that version that was being sold in Europe; however, ours would have a larger engine, probably to provide enough power when emission controls were added. It all sounded great! So off I went in the 365 with the automatic transmission—after giving them a bank check for the car—and headed back to Cohasset.

This Ferrari was big, very big, and the engine sounded beautiful and the automatic—well, it worked just fine, and not only was it an automatic but it also had power steering and a self leveling rear suspension, it was very deluxe. You really couldn't feel the power steering work except at very slow speeds, but it was probably a good addition to that size vehicle. The transmission was perfectly mated to the engine, and although it was only a three speed, it really moved it along. When you gave it close to full throttle it would accelerate in first gear and as it approached the red line (no break-in period here) it would upshift and the tachometer would drop down to the beginning of the torque curve and wham, it would put you back in your seat with a powerful surge forward. I liked it, and so did Mr. Remick.

8

And Then There Were Two

WE NOW REALIZED THAT OUR FUTURE was with Datsun, BMW and hopefully soon Ferrari as they were still trying to federalize their European models that we were salivating for. That included the 246 Dino GT and the Daytona, which was the biggest tease of all as the car was not only sensational looking but fast as hell.

BMW sales were increasing as they had recently introduced a new model, the Bavaria, to replace both the 2500 and 2800 series. The Bavaria model was requested of the factory by Max Hoffman, who had a real sense for what the American market wanted. He was an Austrian immigrant who was instrumental in bringing many European brands to the U.S., by contracting with factories as distributor and eventually selling those rights back to the manufacturers. He was hugely successful with brands including Volkswagen, BMW, Alfa Romeo, Porsche and Mercedes-Benz. His urging of the creation of the Bavaria was right as it proved an instant success, being priced at $5,550 with a standard shift (with no power steering) and a 3.0 liter six cylinder engine. It was quite a package.

The 2500, 2800 and Bavaria also introduced a new type of ignition/door key that was different than any I had seen before. It didn't have notches cut from the edges but rather round depressions of different sizes and depths that BMW claimed reduced, if not eliminated, illegal copying of the keys. In fact if we needed a copy we would have to order it from BMW in New Jersey as our key cutting machine could not duplicate one, leaving us with mixed feelings about the new design. But it was here.

Again in 1971 Fritz and Alice wanted to return to Europe, as did I, so we made the same sort of arrangement where they would order a hard-to-find BMW coupe for Munich delivery, and then I would pick it up in Zurich after they returned. We had inquired through Chinetti if we could arrange a similar delivery with a Ferrari in Maranello. They replied by saying we could purchase a new car but it would be a European model so that we would not be able to bring it back to the States (legally). Well, that wouldn't work, for as much as we wanted a Daytona, leaving it in Europe for the occasional use seemed extravagant beyond our means.

Fritz and Alice picked up the BMW in Munich and then went to Zurich and Italy, where Fritz's sister lived and where there was no speed limit; this car also would be well broken in by the time I got to drive it, and essentially it was the same vehicle as the 1970 model. This time my itinerary was different as I wasn't going to Spain but visiting my relatives again in Torino, then driving to the French Riviera and on to Paris. From there I would go to Le Havre to embark on the *SS France,* again, and with

SALES DEPARTMENT

8:00 a.m. - 9:00 p.m. Weekdays
April–October
8:00 a.m. - 8:00 p.m. Weekdays
November–March
8:00 a.m. - 5:30 p.m. Saturdays
All Year

SERVICE DEPARTMENT

8:00 a.m. - 5:30 p.m. Weekdays
All Year
8:00 a.m. - Noon Saturdays
All Year

*Service is available
for all imported makes.*

*For your convenience
Rental Cars are available
at nominal rates*

autohaus

1970 PRICE LIST

Cushing Plaza, Route 3A
Cohasset, Massachusetts

617-383-0095

February 1, 1970

ROVER

2000 TC 4 door	$4350.00
2000 Automatic	4350.00
3500S	5398.00
Air Conditioning	478.00
Tinted Glass	50.00

RADIOS Prices include Installation Speaker and Antenna

Blaupunkt
AM Hamburg	95.00
AM-FM Montreal	145.00
AM-FM Frankfurt	195.00

Becker
AM-Europa	95.00
AM-FM Europa	175.00
AM-FM-LW-SW Mexico Automatic	225.00
AM-FM-LW-SW Grand Prix—Automatic	250.00
AM-FM Stereo—Europa	275.00

##

1600 2 Door	$3082.00
2002 2 Door	3450.00
2002 2 Door Automatic	3756.00
2500 4 Door	5750.00
2500 4 Door Automatic Power Steering	6300.00
2800 4 Door	6800.00
2800 4 Door Automatic Power Steering	7330.00
2800CS 2 Door Coupe	8100.00
2800CA 2 Door Coupe Automatic	8440.00

Accessories
1600, 2002
Sun Roof	135.00
Tinted Glass	65.00
Special Paint	65.00

2500, 2800
Sun Roof	220.00
Tinted Glass	75.00
Leather	320.00
Air Conditioning	493.00
Special Paint	100.00

##

PL 510
2 Door Sedan	$1985.00
2 Door Sedan (automatic)	2175.00
4 Door Sedan	2085.00
4 Door Sedan (automatic)	2275.00
4 Door Wagon	2315.00
4 Door Wagon (automatic)	2505.00

SPL 311
Convertible 1600	2841.00

SRL 311
Convertible 2000	3171.00

240Z
Sport Coupe	3500.00

PL521
Pickup Truck	1925.00

Accessories
Radio – Hitachi Antenna	65.00
Stereo Tape Deck	125.00
Roof Rack – Wagon...	60.00

Please add $50.00 Inland Freight to all models listed in this pamphlet.

Autohaus 1970 price list: Rover, BMW and Datsun.

the BMW as part of my luggage, sail back to New York—all in less time than the previous year's trip. So in mid–April I was heading back to Europe and to Zurich, which I was getting to know pretty well. It was a clean and vibrant city where many people spoke English, which made things easier for me.

I always tried to include the Riviera in my trips as the scenery was great, the roads challenging and the people interesting—and the cars! Vehicles seldom seen in the U.S. were often tooling around there, making a visit worthwhile on that basis alone. On this trip I was planning to meet my brother Dick, who was in the Army and stationed in Germany (better than southeast Asia), and his wife who had joined him for the last year of his assignment. We were going to meet in Beaulieu, in the south of France, but our wires got crossed and we missed each other, to our disappointment.

My friend Ernest, who always seemed to put me in the best hotels, had arranged my lodgings. At one time he wanted me to join him in his travel business even though I was running Autohaus. He suggested starting part-time with the idea that I might enjoy it enough to change professions. He had a solid business with an interesting clientele and was connected with the finest hotels and restaurants in Europe. As a result he would create itineraries that took me to fantastic places, and much of it was gratis as I think he told hotels that I was a representative of his agency. As tempted as I was by his offer, I liked cars more than traveling, so I never seriously considered it although we remained friends for many years.

BMW 3.0CS ad, *Quincy Patriot Ledger*, March 1970. The photograph was taken near Plymouth Rock.

After the Riviera I headed to Paris on the autoroute where everyone was enjoying their car's top performance and where I was getting into the high speed groove again. The only down side of this type of driving was that when you returned to the States you started off driving the same way, only to be jolted out of your dream by a siren, sometimes from a police car but hopefully from a different type of vehicle. The roads were good and not many cars were passing me until I was about two hours

Citroën SM, combining a streamlined body with a Maserati engine and Citroën quirkiness. I liked it. This one looks like the one I raced against in France (Hotlorp at English Wikimedia/ Wikimedia Commons).

south of Paris, when I looked in the mirror and a car was flashing its lights. I was so used to being "in the lead" in the left lane that I sometimes forgot that someone might try to pass me. I reluctantly merged into the right lane while this stealth gray Citroën SM coupe, with four people in it, went by me at a pretty good clip.

I let them sail ahead and then slowly increased my speed until I was approaching them ever so gradually. After about ten minutes I passed them, not knowing whether they had slowed down—I doubted it—or my speed had been steadily increasing. Once I returned to the right lane, they passed me, etc. Not a game I hadn't played before, although this type of driving you rarely encountered in the States as—well, there were laws, you know. The next time I passed them, or tried to pass them, they kept up with me so I couldn't get ahead of them. Well, this wouldn't do, that was a French car and mine was German, so I pushed some more, and they pushed some more until we were both going close to 130 on this lightly traveled autoroute. Something had to give, and sure enough the BMW started to pull ahead, ever so slightly—I think I had turned off the A/C—until finally I was in front. I had to slow down for traffic, and as an exit appeared for Versailles the Citroën driver pulled up beside me honked the horn, with all four people smiling and waving at me as they exited to the right. What a race!

I was convinced that the 2800CS was a formidable coupe, and as a result of that we sold more than our share compared to larger dealers. One I sold to a Mr. Nelson, who was a customer of A/E and had bought one of the two 1966 Ferrari 330GTs that had been sold on the same day back in 1965, the other being the burgundy one I sold

8. And Then There Were Two

to Dr. Riemer from west of Boston. Mr. Nelson had not serviced his car with us but he called me a few times about new Ferrari availability, and I relayed to him what I had learned from the factory visit and also from Chinetti. He really didn't want to wait another year to change cars so I suggested the BMW 2800 and told him of my experiences in Europe and in the U.S. with the car. He agreed to come down and drive one and liked it a lot, and after a bit of negotiation bought a tan one that we had in inventory, trading the light metallic blue 330GT. He had taken perfect care of it, and like most owners he never drove it in the rain or any type of bad weather, whereas I had the impression that Europeans drove their cars in all weather conditions. We were thrilled to have this perfectly maintained car in our showroom.

This Ferrari has an interesting story. Cohasset was not the place where you might expect to find a dealership that handled exotic cars, but as I have said we attracted customers from a wide area, in part because we stocked many unusual and hard-to-find vehicles. Because of our location and the communities that surrounded us, we never thought too much about crime. Yes, we had the occasional hubcaps stolen, and sometimes even tires and wheels, but aside from that we really had no problem—that is, until we had the Ferrari 330GT. When taking in trade a car like that, it's always good to have some potential buyers, or at least some customers that might be interested in a performance car such as that. We did have a few who had expressed interest in a Ferrari, but most wanted a two seater, either a convertible of a coupe.

A few weeks after trading the car, I had a call from Alice at about 6:30 in the morning telling me I had to get to the dealership right away, and when I arrived I found the Cohasset police talking with Fritz. Well, we had been robbed. We always kept the more expensive cars inside the service building at night, but thieves had broken in and stolen the 330GT and a Porsche. At that time we had no alarm system, or even a secure fence around the parking lot, and we paid the price for that. We found out from the police that there was a gang of auto thieves working on the South Shore—thanks for the heads-up, I thought—and that the same night they had robbed a Ford dealership and others. Quite a big gang, I thought, and it was. The Porsche was discovered the next day, but the Ferrari had disappeared, and stayed missing.

A few months later, our dealership now protected by a chain link fence surrounding the rear of the property as well as a state of the art alarm system, Alice received a telephone call from a man in Georgia inquiring about a Ferrari that he was looking to buy. I took the call and spoke with a man with a heavy southern accent, who said he was a car aficionado from Albany, Georgia, who had recently been approached to buy a blue 330GT that was from Massachusetts, and hence had no title with it (Massachusetts title law didn't take effect until September 1972), but only a bill of sale. He was calling to see if we knew about it as we were the only dealer in Massachusetts at that time. This had to be the stolen car. And it was. But at about the same time the man was contacted by the FBI, who had been following the thieves and apprehended them between the time he had seen the car and had called us. How timely was that? A week later Fritz and Alice flew to Georgia to pick up the Ferrari and had a heck of a drive coming back. I could only imagine!

The Ferrari hadn't been too badly abused, though it had collected a few scratches

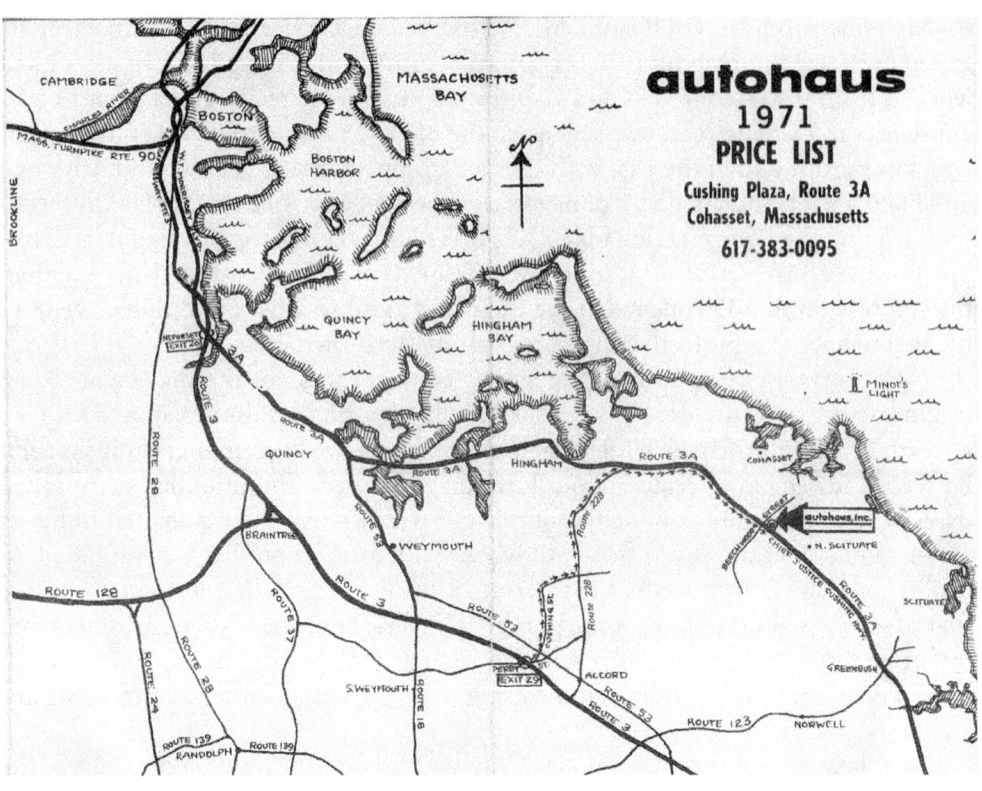

Autohaus 1971 price list. We had only two brands now while still waiting for Maranello to comply with U.S. standards.

and about 2500 miles more than when we traded it. Fritz checked it out thoroughly on the ride back and all the mechanicals on it seemed OK. Our insurance had paid us for our loss so they agreed to let us sell it (at that point it belonged to them) and make a profit on the sale. We sold the Ferrari to a local woman, the first time we had sold a Ferrari to a woman, and although she enjoyed driving it, she didn't keep it very long. In 1972 selling a Ferrari to a woman was unusual, but so was selling any car to an unaccompanied woman.

In the 1960s and until the early 1970s it was my experience that women seldom bought cars by themselves. I don't mean that another person was usually the co-buyer, but that there was usually a man involved in the purchase of the car. It was rare to have a woman come in alone to look at a vehicle (as Mrs. Dane had with the 230SL) and if they did they often returned with a man to look at what they were considering to get his approval or at least a tacit acknowledgment that they were making a prudent decision. Such were the times. There were exceptions of course, but that was rare as women generally either didn't like the automotive negotiating and purchasing process or were unsure of their ability to "get the best arrangement." This trepidation was one of the things we were trying to allay by the way we did business, and to some extent I think we succeeded as by the mid–1970s we were selling more and more cars, mainly BMWs, to women who came to see us alone. Sales to unaccompanied women Datsun buyers were slower to grow, and to help attract their business Datsun published a 14-page booklet entitled *Things No Man Ever Told a Lady About Buying a Car,* outlining car buying procedures and subsequent service needs. The table of contents included a section titled "What happens when the thingamabob goes 'glitch'?" How chauvinist was that? But things changed and within a few years women buyers constituted more than 50 percent of our sales of BMWs and Datsun, and we were glad about that.

The Datsun story of course included the 240Z. The car proved incredibly popular and therefore desirable, so much so that many dealers were charging over the sticker price to take advantage of the lack of availability. We, however, offered the cars at sticker price, which remained part of our sales

Datsun Ladies Pamphlet. I think they already knew most of this.

philosophy as a different type of automobile dealer, and soon we had a list of buyers that would take at least two years to satisfy. We knew that many buyers had placed orders with multiple dealerships waiting for the first one to appear, and then either asking for their deposit back or forfeiting it, but if our buyers canceled we always made a refund. A different type of dealership, we thought. And we were right. Even though they were so hard to get, I was driving one as a demo. It was yellow with black vinyl interior, really good looking, and they were fast. My only complaint was the suspension—the shocks weren't stiff enough—but other than that the 240Z was a hard car to beat. It listed for about the same price as a new BMW 2002, so we created an ad that showed me standing between the two cars, with a doctored photo showing me looking at both cars and ad copy saying "*Which of these $3600 cars would you choose?? We have them both*" Autohaus. Some potential Z buyers were convinced to buy a BMW, but not many.

On one dealer trip to California I met with the Los Angeles regional manager. Considering Datsun's growth spurt, I found him very approachable and very polite, and he listened to my thoughts and ideas, and the same had been true of most Datsun executives I had met since 1967. This included Yutaka Katayama (Mr. K), who was president of Datsun and developer of the 240Z, and who outlined to me at

Datsun ad, *South Shore News*, March 1971. Advertising copy by Yutaka Katayama—Mr. K, first President of Nissan Motor Corporation USA and "father" of the 240Z.

a luncheon one day the different philosophies between Datsun and Toyota. Datsun was putting a lot of emphasis on its engineering and performance while its competitors like Honda and Toyota seemed more interested in economy and appearance to sell their vehicles. It was very enlightening, and when I told him about an advertising program I was thinking of using that had Japanese characters as the lead-in, he responded that he would be pleased to translate my copy into Japanese, which he did. Remarkable.

Returning from this California trip I was driving cross country with some friends, the first time I was to do that, and the first stop was in Sparks, Nevada, to see Bill Harrah's automobile collection, which I think at that time was located in a mammoth warehouse and contained some 1400 cars or thereabouts. I had never seen anything like that and never did again.

Every car you could imagine was there—old, new, domestic and foreign—and I'm not sure but he might have had one of everything, or so it seemed. But once I found the Ferrari 166 MM Barchetta I was the happiest. It was the first time I had seen one and was astonished at how small it was; you never got a sense of that from pictures, and it was beautiful as well. It was the first car that I wanted to get into and just drive away—but I couldn't and didn't. That one sighting was worth the whole trip.

Harrah at the time was the West Coast distributor for Ferrari (Chinetti had the East), and we rarely heard much about him, so separated were we from that part of the country, but his importance was noted when Ferrari first set up their U.S. headquarters in Burbank, California, and not someplace in New York. After Harrah's death in 1978 the car collection was broken up and sold and I never knew where the Barchetta ended up; I hoped it would be at another public place so others could see its beauty.

Ferrari 166 MM barchetta. Unknown driver at Palm Beach International Raceway, Palm Beach County, Florida, 1981.

Harrah Auto Collection catalog. It was the biggest car collection ever when I saw it. Incredible.

While BMW and Datsun were selling well, Rover was not, and it was then that we decided to relinquish the franchise, much to the disappointment of the distributor and some of our customers. Although we were still allowed to perform warranty work on the cars, that didn't continue for long as people eventually found their way to other dealers or traded their cars for a different brand, mostly BMWs. Now we had two lines of cars again, although I guess we could still include Ferrari on that list as Chinetti had said that we would be receiving cars again as soon as the factory began exporting again to the States.

Anticipation—both ours and our customers'—was building to a high state for their arrival.

9

Sixes and Twelves

AND THEN WE HEARD THE NEWS: Ferrari was coming back to the States with two series, the 246GT Dino and the 365GTB/4. We were going to have quite a year in 1972! We were to receive our first 246GT Dino in February (it actually arrived in March) and there was already considerable interest in the car from our customers and the general public—at least those that followed Ferrari.

The name Dino name derived from Alfredo (Dino) Ferrari, the son whom Enzo Ferrari had once been grooming to be his successor. Dino studied engineering and went to work at Scuderia Ferrari, the racing division, before succumbing to muscular dystrophy in 1956 at the age of 24. Ferrari subsequently named the V-6 engined road cars and racing cars in his son's honor.

Ferrari was now able to meet the U.S. emission and safety specifications and would be bringing over not only the Dino but also the 365GTB/4 Daytona in both

Dave Riggs and his Dino 246GT in Marshfield Hills, Massachusetts.

Autohaus Five Year Anniversary announcement introducing Dino 246 GT, *South Shore News*, February 1972. We were all revved up at Autohaus with Ferraris now being built for the U.S. market!

coupe and 365GTS spyder versions, cars we had been lusting after seeing them at the factory a few years back. Those models were beautiful; in fact so was the Dino coupe (the spyder would come later), being much smaller than previous Ferraris and the first road car with a mid-engine configuration and with a V-6 engine as well. It was a Ferrari, even though it was badged as a Dino and many purists—including some of the motoring press—thought a Ferrari had to have a V-12 engine to qualify as a true Ferrari model. But if Enzo said it was a Ferrari, it was good enough for us. The sticker price of $14,500—just add for leather and air conditioning (of sorts) and you sold it for $15,600—was not bad when a BMW coupe was close to $11,000. And so we sold all we could get, which wasn't many, and we got them from Chinetti, which was always an adventure in itself.

The Dino was a snarly car to drive and very, very low to the ground. It seemed to have no hood in front of you, and not much behind as the car afforded almost no rear visibility. It was difficult to keep an eye to the rear to see if anyone might be catching up, perhaps to interview you, and the outside mirror was too bouncy to help much. Oh well. The engine sounded snappy and very responsive; although slower than the 12-cylinders, it seemed just as fast as you were so low you seemed to pass by everything at exhilarating speed. The gated shifter was the same configuration as other Ferraris but the engagement of second gear always seemed balky at first, requiring time for the gearbox oil to warm up before you could do any fast first to second shifts. Other than that the car was a blast to drive and the handling was superb as it was the first mid-engine Ferrari we had driven. It was beautiful

Getting the Dinos from Greenwich to Cohasset was not difficult as we'd purchase by phone with either Ivo Brillo or Dick Fritz and then two of us would drive down—along with a check—to pick up a new car, hopefully in the color that they said

9. Sixes and Twelves 111

they had. Occasionally the designated car wasn't "new car presentable," so after much discussion we would have to chose something different and after settling that, the two cars would drive back, always keeping the other car in sight in case any mechanical problem developed or one of the drivers got interviewed by the authorities. The idea of keeping the other car in sight was good in principle, but in reality there was no way a gentlemanly race wasn't going to happen. The stories of those drives could fill many pages themselves, but fortunately they were mostly kept quiet, at least from me.

Early in 1972 we received word that a new entity would be importing Ferraris for the eastern U.S., Chinetti–Garthwaite Imports, while the western part of the country would have Bill Harrah's Modern Classic Motors as importer. This new company was an association of Chinetti and Algar Enterprises, owned by Al Garthwaite, a successful tire distributor and, we thought, the money behind the endeavor. The car distribution would be out of Paoli, Pennsylvania (where?), and the company would handle all aspects of Ferrari merchandising, warranty and service related issues. Bob Turney was the general manager and a real nice guy who was easy to deal with and reasonable on most issues.

It was going to be a good year. What with two new younger salesman, Lanny Chase and Jim Theriault (who would remain with us for almost 20 years), plus Chuck Kay, we had a very strong and professional sales staff. I was proud of them and felt lucky to have such a competent, trustworthy group. As most business people know the biggest problem running a small business is not the customers but the staff. But with us it wasn't the case. The factories were always holding sales meetings of sorts where the salesmen would go and learn about the latest models and how to sell them, at least as the factories wanted them to be sold. Often they would have competitive driving events where the sales people from different dealerships would compete in driving skills, etc., and our

Dino 246GT ad, *Vincent Club Program*, 1972.

man Lanny was always coming home with trophies. Jim, who had just bought a 2002 before starting with us, was another frequent winner.

Chuck, who had joined as a salesman in 1969, was an older man who was a gentleman by definition. Accommodating to both men and women, he had a beautiful way of speaking and explaining the products we sold. He sold the first Dino to a contractor of Italian heritage from Duxbury who traded a Lincoln Mark III, which was at least three times as large as the white Dino. Talk about a change, but he loved the car and used it all the time, not just on weekends as a Sunday driver. The second Dino we received was burgundy—*rosso bordeaux*—and we sold it to a salesman who also used it every day. When he traded it back to us a few years later it had over 50,000 miles on the odometer. He too was of Italian extraction, as would be many of our Ferrari buyers. Many were probably first or second generation Italians and still felt a connection to Italy, and what better automotive representation was there than Ferrari.

Ferrari Daytona arrival announcement, June 1972. Quite the party. Quite the car.

9. Sixes and Twelves

One of the first sales we had under this new company was for a 365GTB/4 Daytona, purchased by a doctor for delivery in Modena at the end of March. The savings were considerable at that time for an overseas delivery, the car selling for $18,000 vs. $24,800 here. The only thing was that he didn't have the time to go Italy to take delivery, and asked if someone from the dealership could go. Before I organized myself, Fritz stepped in and said he and Alice would go. That was fine with me as it was going to be a busy year and I really wanted to stay around, even if the thought of the autostrade in a Daytona was quite a picture. So they went to Modena to take delivery of the gold (*oro*) with black Daytona, the cars being delivered at a facility there rather than at the factory in Maranello. I just got one postcard telling me that all had gone OK with the delivery—they were probably going too fast to stop and send another—and at the end of their trip they were leaving the car in Zurich to be shipped back from there. It arrived in the States in the middle of May in perfect condition with the exception of a missing tool kit, the loss of which was covered by insurance. The customer was happy, so pleased in fact that in June he and his wife had an afternoon cocktail party celebrating the (safe) arrival of their car. It was quite an affair.

So we had sold our first new Daytona, and I finally got to drive one, and it was sensational. So different from the 275s and 330s and certainly from the Dino; the sounds, the gearbox with its gated shift, its rugged feel, and of course the design. And was it fast! It felt heavier and more substantial, which it was, and the acceleration and torque were way more impressive. It also had a transaxle so the balance seemed perfect; although at low speed it seemed brutish, once you got going it felt nimble and aggressive.

Ferrari GTB/4 Daytona performance specifications, from factory brochure. Note the performance curves!

Leonardo Fioravanti of Pininfarina, who designed the car, and whom I was to meet many times over the years, was churning out one beautiful design after another including the 206/246 Dino. They just weren't gorgeous, they were made incredibly well. The Daytonas, in competition configuration (one of which was bought by a customer, John Kelly, who had it serviced by us, also had bought a 308GT4), were to compete and win at countless races for many years. We were a 15 minute drive to the divided highway, Route 3, where especially in the mornings heading south you could experience what a car had to offer; and this machine offered so much. Of course, Fritz and Alice had broken it in driving in Italy and Switzerland, so the car had no problem living up to its reputation—at least that's what I heard. The factory stated top speed was a stunning 174 mph. How could any car that purposeful be that beautiful? But it was. And it was a dual purpose car that could be driven on the road or at the track, and successfully at that. I think that was always Ferrari's wish, and this car combined both ideals superbly. It really blew me away; in fact each successive new Ferrari I drove blew me away, showing evolving mechanical prowess and design that was really in a league of its own. At least that was my opinion.

To improve my Italian I had taken a night course in Quincy and was able to increase my conversational ability somewhat. The teacher was very good, an American whose parents had emigrated from Italy to the U.S. One of the hotels I stayed at in '71 was the Villa D'Este, on Lago di Como, a palatial hotel that formerly had been the residence of one of the leading families of that area. (My travel agent friend had insisted I stay there.) When there I sent a postcard to my teacher, in Italian, to show how the trip was improving my ability. When I saw her next in the autumn she told me how much she appreciated the card, so much so that it brought tears to her eyes. That surprised me—but it wasn't that my grammar had improved so dramatically, it was the fact that her mother had worked as a seamstress in that palace for the Este family when she was a young girl, before emigrating to the United States.

Shortly after we received the Dino, BMW also started sending us new models starting with the 2002Tii, the first fuel injection model to come to the States, It was a real goer. We lost the 1600 but gained the Tii—a fair exchange, we all thought. No more carburetor icing on those drives to the ski areas, and no more troublesome start-ups. I think BMW wanted to improve the lineup but also were testing how well the system would hold up with the ever more stringent emission laws. They also replaced the 2800CS with the 3.0CS, which gave that car more oomph (did it need it?) while the body stayed essentially the same. Datsun added automatic transmission availability to the newly introduced 1200 coupe and sedan that gave the line a good price range, while the 240Z stayed unchanged as did the wait to get one. Interest had not died down one bit. But we were starting to hear rumors about some dealers getting more Z's than they should based on Datsun's allocation guidelines, and those rumors would prove fact later on.

We received some interesting trades that year including some Citroëns, Jaguars, Bentleys, Porsches, some right hand drive vehicles, and even a Spanish Seat, like the ones I had seen in Madrid. A man from Duxbury had rented one while vacationing in Spain and liked it so much that he negotiated its purchase and brought it back here. Talk about hard to find parts! As long as the car was produced before 1968 it could be

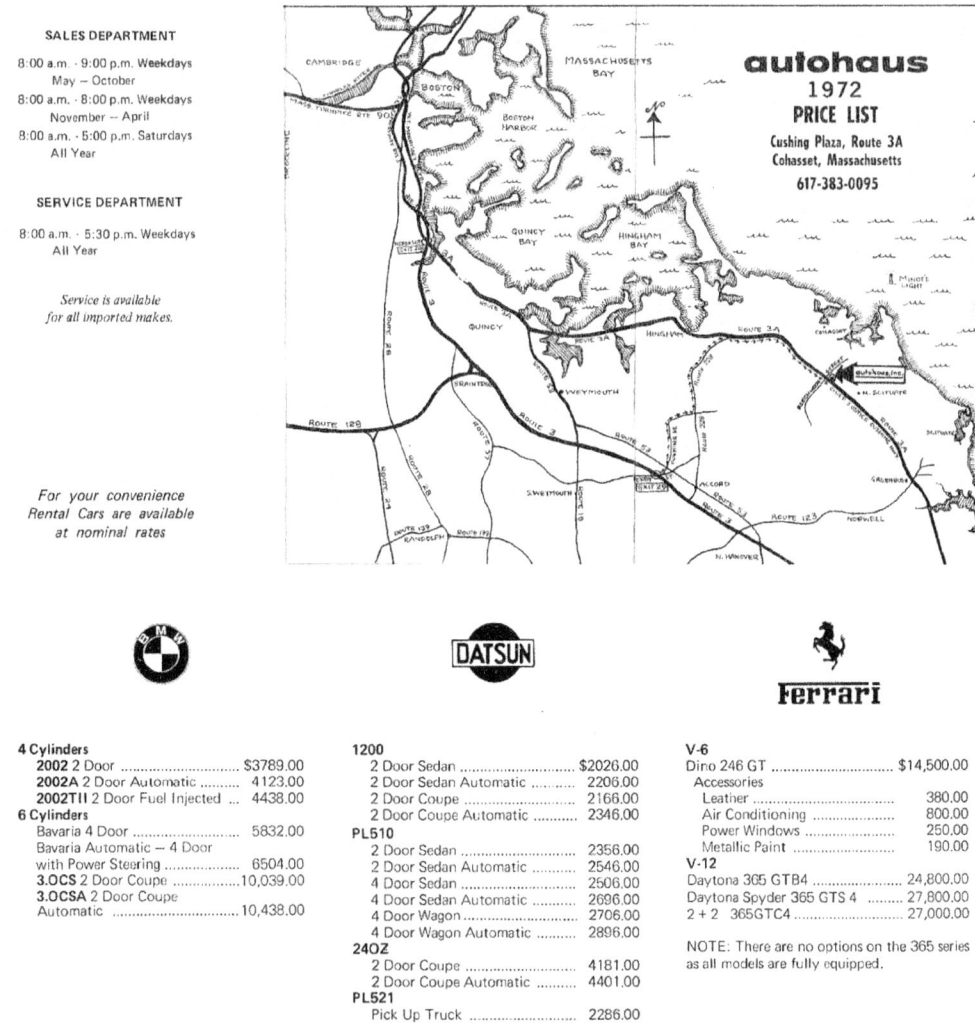

Autohaus 1972 price list. Ferrari is back in the USA!

brought back here with no problems, although that would change. I always liked the Citroën DS21; it was so comfortable and so quirky.

Many people came to the dealership to see the new Dino and also the Daytona that was there for a short time. One of the visitors was a man from the North Shore who was in the advertising business and whom I had met someplace before, maybe at A/E. He was driving a rare Ferrari 365 California convertible, a brown one that was really a big car, almost the size and shape of the 365GT automatic that we had sold. He wanted to drive a Dino, so we did, and he liked it. He wanted to trade his California, but we couldn't work out a price that was satisfactory to both of us. As he drove away I regretted that we had not been able to strike a deal, as his car was so unusual I doubted that I would ever have the opportunity to trade one or even see one again.

We did, however, trade an interesting Ferrari that I had seen before. My top salesman, Chuck, was pretty low key but liked to talk, and being older, maybe 60 or so, he had a connection with events from before World War II. One day he had a call from a Mr. Hall from Fitchburg who was interested in a new Dino. He had read about them and thought it would be an easier Ferrari to drive than the one he currently had, which turned out to be a 1965 275 GTB coupe, a beautiful car with a two cam engine with six carburetors (three were standard) and a short nose. I remembered him having it serviced at A/E. He traded for a Dino, a white one that we had planned on putting in the auto show; of course the customer came first so we put a red one on the display instead, probably a better show color choice anyway. The 275 he traded was perfect and I sold it to a man from New Hampshire before the auto show even started. I think everyone involved in those sales was very happy. I know we were.

So now we had sold two out of the three current Ferrari models that were available in the U.S., the Dino 246GT and the Daytona 365GTB/4 (not the spyder) but what we hadn't sold—or even seen—was the 365GTC/4. This car, which had two small jump seats in the rear and power steering as standard equipment, arrived quietly on the American scene; we had hardly heard about it before the new importer sent us some specifications on the vehicle, including the sticker price: $27,000! In 1972 that was a lot of money for any car, even a Ferrari, but I thought if we were going to be a full line Ferrari dealer, which we were, then we had to have at least one

Our first Ferrari 365GTC/4. Its sounds were inimitable.

12 cylinder car as well as the Dino. Since the price of a 365 GTC4 was less than the price of two Dinos, it sort of made sense to have one. The other factor was the annual auto show in Boston where we were offered free space if we would show Ferraris; it would be the perfect venue to introduce not only the Dino but the 365GTC/4 as well. So after considerable arguing back and forth between Fritz, Alice and me, we finally decided to get one. The only color available then was a metallic brown, called *marrone Colorado*—not exactly what we would have chosen if there had been a selection. So we ordered it. We didn't have time to send a driver (probably me) down to get the car so the importer was able to have it delivered to us on a truck—the last time that delivery mode was used for many years.

That year we had our own display at the New England Auto Show at the Hynes Auditorium, showing Ferraris which involved setting up our own booth. The show people contacted us wanting to have as many exotic draws as they could get, so we were able to find a well situated display space free of charge. They also gave us carpeting, railings to keep the kids out—as well as adults that liked to touch too much—and even a desk and chairs. It was really generous of them, but maybe they were rewarded by increased attendance due to our presence. We added a couple of potted palms and there we were. On opening night we served drinks and canapés and invited many of our customers to the show, giving them free passes to get in. Our presentation was a real hit, and amongst the viewers were a great many other dealers and factory personnel that had never seen a Ferrari up close, as we had a Dino and the 365GTC/4 both on display. It was enjoyable but the show, which lasted ten days, took a lot of salesmen's time as we had to not only staff our exhibit but also provide manpower for the Datsun and BMW booths. It was a success, however, as we sold a Dino right from the show that year. We were to repeat the event for many years.

We didn't sell the 12 cylinder at the auto show so we still had the GTC/4 and it was January; no Ferrari buyers now, we thought. But starting in the spring the Ferrari buyers reappeared, from wherever they went during the winter, and we started to sell quite a few Dinos which meant there was a lot of driving between Paoli and Cohasset.

I really enjoyed showing the 365GTC/4 to people as it was not at all like the Daytona; the only similarity was really the V-12 engine size, but the layout was not the same. While they both had six Weber carburetors, the six in the Daytona ran in a neat row down the center of the engine between the two cylinder head banks, and on the GTC4 they were on either side.

I have to describe the engine compartment of the GTC/4 as it was really something. To open the hood you had to reach inside the driver's side to release the hood latch and the hood would pop about three inches, being stopped by an additional latch which was located just under the windshield wipers. This secondary latch was designed to prevent unwanted opening at high speed, although the hood opened with the hinges at the headlight area minimizing the chance of an unwanted hood flying up to block your vision. Then when you released the second latch the hood would slowly raise itself, guided by two pistons that let out a sort of mild *whoosh* until they stopped the hood at a nearly vertical position revealing the most magnificent Ferrari engine. This V-12 setup was totally different than the Daytona as the V was quite a bit wider; that is the two camshafts (actually two per bank giving a total of

Ferrari 365GTC/4 engine, from a factory publication. All six carburetors along the sides. These were the days when you could actually see the engine when you opened the hood.

Ferrari 365GTB/4 motor, from a factory publication. All six carburetors neatly in a row on top.

four camshafts, hence the GTC/4 designation) were farther apart, therefore lowering the height of the engine, and in turn the hood, while the carburetors—six side draft Webers with three on each side—were mounted on the outside of the V's camshafts, giving a very low profile. The first time people witnessed this—what I could call a ceremony—their mouths and eyes would open wide. It was truly breathtaking.

But that was only part of the presentation because if someone actually wanted to test drive the car, we would start it in the showroom to move it out to the parking lot. The starting of the car was even more impressive than the hood opening, as once you turned the ignition key to actuate the starter motor, the engine would turn over slowly as though it wasn't going to start at all, then suddenly the spark plugs would fire and you would hear this mechanical bellow that reverberated through the showroom, the building, the parking lot and even your chest. It was inimitable; there was nothing else like it in the regular automobile category of sounds. The exhaust notes were rhapsodic when heard in an enclosed space, with the only other equally acoustic moment being when you were traveling through a tunnel of some sort and hearing the echoing exhaust. The Daytona produced similar sounds but of a slightly higher pitch; the GTC/4 was the best sounding Ferrari I had ever heard.

Interestingly, the delay in the motor firing was due to an oil pressure monitoring switch that prevented the engine from starting until the oil pressure reached the recommended amount. It was innovative for them but soon proved problematic.

The 365GTB/4 Daytona had been first made available in the U.S. in 1972 but was still a very rare car, so when Fritz had a call from a man who lived west of Boston, and had a Daytona that was recently in an accident, he was surprised. The man knew of us although he had purchased the car in New York, and now wanted us to arrange the repairs to his car. We had it towed to Autohaus for an insurance inspection and found that it had quite a bit of damage to the front end, so after considerable bantering back and forth between the insurance company and our body shop, the customer agreed to have us repair the vehicle.

It was a very low mileage car, just over 2,000 miles on the odometer—again not unusual for Ferraris—and was perfect except for the mangled front end. After a considerable time—maybe four months—the car was repaired, so we informed the customer that it was ready, but he didn't come to pick it up. He was hard to get in touch with, which was not unusual among our customers, but after leaving several messages with his home, we finally heard from him. He said he was in no hurry to get it as he had another Daytona that he was driving and would let us know when he could come down to Cohasset to see it and retrieve it.

Well, that didn't happen. We never heard from him again. We ultimately decided to sue him for the amount involved for the repair bill was sizeable—just over $20,000—and we wanted to get paid as we had already paid the body shop for the repairs. His insurance company was no help as they said he had to approve the repairs and hadn't done so. We found out in short order that in fact his insurance had been canceled, so he had no insurance on the car! Now what? The only way to recoup the repair costs was to bring suit against the owner in court and have a judge decide if we could claim the car in payment for the unpaid bill. And so we went to court—bringing the Daytona along with us—to visibly show the judge just what we had done to the vehicle. It was quite a scene, for after presenting our case we suggested that the judge come outside to see the car itself and to show that we should be given ownership to satisfy our bill.

The judge was an older man—maybe in his late 70s—who looked conservative, but when he saw the Daytona his eyes opened wide, and when Fritz opened the hood wide to show him the expert body work that had been done on the engine

Ferrari 365GTB/4 repaired. For a new model, this Daytona already had quite a story.

compartment and that magnificent 12 cylinder engine, the judge's mouth opened wide also. Eureka, we won the case and were given ownership of the car and after getting a clear title we were able to sell it on the open market. From the sale we were able to recoup the repair costs.

We never heard from the owner again.

10

No Gas for the Speedy

THAT SPRING I DECIDED TO GO BACK to Europe and take along my younger brother Gerry as a copilot. I tried to arrange for a Ferrari 365 or even a Dino, but the factory couldn't guarantee availability due to intermittent production as a result of more strikes. Politics were in upheaval in Italy so it was not that much of a surprise. So once again it was going to be a BMW, although this time I would be driving the new 3.0CS, which had more power than the 2800s, plus we were going to take delivery in Munich and visit the BMW factory from which so many great cars were coming. Gerry was now working at Autohaus in the parts department under Gayle Fortier, our really excellent Parts Manager, so I thought it would be a good idea to include him on the business trip. We flew to Munich where we picked up a silver 3.0CS standard shift, and this time *we* were going to break it in.

From there we went to Torino to introduce Gerry to all the cousins that I had met a few years before. They were all there as well as Aurora, a daughter of Aldo's from Sardinia who was presently going through a divorce. Her two small daughters were the cutest girls and the biggest brats that we had ever seen. But Aurora, well she was beautiful and an exact double of Gerry. They were *gemelli,* twins. Those genes work in curious ways. After a few fun family days we left Torino and our relatives, promising to return soon and inviting them to come and visit us. We had decided to go to Greece by taking the ferry from Brindisi to Patras across the Aegean Sea. On the way we spent a couple of days in Rome as Gerry wanted to see the Vatican and I wanted to do some walking around the city.

We arrived in Brindisi in the late afternoon with plenty of time to board the ship, having left the BMW with the steamship line. The voyage was overnight so we arranged for a cabin for two—it was more like a cabinet than a cabin—and after boarding headed for the dining room or the bar, I can't remember which. But it was a nice passage, although I don't think Gerry ever came back to the cabin that night, and we arrived in Patras the next morning to the beautifully warm Greek sunshine and the gorgeous blue Aegean. It was dazzling. After going through customs with the car we headed to Athens and to the Athens Hilton.

After a few days of sightseeing and imbibing the classical Greek culture it was time to depart. We had to return the BMW to Munich to be shipped home and we had return flight reservations with Lufthansa that we couldn't miss, so we decided to drive to Munich through Yugoslavia rather than return through Italy. On our day of departure we were at the front desk settling up our hotel bill when I asked the

Easter dinner, Torino, 1973. Family with Aurora, Gerry and author in rear.

desk clerk if he had a map of Yugoslavia (no advance planning for us). An American couple checking into the hotel heard our question and the woman said, "You're not thinking of driving through Yugoslavia, are you?" and when I confirmed that we were, she recounted a tale about their drive through there that they had just completed, adding, "We're lucky to be alive." She said the main roads in many places were nearly impassable, there were bandits everywhere and the roadside accommodations were virtually nonexistent. Bad roads definitely were not for us, and with that we changed our plans by arranging shipment for the car directly from Athens and then flying to Munich and home.

Not long after the BMW returned I sold it to a Mr. Gannet from the North Shore who actually liked the idea that the car had been "broken in" on the European roads. He didn't have the car very long as it was stolen in Boston and wasn't recovered for a long time, maybe three or four years. It was found abandoned out west, I think in the desert someplace, and although the car belonged to his insurance company as he had

Author on the road to Brindisi with BMW 3.0CS, 1973.

been paid off, he had liked it so much that he repurchased it and drove it for quite a while.

Business had been good while I was away (why did it always seem to go better when I wasn't around?). In my absence we had received our first Dino spyder, a red one with tan interior, quite striking I thought. It had a removable roof panel, not unlike the Porsche Targa, although the panel was stored behind the seats, not in the trunk as in the Porsche. It was sure to be popular, and one of the salesmen already had someone very interested it. But the 365GTC/4 was still sitting on the showroom floor, without a "sold" tag on it. That was the status until about one month later when Jim had a telephone call from a man in Springfield who wanted to know if we had any 12 cylinder Ferraris in stock and Jim said, "Oh yes, we have one on display in our showroom."

The next day the man arrived in an older Pontiac wagon and Jim showed him the GTC. As he walked around it I could see that he wasn't getting too excited (had he imagined we had a Daytona?), until Jim opened the engine compartment; then,

Gerry at the Acropolis, May 1973.

almost on cue, his eyes opened wide and he shook his head saying "That is unbelievable." Upon their return from a test drive, the man said he'd like to buy it—today. In fact he wanted to take it right then and there. Great, said Jim, but there was a problem in that the customer didn't have any money with him, not even a check, as he hadn't really expected to want the car right away. As this was long before the days of instant wire transfers, we were in a quandary until Alice remembered that you could write a check on any piece of paper and as long as your bank (and his) accepted it, you had a negotiable instrument. So we called our bank and they said yes it would be OK though very unusual; and we called his bank who said the same (at the same time we confirmed that he had sufficient funds to cover the check) and we then created the check. We did it on one of our envelopes and wrote it so it resembled a normal check—for $27,000—and he signed it. Of course he didn't have a license plate to put on the Ferrari, so we loaned him one of our dealer plates, which was always a good idea as we were assured of coverage from any type of loss by our insurance company. So he signed the check, shook our hands, got in his new Ferrari and drove away, leaving the Pontiac to be picked up another day. What had we done? Fritz didn't have a good feeling about it, but he got over that as the check cleared and we had sold our first 365GTC4—but not our last.

But a word about dealer plates. Issued by the Massachusetts Department of Motor Vehicles to new and used car dealers, these plates were really valuable—not that they cost a lot to purchase, but because they were so important to running an automobile business. They could be used on any car, registered or not; they could also be used on trucks, motorcycles (although they didn't fit that well) and commercial vehicles. They enabled the dealership to transport cars anywhere, even to Canada, and they could be affixed to cars that were being loaned out to customers either for a test drive or as a "loaner" when their car was in for service. All good and important uses, but second only to missing keys, they were the most frequently lost or misplaced item in the dealership.

Over the years we had between six and ten dealer plates (not a great many compared to larger dealerships) but at any one time 80 percent of the plates were out of the dealership on some vehicle on some errand or something unknown. Everyone was always hunting for a plate—the mechanics to test a car, the salesmen to drive a car, etc.—and even though each plate was assigned to an employee they were always losing track of them. When being used some were bolted on, some were held on by magnets (where they could scratch the finish), some were in the rear window (where they could damage the rear defroster elements) and some held on by plastic straps that went into the trunk (and were always flapping around). But no matter what ingenious method was used they were always falling off, being run over and sometimes found but often not. It was like we needed a full-time employee just to track the plates. And of course it was always at some time of crisis that a tag was needed most, but not located until someone remembered that they had left it on a car out back, or left it in a car that was at the body shop, etc., etc., etc. It was a never-ending problem that was never really resolved—and probably isn't to this day at many dealerships.

One of the recurrent problems we encountered

Autohaus dealer plate. The "B" was for Bob.

was price changes on vehicles due to currency fluctuation between the dollar, the German mark, the Italian lira and the Japanese yen. We were subject to those vacillations with no recourse and no alternative other than to pass the changes on to our customers, which made nobody too happy. But those were minor problems compared to a major change in the price and availability of the one product that all our vehicles depended on—gasoline.

In the fall of 1973 there was a shortage of oil coming to the U.S. due to an oil embargo instituted by OPEC member states against the United States and European nations. Prices shot up and long lines developed at gas stations where gasoline was being rationed, so joy riding became a thing of the recent past. Sometimes you just couldn't find any gas to buy, and for a period it was being allocated by license plate numbers, though fortunately dealer plates were exempt as gas was essential to our business. The value of gas-guzzling V8 cars, which included many of Detroit's best selling products, plummeted. In a relatively short period of time, cars that once were known for keeping their resale value became dinosaurs in the marketplace. We were swamped with requests to trade these large cars for vehicles that got better gas mileage, including not only Datsuns but BMWs as well. The wholesalers were no help as they wanted to buy cars for 50 cents on the dollar, and while some consumers went along with that, many just kept their cars hoping for a return of saneness to the marketplace. That took a long time.

But the gas crisis didn't seem to affect the value of Ferraris, perhaps because few owners drove their cars many miles in a year. So we decided to continue ordering Ferraris. One of the next ones we sold, a red with black 365GTC/4, was to a man from west of Boston who traded a 365GT4 like that automatic that we had ordered, except his was a standard shift. I knew that some had been sold in the U.S., but this was the first one we had ever seen. Then in November we sold two more GTC/4s, a silver one that had been in the auto show and also a light blue metallic which was purchased by Mr. Hall from Fitchburg, who traded the Dino that he had bought the year before. He missed the power and sound of the V12, like what was in the 275GTB that he once had.

Ferrari Daytona ad, *Harvard Magazine*, July 1974. We were experimenting with targeted ad publications. The exposure paid off.

10. No Gas for the Speedy

Three of us had driven down to Paoli in a BMW to pick up two cars, that silver GTC/4 and a Dino spyder. Jim and I drove the Ferraris back to Cohasset while a third employee drove the BMW back. Between Paoli and NYC there was way too much traffic so you really couldn't enjoy the cars, but once we crossed into Connecticut all hell broke loose. The Connecticut pike was a good road but it was littered with toll booths that seem to appear every five minutes, and before the day of EZ Pass and dedicated lanes, everyone had to stop at a toll booth. If you had exact change, however, you didn't have to actually stop as you could set up a sort of trajectory with the coins and as you slowed down start hurling them out the window into the basket, hoping they would hit the target. That being accomplished you had to ignore the bells going off as you had passed out of the area before the change had been counted by the machine. I guess that really didn't matter as we never were pursued because of a missed toll. So it became more of a game of guessing the fastest lane and having the correct change for the tolls, and we were both prepared for that. But if you got in the slow toll lane, by the time you got through the other car was way ahead and you had some catching up to do. The top speed didn't really matter that much as we couldn't get near it, but acceleration was really handy leaving the tolls.

So on that day it got dark early and I was able to stay a respectable distance ahead of Jim in the Dino when it started to rain; not too hard, but enough that we had to use the wipers. I knew I would have an advantage as visibility in the Dino was not great in the rain; it was so low that every other car's spray was right at windshield level, the headlights weren't that great, and because they were so low, you could easily outdrive them. They all needed Marchal driving lights (some of which were so powerful they could melt the pavement in front of the car, as the adage went) for which we were a distributor and always looking for dealers. So I was sure I would be first to Cohasset until suddenly the wipers on my car started to shudder, then bind and finally stop completely. No wipers! Probably a feature not tested by those technicians at Maranello as they wound out the V12s on their way to lunch someplace.

Now I couldn't see anything—but how could I stop and allow Jim to pass me? There was nothing I could do as he sailed by unaware of my problem, so I put down the window and tried to work the wiper manually. That was dumb as I could only make it move a few inches. So I slowed down, way down—what I wouldn't have given for Rain-X—and just went along barely able to see ahead.

We were north of Providence on I-95 when the rain finally stopped—could I catch him? Ah, this is where those 12 cylinders were going to pay off. I sped up, to what speed I don't remember, but the car was running perfectly; what a test ride this was! Just south of Mansfield I passed him, unfairly as I knew his headlights were holding him back, and he tucked in behind me and we continued that way to Cohasset. After getting back Jim said he was worried because I wasn't catching up to him until he saw way in the distance the telltale wobbling of the low headlights and he knew it was me. The 365GTB and 365GTC both had concealed headlights that were in a pod that closed when the lights weren't being used, but when you turned them on the pods would pop up and the headlights would go on. But the pods were not strong enough or aerodynamic enough to prevent them from wobbling and giving away the identity of the rapidly approaching Ferrari.

Jack Crusoe from Porsche Cars had retired, but he still kept in touch with us and I would see him at the opera occasionally. The Opera Company of Boston's executive director was none other than Miss Sarah Caldwell, to whom I had sold the Lancia coupe not that many years before, so I was pleased to support her any way I could, including placing advertisements in the opera program. I met her again a few years later at a fund raiser and as I introduced myself she smiled and said, "Of course I remember you, Bob, you were my driver's-ed teacher." I was surprised, and pleased.

Jack's lady friend from A/E, Liz Donahue, for whom we had sold her Maserati 3500, was a patron of the opera. One night at a performance that I was attending they were there, and when Jack went to get another glass of something she pulled me aside and said, "You know Bob, I would really like to have a Ferrari, but you realize how Jack feels about it." Jack, a true Porschephile, really didn't like Ferraris—although he did like Alfas. She said she would call me in a few days and she did, saying that she would like to buy a Dino coupe but that we couldn't let Jack know. "OK," I said, "once you make a decision I'll handle the arrangements myself and drive it up to you myself." She replied that she had already made her decision and wanted the dark red one that we had on display at the auto show.

We arranged a delivery time a week later and I started out for the North Shore—always a memorable trip—going through Quincy, and when I was just approaching the expressway ramp I gave the gauges a quick look (always a good idea in any Italian car) and noticed that the ammeter seemed to look grayish, at least grayer than the other instruments. When I looked at it a few seconds later it seemed to be almost melting! What was this? I pulled over to the side—always a tricky maneuver in Boston traffic—and when I looked at the gauge again it had totally shriveled up and was smoking. Oh boy! There was some electrical fire happening with the gauge and maybe with the wiring behind the dashboard.

I had to disconnect the battery and quickly, or I might lose the whole car—and the sale. So I popped the latch for the rear trunk lid, raced around to the rear, opened the trunk where the battery was supposed to be—or so I remembered—and searched vainly for it, pulling up the carpeting etc. I knew the "dinoplex" (an electronic ignition device) was there but no battery. Yikes! Then I remembered it was in the front trunk. I raced around and opened it up—carefully—and all that was there was the spare tire. Flash! It's under the spare. But it was under a cover which had to be unscrewed—with a coin? Did I have any? No. How about a screwdriver—and there was the tool kit. Got the screwdriver, got off the cover, found the battery, needed a wrench, found the wrench and finally disconnected a terminal. Fire aborted! But so was the delivery—at least that day.

The dealership sent a tow truck to get the Dino while I waited with my head turned away from the traffic—no need for publicity right now. Back at the garage I called Liz and told her what had happened. She was totally understanding as she knew Italian cars well, saying we'd arrange another delivery time when the car was ready to drive. We fixed the problem, which turned out to be in the gauge itself. Always check your gauges! And Liz got her Ferrari, and Jack never knew, or so she said.

We had sold another red Dino coupe at about the same time, but the fellow left it one night in a parking lot in Cambridge and it was stolen, the first Ferrari theft we had heard about other than our own a few years before. It was never recovered but he obviously never lost the bug as he showed up a few years later in a 365GTS Daytona spyder. It was black with black leather—absolutely beautiful and sinister at the same time. He said it had originally belonged to Cher, and it was easy to envision her driving that car down Rodeo Drive, although when I met her a few years later I realized it couldn't have been an easy car for her to drive because of her diminutive stature.

We finished off that astounding Ferrari year with another 365GTC/4 sale to a man from Quincy who traded a Maserati Ghibli spyder, a very rare and beautiful car that I had only seen pictures of before. Why didn't we ever see any of these cars on the road? Or why didn't any of our highly car conscious clientele report seeing this car? It was a mystery. He picked out a light metallic blue car that was in inventory at Paoli and wanted to accompany our driver on the trip. We said yes, of course, and I sent my brother Gerry down with the buyer to get the car. My brother said the trip back was uneventful and every hour or so (it was a six to seven hour trip—in a Ferrari) he would suggest that the buyer drive, but he never wanted to.

Gerry went frequently to Paoli to pick up cars, and on one memorable occasion he went to pick a brown Daytona coupe that we had sold to another man from Quincy. My youngest brother Doug (who helped out from time to time and who of course was a Porsche lover) drove Gerry down in a BMW 2002Tii and was tailing the Ferrari on the way back. He said—ahem—that they were going moderately along until they reached Providence, when Doug saw a Lamborghini Miura flying down an entrance ramp onto 95, obviously having seen Gerry in the Daytona. And then Gerry saw it too and that started a competition of the two cars that Doug said disappeared like a flash through the esses ahead. Gerry later related that after a few miles the Miura, bearing Rhode Island plates, slowed down and took another exit, never catching the Daytona.

The year of 1974 was going to be bittersweet for Ferrari as it was going to be the last year that we would receive the V-12 cars. What were they doing? The cars were still magical and drawing interested buyers although sales had slowed down—had we exhausted the market or had our clientele been reading the European press? We had read that there was a new model, the 365BB, that was just going into production in Europe and would eventually replace the Daytona. It was going to be a mid-engine setup like the Dino but would have 12 cylinders in a boxer configuration, like a Porsche; hence the BB, or Berlinetta Boxer, designation. We couldn't wait to get this car from the factory, but we never did. That story continues, but at the same time we learned that the Dino Spyder was also being discontinued (we had received the last 246GT the year before). This was a major shakeup in the Ferrari market, and by talking to other dealers and to friends in Europe we learned of another new model that we would definitely—no, probably—receive in the fall, a mid-engine 2 + 2 V-8 Bertone designed coupe. A what? By who? With what specs? It all seemed so out of Ferrari character, but we were to find out soon enough that it was all true.

Realizing that there were to be no more Dinos available, Fritz decided to order one for overseas delivery and pick it up at the factory. While European delivery was available this year, in other years Ferrari might or might not make factory delivery

Fritz's 1974 Ferrari Dino 246GTS with flared fenders and Campagnolo wheels. This car turned heads everywhere. The sound was all Ferrari.

possible. Whether it was due to availability, or because of U.S. or Italian regulations at the time, we did not know, but the policy was subject to revision or cancellation at any time. Hence it was rare that we took delivery of a Ferrari at the factory, and often chose a BMW for use in Europe as their plans were always available. So Alice and Fritz ordered a 246GTS in *rosso Dino* paint with a tan leather interior with Daytona seats, a front air dam and flared fenders to accommodate larger tires and Campagnolo alloy wheels (an accessory group that was later described by some as "chairs and flares"). It was quite a package and it was beautiful. The color was kind of medium orange, really bright, and something that made sense in a car that low, and that fast. So they picked it up in Modena and then went to Switzerland where I heard it caused quite a sensation. I bet!

One of the interesting aspects of being a Ferrari dealer was that we frequently had inquiries from dealers that handled other lines of cars but not Ferraris. Sometimes they had a customer that was potentially trading one and they wanted to get an idea of its wholesale value and our possible interest in buying it; and sometimes they were interested in buying one for themselves, usually if they had a very profitable year. We sometimes felt a little guilty about charging another dealer list price for a car, but that was business; and sometimes they already had one that they wanted to sell. That was the case with a Datsun dealer from the Boston area who called me one day to say that he had a 1965 Ferrari Lusso in his garage and wanted to dispose of it. He had traded it on something or other a long time before and now was tired of watching it decay slowly before his eyes. We had a good dealer-to-dealer relationship and his business partner was of Italian descent and we would sometimes say a few words in Italian (he was fluent, I wasn't), so he called me. Fritz and I went to look at the car, which was a medium blue metallic with black leather, and although it sure was in sorry shape we figured we could get it presentable and sell it "as is" to someone. So we bought it for around $4,000 and had it towed back to Autohaus where Fritz worked his magic on it and got it running smoothly.

We advertised it for sale in the *New York Times* and soon sold it to a man from North Carolina who said if the car was as described he didn't need to see it, and he bought it over the phone and arranged delivery himself, all for $5,000. Ah, those were the days!

Another purchase we made this year we had not expected, and that was a parcel of land that was diagonally across the street from us. As I have said, some of the manufacturers would periodically ask when we would build a new and larger facility and hopefully have room for their brand. Although we thought it was too early for that, it was in the back of our minds, so when this land came up for sale we were interested. It was offered to us by the same Mr. Rice from whom we had bought the Autohaus property. He gave us similar terms with no money down and a 20-year, low-interest mortgage, so we said yes, of course. Now we had two pieces of land in the desirable town of Cohasset.

Meanwhile we had heard from Ferrari that the long rumored new V-8 model, the 308GT4, was going to be shipped to us in October, so we decided to have a special showing for it at the Larz Anderson Automobile Museum in Brookline. The museum was located in the former carriage house of an estate, built by a diplomat, that had once included a huge mansion, since torn down. Many of the cars and carriages that the Andersons had collected were displayed. The museum was happy

Ferrari ad, *Boston Globe*, April 1973. It was always exciting to see our ads in the papers as we were making strides and getting good responses.

AUTOHAUS

cordially invites you to attend

The First United States Showing

of the New

FERRARI — DINO 308 GT4

on

Thursday, November 7, 1974

from 7 P.M. — 9 P.M.

at

MUSEUM OF TRANSPORTATION
LARZ ANDERSON PARK
15 Newton Street
Brookline, Mass.

For Directions See Map

Invitation to the first U.S. showing of the Ferrari Dino 308GT4 at Larz Anderson Museum of Transportation, Brookline, Massachusetts, November 1974. We felt honored to provide the first U.S. showing of this new Bertone designed model.

Ferrari Dino 308GT4 at Larz Anderson Museum of Transportation, Brookline, Massachusetts. It was a hit!

to host our showing, which was really well attended by customers and museum members.

From there the GT4 went to our display at the New England Automobile Show at the Hynes Auditorium, where we announced that it was the first public showing in the U.S. of this brand new and exciting Ferrari. Since the New York auto show wasn't until the spring, once again Boston was premiering a new car. The design was immediately controversial, as firstly it wasn't by Pininfarina but by Bertone, and secondly it was very angular, not at all what we were used to. But I really liked it, as it fit me like a glove. It had two small (very small) seats in the rear and had excellent visibility all around, and it was a V-8, a Ferrari first at least for road cars. But it was still carbureted like the Dino, and not that we didn't like carburetors, but they were much more difficult to maintain than fuel injection and they were sometimes prone to backfiring—due primarily to the emission air pump—which could be pretty scary when it first happened. No, it was scary every time it happened.

The last day of the auto show we always had staff there to get the cars out early; otherwise you got stuck waiting for the freight elevators which were slow and unpredictable. Our display was on the second floor so it was important to leave before others did. This year we displayed the new 308GT4, the yellow Dino 246GTS and the gold 365GTC/4, a pretty nice display of Ferraris, everyone said. To bring the cars back it was Jim, myself and Alice because no one else was available. Alice wanted to drive the GTC/4 (she liked the 12 cylinder models—remember the Daytona in Europe), I drove the 308 and Jim took the Dino. We all knew the best way back via Route 3A, not the expressway which could have too much traffic to expose these unsold Italian cars to. Jim and I took off while Alice got caught in traffic exiting the show, but she knew the way. We were enjoying the cat and mouse game down 3A, through Quincy and down to Hingham and the rotary heading south to Cohasset. As soon as the road straightened out and started climbing after the rotary with me following right behind Jim there was this muffled roar as a car went flying by the both of us. It was a gold car, it was a Ferrari, and it was Alice! Could that woman drive or what? She had caught us totally by surprise as we smugly drove along certain that nobody would pass us. When we arrived at the dealership she was just getting out of the car with a huge smile on her face. I don't think we ever talked about it again.

11

The 308

Now we had four Ferraris in inventory; one *oro chiaro* (gold) 365GTC/4 and one *giallo fly* (yellow) Dino 246GTS along with two new 308GT4s. The Dino we soon sold to a man from the North Shore who gave the car to his son for an early graduation from high school present—he had to have been a very good student—but the GTC/4 wanted to stay around for a while.

My brother Jim, who had moved to Ft. Lauderdale in 1963, had entered the real estate business at a time of real growth in that area and started his own firm, Tamarac Realty. He became quite successful, got married and had a beautiful daughter, and remember, he was the one that got me started in this whole foreign car mania that was still continuing unabated. He loved cars as much as or more than I did and had bought a 1968 Ferrari 330GTS, a silver one that was just beautiful. The smaller size of that car was optimum to many drivers as it was much easier to drive than the other 12 cylinders of the day. But after a few years he wanted to sell it since he had no room to keep it inside—you know that Florida sun—along with their other two cars and it was just time, so he asked us to sell it for him.

In the fall of '74 my brother Doug had flown down to Florida to drive it back—that's another story that Doug will have to tell. We had it for sale during the winter—good timing, eh?—and in the spring a local man from Scituate expressed interest in it and after (much) haggling and negotiations Jim agreed to sell it for $9,000. Ah, those were the days! The buyer didn't like the color and changed it to red though we cautioned him about the pitfalls of such a decision. Sometime later we saw the car in its new paintwork. The owner really liked it—I didn't.

Jim followed up the Ferrari by buying a 1964 Morgan Plus 4 in British Racing Green with tan leather interior, a classic combination on a classic British sports car. I drove the car a number of times through the years and it was classic indeed. It was real "seat of the pants" driving as your every movement was recognized by the car and it responded immediately, and the suspension—well, when Jim sold the car after quite a few years, he claimed it was probably the cause of his hip replacements. He said it—not me!

In 1975 I bought a small airplane. No, not a private jet, and no, not alone; it was a Piper Cherokee 140 and I bought it together with my friend Archie who had returned me to flying the year before. What was I, crazy? What did I need a plane for? My friend convinced me that the cost of flying lessons was high and a big part of that was the airplane rental, so, if we had our own plane it would pay for itself over a

Jim and his Morgan Plus 4. Talk about seat of the pants driving! He said it led to two hip replacements.

year or two. Well, he would have made a good car salesman—actually he was a salesman but not of automobiles. So we bought it for around $7,000 and it was in fine shape with low hours, having belonged to a commercial pilot who used it to commute from Marshfield to Logan—not a bad commute, we thought. Although he had all the licenses allowing him to fly into that airspace, it would be a long time before we were able to do that, if ever. So we continued to take lessons and in the late summer of '75 I got my pilot's license thinking that I would be able to use this in the business. I did—twice. Both times this same year.

The first occurrence was related to the 365GTC/4 that we had sold to Mr. Hall from Fitchburg who had traded his Dino. The GTC/4 had a special oil pressure switch, a feature that prevented the engine from starting until the oil pressure was up to the required level. Well, some of those switches were defective and rather than preventing the engine from starting, they allowed it to fire up and then within a few miles they would fail and the engine would lose all of its oil—all 17 quarts. This was not a good thing to happen. Fortunately for us, and for our customers, none of the cars we had sold had any engine damage as all the drivers noticed the oil pressure gauge falling and shut down the engine. Whew! We would have replaced the switches in all the GTC/4s when this problem was recognized, but Ferrari assured us that they were isolated instances and not all cars would have that failure.

Fritz thought that all should have been replaced, once again demonstrating his innate understanding of things mechanical, and the responsibility of manufacturers, so eventually they were. It wasn't long after we had delivered the car to Mr. Hall that he called Fritz and told him that his car had lost all its oil. Fritz explained to him what had happened and said we would get a mechanic up to him right away as we had replacement switches and plenty of Castrol oil. Rather than drive there, I volunteered to fly up with the mechanic and the oil and the switch.

Fitchburg had a small airport and it was bound to be easier and faster than driving, I thought. So off we went to Marshfield, got in the Cherokee and started her up for takeoff. It was a clear day and the flight path to Fitchburg was fairly simple—I had laid out a route before taking off, as one should always do. A driver met us at the airport to take us to the 365, and after the repair Mr. Hall couldn't have been happier, saying, "Now that's what I call good service!"

The second business use of the Cherokee was to transport a spare tire from a 308GT4 belonging to a Newport, Rhode Island, customer. The car had been in for service, but the technician forgot to replace the tire in the front trunk. It was less than an hour's flight, although it was a night landing, which was always interesting at a new airport.

When I met the customer there, he invited me to have dinner at his restaurant and stay at one of his hotel rooms on Bannister's Wharf, which I did. Daylight flights were always better.

And then came the Alfas. The district sales manager for Alfa Romeo Cars had been visiting us off and on for over a year, trying to get us to add their line of cars to our already crowded showroom and parking lot.

Autohaus aerial view, 1975. Where to put the Alfa Romeos?

So in the early spring of '75 we decided to take on the line, which at that time consisted of '74 models (so they were only one year behind) including the spider, the 2000GTV coupe—one of my all time favorites—and the 2000 Berlina four door, whose design was right out of 1962. But the '75 models would appear in April, with the new Alfetta GT replacing the 2000GTV and the Alfetta sedan replacing the Berlina. All the Alfas were great to drive and had a totally different feel than the BMWs.

One of the immediate bonuses of signing on with Alfa was a planned dealer trip to Italy on what was called the *Ciao Tour*. Select Alfa dealers, and new ones like us, were to travel to Milano and see the factory where they would have a new Alfetta sedan available to drive on a tour around Italy. Fritz and Alice went, and over the many years and despite all the incredible trips we took they always said that the Ciao Tour was the most fun. Other dealers agreed with them as they reported racing through most of southern Italy and visiting the greatest restaurants and hotels. The dealers that also handled Ferrari went to Maranello where they had a tour of the factory and met with Enzo Ferrari himself, and of course that included Fritz and Alice.

When we received the '75 models in late spring, they started selling pretty well, including the new Alfetta Sports sedan which had just become available. It was nice to drive, fairly peppy and like the Alfetta GT it had a rear-mounted five speed transaxle, as did like the Ferrari 275GTB, the Lancia Flaminia and the later Porsche 924. One unusual sale was to the same doctor who had bought the Daytona that Fritz had picked up in Italy a few years before. He had decided that he just wasn't using the car enough and wanted to trade it back on an Alfetta in a transaction known as "trading down." That meant that the car he was trading was worth (considerably) more than the one he was buying so that he would receive cash plus the Alfa Romeo in trade for his Daytona. The reality was that we were purchasing the Ferrari for X dollars and he in turn was buying the Alfetta with some of that cash; but since it was a negative trade transaction there would be no sales tax due. We were both happy with the arrangement as he had a new Alfetta and we had a low mileage 365GTB/4 that we were pleased to have in our showroom now that new versions were no longer available.

We also sold parts wholesale to many small repair shops and body shops, supplying them with factory manufactured parts as we didn't like to sell "aftermarket" parts that might not have the quality of factory parts and did not have a good warranty. One of the body shops in Quincy was owned by a man who operated it with his two sons, and they had a very good reputation. The father, who was probably in his late 60s or 70s, loved Ferraris and especially loved our gold 365GTC/4. Normally when body shops bought parts from us, either we would deliver them to the shop or they would send a driver down to get them. But it seemed that every time we sold something to this shop in Quincy the father would show up to get the parts. And every time he would come into the showroom and walk around the GTC/4 smiling and say to me something like "I really like this car, but it's so expensive," but that's all that he would say as he was a very quiet man. He never asked to drive it or even hear it start up but I'm sure he had seen it being moved around once or twice.

One day in April one of his sons came in to pick up parts and came into the showroom and asked for me. Surprised his father hadn't come, I inquired if he was OK and his son said yes he was. The son said his father thought he was bothering me

2000 Spider Veloce

Beneath elegant new Kamm-tail styling by Pininfarina nestles the legendary, race-refined Alfa D.O.H.C. Plus gearbox, suspension, brakes and steering producing handling, road-holding and cornering capabilities to satisfy the most demanding performance enthusiast. Top speed: 118 mph.

Wheelbase	88⅞ in.
Front track	52⅜ in.
Rear track	50⅜ in.
Overall length	161⅜ in.
Overall width	64⅜ in.
Overall height	50⅜ in.
Curb weight	2292 lbs.

2000 GT Veloce

Outstanding styling by Bertone, outstanding performance by Alfa Romeo. Result: a true *gran turismo* car offering race-refined performance, handling and safety in a richly appointed, classically styled coupe. Top speed: 118 mph.

Wheelbase	92⅜ in.
Front track	52⅜ in.
Rear track	50⅜ in.
Overall length	161 in.
Overall width	62⅜ in.
Overall height	51⅜ in.
Curb weight	2292 lbs.

2000 Berlina

Performance so unexpected in a family car that many enthusiasts consider it "a racing car in disguise." Bertone styling. Rigid-unit body construction. Same D.O.H.C. engine, transmission, brakes and running gear as every other Alfa—in a spacious and comfortable four door car. Top speed: 112 mph.

Wheelbase	101⅜ in.
Front track	52⅜ in.
Rear track	50⅜ in.
Overall length	172⅜ in.
Overall width	61⅜ in.
Overall height	56⅜ in.
Curb weight	2442 lbs.

1975 Alfa Romeo model lineup.

Our last new Ferrari 365GTC/4. What would they replace it with? This was my favorite sounding 12-cylinder Ferrari. Showing this model to customers and test driving it was always rewarding.

by always looking at the car and not buying it, but I said I really enjoyed seeing him and understood his feelings for the 365, and he certainly wasn't bothering me. Then the son said that his father really wanted to buy the car but didn't want to insult us by telling us what he could pay for it. He said his father had been a hard worker all his life and this would be a great reward for his efforts, and both his sons wanted him to buy the car. So without him asking, I gave him a price that we could sell it for, writing it on the back of one of my business cards, and telling him to let me know if that price was OK. Well, it was. The son called me back and said it was fine with his father and could they pick the car up in a week? I don't think I ever saw a bigger smile on the face of a buyer than on the day that the father came to get the Ferrari. And as he drove—very slowly—out of the parking lot we all smiled too—it was part of the profession that could be most rewarding. That was the last new 365GTC/4 we sold.

As a surprise, which was often the case with Ferrari news, we started to receive some 308GT4s in new color schemes, some with a two-tone paint job with fly yellow on top and black below the door crease; they looked sensational. They proved a good attraction at the fall auto show.

That year we sold a few more used Ferraris including a '64 Lusso that a good customer had left with us to sell on consignment. It was a maroon color with black interior and we loved having it in our showroom along with the Daytona that we had traded, which had not yet sold as we entered the New England winter. Although the cars were happy in our showroom we would have much preferred that they be in someone else's garage. In the middle of November a man called from the North Shore

Ferrari 308GT4 with boxer paint scheme in our display at the New England Auto Show, 1975.

(were all the big spenders from there?) after seeing our cars advertised in the *Boston Globe,* and came down to look at both of them. He looked them both over but just couldn't resist the Lusso, even at the healthy price of $11,500. It was sensational looking then, and still is today; many have said, including myself, that in the final list of great automotive designs the Lusso will always be in the top ten.

But not everything was great with Ferrari as they had been accumulating a large inventory of the new 308GT4 model; in other words, it wasn't selling well. They advised all the dealers that we were supposed to do something about it—by increasing sales of course. But in addition to that familiar distributor's refrain, we also heard that they were appointing new Ferrari dealers in Burlington, Vermont, and in Cambridge. We had already learned, and were to keep on learning, that dealers had little voice when protesting actions of a distributor or factory. Their decisions were a *fait accompli* that you just had to live with. We were still hoping to get the new 365GT/BB Berlinetta Boxer that was already prowling around the roads in Europe and elsewhere, but it seemed it would be a long time coming, if ever. So it was going into 1976 that all we had to sell was the new 308GT4—but that would change the following year.

The new Vermont dealer had bought a new 308GT4 from us before being appointed as a dealer. I think he had seen the car at the auto show and then driven down with a friend to look at a maroon one we had. He drove it and liked it, then wanted to negotiate on the price, but before I could say anything he reached into his pocket and pulled out a velvet bag and emptied the contents onto another piece of black velvet. They were diamonds, and I guess big ones, but what did I know? He wanted to exchange them for the car, so I called Alice and said you have to come help me with this. I could see her eyes widen when she saw them, and she said they looked beautiful, but we really wanted dollars not carats, so he ended up paying us with a check which was fine with me. He must have liked the Ferrari a lot, but I guess other Vermonters didn't as he only had the franchise a short time.

To encourage 308GT4 sales I started driving one as a demonstrator, a light metallic green color called *verde medio metallizzato*; the name even sounded beautiful, and the car was. I wasn't putting that many miles on that summer except maybe one or two trips to Vermont where it really showed off on those winding and hilly roads. The Ferrari's performance was supplemented by a CB radio, the toy of the day with the handle "green machine," and with that I felt protected from unwelcome attention. I think the fact that we had that car available to be driven extensively by potential clients did help sell a few, which was the real idea behind having demonstrator models.

That autumn we decided to attend the U.S. Grand Prix at Watkins Glen, New York, and were to witness Niki Lauda, Ferrari's top driver, display his skills at a very tough track. So I in the green 308 and Fritz in a maroon 308 headed west to catch the event. Well, I think the real event was on the New York Thruway and not on the track as Fritz and I jockeyed for lead in a non-stop Ferrari competition from Cohasset to the Glen.

Niki Lauda (in striped jacket) leans over the shoulder of racing team manager Montezemolo in conversation at 1975 Watkins Glen GP.

11. The 308

1975 World Driving Champion Niki Lauda and the Ferrari 312 B-3.

Niki Lauda and the Ferrari 308 GT4 at Watkins Glen.

Why is a Ferrari racing car similar to a Ferrari 308 GT4?

Ferrari racing experience is great. In 1975, Ferrari won the Formula 1 Constructor's Championship, and Ferrari team driver Niki Lauda won the World Driving Championship. Since 1948 when Ferraris began racing, Ferrari drivers have won seven World Driving Championships (more than any other team). That's an enviable record, but few people drive race cars. What is important is that this racing experience gets translated into a high performance "street" car suitable for the U.S. market.

To do this, Ferrari engineers work on designing both race cars and "street" cars. The same factory that builds the race cars also builds the limited number of street Ferraris. The same drivers who race the Formula 1 cars also test the prototype "street" cars.

Niki Lauda spent several months testing different versions of the Ferrari 308 GT4. He made suggestions on how to *improve* the suspension, what to change in the gearbox, where the visibility could be greater, how the car could be more comfortable, and where the steering was less than perfect. The engineers then made the changes and Niki Lauda made more tests and suggestions.

Finally, he pronounced the Ferrari 308 "mechanically really good —the best Ferrari ever made for the U.S. market."

A September, 1975 Road & Track article said the Ferrari 308 "has all the traditional Ferrari features and then some. It hardly needs saying that the 308 like the larger Ferraris is a driver's car in the extreme. Outstanding performance, ride and handling are all there. It's an exhilarating car to drive fast, yet it's absolutely docile in town."

Ferrari ad featuring Lauda at the 1975 Watkins Glen Grand Prix; he won both that race and the world drivers' championship for 1975 while Ferrari won the International Cup for F1 manufacturers.

What a time that was! Lauda won that race and also the World Driving Championship for that year, and Ferrari won the Formula 1 Constructor's Championship. Quite a year for everyone. So at the race we briefly met Luca Cordero di Montezemolo, who was the factory team leader at that race and went on to be head of Ferrari in the 1990s. We left "the Glen" in great spirits and the drive on the way back was only a bit less intense than the drive to the race as Fritz and I were constantly being challenged by a flotilla of Porsches, MGs, Jaguars etc. But you can guess who arrived back at the dealership first. Can't you?

BMW rear window sticker. We liked these dealership identification labels as they were less obtrusive than ones attached to the car's body.

Early in the year we were advised by Hoffman Motors, the BMW importer for the U.S. for many year, that a new company, BMW of North America, would be assuming the importation and distribution rights for BMW products in North America. So the factory was taking over after all (I guess they always do), and I'm sure a lot of negotiations with Max Hoffman, who had been the driving force for so many imported makes, had occurred.

A common sight on the back of most cars was some sort of insignia or badge indicating where the vehicle had been purchased, but we didn't like to mess up the rear appearance that way. In Europe we had seen stickers affixed to the inside of the rear windows of cars, much less obtrusively than on the back of cars. We decided to use them beginning with BMW models, and we thought if someone didn't like it they could just peel it off the window with no physical damage to the car. Most people didn't object.

From BMW came big news affecting much of the model lineup: the 2002 series was being replaced by the new 3 series, and a new 7 series sedan larger than the Bavaria and 5 series was coming, aimed more at Mercedes-Benz and Jaguar top line models. But even that wasn't all because BMW was also introducing a new coupe model, the 630CSi, to replace the long absent 3.0CS sport coupe.

BMW introduced the new 7 series at a dealer event at Lime Rock Park (remember the Porsche Sportomatic?) and they were going to allow the dealers to test drive the new sedan on the track—while in the company of a race car driver—and experience a new front end suspension that they were very excited about. I drove down to the event thinking along the way of all my memorable—and not so memorable—drives to that part of Connecticut, which were always worth the trip. This time the driver I was assigned to was Sam Posey, whom I had never met though I had followed his career as he had raced at many tracks including Sebring and of course Lime Rock, so he really knew that track well. His lap times showed that he and the 733 were going around the track faster than many all-out sports cars in SCCA competition. He was an incredible driver, always very calmly in control, and the 7 was an incredible sedan. You could still get it with a standard transmission, increasingly unavailable in luxury sedans, and something I really enjoyed. The 6 series was also impressive, featuring a very refined and attractive design, although I didn't like the seating position as much as the 7 series. I wondered if Italians were helping out in the design studios.

Meanwhile Datsun was getting more popular. The Z car had remained successful through two revised generations since its bombshell introduction. The fuel injected 280Z was still unbeatable in its market, and the 2 + 2 model introduced in the '74 260Z had carried over to the 280Z and added to sales that were increasing dramatically as the Japanese imports slowly ate away at Volkswagen's once insuperable sales lead. Datsun's rise didn't do much for the service department as they needed so little attention that even the warranty claims were sparse. The BMWs liked to visit the shop much more frequently, much of the time for warranty work, which Fritz was eager to do. Ferrari's warranty at the time was one year, but owners tended to drive them so little during the first 12 months that repairs were rare. But there was one common problem with those cars, and also with Alfa Romeo as we were to discover (we won't even talk about Porsche), and that was rust, New England rust. They all were subject to it, some to the extent that entire fenders or rocker panels had to be replaced. One BMW customer's new, very pretty Tundra green metallic 3.0CS, which was always garaged and never driven in bad weather, developed severe rust on the tops of both front fenders; even the BMW service representative couldn't believe that one. But it was true.

Ferraris rarely had mechanical problems, which had as much to do with their quality control as with the slow pace at which they accumulated mileage. It was a little disappointing to discover that some customers didn't even drive their cars to our shop for service, but rather would have them towed in (on the new ramp type tow truck) and then towed back to their home after the service was completed

We were starting to see pictures of a new coupe coming from Ferrari that was designed by Pininfarina and would have similar underpinnings to the 308GT4; then in March we received notification from Chinetti-Garthwaite that the new car would be available in early summer. Although we took that timetable with a grain of salt, they must have been pretty sure about it as they called a special dealer meeting—their first one since assuming importation responsibilities—to talk about the new model. So I went to the meeting and saw the full press release on the 1976 Ferrari 308GTB, and it was absolutely beautiful, a Pininfarina masterpiece designed by Fioravanti. How could Pininfarina continue to create these spectacular designs? How its lines flowed, how it encased a performance automobile underneath was wondrous.

Then we found out that this gorgeous car's body was to be made of fiberglass. What were they doing, copying Corvette? Apparently Ferrari had been experimenting with resin bodies—no body rust on this model—and thought this would be the perfect car to introduce it with. We also received their "estimated" suggested retail price for the car which was $26,445, or about the same as the last Daytona that we had received. Inflation was running strong, and I guess they didn't want buyers to think that they had cheapened the car in any way. Well they wouldn't think that as when the first "actual price list" was released in August, the retail price had increased to $28,580—that lira was getting very expensive. One thing was sure: They'd better have sold all the GT4s before this car arrived. If it was as beautiful in real life as in the pictures, it would totally overshadow its stablemate.

That spring I sold the gold 365GTB/4 Daytona of European Delivery fame to a member of the rock band Aerosmith, and that fall a bandmate would follow him into Italian driving bliss by purchasing a gold 246GTS Dino that was left with us on

Ferrari 308GTB at our display booth at the 1976 New England Auto Show—its first U.S. showing.

consignment by a hotelier from New Hampshire who had enjoyed the car but now was going to be using a company car instead—quite a switch, I'd say. Both of the band members were real car guys, and exceptional musicians, and often would stop by just to gab about Ferraris and Alfas mostly.

That was all before we finally received our first 308GTB red coupe (all the first ones were red) just in time for the auto show in Boston. As it turned out, that would be the first American showing of this beautiful car and we advertised it heavily for the upcoming show. We

Ferrari 335S at our display booth at the 1976 New England Auto Show. The 335S was on loan for the show through our friend Serge Dermanian, the Alfa Romeo dealer in Waltham.

Bruce Jenner signing autographs, 1976 New England Auto Show.

had a great display highlighted by the 308 elevated on a platform that we convinced the show management to provide us with gratis. The other two cars in the booth were a new 308GT4 and a 335S race car from the '50s. The latter car was loaned to us by Serge, another Alfa dealer who really loved Ferraris, and this car belonged to one of his good customers, Peter Sachs, who had quite a collection of Ferraris although I never got to see them. So many private collections were hidden away where few people ever got to see them; such a shame.

It was a great show that brought us a lot of visitors and potential buyers, along with quite a few admirers including Bruce Jenner, the athlete who had won a gold medal in the decathlon at the 1976 Montreal Olympics and was working for the Porsche display. He came over to our booth to look at the 308 and whispered that he would really prefer to have the GTB; well, at least that's what the salesman told me. Before he could get back to the Porsche booth he was suddenly surrounded by fans and admirers and was signing autographs. I never heard what Porsche said about that.

We had decided not to sell our first 308GTB right away as we weren't sure when we were getting our second one and we needed it to demonstrate to potential customers. I don't think Chinetti–Garthwaite knew either when the next fiberglass ones were arriving, but they wanted to make sure that we were serious about notifying them of genuine interest and sales. So they had an order form that included the customer's name and a notation that they had placed a $1,000 deposit with their order. Kind of foolish, we thought, but that was the rule. Well, one of the first deposits on a new 308 coupe came from a third member of Aerosmith, two others of which had already bought Ferraris from us. They were great guys and the fact that a third member was buying from us also made us feel really good that we were doing something right with our customers.

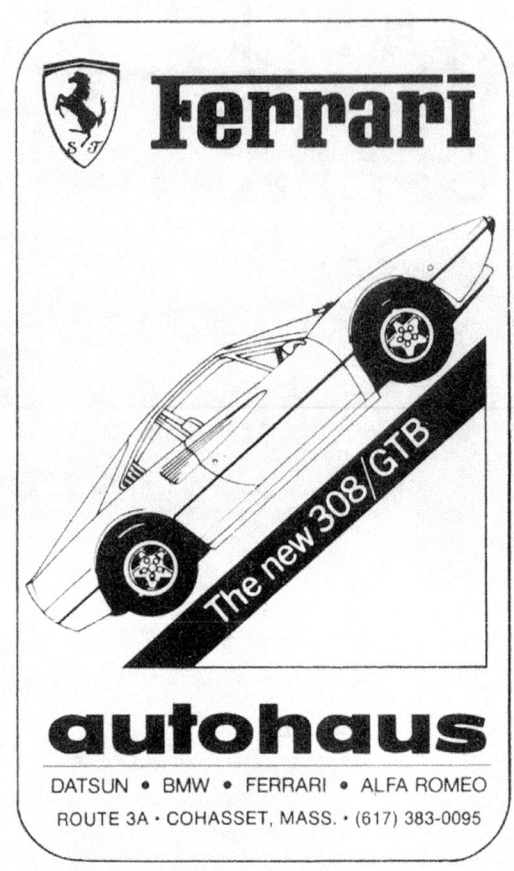

Ferrari 308GTB ad in a Opera Company of Boston program in 1976. This ad really stood out no matter what publication it appeared in.

12

The Boxer

EUROPE REALLY WAS A DIFFERENT WORLD than the U.S. in the 1970s, automotively speaking. European countries had not yet regulated emissions, even though the predominance of diesel powered cars and trucks made smog conditions in certain cities as bad as, if not worse than, California. Thus cars that were expected to be low volume sellers—such as Ferrari's 365 Berlinetta Boxer and 400 series—were never considered for our shores, to our knowledge at least, because of the expense of bringing them into compliance with American regulations. U.S. bound vehicles had to meet stringent emission and safety standards that meant redesigning integral components. It was possible, however to retrofit some cars, at considerable expense, so that vehicles not originally intended for us could pass our regulations—this became what was known as the grey market. Grey market cars became legal once they were converted and conformed to our standards.

We were aware of some Ferrari 365BBs (Berlinetta Boxers) and some 365GT4s arriving here and being modified to be sold by dealers and private individuals. The factory wasn't publicly saying anything about these cars and we weren't hearing from the importer Chinetti-Garthwaite or the newly established Ferrari factory office in Burbank, California. The purpose of this California office (the first ever set up outside of Italy by Ferrari) was to coordinate distribution and information about cars to the two U.S. distributors, Chinetti-Garthwaite for the eastern U.S. and Modern Classic Motors in Reno for the western U.S.

Ferrari had recently replaced the 365BB with the 512BB a car with a larger engine and more performance that would make U.S. emission certification much easier. The 512 designation changed the way Ferrari had historically described their 12 cylinder road cars which had the numbers indicating the displacement (in cc) of one cylinder. Starting with the 512BB the number 5 meant the total engine displacement in liters, and the 12 meant the number of cylinders. Quite an interesting change. So it was then that we started thinking about the possibility of importing one of these new and unavailable Ferrari models. But that would come later in the year.

One of the dealers in California shared a funny story about one of the very first 365BBs delivered. The man that bought it in Italy was a personal friend of Enzo Ferrari and was so pleased that he was able to get this new car virtually before anyone else. He took delivery at the factory with his wife and headed north to Modena, and after leaving the traffic in Maranello he sped up only to feel this serious thumping coming from the rear. He stopped the car and saw that he had a flat tire! How could

Factory brochure for the Ferrari 365GT4 BB, the first mid-engine twelve cylinder Ferrari road car.

this be, it was brand new, but alas, he had run over a metal spike. He knew how to change a tire, but what he didn't know was that the Boxer had one of the new "space saver" spare tires which wasn't a normal road tire, but a much slimmer temporary one that fit in the front trunk and left some luggage room. Not a problem, he thought as he changed the tire while his wife patiently stood at the side of the road, but when he finished he realized that the rear tire was too big to fit in the trunk where the space saver spare had been. He decided he certainly couldn't leave the damaged tire on the brand new magnesium wheel by itself on the side of the road while driving back to Maranello. So what did he do? He put the tire and wheel on the passenger's seat and left his wife on the side of the road saying not to worry, he would be right back. She probably wasn't surprised.

It had been four years since my last trip to Europe and I thought I should return to see relatives, visit the Ferrari factory to check on a *blu montecarlo* 308GTB order for a special customer from Hingham and pick up one of the new 630CSi models from BMW. Once again I had been unable to take delivery of a Ferrari as not only were the strikes continuing but also there was a shortage of the new 308s.

I was also planning to meet my parents, who were going to a theater owners' convention and would be there at the same time. Dad and a business partner had opened the first drive-in theater in New England in the late 1930s in Weymouth and

12. The Boxer

Autohaus ad, *New England Journal of Medicine,* **October 1977. We thought this ad had a European flair.**

they had recently upgraded it to have twin screens and a much more modern concession stand. His full time business was real estate and insurance but he always stayed involved in the Variety Club and their social causes, and along with Mom enjoyed going to the meetings and conventions which were sometimes in Europe. So I was to meet them in Verona and then drive to Comacchio, where our ancestors came from and where Mom had spent a year in 1930. She hadn't seen these relatives since that time and was very excited to return.

I arranged to have the BMW delivered in Zurich so I could meet up with Fritz and Alice's relatives and enjoy the Swiss hospitality. Everyone was looking forward to BMW's replacement of the 2800/3.0CS, which was now looking old, especially from the rear with a kind of narrow tread, not like the newer cars with little side overhang. We received our first 630CSi in the 1977 model year in the spring and it looked (not performed) great. More room, cleaner, more modern lines, and great colors that you could special order—as we liked to do to, not only because it livened up the showroom but also because, when someone fell in love with a special color, they wouldn't be able to find it elsewhere (at a lower price)!

But they were scarce! One way to augment the inventory was to have an overseas delivery, which not only provided you with an extra car, but also didn't count as part of your usual allocation; that is, dealers were allocated a certain number of each model, decided by your volume (and how well you knew the district managers). So overseas delivery was a great way to get an additional car, and of course enjoy Europe. At Hoffman I often talked with Sandy in distribution and Mel in the overseas delivery office, who had a great sense of humor, and we often joked about delivering cars to exotic places. He had in fact helped arrange delivery of a 325 to Shiraz, Iran, which is another story in itself

We arranged to have a light metallic Fjord blue coupe (standard shift of course) delivered in Zurich in May and I flew over on Swissair to get the 630. Fritz's brother Rolf and his family lived there and were always happy to help with our plans whenever we were in Switzerland, so it was he who picked me up at the airport. As we were going to my hotel we suddenly found ourselves behind a light blue 630CSi with German export plates with three people in the car carrying on, waving their arms, and they were really moving (not an easy thing to do in downtown Zurich) so we followed them for a while. I exclaimed, "There's my car!" My friend said the odds of it being my car were slim as there were already quite a few of that model in Switzerland and in fact in most of Europe, as we knew the U.S. was usually the last market to get new models. But I thought that the export plates along with the model designation made it probably a U.S. version.

We were to take delivery of the car the next day at a BMW dealership outside of Zurich where our former technician, Ruedi, was now working. Ruedi had enjoyed working for us and living in the U.S. but unfortunately when he went home to visit his family, he had not filled out the proper paperwork and was not allowed back in. It was too bad, although he became successful in his own right and eventually became the owner of a Mercedes-Benz dealership outside of Zurich.

I was anxious to try out the 630 on the autobahns, so after a great evening with my friends we headed for the delivery location the following morning. When we arrived at the dealership there was the *same car* that we had seen the day before! A representative from the factory in Munich, whom we had seen in the car, was there to present the car to me, but before she could open her mouth Rolf was grilling her about the delivery process and why three people were joy riding (my words not his) around Zurich in a car that was already sold—and paid for by an indignant American.

Actually, I wasn't bothered at all by that fact but he sure was—and they went back and forth in high German for a while and that's when I definitely decided to take some courses in the German language. After that discussion was over the representative, a very business-like if not contentious woman, proceeded to show me around the car. But as I was already familiar with the vehicle I really wasn't paying much attention to her, I was just looking to make sure there was no physical damage to the car, and I was certainly experienced in the type of surveying as we did it with every vehicle we ever bought, or had delivered to us. So my walk-around and inspection took maybe two or three minutes, and all the time the woman was talking mostly about the features of the car and the mandatory break in period. She finally became so exasperated that I wasn't following her every word and that I seemed to her either uninterested in the car or in her, that she suddenly said, "You Americans, we don't know why you buy our cars when you don't even appreciate their features and qualities" (and her description of same). At that my Swiss friend started up again with her—in German—and the discussion got quite heated, with aspersions being thrown, I'm sure, at both the German and Swiss personalities and cultures.

Meanwhile I got in the car, started it up and drove out of the delivery area. That finally stopped them talking—and with that I signed some papers, smiled and thanked the woman, said goodbye and thank you to Rolf and headed south to Italy.

I had one important stop to make before meeting my parents in Verona, namely another visit to Maranello where I was going to check on that special order 308GTB for a good customer of mine, Pete Wensberg, to whom I had sold an XKE roadster when I was at Auto Engineering. He was a super guy and had two sons who were real car enthusiasts too and who were always stopping in at Autohaus to gab and gawk. He had ordered a bright blue coupe, almost a French racing blue car, and was anxious to have word on its delivery time; so I had that goal plus I wanted to know more about the soon to be released 308GTS spyder. I arrived there and met with a different person than the last time, a Mr. DiFranco, and fortunately I would be able to have a short tour of the factory as there was only a half day strike going on. Very lucky, I thought.

Well, gone were the huge books with all the entries written in sepia ink, for now when we checked on the car it was on a computer printout sheet with a serial number already assigned to Pete's blue 308.

And so Ferrari was changing too. I was a little disappointed that the huge tomes were no longer the go-to ledgers, but it was encouraging that Ferrari was keeping up with the modern world at least in the recordkeeping department. Italy was deceiving in its infrastructure capabilities as on one hand the telephone system seemed so primitive while on the other they were the vanguard in robot assembly lines for Fiat automobiles.

My factory tour was very short but exciting nevertheless. There was this hum that seemed to pervade the entire factory (or was that my imagination), a hum that talked of excitement and passion for what was being done there. There were the assembly lines, one with 308s, another for Boxers and 365s, and all of them almost stationary. The cars were all being worked on by surprisingly young workers who seemed to be totally engrossed in their work of smoothing out body imperfections or installing seats and door panels, and as I approached with my host, they would look up and smile and then continue with their respective assignments.

Although I didn't see a 308GTS I did get to see where they were testing the engines before installing them in completed vehicles. Their engines were almost entirely made at that factory starting with the engine block being created in the foundry, and every one of them was tested before being installed in the various models. This meant that all the engines were tested at least twice: once on the dynamometer, and again on the road test of the completed car. Pretty thorough, I thought, and another reason why there were almost never any warranty claims on Ferrari running gear. And then our road tests of the cars before they were delivered to the ultimate buyer, virtually assuring them of a perfect running Ferrari.

In the dyno room they had a 308 engine attached to a dynamometer and were testing it for various outputs including the horsepower, and that's when I learned that when Ferrari stated that a certain model had X horsepower what that really meant was that every car produced would have *at least* that advertised horsepower, which also meant that some might have more, and substantially more at that. Now I understood why some new cars we received definitely felt faster than others! That was demonstrated not only by driving the cars from Algar to Cohasset but also when the car was prepared for delivery by our technicians and subsequently test driven. I insisted that the salesman who sold each car was ultimately responsible for the condition of the vehicle before it was delivered to the customer and that included that it was full of gas, that its cosmetic condition was perfect and that it performed as it should. It was a tall order for the sales department, but they did their job and if there was any item that didn't satisfy them they would come to me and I would drive the car to see what the problem might be—and if there was a flaw, it would be rectified before delivery. It was quite a check-up process, but it worked!

I was to learn some startling news on this visit, specifically that Pete's car—and all future 308GTBs—would not have a fiberglass body, but a steel one instead. We had heard in February that the factory might be changing to steel bodies, but we weren't sure when or if that would actually happen so I had sought to find out the real story, and I did. Pete's car was being produced in April with a steel body. No official explanation was given for the change, though everyone kept guessing at various reasons.

Pete's car arrived at our dealership shortly after my return and he was pleased with the car. Unfortunately it caught fire not long after and was a total loss. Following that he decided to import a 275GTB that he found in Europe, and had it shipped back to Boston aboard a freighter. While it was being unloaded onto the dock, the sling holding the car gave way and it was dropped from a considerable height onto its nose, causing extensive front end damage. Pete did not deserve that run of bad luck

After my short but informative factory visit I was off to Verona to meet up with the folks, who were thrilled to see me there. The next morning we headed to Comacchio, birthplace of my maternal ancestors, and my mother's reunion after 47 years. A small town at the mouth of the Po River, Comacchio is called the little Venice because of the many canals and bridges throughout the area. It's primarily a fishing village and the specialty cuisine is eel, which are caught in these swooping nets that are lowered into the river as the tide changes and the eels swim in and out. In earlier times it was noted for its production of salt; in fact one of the reasons Napoleon invaded the area was to gain a supply of salt that was not mined but created in early desalination plants. We arrived on a beautiful May afternoon and checked into the hotel before going to visit the relatives.

The reunion was surreal, and as Dad and I watched there was as vivid a picture of my mother's youth as I had ever seen. There were all sorts of cousins, all with my mother's maiden name or her mother's maiden name, recounting times past and how no one had really changed that much. I was very happy for her. That evening we had a delicious meal, even including the eel, which I had not expected to like. One of the relatives was a young man a few years younger than I who was to take me around to Comacchio the next day and show me the town's history and monuments while my parents went with the older aunts and uncles.

Edgardo spoke no English so communication was all in my not so fluent Italian, but we got along just fine and had a great day, at the end of which he said he hoped I would return to Comacchio and I said I would try and told him that he must come

Cousin Edgardo and the author in Comacchio, Italy, 1977.

and visit us in the U.S. He thanked me for the invitation but said that he wouldn't come as he really didn't want to travel, and that he hadn't even been out of Italy. Thinking of my wanderlust from my college days, I asked him why he didn't want to travel and he replied that he had everything he could ever want right there in Comacchio and was happy with what he had. That comment has always stayed with me.

From there we drove back to Verona, where I left Mom and Dad to rendezvous with friends before traveling to the convention. I was to meet them again in Paris from where we would drive to Cherbourg to board the *Queen Elizabeth 2* for the sail back to New York.

From Italy I drove west to the French Riviera again, where I looked up some old haunts and stayed at the Hotel Byblos, which at that time was somewhat affordable; I don't know about today though. It was enjoyable as always, and in those times May was not too crowded, but after three or four days I left for Paris which was just over 500 miles away. It was an easy one day drive, what with no speed limits and such, and I could really test the 630 at speed while breaking it in properly.

There are some great roads before you get to the autoroute with little traffic, especially in the early morning. After I entered the autoroute the weather was turning darker, which probably meant rain and lower driving speeds, but that was OK. After a couple of hours on the autoroute as I was merrily passing just about everyone with my blinker on and my headlights flashing, I suddenly noticed in my rearview mirror a single headlight approaching me at a pretty good clip. Knowing many of the gendarmerie used motorcycles, I slowed down a bit to let him pass, but it wasn't the police; it was a guy on a BMW R100S, and as he passed me he sort of nodded his head and sped away. Now wait a second, I thought, it should be the other way around with me passing him and letting him see my taillights; this had to change. So I sped up and passed him, which wasn't done that quickly, and then he passed me again and I passed him thinking that these French really like this game on the highways. When he passed me again I pressed the accelerator to the floor and watched the speed climb to 125, but I couldn't catch up with him. This car was not as fast as the 3.0CS. Damn emission stuff, I thought—or maybe it was the floor mat. So I reached down, pulled the mat out from under my feet, threw it in the back seat and pushed the pedal down all the way, hoping I could get it through the floor boards—but it didn't work, 125 was it and I couldn't catch him.

And then it started to rain. Now, I thought, I'll watch him slow down because motorcycles in the rain are difficult. He did slow down, as did I because at over 100 the wipers were useless. But still he was keeping up with me in the rain at 100 mph plus—this guy could ride. Then he pulled up beside me and motioned for me to follow him at the next exit, which was to one of those incredible overhead restaurants spanning over the autoroute's lanes so the traffic heading both ways could access them. They were pretty spectacular. So we stopped beside each other in the parking lot and said hello, or bonjour. It turned out he was a mechanic at a BMW motorcycle dealer in Nice and was going to his family's house south of Paris. We went into the restaurant for a coffee and croissant and gabbed and laughed for quite a while, and that's when he told me that there *was* a speed limit on the autoroute and that I had to be careful because the police also used BMW motorcycles. Turns out, I was so impressed with the R100RS that I would end up riding one a few years later. Things had changed on the French highways since 1971, I discovered. Then we both had to go, but not before taking pictures of each other with my Polaroid. Great race, great guy, great roads. I loved it.

I arrived in Paris late and went to see some friends from Massachusetts, as my parents would not arrive for a couple of days. One friend, Jack DePalma, worked for Barbra Streisand and was always traveling for her and looking for scripts that might work for a movie. He introduced me to a friend of his, Marie, who was a real late night girl and a lot of fun. She in turn had two friends who owned a bar in the Marais district named the Piano Zinc, so we went there the first night to see them. The bar had three floors and they were not above but rather below, and the farther you descended, the smokier it became and the mixture of Gauloises and brandy was intoxicating even if you didn't partake. What a French flavor that place had. As for my clothes, I had to hang them out of the hotel window that night.

The next day I did a lot of touring and went to find the hotel where Fred and I had stayed back in 1963, and it was still there. Everyplace in Paris seems to be ageless, just like Boston I thought. The next day I met up with my parents and we had dinner with some of my friends (we didn't return to the bar in Marais) and they really enjoyed it. Mom could speak French also and she and Marie enjoyed each other's company as did we all.

The next day we headed to Cherbourg to board the *QE2* (which was late) so I went to drop off the car at the pier and then we went to have lunch. When we came out, it was raining and everyone had an umbrella, *comme le film*! We boarded in the late afternoon and found our way to our respective cabins. Mine was a double suite cabin that I was sharing with my friend Dick Murphy, who was on one of his many, many trips on this ship, and really knew his way around.

Dick was on a first name basis with some of the officers and he got us invited to a party in the Captain's quarters, which we all really enjoyed, especially Dad, who loved the sea. When the Captain asked my profession and I told him what I did and that I had a new BMW 630 aboard, his eyes lit up. He loved cars and was in the process of restoring an early '50s Mercedes 300 four door and wanted to know my opinion of the car. So I told him that the cars were indestructible and described the ones that I had driven at Auto Engineering. We had a great talk and I asked him if it would be OK if I put some glasses that I had bought on the ship in the trunk so that I didn't have to carry them off in New York, and he replied sure he would see to it.

The next morning there was a knock at the cabin door fairly early, and there in the passageway was the baggagemaster, who apologetically told me that the captain was extremely sorry, but although he had told me I could store some items in the car it was actually not allowed as the cars were in bond. I think I knew that but had thought the captain might override the policy—but the baggagemaster was in charge of the baggage and had to remind the captain of the rules. My friend Dick commented in his usual flip manner, "It's only you, Guarino, that could get the captain into trouble on his own ship!"

The voyage was smooth as there were usually no storms in May, so it was fine to go out on deck and enjoy the sun. At night there was the casino where I learned to play Baccarat under the tutelage of an older American woman who was always wearing a fur coat. She knew how to gamble, and after watching me lose my modest gains she told me a secret of how to hold on to your winnings.

We arrived in New York on schedule although the crossing time had increased as the ships were now going slower to save fuel. I was giving Mom and Dad a ride back to Milton, of course, and as we were waiting for the car to be unloaded the woman with the fur coat

Queen Elizabeth 2 baggage tag for our BMW 630CSi.

came over and said hello as she was waiting for her car also. Her car was the third one out of the hold and onto the dock, and what a car it was. Actually what car was it? I couldn't identify it! It was low, it was green, it was a two seater coupe and as it approached her I could see the Jaguar emblem on the wire wheels. She looked at me and seeing my puzzlement said, "It's a Pirana," a special bodied XKE Jaguar that she had bought in England and was bringing back to Massachusetts. She had planned on returning with a much more standard looking Jaguar, but when she saw this she just couldn't resist it and there it was. It was quite stunning. The driver left it running for her, always a good idea I thought, and as she drove off she waved goodbye and left the pier with the typical Jaguar sound being following along behind her. And with the parents I returned to the reality of stateside driving, slowly, I might add, as Dad had become very aware of my driving proclivities. We arrived in Milton and after a quick goodbye I headed back to Cohasset.

Meanwhile we decided we had held on to our first 308GTB long enough as we had shown and demonstrated it all the while extolling the exciting V8 performance and the magnificent fiberglass body to most of our potential buyers, some of whom had ordered cars for delivery in the summer. So it was early May when a woman arrived driving a late model Jaguar and wanted to look at the car—and to drive it. As I have said before, there were very few women that had bought Ferraris and the last sale had been quite a few years earlier, so when she approached Fred we all thought that she might be another buyer—and she was. Fred later said that she drove extremely well, probably too well as Fred never liked to go that fast, especially when he wasn't behind the wheel. She bought the car without trading her Jaguar, and after agreeing to our price she paid for the car and said she would return in a few days to pick the car up, which she did. And so our only fiberglass 308 was gone, but it returned about a year later as the same customer traded it back for a steel car of a different color; such was the automobile business.

Another occasion of note in the summer was the reappearance of the first new Ferrari that I had ever sold, the maroon 330GT. I hadn't seen Dr. Riemer since I left A/E but I heard from friends in the area that they had seen the car driving around, so when he called to say hello I wasn't surprised that he still had the car 11 years later. But he said he wanted to trade it for a BMW 530, having driven a friend's and really enjoyed it. So one day he arrived and looked pretty much the same as I remembered him, as did the car, and after a little back and forth we came to an agreement. A week later he picked up the BMW and left the Ferrari with us. I told him that the blue one that he had seen that day in Bedford had also come in trade for a BMW (although six years earlier) and he remarked that both the cars had gravitated back to me—or something to that effect. I thought too that the coincidence was remarkable

That fall, after seeing a number of Ferrari 512BB models advertised in New York papers by Ferrari dealers, we decided to see if we could purchase one in Europe and bring it back here to sell. My friend Dick, who was now also a customer having bought one of the first 320is, had colleagues in Italy who were attorneys and whom we contacted about finding a car to buy, maybe in Rome. The dollar was very strong against the lira at that time and after all the back and forth about availability and price they were able to locate a red one for us at a Rome dealer for less than $40,000. Of

Top salesman Fred Spring with three BMWs.

course we would have to arrange and pay for shipping back to Boston and then have the car modified so as to pass the emission and safety standards, all before we could offer it for sale. We had never spoken with or contacted the Rome Ferrari dealer ourselves but our agent in Rome said they were fine to deal with; their only request was that the car be paid for in dollars, which made sense considering the fluctuation of the lira, and that we pay in cash, not with a draft or something similar. Fritz and Alice agreed to go there and take delivery and bring the funds in the form of American Express Traveler's Checks, the next best thing, as we certainly were not going to carry that much cash overseas.

It was mid–December by the time everything was arranged, so Fritz and Alice left for Rome via Zurich, to which they would return after the transaction to spend some time with their families. Our friend Ernest had selected a nice hotel in Rome near the Spanish Steps, and after they arrived they contacted the dealer to see if all the paperwork, etc., was ready, and it was. As they were walking to the dealership, which was not far from the hotel, suddenly a motor scooter with two riders approached them from the rear and then sped up, and as they passed Alice the one in back grabbed on to her pocketbook. As she tried to hold on to it they accelerated and she had to let go as Fritz ran after them yelling Stop, thief! Alice was unhurt but she couldn't have been more upset at losing the $40,000 and their passports too. There was a lot of that going on at the time, with motorcyclists stealing handbags, and I think it was only after the police started using policewomen as decoys that the rash of thefts decreased,.

Returning to the hotel, they contacted the police and reported the incident, and then they called me to tell me what had happened and to contact American Express.

Of course I had all the check numbers and within two days they had an American Express check for the stolen amount. Pretty good service, we thought, but they still had no passports. For replacements they had to go to the American Embassy, which meant staying a few extra days in Rome—normally a fortunate thing, but the bad experience of the robbery left them wanting to leave Italy as soon as they could. As for the Boxer, they contacted the dealer and explained what had happened after deciding this was a bad omen—doing business in Rome—and the dealer said it was no problem as they could find another buyer easily. No problem?

In retrospect we concluded that it was some type of setup; otherwise why would they have taken Alice's bag as opposed to the hundreds of others in the same area that morning? So as bad as this experience was, when Fritz and Alice finally arrived in Zurich, Fritz's brother told him of a Ferrari dealer there with another red Boxer for sale in his showroom. After all that, here was another car, and a dealer that Fritz could converse with, and the price was just $2,000 more than the one in Rome. So they bought it. The dealer was to arrange delivery to the States by ship and its estimated time of arrival was late January.

At last we would have a Boxer!

13

Snowbound

THERE WAS A LOT OF EXCITEMENT about the Boxer that would be added to our other three Ferrari models: the 308GT4 (still model year 1977), the 308GTB (also 1977), and in March the 1978 308GTS, which was still undergoing the federalization certification at the testing site in Michigan. So we would have four for customers to choose from, but we were still waiting for our 512BB to arrive from Switzerland.

We received word from the shipping company that the car was due to arrive in Port Newark on February 4 and that we could pick it up at the port holding area on or after Monday, February 6, which sounded perfect. We knew a shipping agent in Boston who said they could clear it through customs for us, but it wouldn't happen for at least a week and of course there would be their fee. But they said it was simple to do and we could clear it through ourselves as long as we provided a bond equal to the value of the car, thereby assuring the government that we were going to have the car federalized or never drive it on the road. I found out that our insurance company would issue the bond; all we needed to do was present the bond at the customs office and pay the duty and we would be on our way.

So early Monday morning Jim and I, toting a dealer plate, the insurance bond and a few checks, got a ride to Logan Airport to catch a flight on Eastern Airlines for Newark Airport, which was just a short cab ride away from the port. The roads were clear with just a little snow left from an earlier storm, so the drive shouldn't be a problem, but as we were getting closer to the airport we noticed a few snowflakes in the air—probably the ocean effect, we thought. It was snowing lightly in Newark when we arrived, actually a little more than lightly, but we weren't going to be deterred.

At the port we found the customs agent and went inside for about a half-hour wait. Just as we completed the forms and paid the $900 duty, a man came out from the office behind the counter and announced that the office was closing down because of the storm. What? What storm, asked we New Englanders. In fact the whole port was closing down, so if we wanted to go it had to be now, said a worker who was taking us to the car's location in the parking lot. And there it was, beautiful and red and covered with snow. We hurriedly brushed it off and I got in the car, but it wouldn't fire up despite turning over fine. We lifted the engine cover and there was snow everywhere. As Jim and I looked at each other wondering how to get it started, a man came over and said that they were closing the gates in a few minutes and also that we were wasting our time as he had seen the car being pushed off the ship and around the lot as no one could get it to start. With the snow now really coming down heavily, we had to

Author testing the Ferrari 512BB in the snow!

leave and think of another way to get the car. We needed to get back to the airport but couldn't find a cab in the chaos of everyone leaving at once. We asked how far it was, whether we could walk it, and someone said sure if you're crazy. Feeling we had to at least start in that direction, we set out and then a cab stopped for us. Seeing us walking, the driver had figured we were headed for the airport and stopped to give us a ride on his way home. We considered him a life saver.

Newark Terminal was not that full as everyone except us apparently knew about the storm and either left on the last flight or never came to the airport at all. It was a new, modern terminal, which was great because we were about to spend the next two days there! With the office being closed in Cohasset, I reached Alice at home by phone and she was glad to hear that we had left the car and weren't stranded someplace on I-95 (thank goodness the car wouldn't start) with the Boxer in a snowdrift. She had spoken to Jim's wife Sandy, who was expecting her third child, and all was OK with her and their two children.

The first hint of the storm's magnitude was through a loudspeaker announcement saying that there would be no more flights either inbound or outbound until at least the next morning. That we understood, as it was snowing so hard that you couldn't see the tails of the planes parked at the terminal. Eastern Airlines had one of those semi-private clubs designed for frequent travelers, named the Ionosphere Club, that for a modest annual fee you could enter to enjoy soft chairs and drinks. Once we found out it was going to be an overnighter I decided to join it so that at least we would have a soft sofa to sleep on rather than a fiberglass chair or bench in the terminal area. It was very comfortable and relatively quiet until the management decided to open the doors to others so they could at least sleep on a carpeted area rather than tile. That was nice of them, I guess, but at least we had already claimed couches for ourselves. We ate and watched the horror stories on television, which included reports of coastal flooding in the northeast. It was the start of the Blizzard of '78!

Jim's house in Cohasset was in a marshy area, and he was worried but knew that Sandy would be at a neighbor's house at a higher and safer elevation. So we ate sandwiches and watched TV and slept well after that day. The next morning it was still snowing. When we started chatting about conditions with an Eastern Airlines representative who came by to see if all was OK, he invited us up to a conference room where every morning he would speak to the Eastern managers in about a dozen cities up and down the coast. This morning it was quite a conversation, and as he called off the name of the airports they were all reporting closed with no idea when they might reopen. Portland, Boston, Providence, NYC, Philadelphia, Washington, Charleston and Atlanta all had the same report. Only Jacksonville and Ft. Lauderdale were open, but they might have well as been closed as there was no place for their planes to go other than farther south. It was a fascinating morning.

That afternoon there was still no word when the storm might let up and we were watching TV footage of miles and miles of snowbound cars clogging all the highways in New England. What a mess! With people getting antsy, the manager announced that we could all board the plane to watch a movie; well, at least it was a distraction. Quite a few people boarded an eerily silent airplane with the only sound being the ventilation systems, as the engines were off. As we found seats and sat down, there was this hilariously funny sound of *everyone buckling their seatbelts*! The whole plane started to laugh.

Later the weather report said that the storm was finally letting up, but there wouldn't be any flights for at least another two to three days and the roads were only slowly being cleared; however, the Washington, D.C., to Boston train would be running starting the next morning, and for those who were heading north it would be a good time to get going. Jim and I agreed to seize our chance and the next morning we were able to take a bus to the virtually abandoned train station, where we waited and waited until finally around ten the train could be seen approaching from the south. As it pulled in the station it resembled what you might have thought the Trans-Siberian express would look like—totally ice and snow encrusted with passengers crammed in and all peering out the frosty, fogged-up windows. To our relief we were able to squeeze on and away we rumbled.

By the time we arrived in Boston in the mid-afternoon the sun was out and reflecting off the glass sheathed office buildings, giving an even brighter whiteness to an eerie scene that was devoid of people and cars. It was there that we discovered what havoc the Blizzard of '78 had wrought along the coastal towns and what snowfall amounts had hit so much of Massachusetts. The governor had ordered all nonessential businesses to close and was working out a plan so that employees could be paid a certain amount in place of their regular wages. It was a real national emergency which also meant no driving on the roads except for emergency vehicles.

But how to get to Cohasset? We decided to go to the waterfront to see if by any chance the commuter boat that ran to Hingham might be operating. What luck! They were about to try their first voyage in three days as the Coast Guard had just opened a channel with one of their icebreakers. It was leaving at about 4 p.m., just before it started getting dark, and we were able to get aboard along with hundreds of other unwashed and unshaven passengers. As we sailed into the harbor the daylight was disappearing and it was the strangest scene; there were no lights coming on in the buildings or in the houses. There was no airplane traffic, of course, so we were going along in ice floe laden water in descending darkness with a surreal quiet interrupted only by the muffled voices on the boat and the occasional thump of the hull colliding with the ice. It was like a setting in a Bergman film.

Arriving at the pier in Hingham, we found there was more ice than had been expected so they were forced to tie up at an adjacent pier. Now we had to get to Cohasset, which was not possible on foot, but many people started walking out of the area and onto the deserted Route 3A and heading for home or some refuge. We decided to walk to Weymouthport, less than a mile away, where we had left our cars. Since the few trucks that had traveled the road had left large ruts that were easy to walk in, we made it there in less than half an hour, only to discover that the lower garage level, where my storage unit and Alfa GTV were, had been flooded with sea water. But we were lucky; although some items in my locker got wet, the water never touched the underside of the Alfa, just the lower half of the wheels. Whew! We decided to try to drive to Cohasset, thinking that if we got stopped we would say we didn't know about the road closings—with the travel saga we had just endured it was believable, and surely they would let us keep going, for where would we park the car? The Alfa started right up and out we went into the desolation that had become Route 3A. It was a little hairy keeping in the ruts as they had been made by vehicles with much wider tracks, but we managed, encountering only two vehicles heading the other way and no National Guard checkpoints. They must have been too busy on the coast to bother with the roads, I guessed. We finally made it to Jim's house, where I was going to stay and where some of his friends were underneath in the crawl space trying to thaw out the water pipes with a blowtorch.

The next morning I went to Autohaus and found Fritz already there, along with a man in a snowplow that was getting nowhere fast. They had put as many cars as possible into the shop area in anticipation of the storm (I think they managed to get 24 vehicles inside, which remained a record for many years) to facilitate the plowing when the snow ended. Moving each car took ages since first a space had to be cleared and then the car had to be broomed off (the snowbrushes wouldn't do it) and then be started (hopefully) and driven (or more likely pushed) if they could gain traction (the BMWs all had to be towed as the '70s and '80s models were hopeless in the snow) and finally put in the new spot. Car after car had to be moved that way. Toward the end of the week one of the technicians appeared and made it a lot easier. Then there were the customers' cars, some of which had been towed in for service and not worked on yet—well, you can imagine. The crowning moment was when everyone came back to work the following Monday and looking at the yard said, "Gee, it doesn't look that bad!" Fritz and I could only look at each other and laugh.

About a week later after the chaos of the Blizzard of '78 had dissipated we sent a trusted tow company down to Port Newark to pick up the Boxer. Driving the latest ramp type truck that could safely load the car onto its ramp—even with the Ferrari's low front air dam—and then secure it, and also supplied with the customs paperwork that we had obtained that incredible day in Newark, the driver successfully brought the car back to Cohasset. Fritz found that the sparkplugs were soaked in gasoline and replaced them with a new set, and vroom, it started right up with the whole shop smiling and clapping. I couldn't wait to drive it after Fritz did. It was different than the Daytona, so much more modern.

Driving the Boxer was different than anything I had experienced as the mid-engine configuration along with 12 cylinders made for a surprisingly light feeling car compared to a Daytona or GTC/4. The throttle response was immediate and the seating position provided remarkable forward visibility which allowed the driver to be in total control of the car. Although mid-engined, it had no similarity to the 246 Dino, being much larger and faster. I loved the car. But any speed trials would have to wait for dryer roads in the next few months.

To have it federalized, we had decided on a shop called Amerispec in Connecticut that was operated by Dick Fritz, whom we knew well from Chinetti Motors, and who had bought a Porsche 912 from us a few years back. We sent the Boxer to Connecticut and some three months and $16,800 later, we received word from both the EPA and the NHTSA that the car was now federalized and could therefore be sold. The company did an excellent job as you could only see that the bumpers were slightly different and that there was now an air pump in the engine compartment. I went down along with a friend, Dave Riggs, my flight instructor who owned a beautiful 246GTB Dino, to drive the car back, and it performed beautifully. This Ferrari, I thought, had quite a story to tell.

Ferrari 512BB after federalization, with bigger bumpers front and rear. Performance was just the same.

Not long after we got the Boxer back, we finally received the first 308GTS. By this time the cars were being delivered to us by enclosed trucks; there were no more memorable drives back from Paoli or Greenwich and no more tales to tell, although we were forever to relive the ones that had occurred. So we got a red with tan leather GTS which was sharp and immediately popular, and at the same time we were informed that the 308GT4 and 308GTB were also all to be 1978 models (although they still had a few 1975 308GT4s in Paoli that they were selling at greatly reduced prices).

Meanwhile our sales staff were satisfied (mostly) with the commissions they were earning and also able to handle the great variety of customers that they dealt with. We were pretty sure that we were the only new car dealership that had both Ferrari and Datsun in the same (smallish) showroom, and when you added BMW and Alfa Romeo as the other two makes on display, it was something to see. As we all knew, when a new customer arrived you seldom could tell what he might be interested in, and the sales department's ability to engage all different types was a credit to them—and to us. I never heard a Ferrari buyer complain about having much less expensive cars for sale adjacent to what they were looking at, and I rarely heard any Datsun buyer talk negatively about the higher priced vehicles other than to occasionally say, "Wow, that car costs as much as my first house!" The manufacturers didn't mind it too much at first; later they all started to want stand-alone facilities for their brands, but that's a future story.

We had the Boxer through the summer and it got a lot of attention as we advertised it in national newspapers, but as autumn started we still had not sold it. We were planning to display it at our booth in the upcoming auto show when in early October we had a call from a man in California who wanted to buy the car sight unseen. He said he would send his brother out to see it and bring along a "purchase draft" (which we were not familiar with), and if the car was as we stated he would buy it. That sounded fair enough once we found out what kind of draft that was, and that it was negotiable. So we said OK and a few days later in walks this 18- or 19-year-old young man who was the brother of the buyer. He looked the car over, said it looked fine, called his brother whom we then spoke to, and said it's a go and he'd like to drive it back today.

Well, we were concerned on a couple of accounts; first, giving a teenager a Boxer to drive across the country, and second, it had just started snowing! It was one of those early October snowfalls that probably wouldn't amount to much—at least not here at the coast—but heading west, who knew? So we called the brother back in California and told him our concerns and he very nicely said it was up to his brother whether to proceed in the snow, because he said his brother was a very accomplished driver. So after we almost pleaded with the fellow in our showroom not to drive now, he thanked us for our concern but declared that he was heading west, snow or no snow. And he did. A few weeks later the brother called from California to tell us the car had arrived in perfect shape after an uneventful drive from east to west coasts and that he was very pleased with his new Ferrari. End of story!

BMW must have been listening to my cursing the lack of speed in the 630CSi because for 1978 they introduced the 633CSi, with more horsepower and more

13. Snowbound

The author and Fritz on Autohaus' Tenth Anniversary. It had snowed, of course.

oomph. Thank you! The rest of the models stayed the same with some tweaking of emissions, etc., while Alfa Romeo and Datsun kept going with what they had, although we did hear that the Z was going to be totally revamped for 1979. We hoped they wouldn't ruin it.

It was that summer that I decided that I wanted to have a real house with a yard and not a condominium anymore, so I went house hunting on the South Shore. I was looking primarily in Scituate and Marshfield—close to the airport—and there in Marshfield I looked at some houses near the North River, but they were too small or had too small a yard. The realtor said there really wasn't much else. But then she paused and said, "Well, there is the old Judge place, but that's on an island so I'll have to check the tide to see if we can get over the road to it." Bingo! It sounded just like someplace I was looking for, and it was. The access road, which was occasionally covered by the tide, ran through the marshland out to the island named Macomber's Island, and then beyond to another island that was on the South River. There was a creek that paralleled the road and had a small pier that was attached to the marsh so that a small boat could be moored there. The house itself was built in the early 1900s and had been for sale for about a year. The realtor told me also that it was winterized but that the blizzard had damaged it somewhat so the owners were anxious to sell.

The house was built on pilings, always a smart idea when near the ocean, and although water had evidently come into the house during the February storm, unlike many of the neighboring houses, it was still there! I loved it in May and I could envision how beautiful it would be in the summer, so I decided to buy it together with

Jack, a friend and customer who was the financial type and forward thinker, as I knew that the house would need a lot of expensive work. It was close to the airport and 15 minutes to Autohaus. Too ideal!

Meanwhile Ferrari sales were going pretty well despite the frequent price changes (up but never down), but there were rumors that the factory in Italy was going to take over the distribution rights from Chinetti-Garthwaite and Modern. We figured, correctly, that it was only a matter of time before they were successful.

We continued to take interesting cars in trade, and in December we sold a red 308GTB to a man from the North Shore who traded a red 1972 Lamborghini Jarama, a car that I wasn't very familiar with. Checking around, we found that no one else seemed to know much about that model either. It was a brawny car to drive and very powerful with its V-12 engine, but didn't seem quite as refined as the 365GTC/4. There were a few dealers in New England that sold Lamborghinis new, but we thought it would be difficult to find parts if they were ever needed; this turned out to be very true. We sold the Jarama a few weeks later to a conservative man from the South Shore who had wanted an Italian exotic 12 cylinder car and who, when he saw this, had to have it. In a crowd you would never have selected him from a group of peers as the Lamborghini owner, but that was part of what made this business so unpredictable and so interesting.

BMW surprised most of the dealer network—I think—by announcing a national

Our Ferrari display booth with 275GTB4 (front) at the 1978 New England Auto Show. The 275GTB was on loan through Serge Dermanian, the Alfa Romeo dealer in Waltham.

dealer meeting for the fall in Hawaii. We had never been there before and Alice was especially excited, as was I. They were going to introduce a new model, the 320iS, and decided to make a real splash with this upgraded 320i. I decided to stop off in San Francisco on my way there to see my Uncle Chester's widow, Denzel, whom I had visited in Milano in 1963. It was great to see her and we spent one day and evening together reminiscing. She was as lovely and vibrant as I remembered and always kept in touch with the family, most frequently with my brothers Gerry and Jim in Florida.

The BMW meeting was spectacular and of course everyone was in the best of moods. I happened to meet the BMW dealer from Maui, who was a native Hawaiian, and whom I would see a few years later in a dealer organization, a real fascinating person who kept on saying "Welcome to paradise," and rightly so. I also met the Ferrari dealer in Honolulu who also handled BWWs. Where were you going to exercise a 308 there?

As I've written, one of the continuing issues we were always dealing with was the fluctuation of the dollar with foreign currencies so that every three of four months we would have a price increase, never a decrease, and if the dollar got stronger against other currencies there were a whole slew of reasons why the prices couldn't go down. The main reason, we were told, was that the customers who had recently bought at the higher price would be outraged if the price went down and might sue or something to that effect. So prices never decreased, at least to the dealers.

In January of 1978 when the 308GTS was announced, the estimated price was $33,500; in March when the car was first released, the list price was $35,000; in July the new price was $36,600; in November when the '79 models were announced the price was $37,950; in January of '79 the list price jumped to $40,400; and in May it was $41,750; and in July of '79 the list price had become $43,185! In a little over a year the list price had increased almost 30 percent or $10,000! Some of that was surely the dollar/lira dance, but some of it also had to be based on the salability of the new model. You would have thought that customers would have balked or questioned these increases, but no they didn't. The car was that much in demand; it was something that we hadn't experienced before in Ferrari sales and it was quite remarkable, and something that would continue.

Of course the same thing was happening to BMW prices, but not to the same magnitude, and their customers did complain. They were always asking to find one of the older cars "at the lower price" which was not easy to do. And then the leasing companies were getting confused as the selling prices were going up; it was difficult for them to calculate leasing rates even one or two months ahead. Datsun prices, however, rarely changed as the factory was probably absorbing the increases without passing them on to us and the customers.

Datsun finally replaced the 240, 260, 280Z body style with the new 280ZX, which, although a much improved car technically, lacked the unity and simplicity of the original design. It was more luxurious (some said T-Birdish) and larger both inside and out—and it was selling well, which always was the bottom line (well, almost always).

This was also the year of the Iranian Revolution that overthrew the Shah and replaced him with a theocratic form of government. Its relevance here is that up until

Importer Chinetti-Garthwaite ad for Ferrari models, 1978.

1979 the Iranians often represented the wealth factor in purchasing power, not only in real estate, investments, etc., but also in cars. They were big spenders and they let you know it. But they were just one group in a series that were the spenders at any particular time period. When I first started selling cars the doctors were the revered buyers of expensive cars. Wednesday was the traditional "day off" for doctors and

Ferrari factory ad depicting a 308GTS and Carlos Reutemann, winner at the Watkins Glen Grand Prix in 1978.

the day when they might visit a dealership to look at cars. That meant that any smart salesman did not want to have that as his day off; rather, he wanted to be on the salesroom floor or near the telephone to meet or talk with a potential doctor buyer that might appear.

The doctors were followed by stockbrokers and briefly by some high profile attorneys, but following the Iranians were Middle Easterners in general. Any of the oil producing countries generated big spending individuals who could be found in any high price automobile showroom. This included Nigerians, who were followed in the mid–1980s by the Japanese. The Japanese economic miracle showed up as students studying in the Boston area and had seemingly unlimited buying power (although it had to be approved back home) to purchase what pleased them, and for many at the time that meant Ferraris and BMWs. The '80s also created a great many tech investors, some of whom we saw.

My friend Loring's husband (they had recently bought a *prugna* [plum] 308GT4 from us) called me one day and told me that a friend of his, a technology company success story, was considering investing in a Brazilian car that a group wanted to bring to the States. He asked me if I would come to a showing of the car and give my opinion of its sales potential in the U.S., and I guess particularly in the Northeast. I agreed to go and asked if he had some info on the car so I could do some research beforehand. He sent me a brochure on this VW-based coupe that was actually very good looking; in fact I was familiar with the car having seen it in Brazil a few years prior.

Brazilian Volkswagen coupe near beach at Salvador, Brazil, 1974. Best looking Volkswagen I had ever seen.

In 1974 I had gone on a trip led by a magazine group we advertised with which also had a travel section that sponsored trips for very little money. So I had traveled for a week to the cities of Rio de Janeiro and Salvador where I had a chance to have a good look at this Volkswagen Brazil based sports coupe. As I remembered it had beautiful lines, very European in style with a handsome interior, and I wondered at the time why no one had thought of exporting the car to the States. Well, now someone was thinking of doing just that.

So one day we went to this fellow's house where the car was to be shown to a group of potential investors. There were quite a few people there gathered around the coupe and my friend introduced me to the owner of the house. He was very pleasant, a real car guy who had an incredible car collection housed in a big barnlike structure on his property. He had a real variety of cars, prewar, postwar, domestic and foreign, and talked about them lovingly. Here was another private collection that few knew about, as far as I could tell, and I told him that someday he should make his collection available to the general public to see, which I think he eventually did. After the tour I talked with him briefly about the Brazilian VW and told him that although the design was stunning, the marketability of the car was questionable because of its running gear, which would need to be upgraded in order to be successful in the U.S. Eventually he decided not to invest in the project, and I think the sponsor group also gave up the idea at some point.

We understood that the winds of change were blowing when we received a mailgram from Chinetti-Garthwaite saying that effective July 10, 1979, they were no longer importer or distributor of Ferrari automobiles for the eastern U.S. and that Ferrari North America (FNA) was now the sole importer and distributor for the same area.

One of the first communiqués from them was the announcement that they were having a dealer convention in Montreal at the end of September to coincide with the Canadian Grand Prix. Hoorah, a foreign Grand Prix! Well, not exactly Monza or Monaco, but still it sounded exciting. We were to meet for the first time the new president of Ferrari North America (FNA), Gary Rodrigues, and get together with all the other dealers from the states and eastern Canada.

The meeting in Montreal was a great success, starting with an evening reception featuring a surprise appearance by Ferrari's Formula One drivers who would compete the coming weekend, Gilles Villeneuve and Jody Scheckter (no wine for them). They were the first Formula One drivers I had shaken hands with and I was surprised at their slight appearance; all the better to fit in the cockpit and minimize the gross weight of the car. FNA had the business meeting the following day where they discussed plans for the coming years. We also got to meet again with the American dealers and for us the first time to meet with the Canadian dealers, who were all true blooded Ferraristi.

Some of Ferrari's marketing plans for the U.S. were revealed at the dealer meeting in Montreal and in a couple of articles and press releases towards the end of the year. It was interesting to note the sales figures for the States during the past ten years. According to statistics from R.L. Polk & Company, sales were negligible (less than 100 cars annually) for 1970 and 1971; then in 1972, the first year for the Dino, sales jumped to 255 units; in 1973 sales increased to 410 cars as we also had the Daytona and 365GTC/4 to sell. They dropped in 1975 to 188 cars, when just the 308GT4 was available, and then leapt to 617 cars in 1978 as we had additionally the 308GTB and GTS. But still, it was a very small number of vehicles sold to support the New Jersey operation, so we were not surprised when the factory said they expected sales to reach over 1,200 cars in 1980.

We were told that we would only have the V-8 cars, not the 12 cylinder models as the federalization expense was too great for the existing models, but they did hint that maybe something new with 12 cylinders would find its way to us. We certainly hoped so. There were also rumors about revisions to the 308 series that would include fuel injection, and that meant no more exhaust thermal reactors, etc., which made us glad. Thermal reactors were installed on all the cars starting with the 1976 models in order to comply with emission regulations. They ran at a very high temperature and provided a place for afterburning of exhaust pollutants, allowing the exhaust gases to pass the new standards. We were relieved to find out that starting in 1978, the factory would be installing catalytic converters instead of the thermal reactors.

With the small number of dealers and the relatively high gross margin per vehicle sold, the factory, the U.S. arm and the dealers were all going to be happy about the franchise into the foreseeable future. Traditionally Ferrari sales were one third in Italy, one third in the U.S. and one third for the rest of the world, but from what Ferrari North America was saying we would be allocated almost 50 percent of the factory's production in the coming year, and that would be fine with us if it really did happen. We would see.

The Grand Prix race itself was exciting as the Canadian driver Gilles Villeneuve was neck and neck with Alan Jones, driving for Williams, for pretty much the entire race. At the finish Jones won over Villeneuve by just one second. Villeneuve won the following Grand Prix at Watkins Glen while Scheckter went on to win the World Championship that year, and Ferrari went on to win the manufacturer's championship once again for that year. Alfa Romeo was also in that race but the car retired before finishing.

This was the first Grand Prix that we had attended under the Ferrari umbrella, and what a tent it

13. Snowbound

was. There was a special section set aside for us in the reserved area of the grandstand and in another area there was also a tent emblazoned with the prancing horse where we could sit down for coffee and just rest away from the roar and whine of those beautiful machines. It was quite a scene. It was the first of many, many events we were to attend where Ferrari was the host and where we learned how magical that name was to the catering and hospitality industries.

Opposite, top: Grand Prix of Canada Program, Montreal, 1979. Villeneuve for Ferrari placed second behind Jones driving a Williams in a very exciting race. *Bottom:* Autohaus aerial view in 1979. We're now fenced in. In front are two 308 Ferraris, gray and silver, and in the rear is the 1970 365GT 2+2 automatic that we had traded back in. Also barely visible in the rear is the Monteverdi 375 waiting for parts.

14

Mondial

That we would finally have fuel injection in the 308s (the "i" suffix was for *iniezioine*—fuel injection) was the good news, but the bad news was that the car would be less powerful and therefore slower—noticeably slower as it turned out. And to add to that embarrassment, a new regulation of the National Highway Traffic Safety Administration (NHTSA) mandated that all manufacturers install speedometers with a maximum indicated speed of 85 mph! This was to go along with the 1974 National Maximum Speed Law that capped speed limits at 55 mph to save gasoline by reducing speeds on highways. (The NMSL was not repealed until 1995.) How, we asked, could that be allowed in this free country? Our customers creatively requested that their speedometers be replaced with ones that at least showed an available 160 mph top speed. But of course it wasn't only Ferrari that had to obey; it was Alfa Romeo, Datsun, BMW and all the others, and although this foolishness only lasted for a couple of years it denigrated the soul of these cars and created a backlash that became apparent when a study showed that the average interstate speed was 15 mph greater than the allowed 55 mph.

Fortunately most of the vehicles we were selling, except for Datsuns, were still standard shift, and we would explain to customers who purchased cars with the 85 mph speedometers that it was possible to estimate your speed fairly accurately if the speedometer needle was pegged at the 85 mark; you could just double the tachometer reading in 4th gear and you would have close to the actual speed. Not that we were encouraging that, but if drivers happened to find themselves on a race track it would be handy to know how fast they were really going. That information was really appreciated by some.

I had to get back to Europe and get this 55 mph slowness out of my system. Fritz, however, never seemed to adhere to the speed limits, and if he ever got interviewed (which he did often) his Swiss accent and mechanical prowess inevitably got him out of trouble. He was incredible! And while Alice's speech became more Americanized, Fritz's seemed to become more Swiss.

Speaking of foreign languages, I had decided that having at least some knowledge of German would be beneficial to me, not only in Germany but maybe in Switzerland also. So I decided to take a basic course in German at Harvard night school. Actually at Harvard I found out there is not such a thing as a basic course as it was pretty intense learning. The course met twice a week for a couple of hours each night and there was considerable homework. I actually liked the course and the professor,

Ferrari 308GTBi/308GTSi factory brochure. Say goodbye to carburetors.

a German lady who also taught Harvard day classes. But this was not Swiss German, as any German speaking person will tell you. Swiss German was not only a dialect of German, but also very difficult or impossible to understand if one was accustomed to speaking regular—or high—German. However, since I had been listening to Schweizerdeutsch for some 15 years, I could somewhat assimilate them so I began to comprehend. I was happy about that!

This was also leading up to a trip I was planning to Germany in late April that would include taking delivery in Munich of one of the new BMW 528i models that had been introduced in 1979. There I was to meet my traveling friend, Jack, who had business in Germany, after which we were going down to the French coast to get some Mediterranean sun and see what was going on. He spoke fluent French and with my newly acquired German prowess it was bound to be an interesting trip.

We picked the car up at the Munich delivery center, which was highly organized and where the people were much more pleasant than those I had encountered in Zurich when I took delivery of the 630CSi. They even had a restaurant, so we had some café, etc., while we waited for the car to appear, and after checking it over, off we went. We stayed in Munich for a few days and visited some sights, and I wrote some postcards back to the office and also to my German teacher—in German of course. Then we headed to southern France for a few days to hear Jack's expertise. The 528i performed well, and on the autobahn, it really felt fast and solid.

From the coast we headed to Paris where we visited with the friends who had the smoky bar in the Marais district, and they were as friendly as before, so we got together at a few dinners and thoroughly enjoyed the time there. I was leaving the BMW at a factory designated dropoff point in Paris for the shipment back to the U.S., and it was there that they would install the catalytic converter on the car. Although the trip was short, I did manage to get the speed demon out of my system—for a while.

Once again sales were going well in spite of my being away for a few weeks. The sales staff had changed somewhat as one of my best salesmen, Fred Spring, left to go sell Cadillacs (although he returned to us about a year later) and I hired two younger men who were car savvy and energized. Although I gave the old sales staff authority to make deals (approved by Alice) in my absence, the new fellows had to consult with the seasoned salesmen before making any agreements. It worked really well and I was fortunate to have such a dedicated staff. As I have said before, I was forever emphasizing that they always had to get a customer's name and telephone number as they might make a strange request that you would never think you could fill.

That very event happened in July when a well dressed man came in looking for a purple or lilac 12 cylinder Italian car. The salesman talked with him for a short time but, as I found out later, considered him a bit of a flake. Well, that's not OK as it could describe many people who, while giving that air, in fact are serious buyers, and that's who we wanted to do business with. A few weeks later the story came out that the salesman hadn't gotten the man's name so we didn't know who he was—and that revelation was precipitated by a visit from a Rhode Island man driving a lilac colored Lamborghini 350GT that he wanted to sell! Needless to say we couldn't find the man interested in a "purple Italian car" and we couldn't convince the Rhode Island owner to leave his car with us on consignment, so nothing happened other than that was the last time that salesman failed to get a person's name and number. Or so I hoped!

Selling cars on consignment was not always an easy thing to do, as once we had the car in our possession we were responsible for it both mechanically and cosmetically, so we tended to provide that service only for customers and cars that we were familiar with. We normally charged a 15 percent commission on the sale price, but by the time we paid a salesman's commission, provided a warranty on the used car (which we always did) and put the car in good running order, we seldom made money. It was really just an accommodation to our good customers.

This was the year that many manufacturers started using the federal government vehicle identification number (VIN) system, the 17 character alphanumeric structure that had to appear on every car manufactured after January 1, 1981. The VINs looked incomprehensible at first but with a decoder you could tell at a glance where the car was manufactured and the model year of the vehicle. The first characters were letters indicating the country of manufacture and the 10th digit represented the model year. Ferraris and Alfas had a Z in the first place, meaning Italy, while BMW used W (probably because of West Germany) and Datsun had J as the first, but the cars manufactured in the U.S. had a 1 in first place. It made identification a lot easier, but of course with the earlier models we still had the same difficulty of knowing the correct year unless there was a title with it, and even then you weren't always sure.

One of the more interesting trades we received—at least I thought so—was a Porsche Speedster replica that came in trade on a new BMW. There were a number of firms making replicas of this famous Porsche with which I had been so familiar, and in many respects they did a remarkable job of recreating the car. The fiberglass body was virtually identical to the original, as were the bumpers and wheels, and the interior also was close to what Porsche had produced. The gauges were VDO and probably were OEM, but that's where the similarity stopped. The seats were OK but not great and the running gear—well, that was VW. Driving the car certainly brought back the memories as it felt very Porsche-like aside from the engine and gearbox, which were not at all similar; however, it was certainly less expensive than a real one. Every time I would see a Speedster after that I had to do a double take to make sure it was just a replica and not a real one. I couldn't tell from the outside; it was only by looking at the interior that I could be sure.

There were other replicas being made, including those of Bugattis and Jaguars, but they were rarely seen in our area. One sunny summer day I thought I saw a racing Jaguar of some sort, maybe a C type, parked across the street so I went to look at it. It was a pale blue C type Jaguar, a very rare car indeed, and while I was looking it over the owner appeared and didn't say much other than hello. Assuming I was looking at a replica, I told him that they were really making these reproductions look real. He responded huffily, "It's not a replica—do you think I would drive one of those, I am really insulted." Well, I didn't know who he was and I don't think he knew me either, but I was flabbergasted at his remark as first of all his tone was unnecessary, and secondly I should have kept my mouth shut before I knew what I was looking at. An honest mistake, I thought. He then started the car and sped away. I could tell it was a real Jag for two reasons: first was the sound, and second, on the pavement where the car had sat was—you guessed it—a puddle of oil.

The fuel injected 308s became very popular and we started to trade some of the earlier carbureted models including an early 308GTS that I had sold to a Mr. St. Onge, a businessman from New Hampshire. He had wanted to order one of the first spyders in 1977 when the rumors about their imminent arrival were flying about. He was driving a highly desirable 365GTS, a Daytona spyder, that he wanted to trade, but

Speedster Replica brochure. At first glance it was difficult to tell the replica from an original.

Ferrari 308GTBi ad in the program for a 1980 Metropolitan Opera Company production with Pavarotti in the cast.

we couldn't get him the 308 spyder because they didn't exist yet for the U.S. Thirsting for the Daytona, I tried to persuade him to leave it with us as a partial trade-in while awaiting the 308, but to my disappointment he didn't want to do that. But in 1978 he came back to buy a blue spyder, this time wanting to trade an Alfa Romeo Montreal that was a beautiful car. As I have mentioned before, it was not unusual to find that some of these customers, while appearing to have only one or perhaps two exotic cars, in fact had a collection of them, and so it was with this gentleman.

I had seen the Montreal at an auto show in Europe, but in our driveway it seemed diminutive, not as large as I remembered. It had a small V-8 in it and Roland insisted I drive it; it was fast and fun like all Alfas but much quicker than either the four cylinder models that we were familiar with or the 2600s from the 1960s. The only problem with the Montreal was that it was not legal in the U.S., and for us to sell it we would have to federalize it, whereas a private party … well, it was up to them whether or not to federalize it. So we couldn't trade it, and now we had twice been unable to trade one of his cars, first the Daytona Spyder, which he sold on his own, and now the Montreal. Undeterred, he had bought the blue 308GTS spyder after all, and now wanted to trade it on a new red 308GTSi, and that was OK with me. So we concluded the transaction over the telephone as I had no need to see his trade-in as he kept perfect care of his cars. He was one of our northern customers who dreaded the drive south either going through or around Boston, and I couldn't blame him, as it could often be the ride from hell, so I offered to bring the car to him myself and he was thrilled.

Both Fritz and I enjoyed delivering cars to our customers; it was just another aspect of our personal service that made us a different kind of dealership. And to us it made being dealers all the more enjoyable as every day in this business was interesting and often very exciting. There was really nothing predictable about it. Sure, there were the regular routines of opening up in the morning and receiving customers, but beyond that you never knew what surprises lay in store as the day progressed. Although problems arose, none seemed insurmountable as we followed our beliefs in straightforwardness and fairness.

Our appearances at the New England (Boston) Auto Show had always been well received, so much so that the exhibitors that ran the show asked us about participating in the Providence Auto Show that occurred about one month before Boston. The arrangements would be similar with them providing the space, carpeting, etc., and us providing the Ferraris, in this case two 308s, one coupe and one spyder, and the staff. Since our Ferrari business in Rhode Island and environs was increasing we thought it would be a good idea and agreed to provide two 308s and one salesman. Unfortunately the show was a lot different from Boston, as was the market I guess, as the only leads we got were from people that we already knew.

I think most people just wanted to see the Boston show since there were more cars displayed there and it ran for a longer time. In reality the best part of that was the drive back from Providence to Cohasset after the show had closed and we had removed the cars. The only problem on this particular occasion was that we had forgotten to bring dealer plates with us when we were driven down by an employee, which might put us in an embarrassing position if we were stopped along the return drive. To compound that fact was that one of our best Rhode Island customers had invited us to join him at a well known Italian restaurant on Federal Hill for dinner after the show closed. Well, we couldn't disappoint him, so we cautiously drove up in front of the restaurant where a valet had been instructed to care for our plateless cars while we were inside. After a great dinner and a friendly thank you to our host, we slunk out of Providence and sped back to Cohasset, which turned out to be

Our Ferrari display booth at the 1980 New England Auto Show, Hynes Memorial Stadium. People of all ages stopped to admire the Ferraris.

another nail biter to the finish line at Autohaus between Jim and myself both in the same model.

One day in October between the two auto shows, I was in my office on the telephone when one of the salesmen called to me to come and look at a car that had just driven into the parking lot. There stood a silver coupe that I couldn't identify; it was sleek and definitely Italian looking and looked vaguely like a Ferrari. Well, it was. Jonathan Thompson, a man who lived in the neighboring town of Norwell, was a freelance automotive writer for various sports car magazines and had visited us before, often saying that he was "just looking around but enjoyed talking cars." This time, however, he came in with a purpose as he was testing a new Ferrari model that the factory might be bringing to the U.S. and wanted to get some feedback from dealers and prospective customers. But why didn't we know about this car, which was named the Mondial 8 and would replace the 308GT4? In fact, I had seen a picture of it from the Geneva auto show that spring but had been unimpressed by the photograph as it looked pretty plain compared to the 308 series, and it still was.

So we eagerly looked it over and drove it. Although it felt different than the two seaters, it was a Ferrari, the V8 engine was definitely Ferrari, and the looks it got on that short drive also cemented the fact that it was a Ferrari. My only objection was that it seemed to be a little loosey-goosey, but it was a preproduction car, wasn't it? It was bigger than the GT4, and had more interior space which probably would be used to justify its purchase by a husband who had to convince his spouse that the kids could come along too, making it a real "family car." Jonathan spent about an hour

Author with Ferrari Mondial factory test vehicle in 1981, a surprise visit to us.

with us talking and taking pictures which I assumed he was going to include in whatever type of report he was going to give the factory. He was a nice guy, and after that introduction we often talked with him about cars on the phone, but eventually he left the area and I think moved to California. About six months later a book came out showing this new model with a few pictures of Autohaus in it. We liked that. And the Mondial? We would see it in the middle of 1981 as a new car for the U.S. market.

Being a Ferrari dealer, we were on every aftermarket business's mailing list, including some firms that were creating Daytona spyders from Daytona coupes. They were literally cutting off the roofs of these beautiful cars to transform them into ersatz convertibles. They looked fine but they had all sorts of structural problems such as cowl shake and strange body movements. It happened to quite a few of the coupes and buyers had to be cautious about whether the car was an original 365GTS or a conversion, as there was quite a difference in value and quality of performance. And if you look at today's prices for Daytona coupes, it seems like a very foolish move to destroy the car's integrity and not only lose the coupe, but create a spyder that will never be as valuable. Some firms were also doing it to the 400 series, which was another non–U.S. vehicle that some dealers were bringing here to sell after having them federalized, and a car on which we had received some inquiries.

One such inquiry came from a New Hampshire BMW dealer that I knew well and whom I would often see at dealer meetings. At one gathering he asked about availability of the 400i as he might have a customer for one, and I told him that while we could certainly get one we just couldn't say what the delivery time would be for a special order car. He said he would talk further with his customer to see if he was serious about it, and he did. The factory at that time was not planning any direct exporting of the 12 cylinder cars, we learned from the new president of FNA, John Spiech, who had replaced Gary Rodrigues, so we would have to go outside the Ferrari network to purchase any 400is. That inquiry would soon lead to some interesting business arrangements.

At the auto show that year that we heard that Datsun was going to slowly change its name to Nissan. The Datsun company was actually called Nissan Motor Corporation in the U.S., but the product was marketed under the Datsun name and we were just about the only country in the world that still used the name Datsun. Nissan therefore thought that there should be a universal conformity with the product and our Datsuns started arriving with a subscript under the Datsun nameplate that read "by Nissan." We also got to see the new 810 Maxima sedan and station wagon that replaced the old 810 series, a car with modern engineering but a very dated look which didn't excite people to buy it. Nissan had also announced their choice of a location in Tennessee to build their new assembly plant for trucks. Did that mean that we would now be selling domestic vehicles?

BMWs continued to sell very well with the only problem being the radios. Not that they weren't good quality (although the speakers were marginal) but they were too attractive—to thieves. It had started with the 2002 series that cars were being broken into and the radios stolen. As if that were not bad enough, with the 2002s and the 320is it also meant that a window had to be broken and the dashboard console was being destroyed at the same time.

Finally BMW started producing cars that had a deadbolt locking system on the doors so that if the door was locked in a certain way from the outside, and if someone broke a window and reached inside the car to pull the door button up, it wouldn't move so they would have to crawl in through the window and the broken glass. Well, that helped some more and eventually the break-ins decreased until it was just a very occasional problem. At a BMW meeting in New York City the same year I heard the quip that the BMW acronym for Bavarian Motor Works had changed to mean "Break My Window"! How fitting.

In fact 1980 had not been a great year for sales as interest rates had soared to close to 20 percent for auto loans and that kept a lot of people away unless they were paying cash, which didn't include too many buyers other than Ferrari and the occasional BMW purchaser. It also affected our operation directly as the interest rate on the floor plan—which we wanted to keep as low as possible—was about the same figure.

This also meant that the factories wanted us to buy as many cars as they could convince us to, and we wanted to keep the least possible number of vehicles in inventory so as to minimize the floor plan cost. From what we were reading and hearing, 1981 would also be a year of high interest rates, so we felt fortunate that we weren't paying for a brand new building on our land across the street—which we were still considering—at these high interest rates. We wondered if we would ever be able to build and be profitable, but we would have to wait for that decision.

15

Madame Ibarra

Although sales were slow during the winter, the new offerings from Datsun created a lot of traffic in the showroom starting with our annual Washington's Birthday festivities highlighted by our 15th anniversary "Open House at Autohaus" slogan. It worked well and we were adequately stocked with inventory of the new models. The Maxima, as it was now called, was good looking and had a great six cylinder overhead cam engine—not unlike the BMW six cylinder 5 series (more corporate espionage?), and it performed really well. We were also getting the new 280ZX turbo that was going to be a real stunner, although initially it would only be available with automatic transmission, the rumor being that Datsun's five speed transmission could not handle the torque from the turbo. Datsun was putting a lot of emphasis on its engineering and performance while its competitors like Honda and Toyota seemed more interested in economy and appearance to sell their vehicles. This was essentially the same philosophy that Mr. Katayama had expressed to me at a meeting some years before.

We were actively searching for good used or pre-owned cars, as some like to refer to them, and although most sedans were somewhat easy to locate, sports cars were not, especially Alfas and Ferraris. We did find through one of our contacts a beautiful 1966 Ferrari 275GTS in light metallic blue with tan interior. It had few miles and was strong mechanically, the only defect being the paint as the finish had crazed; that is, it had hairline cracks running through the horizontal surfaces, probably as a result of southern sun exposure, but really because of a less than perfect factory finish. We were able to purchase the car at a reasonable price and decided to have the car refinished with a new paint job—in the same color of course.

Before it even got to the paint shop we had two customers very interested in the car, one being a well know Boston architect who fell in love with the car and actually purchased it before the car was painted. He said he would wait for it as we all thought it would be ready in less than four weeks. Well, that didn't happen. All the trim work had to be removed before the paint removal process could begin, and that led to broken trim pieces that were difficult to replace and rubber gaskets had to be specially ordered. So the one month turned into two, then three, and finally after almost five months the car was completed. And it was beautiful; as the old saying goes "good things come to those who wait."

BMW (and some Ferrari) customers were changing their buying habits as a result partially of the continued high interest rates, with many choosing to lease rather than purchase. At first we weren't recommending it to our customers as the monthly payment for a three year lease was about the same as a five year note if you financed a new car with little or no money down—and at the end you would own the car if you purchased. With the high interest rates on auto loans, though, the leasing option became more attractive. There was almost no money down and the monthly payments included sales tax and the irritating Massachusetts excise tax with only the insurance costs being separate. So from the custom-

1966 Ferrari 275GTS. Speaks for itself.

er's perspective it was beneficial, and hence we started to lease quite a few cars. What happened to the car at the end of the lease was the lessor's concern. We were offered many of the "off lease" cars to purchase, and they turned into a profitable segment of the used car department, as they were often low mileage and very clean—often, but not always.

Meanwhile Alfa Romeo was about to present us with a new coupe model named the GTV6 which was an updated Alfetta GTV coupe with a V-6 engine and lots of "go." On the racing circuit Alfa still had a strong Formula One team and we followed their (rare) successes as we did Ferraris, although in the U.S. Alfa said little about Formula One in their press releases and product advertisements. The new coupe proved to be a beautiful car to drive and, like many Alfas, seemed to have more soul than the competition. The straight arm driving position was more comfortable and allowed the driver to control the steering more directly, I thought, although it had a tricky clutch and was a handful to manage until you got used to it. You had to keep the power on most of the time to make it obey you in the corners and exit ramps off the highways. We saw a lot of cracked front spoilers with damage that looked suspiciously like curbs, and not parking lot curbs either. Alfas were always very engaging to drive, demanding your attention but rewarding you at the same time. All the first ones that dealers received were silver with blue leather—kind of an odd combination, we thought, as did everyone else.

To launch the car, Alfa Romeo had an introductory meeting for dealers at New York's Tavern on the Green where they wined us and dined us while showing the attributes of this impressive new six cylinder engine. Most dealers had already

15. Madame Ibarra

Alfa Romeo GTV6 factory press photo. Another of my favorite cars—not very easy to drive as you had to work to learn its ways, but then pure pleasure.

received their first one, so in deference to Alfa many dealers drove to Central Park in their brand new GTV6. It was only after the meeting ended and we all went outside to give the valets our tickets that we saw the valets in total chaos as *everyone* had arrived in exactly the same car—their new silver GTV! You should have seen and heard the attendants as they tried to get the right ones. They certainly earned their tips that day.

This was the second year for the fuel injected Ferrari 308s, and although the service department liked the serviceability of the new model, the sales department was less than enthusiastic. The continuing price increases along with the decrease in performance had everyone—including me—unhappy with the car. It occurred to me that we were experiencing a similar situation as I remembered from my first days selling Porsche 356Cs and SCs versus Corvettes and Jaguars. Against the competition of 1981's pricey Porsches, Ferraris were slower and very expensive, but they had redeeming features such as drivability and product quality, and the gorgeous design, and that's what we had to emphasize in the Ferrari 308GTis. They were still beautiful cars and good performers and the quality of the bodywork and interior appointments was continuing to improve. And of course they were the most profitable car that we were selling to a still strong market. So we counted ourselves fortunate and looked forward to the rumored engine change for the next year. Ah, those Italians and their rumors.

One rumor that did come true was the announcement of the new Mondial 8 that arrived in our showroom in the spring. Presented as the replacement for the Bertone designed 308GT4, it looked nothing like it as it was designed by Pininfarina instead. The car was virtually the same as what we had seen the year before on its marketability tour, and we liked it. The rear had more room than the 308GT4 and the driving

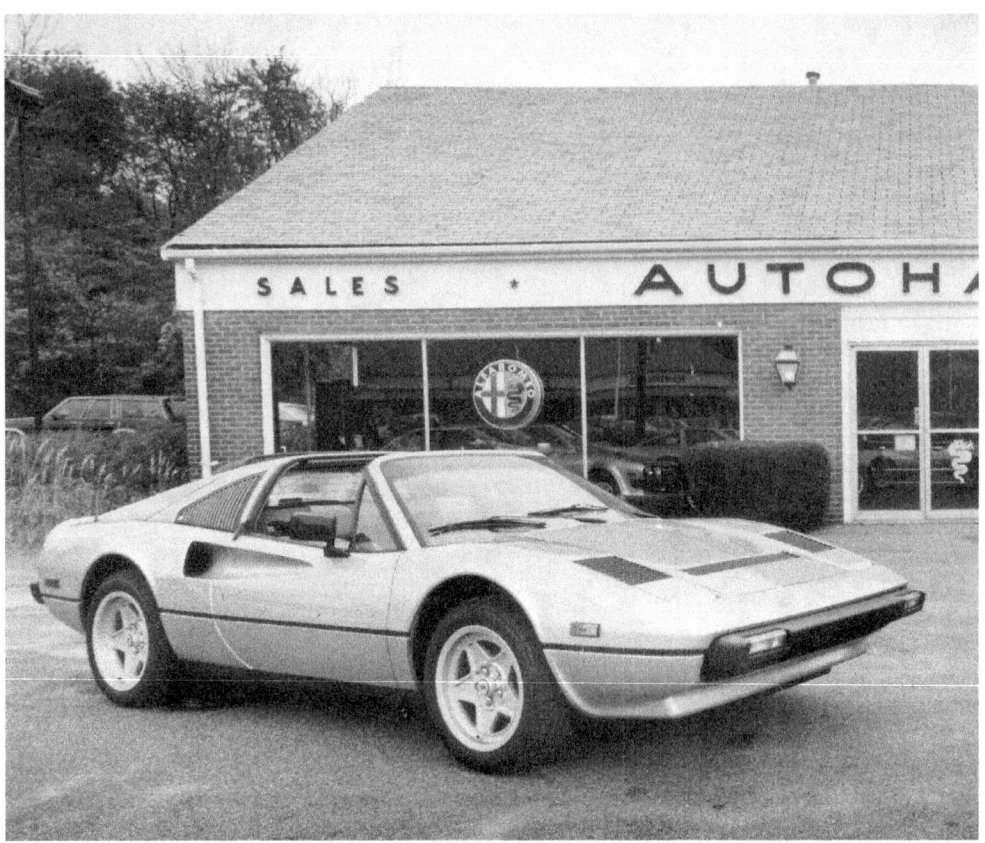

A 308GTSi like Tom Selleck drove in Hawaii in *Magnum, P.I.*

position was more typically Ferrari with excellent visibility out of all the windows. Now all we needed was a 12 cylinder car, like a 400i, Fritz said, as he and I went out for a first drive in the new Mondial.

Actually Fritz and I rarely test drove a car together, and when we did he seemed to prefer that I drive—I think that was because he was driving cars all day long, testing them, checking over the mechanics' work or helping them to correct an annoying problem, etc. And then there was the remote chance that we might have been involved in some sort of accident that might disable us and prevent us from operating the business. I think we had a payroll of about 20 employees at that time so there were a lot of people and their families depending on us for their livelihood and we had to think of them also.

Then, from an unexpected source, came a phenomenal wave of free advertising and promotion in the form of a new television show titled *Magnum, P.I.* that starred Tom Selleck as a private detective in Hawaii on the island of Oahu. Selleck lived in a palatial compound and provided security for the owner while having use of his Ferrari 308GTSi among other perks that went with his job.

Until that time most people probably recognized the Ferrari name from racing news, celebrity news, or car auction news and pretty much everyone had a different mental image of what a Ferrari looked like. However after this TV show became popular the image people had of Ferrari was Magnum's 308GTSi (and of course Tom Selleck too) and they loved it. It became the opening conversation line as people entered our showroom and after a while contributed to a number of sales—especially red cars. Maybe it was that car, in that show, that made everyone want a red Ferrari. Maybe people were identifying with Magnum, or at least his lifestyle, and that helped make a decision for them. We all liked the show and watched it every week to see if he was driving the car correctly and if everything that appeared in or on the car was accurate.

In an effort to reward our loyal and long term employees, we had set up a pension plan and profit sharing plan. Although they saw nothing from it from year to year, when some eventually retired they were surprised by how much had been set aside for them. We also paid for a good portion of employee's health insurance, although our contribution declined somewhat as the costs continued to increase. We really were employee oriented as their families were well known to us and Alice really enjoyed meeting socially with the families and numerous children. My office was always open to problems or disputes that might arise and I tried to be equitable in solving them. To outline all the benefits that were available to them, we produced an "Employees Handbook" that served them, and us, well over the years.

Our parts department was always busy and profitable under Gayle, but the paperwork was mountainous. Not only did we have to keep inventory for our franchised lines of cars but we also needed to have quick access to parts for other cars that were being serviced, such as our varied used cars and other makes that responded to our service department solicitations. We did have a company that provided us with a weekly computer printout of what parts we had in inventory, what we had purchased, and what we had sold. Or course the accuracy of those printouts depended on the accuracy of our input figures and the provider's accuracy as well, so we started to think about getting our own computer. We found out they were expensive and they took up a lot of room and they needed all sorts of weird care and feeding to operate successfully. After talking to the few dealers we knew that had computers, and some vendors, we finally decided on one called Display Data.

The computer's size was about the same as a refrigerator, maybe a little bigger, and it needed a temperature controlled room. But we didn't have air conditioning in the building (that would come later) nor in the attic above the parts department where we were going to install this monstrosity, so we had to build a small room to house it. The room had a door, of course, and many shelves to hold giant tapes used to store and unload data. The whole apparatus looked like something out of a 1960s science fiction TV series or movie and it was noisy and heat producing, hence the air conditioning. We also had two keyboard terminals and CRT screens for the operation, one in the parts department (along with a massive printer) and the other in Alice's office. I remember how quickly (and maybe grudgingly) she changed her habits to make this new machine help us. Now we entered the data into the computer and had available at our fingertips all the info about purchases, sales and inventory of all (well most) our parts. It was the modern world at last.

It was late spring when I had a call from the New Hampshire BMW dealer I had talked with in Hawaii who said he might have a customer for a Ferrari 400i. He now

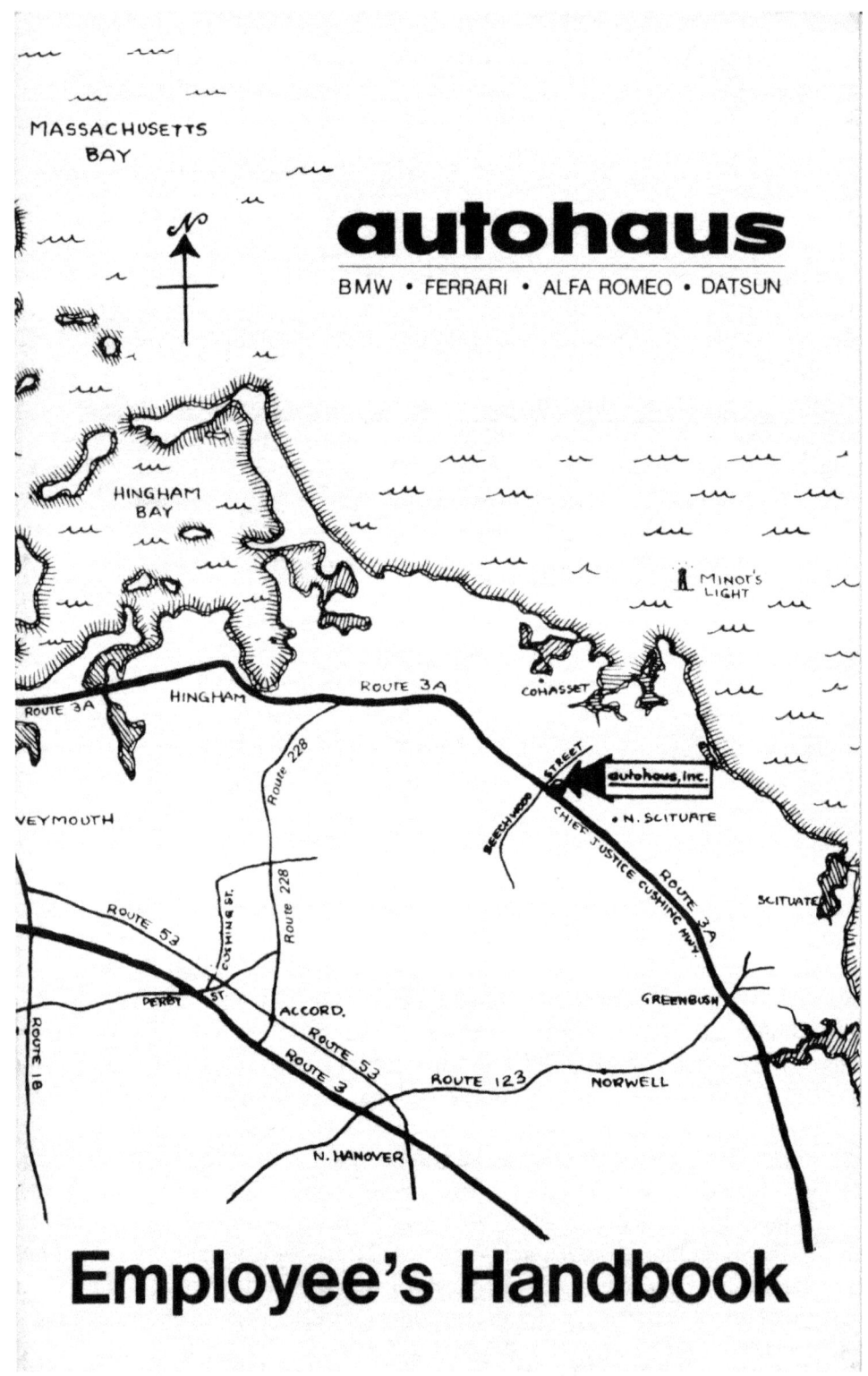

Autohaus Employee's Handbook. A very generous employer.

thought that his customer was closer to making a decision so he needed some questions answered, such as what options were available and what we recommended, how much it cost and how long was the delivery time. The last question, of course, was the toughest to answer as we really didn't know a source other than the dealer in Zurich where we had bought the Boxer a few years before. There had been a big swing in currency valuations and now the Swiss franc was very strong at least as opposed to the lira, meaning the car would be very expensive. We did find out that the weakest currency against the dollar at the time was the French franc, so we looked for a dealer in France that we might get a quote from. I found through the Ferrari dealer book that came with new cars that the dealer in Paris, Pozzi, was also the importer for France and that they might be the ones to ask about the 400i. So I called them and fortunately I didn't have to condemn them to listen to my French as the lady I spoke with, Madame Ibarra, was fluent in English, which was really becoming the international language, as even the French were comprehending.

She was very pleasant and said yes, the 400i was available through special order and the only option that she might recommend in addition to the automatic transmission would be dual air conditioners. That meant the standard one for the front passengers and an additional one for the rear passenger area as there was so much glass. So I requested that she give us a price, in francs of course, and also include the charge for air freight from Paris to Boston—no more Newark, thank you. Delivery time would be about four months from the confirmed order date—depending on when it was ordered and taking into consideration *ferragosto*, the Italian vacation period—and a 10 percent deposit of the selling price would be required. So, in July, after receiving a firm order from our New Hampshire friends—and a deposit—we ordered the car in *rosso chiaro* with black leather and dual air conditioners at the price of F.F. 284,650 (approximately $50,000), to be delivered in October as a 1982 model. I hoped this venture would go better than the Rome fiasco, and indeed it did.

The purchase of non–U.S. Ferrari models and their subsequent sale in the U.S. was troubling both to Ferrari of North America and Ferrari S.p.A., and in a letter to dealers they outlined the procedures they were enacting to curtail the practice. They weren't referring to cars such as the 400i and 512BBi, but rather the 308 series and now the Mondial 8; cars that had U.S. versions. Some non–U.S. versions of these cars were being imported here and then federalized, meaning that their sales were in competition with the franchised dealers, and importers often could sell the "grey market" vehicles at substantially lower prices than vehicles produced for the U.S. So when the factory learned which European dealers were selling these cars to U.S. buyers, they withheld the certificates of origin so that the vehicles would have difficulty in being registered in certain states. They backed up this policy with a series of ads in the national press where they recommended in the headline copy that prospective buyers should "Purchase and Service your Ferrari through an Authorized Dealer" and then they listed all the dealers in the U.S. and Canada, some 48 in all. I don't know how successful this new policy was at slowing down the grey market influx, but it did show that the factory was concerned about the reputation of their product and, equally important, the profitability of their dealers. Thank you very much!

About the same time we received notice that Ferrari was holding a dealer

Author testing a Mondial at Riverside International Raceway, Riverside, California, in 1981. No Nomex suit here.

meeting in California in early September to officially launch the Mondial 8 and was combining the meeting with track testing of the car at the Riverside International Raceway. The Bob Bondurant racing school was going to show the dealers how to drive the cars, and so after instructions about the track and walking around it (just like the Formula One guys), we dutifully donned helmets and went racing around the track—under supervision of course. I had read about Riverside since my Speedster days, and knew that Bondurant had raced a lot here including driving Ferraris at one point. This was my first time being on a West Coast track and we were all excited to see if it was going to be like western skiing where the conditions were always perfect and the sun was always shining. Well, it was a blast and became the first of many Ferrari events at race tracks that were all to be memorable. The Mondial performed very well on the track, and we were timed so that we could see how we stood against our fellow dealers. I wasn't at the top, and I wasn't at the bottom either, but I think the surface was too smooth, with no frost heaves or patched places, nothing a New Englander would be used to, and on top of that the California sun affected my vision or I would have done better, a lot better. I wish I could have had a second chance.

When I returned from California I had word that the Ferrari 400i would be shipped to the French importer in Paris in late November (close enough) and could

15. Madame Ibarra

be forwarded to us upon their receiving our final instructions and payment. At some point I decided that to ensure that all was correct with the vehicle, both the equipment and its physical condition, I should go to Paris, meet the people there and check out the car. So I made arrangements through my friend Ernest, who suggested that since it was going to be a short trip I should consider flying on the *Concorde*. That would be a treat but it was way too expensive, or so I thought until he told me about a special program Air France had with travel agents to provide much lower fares for good customers and provide them with the *Concorde* experience, in hopes that they would fly with Air France again. So that's what was arranged.

After flying on December 1, I was to visit the dealer the day I arrived, then spend two nights with friends and return. Was I ever excited as I was going to fly on the fastest nonmilitary airplane ever built; being a pilot, I figured it was as close to the stratosphere as I would ever get. We were departing JFK at 5 p.m. when it was still light so as to see the plane rush by the parked aircraft. As we took off the plane seemed to skitter over the runway surface and as it was accelerating it was the only time that I had the impression of incredible speed because once we were aloft there was none of that sensation, at least for me.

The plane itself was very small inside, smaller than a 727 I think, with not much headroom, but the seats were luxurious and just two abreast. I was seated beside a man from Mexico City, which is where the flight originated before stopping at Washington, D.C., and now New York. He told me that they were able to go supersonic for just two short bursts when they were over the Gulf of Mexico as it was prohibited over land to avoid a sonic boom. There was a dial at the front of the passenger compartment showing air speed in knots with marks indicating Mach 1 (the speed of sound) and Mach 2, all too exciting as my Piper could only go 0.1 Mach—with a tail wind.

The flight actually was just one long and delicious meal with wine and after dinner drinks helping passengers to take a short nap. After dinner I asked the lovely stewardess if it might be possible to take a look inside the cockpit as I was a pilot, and after checking she returned to say that the captain would be happy to show it to me. Oh how sadly things have changed.

I entered the area through a small door and the captain, copilot and navigator greeted me warmly and asked me questions about what kind of plane *I* flew and how I enjoyed it. They all knew about the Cherokee and the copilot had spent quite a bit of time in one, and they were all very interested in private plane flying in the U.S. They showed me how the *Concorde* operated under these overwhelming banks of instruments, and was I impressed. The nose of the plane was hinged so that when taxiing and landing it could be lowered to give a better view of the ground and then when in flight it would be raised for aerodynamics. The windshield was protected by a set of "buzzard bars" (vertical steel bars) whose use was pioneered by Mercedes-Benz 300SL gullwings in the 1952 Carrera Panamericana road race to protect the windshields from low flying buzzards and here it was again protecting the ever so fast *Concorde* from errant large birds. It was all too much. All the time I was in there we were traveling close to Mach 2 at an altitude of around 50,000 feet, with the only clue being that we could easily see the curvature of the earth and an indication that

FAST COMPANY at autohaus

1982 Ferrari Mondial 8 rosso chiaro	new
1981 Ferrari 308 GTSi bluescurro/black	new
1982 BMW 733i 5 speed black/tan	new
1982 BMW 633CSi 5 speed graphite/tan	new
1982 Alfa Romeo GTV6/2.5 silver/blue	new
1981 Alfa Romeo GTV6/2.5 black/tan	new
1982 Datsun 280ZX turbo silver/black	new
1982 Datsun 280ZX 2 + 2 burgundy/red	new

All new and are prepared for immediate accompaniment to your particular and personal needs!

autohaus
BMW • FERRARI • ALFA ROMEO • DATSUN
RTE. 3A • COHASSET, MASS. • (617) 383-0095

One of my favorite ads for 1981, this ran in the *Boston Globe* in December. It was somewhat controversial as the term "Fast Company" had an early 20th century connotation that worried us. After surveying friends and customers we decided the term was now innocuous.

we were at the edge of the atmosphere. They finally made me go back to my seat and before I knew it, we were approaching Paris. What a ride that was!

We arrived early in France and by the time I got to Paris and had some breakfast it was time to go to the dealership. It was in a modest building that did not stand out from the adjacent structures but was fairly large inside, not unlike Chinetti Motors, I thought. I met with Madame Ibarra, who was very pleasant, businesslike and certainly knowledgeable—almost like a French version of Alice—and who took me on a tour of the facility after offering me croissants (of course) and coffee. I didn't know how many Ferraris were sold annually in France as I hadn't seen many on my trips to the country, but some of the scarcity might have been due to the political climate there—and in Italy—where well off people tended to downplay their status by driving less flashy cars except at night. There certainly were quite a few cars at that dealership including the *rosso chiaro* 400i. It was stunning and perfect with all the accessories, the impressive tool kit, and the dual air conditioners.

She showed me the leather bound owner's manual packet, which she suggested that I take along with me, and gave me the spare set of keys, also a very good idea. I didn't think it necessary to drive the car even though I was anxious to try it out, and decided I would get to drive it after it arrived in Cohasset. The streets of Paris are fine for Renaults and Citroëns, but not for this car, at least not now. After chatting for a good hour and making the arrangements for air shipment—and for payment to her—I left, thanking her for her attention to all the details and assuring her that if we were going to purchase additional 12 cylinder cars they would be bought from her. We would make good on that pledge.

I returned after just two days in Paris and upon arriving back at Autohaus (having flown back in a 747) I phoned my customer in New Hampshire and then instructed our bank to wire the balance due to Paris. Ten days later the Ferrari arrived at Logan Airport in perfect condition. Now we had to have the car federalized, which would be another story.

The Ferrari market started to slow down as more potential buyers became aware of the fuel injected 308's slow performance, but we were being told that a new engine was coming for the '83 model year. That information needed to be kept quiet or revealed as only a rumor because if people knew about it, '82 sales would stop completely. It was a similar scenario to when fuel injected engines were replacing carbureted engines, in that we thought it might affect interest, but it did become known and in fact it didn't affect potential buyers' decisions greatly as some were not buying the 308 for its performance so much as for its looks. Hmm, we thought, what did Enzo think about that?

As uncertain as this all was, we had increasing interest in the 12 cylinder cars since the arrival of the red 400i. I finally got to drive it and found some similarities to the 365 automatic; the shift sequence and torque curves were similar and this car too had a heavy feel. It was sprightly off the line under full throttle and fortunately

Ferrari 400i automatic with factory friends. This car was a special order for a customer, in rosso chiaro.

retained some of the glorious 12 cylinder exhaust noise that we all treasured, but it was more a grand tourer with legitimate room for four adults and some luggage too. The fuel injected 12 idled smoothly and responded quickly; we liked it. We had the car at the dealership until we could transport it to the firm that would perform the federalization; unfortunately the shop that had done the first 512BBi was overloaded with work and couldn't do it for many, many months. That delay was unacceptable to the buyer—and to us—so through others we found a well recommended firm in Pittsburgh that could start the work in February and have the car completed and ready for federal testing by the beginning of March. That was acceptable to all concerned.

As promised, the Ferrari was federalized and passed the tests fine, so we picked it up and brought it back to Autohaus for our final inspection, where it received our approval also. Subsequent to having the car tested the EPA and NHTSA would issue separate letters of compliance so that the bond (which we had put up when the car entered the country) could be released and the car registered, and all that could take time. That fact didn't bother the buyer as the New Hampshire dealer was going to provide him with a dealer plate until the proper papers were received. The dealer came to Cohasset, paid the balance due and left with that very pretty 400i. One revelation came when he was taking the car, and that was when he mentioned for the first time the ultimate buyer's name. I think it might have been a slip on his part, but when he said it I was startled as it seemed to me to be the same person from New Hampshire that I had shown the Ferrari Lusso to in Auto Engineering's showroom some 18 years before. Could it have been the same buyer, John, who was returning to thank me for my time and enthusiasm? I never knew.

16

Maranello

That spring we received the first of many inquiries from Hollywood about the use of one of our Ferraris in a film. They were very secretive about it, not even telling us at first what stars were appearing in the film nor even the title of the movie. We found out later that was because the title often would change (as would the stars) according to the producer's whim. They wanted a silver 308GTS that we had in inventory for two or three days of filming in Cambridge in May; one of the "young stars" would be driving it for a short while and putting only a few miles on it. We had many questions, including how the car would be covered by insurance and how much they would pay to rent it.

My friend Jack DePalma, who had all sorts of connections to the movie industry, did some investigating and came up with a ballpark figure that they were likely to pay, and it proved accurate. The week of the shoot, one of the salesman, Greg (who was very excited), drove the car into Cambridge to meet with the crew—and the stars. Up to that time we didn't know who would be in the movie or who would be driving the car so it was all speculation. Greg called at a break and said a very young guy named Rob Lowe (he was 18 at the time) would be driving it and he had to instruct him as the actor was nervous about handling the car, and the gated shift pattern intimidated a lot of people. They shot the scene a number of times, as they always do, and after two days of filming it was over. We all couldn't wait to see the movie, eventually titled *Class,* and check out the car in the movie, but we were disappointed to find that the scene had ended up on the cutting room floor—what a let-down. Maybe someday in the future they'll restore it and add our silver 308, who knows? We sold the car shortly thereafter with the historical footnote of its brief stardom.

Pleased with the Pittsburgh dealer's work on the Boxer, we asked whether he could give us an even better price if we imported some additional cars—volume lowers the price, doesn't it?—and he said he could, but only slightly. We were contemplating bringing another 400i in on speculation, meaning we didn't have a buyer and would be taking a chance on its salability as we had done in 1972 with the brown 365GTC/4. In one of the conversations they told us they had a 512BBi that had already been federalized, had all the correct paperwork and was available for sale. It was metallic gray with red leather and sounded beautiful. As it turned out one of our salesmen, Fred, had been speaking with another man from New Hampshire—understandable as New Hampshire had no sales tax on automobiles—who had expressed interest in a Boxer. When we relayed the information to him, he was interested but

Ferrari 512BBi. The four carburetors had now given way to fuel injection. Our first one in grigio ferro metallizato (metallic grey).

not for a few months as he had a 365GTC/4 that he was trying to sell. We offered to try to sell the car for him on consignment if he was unsuccessful himself, and he said he would consider that.

The 512 BBi was similar to the 512 BB we had purchased in Zurich, but this car had the Bosch K jetronic fuel injection system in place of carburetors, making the engine cleaner running and able to pass U.S. emission regulations more easily. It didn't sound quite the same without the whooshing of the carbs, but the exhaust retained that snarly sound, and it was fast, really fast.

Meanwhile Fritz and I decided to go ahead and get another 400i from the dealer in Paris as it had worked out so well. I contacted Madame Ibarra and inquired about color availability (if any), and she replied that they were receiving shortly from the factory a *grigio scuro metallizzato* (dark metallic gray) 400i with tan interior, automatic and dual air conditioners—a perfect car for the U.S. and for us. So we ordered it, and although the price had increased we were happy that she gave us a considerable discount at the same time, so the net cost to us was close to what we had paid for the red 400i. The car arrived in June—air freight of course—and no sooner did it arrive than a number of interested customers showed up to look at the car as we kept it in the showroom briefly before shipping it to Pittsburgh for the federalization magic. Everyone seemed pleased with this: the dealer in Paris, the federalizing firm in Pittsburgh, and us. Now we only had to add a pleased customer, and that was to come soon.

We were able to properly service these 12 cylinder Ferraris as both Fritz and our

Ferrari 400i automatic in grigio scuro metallizzato.

top Ferrari mechanic of the time, John Tirrell, were well schooled in earlier versions of the engines and the Bosch fuel injection system was similar to what was used on some BMW and Mercedes-Benz models. It didn't mean, however, that we had lost our ability to care for the magnificent six-carbureted 12 cylinder engines from the '60s and '70s that still came in regularly for maintenance. When one of these cars arrived with a problem, Fritz often would assess it himself. If it was an audible problem he would reach into his nearby toolbox for the stethoscope, put it around his neck and put his head under the hood of the idling Ferrari.

Owners of 12 cylinder Ferraris sometimes did not realize that their cars were not operating as they should. Many of them didn't really push the cars hard, so that a spark plug could foul occasionally and cause the engine not to run correctly. If the Ferrari was running on only ten or eleven cylinders it was not that noticeable. But when Fritz listened (and truthfully some of us in the sales department also) we could detect the misfiring.

I recall one time when an owner of a 275GTB brought the car in reporting that it seemed to be coughing a little, and Fritz detected that one or two of the twelve cylinders were not firing, or missing a beat occasionally. We all watched Fritz place the stem of the stethoscope (the chest piece having been removed) on different areas of the cam covers until he stopped, saying, "Ja, Ja, it's just number eleven that's not firing, we'll see if we can fix it without taking it apart." And with that he closed the hood, got into the driver's seat, inviting the owner to join him, and off they went down Route 3A, leaving the eleven cylinder sounds in their wake.

So his nonintrusive fix was to take a good run down the road, get the engine up to the redline repeatedly, and see if he could clear up the problem, which he often did. This fix didn't only work on Ferraris, but on BMWs, Alfas, even Datsuns, the difference being of course, that when you redlined a 12 cylinder Ferrari, everyone knew it! Everyone within earshot, especially the owner of the car who was sitting motionless to Fritz's right. Fritz was a very fast driver, as I've said, and so this fix would often work, and he would return to the dealership with the car running perfectly, while the owner was still frozen in the passenger seat. I don't think many owners went for a second drive with Fritz, but all of us at Autohaus would jump at the chance.

We also serviced other exotic cars such as Lamborghinis and Maseratis and even a very rare Swiss made Monteverdi 375S, which was powered by a large Chrysler V8 motor and which Fritz thought was very special. Well, it was so special that we couldn't get parts for it, and it stayed around for many months with the customer getting impatient until finally Fritz was able to locate the parts through family connections in Switzerland and we had them shipped. At last the car left under its own power and in the hands of a very happy customer

Meanwhile our salesman Fred had been talking with his New Hampshire customer, Eddy Nicholson, to see if he had sold his 365GTC/4. He hadn't but was still interested in the Boxer if it was still available. So I called Pittsburgh and found that it was still there and they were willing to sell it to us at a reduced price from a few months prior. Ultimately the customer agreed to buy the car and at the same time to let us sell his car on consignment for him (we weren't going to take it in trade). When the Boxer arrived Fred and I agreed to deliver the car to him and then take back the 365GTC/4 which we had never seen. The customer lived in a beautiful colonial house that was full of important antiques—I learned about that later—and had quite a car collection in addition to the black Ferrari, which was in good condition. He thought the Boxer was sensational and thanked us for our patience and effort to find him the car; now we had to sell the GTC/4 for him, which we eventually did.

In the meantime the grey 400i returned from being federalized, and about a week later a customer of ours from Cohasset, to whom we had sold a number of Datsuns and an Alfa, arrived driving a bronze colored Aston Martin V8 Volante. Where did that come from? It was a convertible and he had the top down and I thought that car looked a lot better than the coupe. He was interested in the Ferrari 400i. Although he liked to shift, he had a bad left knee and was medically advised to drive an automatic, and this Ferrari fit him perfectly. He drove it and liked it—naturally—and asked to see if we could take his Aston in trade and give him a fair price. I kept asking myself if I had seen this car around town and really couldn't remember it, although Jim said he had seen it but since the top was always up he didn't know who the driver was. So we did some calculations that were fair to him and he bought the car and traded the Aston automatic. He was delighted with the Ferrari and that winter he and his wife drove it to their house in Florida.

We sold the Aston Martin within a week after advertising it, again in the Boston papers. The buyer was already a customer of ours who had bought one of the early Ferrari 308GTS models, and although he liked the Ferrari he too was looking for an automatic. The 308 he traded was also sold in a relatively short period of time,

16. Maranello

making the sequence of sales starting with the grigio 400i automatic a string of very happy events for the three owners—and the dealer too.

In the meantime we had learned from Ferrari North America that they were having the first U.S. dealer meeting *in Italy,* which included not only a trip to the factory but a visit to Florence also, and we were not going to miss that. We were flying from New York to Paris on Air France and then to Venice. Why not fly Alitalia to Italy? Because the Air France *Concorde* didn't fly there, only to Paris. Yep, I was going supersonic again.

This was the first of many unforgettable trips to Italy that Ferrari provided every other year for its North American dealers. They all included a visit to the factory in Maranello but also stops at many of Italy's magnificent cities and remarkable sights. Although I had been to the factory twice before, it was just as exciting, maybe even more so as this was going to be a completely guided visit. Although I knew my way around—sort of—most of the dealers on this trip had never been to the factory before, and we all shared in their excitement.

This trip started in Venice with a tour of that city's magic, then to Maranello and a tour of the plant where we would spend an entire day—except for a lengthy and delicious lunch—and on to Modena to stay at the Fini Hotel and eat at their restaurant, which I think at the time was probably the best in Italy (and that's saying something), then to Florence and finally Rome. I think every dealer was able to go on this trip and many brought their spouses or a very good friend or customer, as we knew it would be memorable.

The visit to Maranello began with a welcome in the factory courtyard and then we all walked across the street to the Fiorano race track. Adjacent to the entrance were some buildings where the race cars were constructed; the area was definitely off limits to most, but we got to peek at what was going on inside (though we could not take photos). The track was a place of legends and now we were going to be a (small) part of it too. The model we were getting to drive was the new Mondial 3.2qv (four valve) Cabriolet, which I think Ferrari was emphasizing as some dealers were questioning its position in the Ferrari lineup of cars; i.e., who were we supposed to sell this model to? To most, the design was not the equal of the 308 series, and its performance seemed questionable; hence its appearance at Fiorano with the new engine which was also to be in the 308 series. We would all have a chance to drive the car around the track alone after circling a few times with one of their test drivers or factory managers, so everyone was eager to be first in line. I sort of waited a while but Fritz was up at the front of the line as was his friend and former employer, Gaston Andrey, who had been appointed a dealer in Massachusetts after the dealer in Cambridge gave up the franchise.

When it was my turn to ride with a factory person, who gets in the driver's seat but Piero Lardi Ferrari, Enzo's son. I had seen him earlier and exchanged a few words as we were walking over to the test track. He appeared so Italian, with large sunglasses and his sport coat over his shoulders, and spoke good English with a mild demeanor. So we fastened our seatbelts and off we went. I don't know what I was expecting, but could he drive or what? I felt like I was a passenger in a Formula One car, as not only was he in complete control of the car, but the car itself was performing like I never would have imagined! It certainly was a Ferrari, and he certainly was a Ferrari also, there was no doubt about that. It was so exhilarating that all I could do was hold on and try to remember how he entered the turns and where he was using the brakes (*freni*), but it was tough to remember all the nuances as I was too excited. When we finally stopped he looked at me and smiled and said, "How do you like the Mondial Cabriolet?" I could only grin in response while saying "*fantastico*" and then thanked him for the lesson at Fiorano, and we both laughed.

How do you follow that act, I wondered. As he got out he motioned for me to take the driver's seat, and just then Alice appeared saying she would love to go with me, so Piero opened the door for her. We buckled up and took off with me giving it as much power as I could with Alice laughing and me trying to recollect the ride I just had, shifting where I remembered he had shifted and guiding it, not steering it, into the turns. The car was incredible, and I reflected that this was the way to demonstrate Ferraris to customers, not just a short drive down Route 3A. After circling twice—with nary a spin—we got back to the starting point. Alice and I hadn't said a word to each other as the whole experience was too intense, but she said I did pretty well and now it was her turn. Opting to go around by herself, off she went, with the engine screaming and her hair flying in the wind. Oh yeah, we had the top down on all these drives, and no one wore a helmet either—it was the real wind in the face experience. I bet they don't allow that anymore!

After we tried our best at being F1 drivers, Rene Arnoux showed up (we were to meet him later at a reception) looking like a typical Formula One type accompanied by a beautiful French girl, and wearing a Nomex suit. He had broken the lap record the day before with his car #27—and now he was practicing a few laps for our benefit

Ferrari's Formula One drivers for 1982, Arnoux and Tambay, at Fiorano. Press photograph.

Ferrari factory at Maranello, 1982, where we were allowed to inspect the production lines. Here we were looking at the Boxers and hoping that Ferrari would import them to the U.S. They didn't, so it was up to us to find them for our customers.

to show the car's capabilities. The machine was so quick and he was shifting so fast and with the strident exhaust echoing off the hills on all sides of us it literally took your breath away. Truly exhilarating!

With all those sounds still ringing in our ears we walked back across the street to start our tour of the factory itself. The Ferrari people were so hospitable, and although the factory tour was guided with every different facet of production explained, they didn't mind if some people would tarry or wander off to see other areas that were not on the tour. There were no warnings from anyone other than where there might be a danger sign—it all was very casual.

One area where everyone was lingering was the production line of the Boxers and the 400s as we were all lusting after those models. We were told to be patient because there was a possibility of the U.S. getting a twelve cylinder car, but it might not be one now in production. That set us all abuzz, but it would be quite a while before we knew what they were talking about. They did address the "grey market" cars and assured us that they were really trying to eliminate that problem although there was no mention of the 12 cylinder ones we were importing. I think they were so polite and figured it was not the time to mention it, if at all, or perhaps they liked the additional sales and exposure in the U.S.

At that time Ferrari made over 80 percent of the components that went into their cars, including engines, transmissions, running gear, bodies (made at their Scaglietti plant in Modena) etc., excluding electrical instruments and gauges and the like. That way they could have complete control of the quality of the cars and not

Ferrari 308s on the production line, 1982.

Finishing work being done to a 308 GTB body.

blame anyone else for problems. And the quality was exceptional; every engine was tested for eight hours, every car was road tested extensively and that accounted for the fact that all the Ferraris we received had varying miles on the odometers due to the amount the car was driven (and where the test drivers went to lunch, we would joke). So when the cars arrived at our dealership any problems that we encountered were almost always due to shipping or port handling and were usually remedied easily. As the factory tour was ending, we went into the final checking area where there were a number of cars readied to be shipped out that day and a few in another area that had small X's marked on them in colored crayon. When one of the dealers inquired as to what the crosses meant, our guide said, "Oh, those are the ones with imperfections, they are the cars destined for the States"; it took a second but then we all looked at each other and laughed and so did our host. Following the tour there was a short business meeting where the Ferrari management discussed their future plans including the four valve engine for the 308 and the Mondial which we had just experienced (read more performance) and a few surprises that we would all like.

Putting a 308 together.

We then all assembled in the main reception area to depart for lunch, but as we were waiting all the top management of Ferrari appeared and looked toward a door on the far side of the room, acting very nervous, when suddenly there appeared an older man with a raincoat and sunglasses. There was a hush as Enzo himself walked through the room, sat down at a microphone and gave a heart-warming welcome to us all. It was almost a religious experience as we all applauded when he departed, but it gave us all a true feeling of belonging—and being a part of Ferrari. It was unforgettable.

After that extraordinary morning and then lunch, we had some free time, which is rare on these trips as everything is planned out, especially in Italy. I had been talking with three other dealers who wanted to visit both the Lamborghini and Maserati factories which were not far away: Maserati was in Modena and Lamborghini in Sant'Agata Bolognese. They had rented a car and wanted me to drive—why I didn't know, although one later admitted that they were all petrified to drive in Italy, not having had the Boston training that I did. I was always game to drive in Italy, and we all piled into a big Fiat and headed for Lamborghini, which at that time was owned by a couple of Swiss brothers and had been in financial difficulties.

Before we left, Fritz had told me about the Lamborghini Jarama that we had sold the year before, whose owner had missed a turn and ended up with a badly damaged right front fender for which we were unable to find a replacement. Even our premier body shop, whose owner we affectionately referred to as the "Botticelli of Bondo," couldn't straighten the metal, so we had been trying in vain to find a new fender.

The factory was more like a huge warehouse, very different than what we had just visited, and there were very few cars being completed. We saw a few of their off-road LMs and a wild looking right hand drive Countach painted glistening black with white interior. When we asked if it was going to England the manager said no, it was destined for Hong Kong. Whatever was someone going to do with that car there, we wondered. We also saw the recently released V8 powered Jalpa coupe that was designed to compete with the 308, but it wasn't very good looking.

I asked about the fender and the manager took down all the information about the car, as Fritz had given me the serial number, and said he would check into it and contact us in a week or so. We wandered around outside and that's where I saw a Miura convertible. Well, it was more like a Porsche Targa configuration with a fixed rear window panel and a removable roof section. None of us had ever even seen a picture of that car so it was a rare sighting and I regretted not getting a photograph of it. I got the impression that the people there were very excited that we were visiting them as the four of us represented just about the whole country; there were dealers from the San Francisco area, Chicago, Houston and myself from the northeast. They were definitely looking for more dealers in the U.S., and although I had no interest I think the dealer from California did.

From there we went back to Modena and to Maserati, which I think was in sadder shape than Lamborghini. The factory had been taken over by DeTomaso in the 1970s after being changed considerably by the Citroën ownership the decade before, resulting in the production of a number of vehicles that combined technologies from both Maserati and Citroën such as the Citroën SM Coupe, the Bora (first roadgoing Maserati with a mid-engine configuration) and the Merak. Alejandro DeTomaso was an Argentine who founded the company in Modena and was best known in the U.S. for the mid-engine DeTomaso Pantera, which was powered by a Ford motor and sold by Lincoln-Mercury dealers.

We introduced ourselves to the manager and went into a large showroom type area and never got to see the factory, which occupied another part of the building. I don't know if they were manufacturing much at that time although we were told about the new BiTurbo model that we didn't get to see. There was a Kyalami, a sedanlike car that I think was a rebadged DeTomaso Longchamp, not a great looking machine. So they were struggling, as was Lamborghini, and we all thought that as much as we might have disliked Fiat's involvement with Ferrari in the past, it probably allowed the cars to continue to exist and to remain the leader in the high performance market. After the visit as we were returning to the Fini, I remarked that I had felt a little funny about going to visit the competition while we were guests of Ferrari—to which my friends replied, almost in unison, that Ferrari probably would be happy to have us see what their competitors *really* looked like. I guess they were right.

That evening dinner had been arranged at the 18th century Villa Meridiana in Modena, a beautifully restored building that housed a sports club in addition to a renowned restaurant. Before dinner we were guided out to the gardens where we were shown a secret project that was in development by Pininfarina and Ferrari: a four door sedan named the *pinin*. It was an elegant silver-white car that had a true Italian flair to it—as all Pininfarina's designs did—and we were being shown the car to solicit our opinions as to its potential marketability in the U.S.

It was hard not to be impressed with the car as its finish and interior were magnificent and we could only assume that it would be equally impressive to drive. The only design negative I could see was the front end which had a GM look to it, which I noted on the questionnaire that they asked us to fill out. The presenter was the car's designer, Leonardo Fioravanti (also the creator of the Lusso, Daytona and the 308 amongst others), who was the head of the studio at that time and a very engaging man to talk with. I wrote to him after the meeting to express my views on the salability of such a car, saying that although I thought a four door Ferrari had enormous potential the particular design we were shown too much resembled an Oldsmobile. I hoped that I hadn't insulted him! I guess I didn't for he responded to me in a very sincere and thankful letter a short while afterwards.

From there the group went to Florence where we had an exceptional guide, but that is where I parted from the group as they were going on to Rome and I was returning to Torino to visit relatives. The children I had met in the early 1970s were now adults so now we could really talk about cars, food and politics, things that every Italian loves to talk about. After a memorable reunion I promised to return on my next trip to Italy.

That fall BMW brought out a revised 5 series designated the 528e, with a new low revving "Eta" engine that delivered better fuel economy and a lot of low end torque, but unfortunately it was not as fast as the previous 528i.

At a regional BMW meeting we heard that to mollify the fast driving 5 series owners, there might be a new model 5 in 1983 that would use the engine from the 733 series and therefore have a lot more oomph. We couldn't wait to see that! At a dealer meeting in Boston we were introduced to the new CEO of BMW AG, Eberhard von Kuenheim, who was visiting the U.S. primarily to meet with the North American management and to visit a few dealers. He seemed much more approachable than previous high ranking management we had met. It was his first visit to meet some of the dealers so I tried my halting German with a short conversation. He said my accent was very good and wanted to know where and why I was studying German. I mentioned I was at Harvard night school and hoped to be able to understand Fritz, who was Swiss; he laughed at my attempting to learn Swiss German.

A few weeks after that meeting we were to find ourselves in a very uncomfortable situation when we had a surprise visit from Mr. von Kunheim and his wife. She had attended Wellesley College and was showing him areas of Massachusetts that she had enjoyed as a student, and they happened to pass by our dealership and decided to

Ferrari dealer group in Firenze, 1982, still recovering from all that we had seen in Maranello.

stop in. That normally would have been exciting and an opportunity to show him our facility and talk about BMW things with him, but there was one problem—we had no new BMW on display in our showroom! We had an Alfa, a Datsun and a Ferrari 400i, but no BMW, which was a rarity. And even before introducing himself he asked, Where's the BMW? We were embarrassed as we had a blank spot where normally a

Ferrari 400i 5 speed at a special Ferrari event at Larz Anderson Museum in 1983. Jim and Sandy Theriault brought it there to gauge interest. There was plenty.

new BMW would sit. I quickly assured him that it was very temporary as we had just sold the 733 from the showroom and were just cleaning and preparing another one to take its place. Despite that awkwardness, he and his wife were very pleasant and spent almost an hour talking and looking over our modest facility. He said he really liked this section of New England and said he would return on his next visit and see more of it—and to make sure we had a BMW on proper display!

Shortly thereafter we finally received our first Ferrari 400i with a five speed standard shift, a white (not our first color choice) with black interior car. What a difference that transmission made with that car! Why was Ferrari building automatic cars anyway? We had ordered it from the dealer in Paris after selling the grigio automatic; it was the only color they could get without a special order from the factory, which would have taken who knows how many months.

I was anxious to drive it. After it arrived air freight I decided to go to the customs office in Boston myself, and after finishing the paperwork they told me in which airplane hangar I could find the car. There it was, all alone in this mammoth hangar, looking beautiful and pure in a shining white, and as I was looking it over the customs agent said I had to wait a few more minutes because they had a "drug enforcement animal" coming to check the car. I said OK as he told me that drugs and contraband had been concealed in just about every type of vehicle you could imagine (shades of Checkpoint Charlie in Berlin), and their drug sniffing dog could detect anything, anyplace. I was expecting some super German Shepherd or maybe a bloodhound, when suddenly appeared the dog officer pulling along an ancient Labrador

Retriever that I'm sure at one time was black, but now was full of grey streaks and a grey muzzle. Although he was moving slowly when the agent opened the car door, the Lab jumped into the front and sniffed around, then leapt over the console into the back where he sniffed around some more. They then went around to the back of the vehicle as the agent asked me how to open the trunk and when I did, in jumped the Lab as agile as could be and jumped back out just as quickly. The agent said the car passed fine, adding while nodding to the Lab, "He never makes a mistake." With that they both disappeared into the depths of the hangar, and I drove off towards Cohasset into light snow. What was it with these Ferraris and snow?

This Ferrari we had for a while, however, as we discovered the factory's logic in primarily producing automatics: That was the preferred transmission choice for the buyers that model attracted. Was Ferrari creating the automatic market, or just responding to demand? It would be many years before that question was answered. But it was still a beautiful car and even graced our 1983 auto show exhibit, shortly after which we sold it to a customer who was in the hospitality business and kept it for quite a while.

17

The Red Machine

Alfa Romeo, which was trying to increase its presence in the U.S., announced a dealer meeting in Nassau, Bahamas, at which we would get a chance to hear their marketing plans—and get a lot of sun. I hadn't been there before and was a little disappointed with the city, although everyone seemed very happy and friendly.

I met up with some of the Ferrari dealers who had been in Italy the year before and we formed one of those sub-dealer cliques that I hoped wasn't too exclusive; truly it wasn't, as Alfa dealers really liked all Italian machines as did we. One Alfa dealer, Serge Dermanian, was a good friend and had loaned us a few times special Ferrari models for our auto show displays, including the 335S and the yellow 275GTB4. He was also an expert mechanic and had an exclusively Alfa dealership in Waltham, for which he had built a beautiful building to house the cars and some of his customers' more exotic machines.

Although the meeting was encouraging as management talked of new models under development, it was really a pep talk, since we only had the convertible and the GTV6 to sell and the drop top was definitely seasonal in New England.

The flight back from Nassau to Ft. Lauderdale was extraordinary as I booked passage on Chalk Airlines, which flew Grumman Mallards—or flying boats—for the trip. Amphibious planes were seat of the pants, so much so that my carry-on baggage was soaked by the time we arrived in Florida. Quite a trip!

This was one of the many trips that Fritz, Alice and I took together, although the three of us were rarely gone for more than ten days at the same time. They might take a week or two before the meeting to visit relatives and then I might take a week or so after the meeting to travel, so although we seemed to be missing from the dealership a great deal when these trips (especially the ones to Italy) occurred, in reality there was always someone back in Cohasset within a short time. We were lucky to have such a great complement of people working with us: Linda in the office, Gayle who

Rear window sticker showing name change from Datsun to Nissan.

ran the parts department and who took over for Fritz in his absence, and Jim and Chuck in the showroom. They were all terrific and we thanked them for trustworthiness. We almost never heard from them when we were away and would seldom call from overseas to check up on things unless there had been an unusual problem pending when we left. When we returned everything was in order, and if we might have handled something differently had we been at the dealership, we never complained about how issues were resolved or offered any comment unless they asked us to.

That winter we attended a Datsun meeting in New Orleans where we were officially told that the product name would be changing to Nissan and that eventually all the Datsun signs would be replaced with Nissan ones at no cost to the dealers. We wondered what was to become of the Datsun name and goodwill that we had been promoting for the past 15 years. The factory said that it would take time for people to accept the new name and to realize that it was the same excellent product that Datsun had offered for many years. I thought, we'll see about that. To us the name change meant that Nissan was a new product entering the automotive field and it was, to the average consumer, an unknown quantity. I thought this decision would be analyzed in marketing courses for years to come.

In the years between Ferrari's trips to the factory they would often hold a United States meeting at various locations, and this year's was run by the current President of FNA, Claudio Squazzini, who had replaced John Spiech in January and was proving to be a very capable, enthusiastic and sociable replacement. He was the first native Italian who had held that position, and his innate knowledge of things Italian created a comfortable and pleasant atmosphere and gave us confidence that Ferrari news was reaching us as soon as it was available. I missed that meeting but I got to take a different trip that year when we were invited by BMW to attend a meeting in Munich to see and drive the new 524td diesel.

BMW had been working on importing a diesel version of the 5 series to hop on the economy bandwagon as they had already done with the 528e. This diesel engine would also be provided to Ford Motor Company, which would install it in the Lincoln Continental Mark VII in a very limited number. Cadillac had a diesel engine option, as did Oldsmobile, and of course Mercedes-Benz had a long history of success with the diesel. I was meeting my traveling friend Jack in Frankfurt so we could attend the International Auto Show, which was a little disappointing as there were no eye popping new models or even concept cars to drool over. From there I went to Munich to pick up a new 533i at the delivery center so we could travel around a bit after the meeting. It was a dark grey metallic 5 speed with beige leather interior, very nice looking and thankfully fast.

We arrived a couple of days early so as to roam around Munich and go the Oktoberfest the night before the meeting. Big mistake. Neither Jack nor I had been to this beer festival before so when we got there— not having driven, of course—we couldn't believe the size of the grounds. And the tents that we had read about were unlike any tent I had ever seen; they were enormous! We found the Spaten (one of my favorite beers) tent and I could hardly believe the sight—there had to be a thousand singing people in there, all sitting at long tables around a raised platform on which a classic Bavarian oom-pah band was loudly playing German drinking songs that became so imbedded in my brain that I have never forgotten them. And behind the band was a huge open ovenlike arrangement with a gigantic ox being roasted as it turned on a giant spit. All too much. And all the people seated at the tables, many dressed in classic lederhosen, were drinking beer from large steins that were being transported effortlessly by buxom Bavarian barmaids, just as you would imagine. As we were looking for a place to sit, some young people yelled to us to join them and everyone moved so that we could squeeze in. Well, we discovered that the authentic Spaten Oktoberfest beer doesn't get exported to the States. We had never had anything like this before—it was delicious and so easy to drink as it went down like iced tea. My German came in handy as the young people's English was minimal, so we had too much fun talking and telling stories. They warned us not to drink too many of the beers as they could be lethal to the uninitiated, which we discovered we were. Fortunately for everybody, all the tents closed up tightly—like the patrons—at 10 PM, or otherwise there would have been a lot of people passed out on the benches. We parted ways with our new friends (who did send a card one year later) and decided rather than going back to the hotel at this early hour, we would go on a few of the rides in what was a real carnival atmosphere.

The next (agonizing) morning the meeting was at 10 AM—how unfair, we thought—so we hurried over to the BMW headquarters where we were welcomed to a small breakfast and were reunited with other BMW dealers, many of whom I knew. It was not a large group, maybe 40 or 50 dealers, as the diesel cars were going to be targeted to certain areas of the country including New England. The meeting was in a large room where we were introduced to the engineers and managers in charge of this new product, and were promised that after this (hopefully) short meeting we would have an opportunity to drive the car in groups of four per car and would all participate in a rally that would be enjoyable and educational at the same time.

After the meeting they handed out rally sheets that gave us simple instructions to get to our first stop, which was Andechs, a town noted for its beautiful monastery and for the strongest beer made in Bavaria. But since that wasn't our final destination, which was a restaurant on Starnberg See, and since we were driving their cars, we were absolutely forbidden to drink any of the beer at Andechs. To send us to this town where they made the strongest beer in Bavaria and expect us to sit down in their beer hall and order Pepsis—well, it was a lot to ask. But since we were all going to arrive there at about the same time, it being a rally after all, they would be able to assure that we obeyed the beer ban. Drat, we thought.

Outside all 20 or so new 524tds were neatly lined up and we were all assigned a car. The two other people to go along with us were an older couple from the Chicago area who seemed very nice but whom I hadn't met before. I offered to let him drive and his wife could navigate but he declined, saying he preferred the back seat. So I was to drive and Jack was going to navigate. Oh boy, I thought, I'd traveled with this guy before and navigation was not his strong suit, but the instructions were simple, and he knew something of Munich, so what could go wrong?

Directly across the street from us was the Munich Olympic Stadium, which was the first landmark for our list of rally points. I started the car up, noting none of the diesel starting delay that I'd experienced in other makes, asked the back seat

Andechs beer coaster. Strongest beer in Bavaria was its claim, and I think they were right.

passengers if they were buckled in (the man was already reading the *Wall Street Journal*), got confirmation from Jack that he was ready, and off we went, and the first turn we took—was the wrong one! In the space of less than one minute we were lost and heading in the wrong direction. Chaos followed with the emergency unfolding of maps and the reading of signs and the final admission that we would never be able to coordinate the instructions to get in line with the rest of the group. So, after consulting with out back seat riders as to what we should do, we all agreed that we should go directly to Andechs. As a result we were able to finish the two hour rally in less than one hour; what driving!

We got to walk around the quaint town, see the church and learn about how the monks during Lent developed a special beer that provided all the nourishment needed to carry on all their tasks while fasting from food at the same time, and how the same beer was being brewed today and visitors should not miss the chance to try some of the famous Andechsbrau. So we did. Not much, mind you, as we had learned the previous night that one should drink these beers with caution. So we ordered two beers and two giant pretzels and thoroughly enjoyed them. When the rest of the group trickled in and saw us sitting in the beerhall, wondering how we had arrived so soon, we didn't explain, even to the woman who had organized the Andechs visit and who queried as to whether we had drunk any beer. Can you imagine such a question—what, us break the rules? Meanwhile our back seat friends had disappeared but showed up later as we were about to leave for Starnberg See. The drive there was anticlimactic, but the place on the lake was magnificent and the food delicious.

That night the BMW folks had arranged for a special table at the Lowenbrau tent at the Oktoberfest and of course expected everyone to attend. That was going to be a beerful 24 hours, we said, and although we made an appearance at the table, it was very brief as we decided to go to a restaurant instead. That was a good move, as we found out the next morning that many of the dealers had overdrunk while trying to keep up with their German hosts and were now in pretty poor shape. I felt empathy. Now we had experienced the dieselmania that had also infected BMW ... but would it sell?

In the early summer we had finally received the factory information on Ferrari's new engine for the 308 series, to be renamed the 308qv. or *quattrovalvole* (four valve) engine. This is what we had been waiting for as now the 308 could compete—somewhat—with the Porsches' and Corvettes' performance. The bodies remained much the same except for the addition of vent grilles in the hood and a redesigned front bumper—but the engine! That was the major change (along with the price of course), as the car now boasted 230 hp and a 0–60 time of 7.1 sec.—wow! No sooner had we received that information than the cars themselves started to arrive. This four valve configuration was going to be standard on the 308GTB, the 308GTS, the Mondial coupe, and the soon to be introduced Mondial Cabriolet, and it couldn't have arrived at a better time for sales were getting a little slow in anticipation of this revised engine. It made a real difference in performance, even surpassing the carbureted versions from the late '70s, and everyone liked it.

So Ferrari was humming and in July we heard from FNA that Ferrari was considering building a new GTO model, the 288GTO, in a very limited number. This famous name, GTO, had been used in the 1960s and had graced one of the most successful racing cars of the time, and now they were going to resurrect the name on what was sure to be a remarkable vehicle. Subsequently they asked us to send an order in the form of a letter with the names of one or maybe two potential buyers so they could advise the factory on what type of demand there would be. I could have told them that the demand would be great considering the limited production of a car with that name, and I guess others did also as we heard later that the total number to be produced would be fewer than 300 cars, which curiously was about the number of Ferrari dealers worldwide.

Although new car sales had slowed awaiting the four valve engine, used Ferrari sales were going pretty well, especially the 308GTSi and GTBi models. As I have mentioned we would often be called by other dealers to inquire about the value of Ferraris in the marketplace and sometimes concerning cars that they wanted to

Autohaus in 1983: four Ferraris including one in the showroom.

sell. Sometimes they had tried to sell the cars themselves, but Ferrari buyers were aware that the soundness of the mechanics of the vehicle was vitally important and needed to be guaranteed by a place that was knowledgeable about the car. So it was not unusual for a dealer to ask if we would be interested in buying a car wholesale, and we often said yes.

We sold two 512BBi Boxers this year that we purchased from the company in Pittsburgh that had federalized our last two 400is. The customers were impatient to have the cars, and so rather than importing again from France we thought it smarter to just buy cars that were already converted and resell them, and it worked out well for both the customers and us. Both the Boxers were red with black leather and of course had the lower half of the body painted black which was the factory norm. We also could order 308s with the black bottom option, but it didn't really work as well on that model so we sold just a few of them. But the buyers weren't driving the cars. Oh, I don't mean that they never drove them, rather they weren't driving them like they were supposed to be driven—fast! The demographics were changing.

We did buy some 308s locally, but others came from dealerships far away. That included one that we bought in Chicago. The car we were originally interested in was a '79 blue 308GTS at a Cadillac dealer in Cincinnati. I called and spoke with the used car manager, who said they had tried for 90 days to sell it but had no luck so they would be interested in selling it to us (or anybody else) at a good price. The car was purchased new in Philadelphia and had only one owner, was well cared for, etc.; of course it was always the same story, but Cadillac dealerships were usually pretty savvy about a car's salability, so we talked about price and it was a good number, so we agreed to buy it on condition that it pass our inspection. Since it was a used car I decided to go there myself to inspect the car and evaluate its condition and value, and if it was as described I would drive it back to Cohasset. I had wanted to do a long drive in a 308 and this seemed the perfect opportunity, and I thought it would be great to bring my car crazed college friend Larry, whom I had been promising a long Ferrari trip someday. He was all for it and since he was in sales, he had no problem getting the time off.

Larry and I had met during our sophomore year at Northeastern, both studying business administration, but both also wanting to do something else, although not sure at the time what that would be. So we would pal around together, especially after I got the Speedster, which we would take on rallies and go to autocrosses and a few races too. But in our junior year Larry decided to marry, and not long after he had his first child, so that sort of ended our escapades, and sports cars events, until this trip to the Midwest. All we were bringing was a dealer plate, a check, a radar detector and a CB radio to keep in touch with our trucker friends; no overnight stuff as we were flying out there in the early morning and would turn around and drive the car right back all in one day. Not a problem, I thought.

We were picked up at the airport by a salesman driving a Cadillac, who said we would love the Ferrari as he had taken it in trade and driven it himself. Sounded good so far. The Ferrari was parked prominently in front of the dealership—in a ready-to-be-delivered pose—and looked good as we approached it, but as I got closer I could see immediately that the car had been repainted. Now the finish on Ferrari cars had come a long way since the 1960s, but this car had none of that glossy finish that they had been perfecting and that I had seen at the factory. It was a mess. As I looked more closely, the used car manager that I had talked with came out smiling as he was finally going to dispose of this Italian curse that he had owned for over three months, but it wasn't going to be to us. Whether the car was fine mechanically or not was irrelevant as the cost of repainting and the time consumed would leave us with a twice (at least) repainted car that wouldn't be for sale for three or four months, as it took our best body shops that long to do that type of stripping and refinishing of a complete car. So we said no thanks, and now we were in Cincinnati with an unused check and no car.

I was still somewhat determined to drive back in a Ferrari and decided to see if we could find one someplace else—Larry was pushing for that—like at the Chicago dealership with whose owner I had done the factory tours the year before. So I called and although John Weinberger wasn't there, his manager said they did have an '80 308GTB that was perfect, and he quoted a price that sounded fair. We said we would see him as soon as we could get there. When we arrived in the middle of the afternoon, my friend had returned, so we gabbed and gabbed and he showed me his operation which was much larger than ours and seemed very well run. The 308 appeared as it was described, but the check I had was already made out to the Cincinnati dealership. John said that we could just send him the check when we got back, which was really nice of him—so we signed the paperwork, got in the car and headed off due east into the darkening skies.

The car ran flawlessly as we entered the interstate system, on which we would

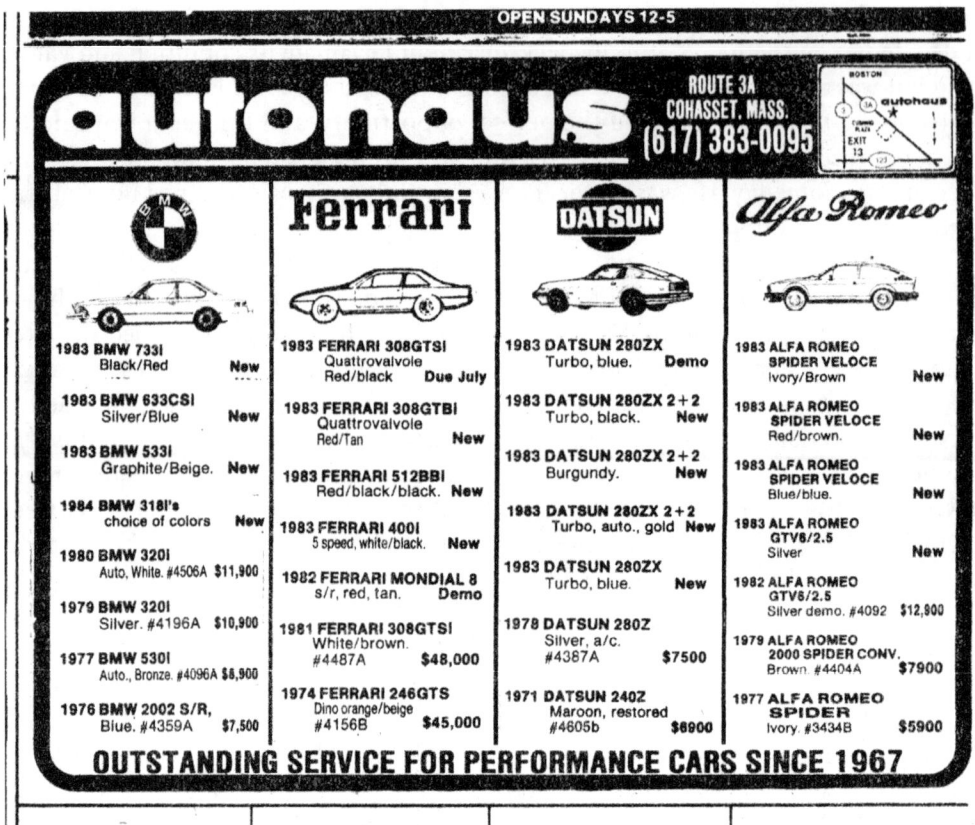

Autohaus ad featuring all four lines in the *Boston Globe*, June 1983.

stay for all but the last 50 or so miles around Boston, so we got up to speed which varied between 80 and 90 mph, and the 308 was fine with that. The car actually hummed; the engine, the exhaust, the transmission all seemed in perfect synch with each other and with us as well, as if the car were becoming part of us. There was little input from us other than a little throttle modulation and the very occasional downshift, and on we went. The only limitation was the bobbing headlights if there was any type of undulation in the roadway, but we became accustomed to that as we were crossing Ohio. The CB radio—what a godsend that was. The truckers could see us approaching fast and could calculate our speed before we even passed them, and they were talking, as were we. I think our handle was the unimaginative "red machine," but they liked it and talked us through on the CB as we heard them asking questions of oncoming traffic and what to expect. We anticipated a lot of police, but we only saw one through all of Ohio and he was going westward at a very high speed. The Ferrari kept going and going, and since we didn't turn on the radio—both of us just wanted to listen to the car's sounds—we could detect the smallest change in the rpms or road surface. It was sublime, and the seats were incredibly comfortable, both for me and for Larry, whose frame was slightly smaller than mine.

As I said I had never gone for more than three or four hours at a stretch in a

17. The Red Machine

50th wedding anniversary party for Mom and Dad on Macomber's Island.

308—even the trip to the Glen was piecemeal—but this was virtually nonstop, except for the mandatory gas fillups and pit stops where we would change drivers and then zoom away, often passing the same truckers that we had recently gone by. We would hear them saying "I think it's the red machine coming up on us again" as we approached. We got to Massachusetts before daylight and saw the dawn and the rising sun that was always right in front of us on the turnpike, sort of guiding us to Boston. I dropped Larry off at his house in Peabody, which we had reached in just less than 12 hours; not bad to cover 1,000 miles! My stay at his house was short as I wanted to beat the rush hour traffic on 128—which I didn't do. But I didn't care as I was in love with that car; the comfort, the sounds the totally relentless power and reliability. That engine never skipped a beat and now I fully realized why the Europeans had such high mileage on their Ferraris—they drove them!

Macomber's Island continued to be a spot of great pleasure and a perfect venue for many, many parties including a surprise 50th anniversary party for my Mom and Dad. Actually, Dad was in on it from the start and gave us the names of their oldest friends, including the couple that had originally introduced them. All my brothers were there as were all the relatives and so many friends. It was a great time and we were playing 1920s and 1930s music that they all could remember and identify with. We had asked the guests to dress in '20s flapper style get-ups and many of them did, making for some great photographs and a lot of fun. I think we really did surprise Mom as she acted shocked when she arrived and saw all her friends and family. As it got dark people moved inside and started dancing, mostly at the urging of Mom, who could never sit down when a good song was playing. They both loved the party.

18

Il Commendatore

When Ferrari sent us the prices for the 1984 models, the new Mondial Cabriolet was edging close to $66,000—a figure that could have almost bought you a 400i or 512BBi a couple of years ago. Prices were climbing for most imports, but it didn't seem to faze the buying public as everyone seemed optimistic about the future of the economy, the housing market, the stock market and the car market. It was then that we began to see the value of earlier 12 cylinder Ferrari models like the Daytonas and the 250 series cars rising. Ferrari was on the move. We received a letter announcing Ferrari's biennial dealer meeting at the factory which would be held in September and would include side trips to Mantua and Verona, plus a "very special secret trip" that they were planning. Whatever could that be, we wondered. All three of us were definitely going on this trip, Fritz and Alice said to me.

Joining us one this trip were the newly appointed dealer Gaston Andrey of Framingham and his wife MaryAnne. He was the dealer for whome Fritz and Alice had both worked before we started Autohaus, and they had remained friends over the years. Gaston (Gus) was a noted race car driver and had campaigned in both Maseratis and Ferraris including a 335s and 500TRC.

Meanwhile on the home front, the BMW lineup was changing this year with the introduction of a new body style for the 3 series and new models including the 318i (still with the four cylinder engine) and the new six cylinder 325e. It was a big improvement over the earlier four cylinder 3 series and was very well received by the public. We still had the 5 series which included the 528e, the 533i and the recently discussed 524td diesel—which created very little interest. Once again we were hearing rumors about a new 3.5 liter engine in the series that might be available next year, and maybe in the 7 series as well. BMW's six cylinder engines were beautifully running motors, smooth, responsive and reliable. Even as their displacement was changed, they still performed as their advertising suggested: "Our Status Is Under the Hood, Not on It." We all knew who they were referring to in that ad.

Alfa Romeo was struggling along with the spider and the GTV6, which was also offered as a special limited edition model with mostly cosmetic changes named called the Maratona. It had similar accessories as the Balocco (named after Alfa Romeo's test track) version offered in 1982. We were having some misgivings about maintaining this franchise as it was not a big income producer, but we still liked the cars and they kept promising new models. When would we learn?

The winters in Marshfield had become too difficult to plan safe travel to work, so

I had found an apartment in Boston, not far from the Public Garden. One of the bonuses of living in Boston was the apartment's proximity to the T & R (the Tennis and Racquet Club) where I played squash as much as I could, about three nights a week. Since I wasn't progressing, even under the tutelage of the pro, that summer I decided to enroll at a "squash camp" that was held at Amherst College and run by Ray Rodriquez, a squash devotee and spectacular player. It was total immersion, not only in squash but also in dormitory living and camaraderie; in other words it was a lot of fun.

Author, Fritz and Gaston Andrey in Mantua during a 1984 Ferrari dealer trip to Italy.

The camp was held in July when few students or faculty were around, and I decided to drive up in a '79 308 Ferrari coupe that had been in our inventory for too long and needed a good wringing out. On arrival, I parked it away from the school so as to not draw attention, but still in what seemed a safe area. But it didn't stay unnoticed for long, as one of the camp goers had a teenage son who saw it parked and, after inquiring, found it was me who was driving it. And then the ribbing started. "Oh, look at Guarino, he can drive, but he can't serve"; "he can shift but he can't return a volley," etc., etc. But I survived it and actually improved my game (slightly), and when we all went to a local lake to go swimming and get the racquet sport out of our minds on the last full day, the teenager begged for a ride. To make it more memorable for him I pulled into an empty lot and let him drive (he didn't have his license yet), and the look on his face made it worthwhile.

But it was I who was driving as we left the lot, and I was too late seeing a large pothole to avoid it completely. As we bounced through it the car died—just stopped completely. What the hell? It turned over but wouldn't start. There was gas; I looked in the engine compartment and all the wires were attached, but no go. Everyone else was already back at the college, so we had to find a gas station—and do what? As if they were going to fix a 308—I had visions of a very expensive tow to Cohasset and who knows when it would happen. Just as we were going to start walking, a car stopped and asked if we needed help, and after I explained the situation, the man said there was a Mobil station a few miles away that he thought worked on foreign cars, and he offered to stop there and tell them of our troubles. That would be great, we said, and off he went. After about an hour had gone by and no one had showed up, we decided we'd better walk or hitch to the college when a ramp truck from the Mobil station suddenly appeared.

The driver hitched the car up carefully and correctly and we both got in for the ride to the station where the driver said they often repaired unusual cars and might be able to fix ours too. When we got there and were watching him unload the car I heard someone yell, "Hey Bob! Bob Guarino!" Who was that? Well, it was none other than a fellow to whom we had sold not one, but two 246GTS Dinos, and he owned the gas station. I hardly recognized him as he had grown a huge beard, but his voice was unmistakable. What good luck!

The problem with the car was that when we went over the pothole, the emergency fuel cutoff switch had been activated, shutting off the fuel delivery to the engine. That switch, which was located under the driver's seat, was designed to activate if the car rolled over, to minimize the chance of a fire being fed by more fuel. In this case it worked, but not exactly as designed, and my friend said he had seen more than one of these cases but it was certainly the first one I had heard of or encountered. All that was needed was to reset the switch—and avoid potholes. I would not forget that incident, nor would my teenage friend, who had a good story to tell for many years.

The red 308 that I had taken to Amherst had been traded in on a new '83 308GTSi by a Buick dealer from the North Shore. It was painted Rosso Dino, the orange color that was on the 246GTS that Fritz and Alice had taken delivery of in Italy back in 1974. It was a remarkable color that never went unnoticed. This dealer eventually traded the GTSi in on a Boxer and that in turn on a Testarossa which was yet to appear. I have mentioned that we sold Ferraris to a number of automobile dealers, and I want to say again that it was always a strange transaction in that everyone was so nice about it. You would think that someone else in the (automobile) business would demand—or at least ask for—some sort of accommodation, but that was never the case, at least with us and our buyers. It was like a gentlemen's agreement on these very special cars that they wouldn't try to leverage their professional relationship for a lower price. If only our regular customers had been like that!

Then came the long awaited Ferrari trip to Italy. On this sojourn I decided to bring a friend, Pauline. We were all very excited about this trip as we were told that we would be introduced to Enzo Ferrari himself; although Fritz and Alice had met him before, it was to be my first introduction. He was in his mid-eighties then and reportedly less and less involved in the operation of the business, but still was there every day. But as if that weren't enough for this trip, we were told at dinner that evening that the next day in Modena we were to see the replacement for the Boxer 512BBi, named the Testarossa. This car would also be a flat 12 but would be made specifically to be sold in the United States market. I don't remember sleeping much that night in anticipation of this new model.

The next morning when we met in the courtyard of Ferrari's Modena facility, there in the center was the new car wrapped in a red cover. Then, in a ceremony worthy of an ocean liner's launch, the cover was removed, revealing the astonishing new

18. Il Commendatore

Line drawing of Ferrari Testarossa, from Ferrari ad copy.

Dealers waiting for their turn in a Ferrari Testarossa during the dealer introduction at Imola Circuit, 1984.

Testarossa. The unveiling was greeted with loud applause and smiles and nods from all the dealers, who knew it was sure to be a hit in the States.

It was a phenomenal looking coupe with unmistakable Pininfarina flair, highlighted by a strong louver treatment along the sides and a very squared rear end; beautiful but rugged and purposeful looking at the same time. We circled around it asking numerous questions and touching and feeling this latest beautiful creation. We all couldn't wait to drive it.

After a meeting dedicated to a technical description of the new car, we were taken to the famous Imola racing circuit where a factory test driver gave us each a ride in the Testarossa. We weren't allowed to drive it (maybe they didn't want anybody trying out the top speed on this race course), but the ride was enough to show us what a car this was going to be. The sounds and performance were breathtaking and as we screamed around the circuit I could imagine for once being a Formula One driver—maybe in the next lifetime, I thought. I couldn't wait to drive it myself back in Cohasset, and was happy to hear that the first Testarossas would shortly be arriving in the United States.

Following the introduction, we went to Scaglietti's new factory where many of the Ferrari bodies were constructed before being shipped to Maranello, where the mechanical assembly would take place. Then, surprisingly, we saw a few GTOs being created utilizing Kevlar in the fabrication. We wondered if it would be a one-time model as the first 308GTB had been when it was molded in fiberglass. The factory also had a few classic models in a showroom including a beautiful 250 SWB Berlinetta.

Next we traveled to Maranello for another tour, which was always exciting and informative. This tour seemed more organized than the last one, but there was still that feel of independent movement so we could roam wherever there wasn't an *Attenzione* sign. The body assembly areas looked the same, although we saw more 308s and looked on as attention was given to final details. There were no work stoppages on either this visit or the previous one in 1982, unlike when I first saw the factory in the 1970s; perhaps there was now a feeling of success in the management and workers which was providing a more stable work environment. But in Italy, who knew?

Since our last factory visit in 1982, a new restaurant had opened across the street named Ristorante Cavallino, and as the name suggested, it was all about Ferrari. From the photographs on the walls to the prancing horse crest on the silverware, you were immersed in the culture of Ferrari, and what a sensuous and beautiful culture it was. We had a memorable meal, with the ubiquitous local wines, and a dessert so good I wish I had a photograph of it. After the meal there were a few short speeches and a brief business meeting, the highlight of which was the affirmation of production of the 288GTO and the news that all the U.S. dealers would receive one sometime in 1985; that note was greeted by a wild round of applause from the dealers.

When the cheers calmed down we left the restaurant and walked back to the factory, where we would get to meet Il Commendatore, Mr. Ferrari himself, in the modest setting of his office. This whole day was starting to overwhelm all of us and we were only half way through it. But first came another surprise: admittance to the super secret racing department—which I had only peeked into before—where few were allowed to visit and no one was allowed to take photographs. It was too short an exposure to the scene but we were able to absorb the activity and the sounds that would be repeated worldwide as Ferrari campaigned for the world constructors title once again with these machines now under development.

Following that, with increasing excitement we all congregated in what was a fairly small room to meet Enzo Ferrari himself. Though 86 at the time and showing his age in some ways, his countenance appeared much younger. Fritz and Alice had met him some ten years earlier when they were on the Alfa Romeo Ciao tour

Ristorante Cavallino menu signed by some of the Ferrari group on our trip to Maranello in 1984. The tortellini were unforgettable.

and spoke of his mild demeanor. I had read and been told by various company representatives that he still was very much engaged in the operation of the factory and in the decisions on new models' specifications and design, plus his passion for the racing arm of the company involved him daily at Maranello.

I hadn't thought that I would ever meet Enzo Ferrari. Even though his company was relatively small and his management staff was very approachable, he seemed like a distant figure. So when we were told that day that in fact we would get to personally meet him, I was thrilled. The scene in his office, with him surrounded by his North American dealers, was like a father encircled by his extensive family, each awaiting their recognition and praise.

Piloti, che gente.... **Enzo Ferrari gave me this book which he had signed when I met him in the Ferrari factory in Maranello in 1984. It was one of the most special moments in my life.**

And then it was my turn, so as I approached the desk Claudio Squazzini introduced me saying in Italian, "Here is Mr. Guarino, the dealer from Boston," and Enzo smiled and shook my hand, and then handed me the signed book. All I said was *piacere* and *grazie* when receiving the book, but the emotion I felt was really unexpected. It was as though I had officially become part of his family and this was his way of personally welcoming me. I don't think it was until that moment that I realized how much I revered him as an automobile revolutionary, and I guess as an Italian one at that. Truly unforgettable. And that was all we could talk about for the remainder of the Maranello visit, meeting Enzo himself.

But this trip still had some surprises as we were ending up with a trip to Venice, a place I could revisit a hundred times without tiring of its charm and seductions. The visit this time, however, was a very short stay as the next morning we were taken to the train station to board the famed *Orient Express* for an overnight train ride to London! The train's route was from Venice across Italy through Switzerland into

18. Il Commendatore

Orient Express Collection catalog had everything to offer. Wish they could have captured the ambiance too.

France, then stopping in Paris for an hour or two, then on to Calais where we would cross the Channel by ferry and then on to the continuation of the train as it would complete the trip to London.

I had read about this train for years and remembered doing a lot of train travel with my parents when very young, but never in this manner. The train was—to sum up in one word—elegant. In addition to the sleeping cars there were several dining cars, the lounge (or bar) car, several parlor cars with general seating for relaxation, games or the like, and a "shopping area" were you could buy necessities along with beautiful gift-type items engraved or monogrammed with the train's logo VSOE (Venice Simplon Orient Express). Pauline and I had a luxurious cabin (they were all luxurious) in the second sleeping car which was attended by a staff member seated in the corridor that ran alongside the compartments in the typical European train arrangement. There were no locks on the compartment doors, so the attendant would keep watch over who was coming and going, and as in any first class hotel the staff knew almost immediately who belonged in which cabin.

That evening there was an absolutely delicious dinner with lots of talk about this incredible trip, meeting Enzo, seeing the new Testarossa and the drive on the Imola race track. It was almost too much to digest at the same time—the dinner and the stories, that is. But we managed to do just that. They had a piano in the lounge car and it was getting pretty late as we approached the border with Switzerland and the access to the Simplon tunnel that ran under the Alps (this was all before the open borders in today's Eurozone), but there was no inspection by any authorities or passport stamps as the stop was not more than 30 minutes as the well greased Orient Express left Switzerland and slipped into France, the next country on our route. It was late when we went back to the sleeping car and there was the car attendant, with his head resting on his arms on his desk, *sound asleep.* We didn't want to wake him as it was all too funny, so we didn't. When I awoke the next morning we were at a standstill and Pauline was gone. We were in Paris and a note from her said she had gone off to meet her sister, who was living there, and would be back before we left for the rest of the trip. As the conductors were calling "all aboard," she was the only passenger who wasn't—aboard, that is. Finally she came running down the platform and literally hopped aboard as we were about to depart. These New Yorkers are so dramatic!

We spent only a short time in London, paid a short visit to Windsor Castle, and then flew back to New York after what has to be called a whirlwind trip that nobody would ever forget. Aboard the short flight from JFK to Logan Airport in Boston came the final interesting point of the trip. I had just settled into my window seat when an older lady dressed in very casual clothes and carrying a somewhat beat-up rucksack sat down beside me. She looked exhausted, and before I could say anything to her she said that she had just finished a lengthy flight from Moscow through London to New York and the she was "bushed." When I asked what was she doing in Moscow, she replied that she had just finished a ten day trip on the Trans Siberian Express train from Vladivostok to Moscow and that it had been the train trip of a lifetime. My expression must have betrayed my surprise as she asked what I seemed shocked about, so I told her of the train trip of a lifetime that I had just completed, and we both howled. Talk about different worlds. So we talked about the Siberian train, not the VSOE as she could imagine what that was like, she said, and I learned about rustic train rides and the real Russian people. We both settled into our respective reflections and soon arrived at Logan.

Back at the dealership we were bombarded with questions about the trip, meeting Enzo, and most importantly, the one for which we had no answer: When would

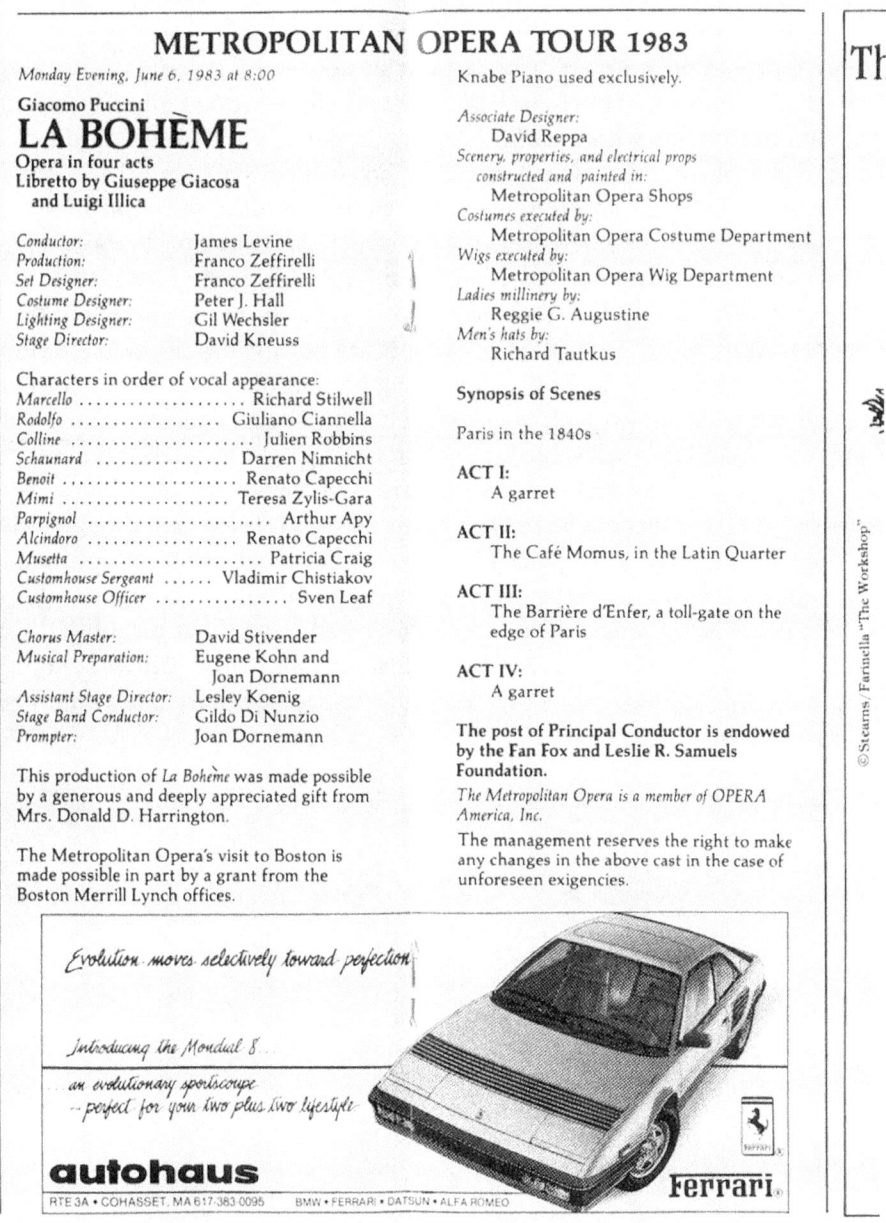

Metropolitan Opera Program for *La Boheme* in Boston, June 1983. They always gave our ads outstanding placement.

we receive our first Testarossa. What the factory had told us was that they were going to produce a version for America and that we would receive the car as soon as it was certified for sale by the U.S. government. That, it turned out, was going to be a long wait. It reminded me of our impatient customers back in the Porsche days who would call two weeks after placing their special order that was estimated to take around four months for delivery, to see if we had any word on the car's arrival date. Now we were the anxious customers.

The 1980s were getting very busy and this increase in business, and resulting increased profitability, was reinforcing our desire to build a new facility across the street on the land we had purchased some years before. We had hired an architectural firm from Boston—to whom we had sold a number of BMWs—to draw up plans for this new building that would be designed to house the BMW, Ferrari and Alfa Romeo franchises, while Nissan would stay in our original building all by itself.

The plans—accompanied by a well constructed architectural model—were very modern and took advantage of the elevated land that fronted Route 3A, while the rear would be built into the wooded (and wet) rear of the 2½ acre lot. There was, of course, an involved process to get a building permit which included numerous site engineering designs dealing with parking accommodations, septic construction, drainage and wetlands protection. This last permit, the wetlands issue, turned out to be the real stumbling block since the property was primarily ledge, and limited natural drainage through the soil meant that there occasionally was standing water on the property. When the inspectors came to visit the site, I was there along with the engineers, and also visiting was a pair of Mallard ducks, merrily swimming and quacking in the lone pool of water on the property. It would be more accurate to call it a puddle, but "pool" is the way the inspectors described it, and that meant that we could not fill it in unless we constructed "compensatory wetlands" someplace on the site. Talk about a stumbling block—this requirement seemed more like a coffin nail. But we decided to see if it was feasible.

19

GTO

This was to be the year of expectations: the new building project, the arrival of the first Testarossa, and probably most exciting, the letter confirming the exact date of our 288GTO availability. There were other expectations as well, such as the long awaited introduction of the new Alfa Romeo sedan, the Milano, destined however to arrive in 1986.

In 1982 I had gotten to drive a 250GTO that belonged to one of our customers from Pennsylvania. He had first arrived at Autohaus driving a 308GT4 that belonged to his business associate, but he liked driving it so much that he would bring it to us for service and spend the day "hanging around" and talking with Fritz and the technician and the salesmen—just about everyone as long as he could talk about Ferraris. After we saw him a few times in the period of a couple of years, one day he showed up driving a Dino 246GTS that he owned himself, and was so proud of it as it was his first Ferrari and a beautiful one at that. It was a long time before I saw him again, and

Ferrari 250GTO factory press photograph. I unexpectedly drove one just like this that belonged to one of our customers. Never drove a car like this again.

that was when he arrived driving the 250GTO. Even then they were very pricey, and we figured he must have done quite well for himself; indeed he must have, as he had just returned from France where he had attended a GTO reunion where 20-plus GTO owners from around the world got together to revel in each other's cars. Quite a "do" it must have been.

Although I usually demurred when invited to drive a customer's car, he had insisted and I did want very much to experience the GTO. Driving it made a totally different impression than what I expected. It was ferocious, it was brutish, it was nimble and it was fast. The sounds were guiding the driving and you knew why so many race cars belittled the speedometer and emphasized the tachometer. You drove with your ears and with the feel of the machine through your body, the sensations augmented by the spartan and purposeful interior. I never drove a car like that again.

Everything was on hold with the new building as the appeals process was very time consuming and there had to be public notice, etc., so it seemed it would be sometime in the late spring that we could even start construction. After all these delays we started thinking that maybe a different area nearer to Route 3 might, in fact, be a better location for the new dealership, and with those thoughts Fritz and I started looking for either existing structures that might work or buildable land on which we could construct a new facility. The few buildings we found were either too big or too small, and the available acreage was either too expensive or unsuitable. As the search went on, all the time we were informing the respective manufacturers of our plans and they were always agreeable to the possible locations we presented.

The question of cost was always a foremost consideration, and we were basing our projections on the assumption of recent profits continuing. Since the BMW and Ferrari lines were both very profitable, we based our ability to sustain a new facility on their numbers, while the Alfa franchise would just add to the overall glamour of the dealership. The Eighties were really on fire and the new Testarossa from Ferrari would greatly add to the very much in-demand lineup. But the expected delivery time for the car was continually extended so that we received our first one in September of 1985, just about one year after first seeing the car in Italy.

There was little interest in the 524td as the idea of a BMW with *less* performance did not appeal to customers, despite its fuel economy. As we had a black one on the lot, I decided to drive it as a demonstrator; I was racking up miles commuting back and forth to Boston, and it was usually easier to find an unused diesel pump at a service station—unless there was a huge semi in your way. I liked the car, although it was only available in the U.S. with an automatic—why couldn't those Germans try harder at educating American drivers to the joy of shifting?

By 1985 the Datsun name had officially disappeared, replaced by Nissan, and the last of the rear wheel drive Maximas were gone; now we had to suffer with front wheel drive on both the sedan and wagon, with the only redeeming feature being the sedan could still be had with a standard shift. But we still had the Z's, now in the second year of the 300ZX model, and there was word of a new four-wheel-drive coming to be named the Pathfinder. We really needed that model since Toyota had introduced a very popular model that needed some competition.

It was also when I decided to try to learn yet another language, this time

Japanese. Since we were selling Japanese cars also, why not attempt the language and then make a trip to Japan where none of us had visited? I think this notion started in Hawaii, on my third trip there, where Japanese tourists represented by far the biggest percentage of visitors and where their cultural presence was felt in many aspects of Hawaiian daily life. How ironic. I had met some BMW dealers from Tokyo at the last BMW meeting in Hawaii, and although they spoke fairly good English, it frustrated me that I had absolutely no idea what they were saying in their native tongue and could read nothing of what they were writing. So in the summer of '85 I decided to enroll in a night course in elementary Japanese at the Harvard College Extension program, where I had previously taken courses in both Italian and German.

That summer we had another Hollywood episode involving the Rosso Dino Ferrari 308GTS that we had taken in trade on a Ferrari 512BBi. This 308 was the car that had been bought by the fellow who traded the red 308 that I had taken to the squash camp the year before. He was a good customer. A studio representative approached us, looking to rent a flashy Ferrari—how redundant—to use in a silly movie that was eventually titled *One Crazy Summer*, starring John Cusack and Demi Moore amongst others.

We didn't know the plotline of the film, but as long as the Ferrari was protected with proper insurance coverage and we could have a person accompany the car to solve any problems that might occur, we would agree to rent it. This time we charged $5,000 and they agreed, and so the car disappeared to Cape Cod for about a week. Since they weren't using it every day, the salesman we had sent with the car returned to Cohasset and waited to be needed again. Well, the day before the final day of shooting he was needed. There had been an accident and the rear of the car had been damaged while something else caused an instrument failure, so there was no functioning tachometer or speedometer. The salesman, Jim, was able to get the car operating and return it to Cohasset, and the insurance company promptly paid the $2,600 repair bill that Fritz figured up after examining the damage. This time the car actually appeared in the film, and as a nod to Autohaus you could see our unmistakable yellow rear window sticker in some of the scenes. The studio and their insurance company were great to deal with, and we decided that anytime Hollywood called us we would say yes. Another call was to come the next year.

In September the first Testarossa arrived, and it was astounding. Seeing it at the

Ferrari rear window sticker. This yellow label really stood out.

Ferrari Testarossa arriving on ramp truck—our last open air Ferrari delivery.

factory and at Imola the year before had not prepared us for how sensational it would look at our dealership, and how excitedly the public would react to the car. It arrived in Rosso Corsa, of course, and all the salesmen who had interested customers were on the phone as soon as it arrived, while Fritz and I were in the driver's and passenger's seats, respectively, and heading south on Route 3A just to see how great this car would be. And it was great. The sound and feel were very different from the 512BBi that it replaced, and the power seemed to be more completely transferred to the rear wheels than what we had experienced in other mid-engine Ferraris. Once again, viewing the longitudinally mounted motor was breathtaking. And now, seeing the red valve covers, it was easier to explain the name Testarossa.

So the car was exceptional and the customers were eager, and at a suggested retail price of $89,200, it would prove easy to sell. It was so much in demand, in fact, and so scarce, that some dealers immediately started charging prices that far exceeded the suggested retail price. But not us. Even when the 240Z had a two year wait for delivery, we never charged above the suggested retail price, for several reasons. Other dealers thought we were stupid for holding the line, but we always kept our prices fair as, looking at the long run, we wanted buyers to feel that they were treated equitably and to have a pleasant buying experience, driving out of the dealership happy.

Another reason for holding the price, especially with Ferraris, was the tendency of some customers to trade their cars back in a relatively short period of time. This often created a problem as new cars, particularly exotic ones, would lose one-third of their value as soon as they left the dealership; a $60,000 car would be worth only

$40,000 if traded after a few weeks on another vehicle. Although some customers understood and would grimace and smile at the same time, others thought it was outrageous to try to "steal" their trades after such a short time. These feelings would only be compounded if you charged a customer more than the suggested retail prices, as the "overcharge" plus the one third depreciation would result in such a loss that often the customer would stomp away and you would lose any future sales. We didn't want that to happen. So we held the prices, and we sold the cars.

Not long after receiving the first Testarossa we finally had confirmation of the delivery time for our 288GTO. We had already paid for it back in the summer by wiring the factory 142,000,000 lira, and now the factory confirmed the availability of the 288 for delivery in late November.

So in late November, Jack, my squash-playing friend Dick and I boarded the *QE2* for a five day trip to England that was memorable in itself. We had a table to ourselves at dinners and the food and service were incomparable. We actually had Thanksgiving dinner aboard, and the Brits did a pretty good job of recreating the grandmother's table that the Americans aboard all were remembering. The only sad part of the voyage was that Dick announced that this voyage was his "swan song," intimating that his health was deteriorating such that he would not be able to take that kind of trip again. I did not realize just how ill he was. Within three years I lost one of my best friends.

Jack, who was returning to his work in Germany and was eager to visit Maranello, and I flew from London to Milan where we rented an Alfa 6 sedan and headed to Modena and the Fini for another fantastic dinner. The next day we went south towards Maranello, and as we went along the weather kept deteriorating so that we arrived at the factory in one of those pea soup fogs.

These fogs made you realize why so many European cars have fog lights both front and rear, as it could get so thick that you could only see three or four car lengths ahead—and that was on the autostrada. When we finally arrived it was already dusk and we met with our contact Emilio Goldoni, whom I had met the year before and

Ferrari factory entrance at Maranello, from a 1985 factory brochure.

who had been expecting us earlier, but understood why we were late. After we completed the paperwork he took us to an area of the factory that I hadn't visited before and where there was only one overhead garage door, which he ceremoniously opened to reveal our 288GTO. It was breathtaking. And there surrounding it were five or six identically dressed technicians, all in red Ferrari jumpsuits and all with huge grins on their faces. They were so proud, and we were so excited. We walked around the car with Emilio explaining different features, all the time closely followed by the red jumpsuits who were listening intently and nodding. Finally it was time for us to try out the car. We had arranged for one month's insurance on the car along with Italian export plates, but had no intention of driving it other than a few miles to check it out, as the factory was arranging shipment back to the U.S. for us, and we didn't want any unforeseen events impacting—no pun intended—the car.

So Jack got in the driver's seat (I had promised him the first drive), started the car, pushed down the clutch, and tried to get the car into reverse. It wouldn't go. He tried again and again with the gears letting out an audible *grrrr* while the red jumpsuits grimaced at the noises. I said to Jack, "What are you doing?" and he replied that it wouldn't go into reverse, and I said of course it would, try again. And he did, but still no luck. Now Jack was a good driver, and although he might have been a bit nervous with such an august audience, if he said it wouldn't go into reverse, then it probably wouldn't. Emilio suggested that Jack get out and let his head technician do it—and he couldn't shift it either. Then, in a sudden flurry of flashing red jumpsuits, we were ushered out of the garage and the door closed, leaving us out in the foggy Italian air.

It was amusing in a certain way that even at the factory level, glitches that were frequently endured by dealers and their staff were being repeated. Emilio smiled and said the GTO would be ready in a few minutes, and we made small talk near the gates of the factory entrance.

In a short time the garage door opened again and out *backed* the 288GTO, ready for its road test. Jack got in the driver's seat and I in the passenger's, and as the gates to the factory slowly rolled open, we left the area, turning right onto the two lane road. Miraculously the fog had lifted and there was virtually no traffic as we accelerated to a most beautiful sound; then after less than one mile Jack turned to me and said, "Your turn."

As I got into the driver's seat, over 20 years of knowing and driving Ferraris seemed to coalesce into this place and this car. It was like my mind was putting it all together, and as I accelerated I could picture the scene from the movie *Back to the Future* when the DeLorean driven by Christopher Lloyd zooms away leaving a trail of fire and smoke. This car was

Ferrari 288GTO export license plate. Wish it revolved like the plate on 007's Aston Martin.

Ferrari 288GTO factory press photograph. It would take a year for us to finally get one.

unlike any other I had ever driven and felt so incredibly fast and so easy to drive. Although it resembled a 308 it was in a totally different sphere and certainly unlike the 250GTO. As we drove through Maranello it seemed as though the whole town was out to watch us pass by, and we figured there must be some sort of silent siren that goes off every time a Ferrari leaves the factory for a test drive so that all within earshot will be able to see and hear it go by.

I was enthralled by it all, and as I went through the gears, hearing the engine and exhaust reverberating off the stucco houses, Jack sat there silently with a big grin on his face. We couldn't go that far, but we did it in record time I'm sure, so after a short drive we returned to the factory to leave the car. Since it was impossible to really test it at night, we decided to come back the next day to drive it in the daylight. We left it with Emilio and the next morning we returned to Maranello where the sun was bathing the factory in bright light, and waiting for us in the inner courtyard was the GTO. We asked Emilio where he might suggest we go in order to really enjoy the capabilities of the 288, and having predicted our questions he had a route already worked out. With his map in our hands, we headed toward route A1 and south.

There really wasn't much traffic and the GTO was ready to make itself noticed, but not by the *policia per favore*. The turbochargers made all the difference as the power surge was seamless and totally exhilarating—so much so that it was as though you were alone on the autostrada as slower cars were melting into the right lane without my even having to flash the headlights. Maybe their radios were all tuned to a secret station that advised them of the latest miracle from Maranello about to overtake them. In any case there was no chance of seeing anybody's face as we zoomed by everyone including a rather pesky 911 Turbo of unknown vintage. Probably thinking it was a 308, he never had a chance against this powerful and beautiful Ferrari.

It was quite plain inside, although not as spartan as the original GTO, and while the dashboard resembled the 308, the seats, door panels and other parts of the cabin were made of very light yet strong materials. The only extra we had ordered on the car was air conditioning as you wanted to keep the car as light as possible in case someone wanted to race (on the track I mean), which I doubt anyone really did. At speed, it felt attached to the highway, and with all that glass there was never any question as to where you were in relation to other vehicles. The insulation seemed minimal so you could certainly hear the engine, and strangely also sounds from air rushing by the exterior rear view mirrors, which stood out from the car like ears on a startled deer. On the way back we took a non-autostrada road and it was just as enchanting and breathtaking as the curves were flattened out and the trees lining the road became a blur as we headed back to the factory. It was one drive and one car that I would never forget.

When we returned to Maranello, Emilio said the car would be shipped back airfreight and that we would have it well before Christmas. With that we thanked him, leaving him with a bottle of Johnnie Walker Black, and pointed the Alfa toward Venice where we spent a couple of days before returning to the States to await the GTO's arrival.

One of our customers, George Higgins, was a well known Boston author of many books including *Trust* and *On Writing* and wrote articles periodically for national newspapers. He drove a BMW and when he came in to have the car serviced, we would often chat about this and that but mostly cars, including Ferraris. On one of his visits he talked about the car that was seen in a certain very popular TV series that took place in Miami, saying he loved the Ferrari convertible that the stars of the show drove around the city chasing the bad guys, but thought it strange that they would use such a valuable car in the show—he knew the value of a Daytona spyder. I revealed to him that the car wasn't genuine, it was in fact a replica—a good one, too, as long as you didn't get too close to it. He was visibly surprised, and I think disappointed too. So we talked about that for a while until I got called away, and the next time I looked for him he had already left as the work on his car had been completed.

Not long after, I received a phone call from a friend who started needling me about my appearance in the *Wall Street Journal* in an article about Ferraris and non-Ferraris. There it was, a lengthy article describing our customer's astonishment at being told of this non–Ferrari–Ferrari. It was quite humorous, especially when he referred to me as a "purveyor of high-priced sleds." All in good fun—at least that's what we thought. Apparently Ferrari thought otherwise, however, as they were gathering information on any Daytona coupes or spyders that we had sold from 1982 until 1987 in connection with a legal case that they had started against the manufacturer of the Ferrari Daytona replica. The Italians were getting serious.

As I had been told in Maranello, the GTO did arrive the week before Christmas, cleared through customs by our import agent and squash friend Brian, who did

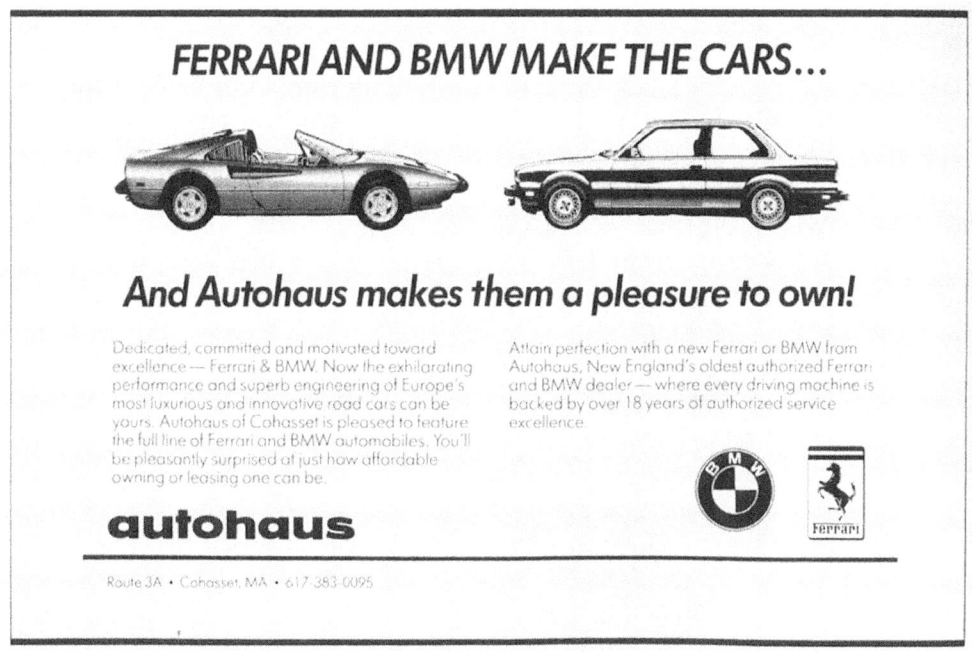

Ferrari–BMW ad from the Boston Open Squash Program, November 1983.

it much faster than I ever could have. He called me the day after it arrived at Logan and said to come pick it up, and I did. Normally we would have sent a truck but the trusted company we used, Smith's, did not have any truck available and the freight offices would be closing down for Christmas. There was no way we were going to leave the car there, so I decided to go get it myself.

Naturally, the next day it was snowing—lightly, to be sure, but undeniably. Undeterred, that afternoon I got a ride to the airport and picked up the car, which seemed to be smiling at me as I approached it with a dealer plate in my hands. I left the airport and tried to remove the value factor from my mind as I merged with the southbound Expressway traffic, which was already stop and go. At the first opportunity I exited and headed south on Route 3A, arriving back at the dealership to eager eyes and a round of applause as I drove into the service department and met the waiting Fritz, Alice, and all the staff.

The 288GTO was a sensation. We (Fritz mostly) had told our customers that the car was arriving around the end of the year and invited all to come and see it—not drive it or buy it, as we had decided not to sell it at this time—but just see it. And come they did. Not only Ferrari customers but others as well, and they all gave it a smiling nod of approval as the rear engine cover was lifted to show the now longitudinally placed V8 engine with the twin turbochargers which altogether produced (at least) 400 horsepower. It was lovely to look at, and although the car was ostensibly a race car, the finish and interior details were almost posh. It was designed to compete in Group B sports car racing and rallying, but the class was eliminated by the FIA before the car could properly show its prowess.

Of course one of the first things was to have it federalized, this time by Dick Fritz at Amerispec. He sent us photos of some of the GTOs he had already done, and there was little visual change to the exterior, including the bumpers, so the car would retain its Euro look as much as possible. He was busy all the time so we made an appointment for June, and with that the car went into our showroom where it stayed off and on for the next six years. Well, not always, as occasionally Fritz or I would take it out on the road to give it some exercise. In this case I was driving it a lot faster than Fritz, who liked to baby it, and that was fine with me.

Our car was one of the last delivered by the factory, so there was already a small history of sales of these cars, both here and in Europe, with prices reportedly in excess of $1 million. We didn't know how true these stories were, and since we weren't planning to sell the car—at least not in the near future—we decided to insure it for what a retail price might be, and to do that we had to get what is called a stated value policy. We would get from an authority such as Amerispec a value for the car and then purchase a stated amount policy for that amount, something that our regular carrier couldn't do for us. As it turns out, Suzanne, a woman with whom I played squash, sometimes worked for one of the biggest specialty insurance agencies in Boston and was able to insure the car for us through Lloyds of London for the appraised amount, starting at $230,000 in 1986 and rising to $1,250,000 in 1989. Talk about leading the curve.

That was starting to happen with the entire Ferrari line—appreciation, that is—especially with the earlier 12 cylinder models and many of the competition cars that were no longer being raced except in vintage racing. The values were even increasing for the still-new Testarossa; we wondered where this was going to lead. It wasn't only rare automobiles that were rapidly gaining value but also antique furniture, impressionist art and just about every type of scarce collectible. It was the Eighties.

In December we had received notice from FNA of the impending arrival of the previously rumored and long awaited 328GTB and 328GTS—meaning that we might see some soon. In fact we received the first GTS, a silver with blue leather car, the same week that the GTO arrived from Italy. The changes from the 308 series were substantial, including a larger displacement engine—more powerful and of course faster—as well as new front and rear bumpers that were color coordinated with the bodywork, making for a much prettier package. Everyone liked the changes.

This was also the year we sold one of our few Ferraris for overseas delivery at the factory. The customer, an investment broker, wanted to pick up a new 412 (which had replaced the 400i) at Maranello, drive it a little over there, and then have it air freighted to us for federalization and final delivery. The total cost of the car with federalization came to just over $92,000, which was fine with him, so we made all the arrangements—this time directly with the factory—and when the car came back it was stunning. Silver with a lot of red leather—just beautiful! After having the car federalized by Americspec we delivered it to the customer and then never saw the Ferrari again. Didn't these Ferraristi ever drive their cars?

I began to sell a few cars to fellow members of the Tennis & Racquet Club—mostly new BMWs, but also some used cars, for which I was very selective. It was a funny situation as I was selling friends cars (which some dealers never wanted to do) and the other side was that people I was selling cars to were becoming friends. In almost all cases it was a genuinely good result as we were proud of the new cars that we sold and the used (or pre-owned) ones were always of good quality, many of them having been sold new and continually serviced by Autohaus until being traded back to us. I offered to take their cars in for service and loan them my car to make the distance factor less important, and we all liked that arrangement, at least for a while. Tom, the manager of the club, brought in an early '80s Alfa spider, a nice cream colored car with low miles, that he wanted us to service. After making arrangements with Fritz he left it off for the work that was supposed to be routine, but after inspecting it we realized it needed a lot of expensive repairs. I gulped when I told him, but he seemed unfazed as he thought there might be more to it than just an ordinary service. But it was an Alfa, and it was Italian, so I guess we were both prepared in some way and he loved the car—at least for a time.

It wasn't only I, however, who was befriending customers, but our salesmen and technicians alike. There had evolved such a sense of trust and mutual appreciation of the cars we sold that Autohaus was becoming club-like itself, with customers socializing with staff and some of those friendships continuing for many years and even until today. This interaction was unusual in a retail environment, especially in the automobile business, but again that's what made Autohaus different, and our customers enjoyed it as did we. Making a business successful obviously included making a profit, but with us it was more than that, it was sharing the uniqueness of the cars we sold and the positive aura about them. It made going to work every day exciting and interesting for many, many years.

20

Italy, Italy

At last Alfa Romeo announced the launch of the Milano sedan, the American version of the recently introduced Alfa Romeo 75, with the dealer presentation to be held in Italy with a side trip to Monte Carlo. In the mid-'70s Fritz and Alice had been to the factory in Milano and experienced Italian industry at a low point, with dissatisfied employees and decreasing production, but now under the Fiat umbrella, things were different—somewhat.

In May 1986 most of the 150 U.S. Alfa dealers met up in New York and boarded a Pan Am flight to Nice where we then traveled by bus to Monaco for the first leg of our trip. The first day featured a tour of Monaco and the surrounding area, and the following day was taken up by a business meeting during which the dealers' guests or spouses were taken to Nice for shopping and museum visits. That evening there was a gala dinner in Monte Carlo with music and dancing and, for those interested, a bit of gambling. The last time I had been in the casino at Monte Carlo was on my first trip to Europe with my fraternity brothers where we had been stunned by the amount of money people were wagering, and what beautiful people many of them were. This time, however, we were able to enter the Salon Privé, where as I remember there was a minimum bet of around 1000 FF—and talk about beautiful people! I didn't bet much, nor did Fritz and Alice, but I at least honed my skills at playing Baccarat. It was quite a night.

The next day we were taken to Italy by motor coach to Alfa's proving grounds and test track at Balocco, not far from the factory in Arese, and where we would drive the cars. But when we arrived in rain, shortly before noon, that seemed in question. In a beautiful low stone building that was a large hall of sorts, our hosts had laid out a magnificent luncheon spread of food and wine as only the Italians can do. The wine probably meant no driving for us—although you never knew. Most of the women had chosen to go shopping in Milan and were promising to arrive back at the hotel with many, many bags (they did), so it was almost entirely the dealers who enjoyed the noontime feast.

Many factory people were there, most of whom spoke English. I started to talk with one obviously older man, smaller in stature, wearing a tweed jacket and tweed cap, but his English was more limited than my Italian so there wasn't much to the conversation—my loss, I thought. After the lengthy meal the U.S. director gave a short talk and told us that due to the weather we wouldn't be able to drive the cars, but we would all be given a ride around the track by one of the four factory test drivers with

Alfa Romeo Milano, from factory brochure.

three of us in the car at one time plus the driver. As the test drivers assembled, it was easy to identify them as they were in their 30s and appeared eager to take us around the track. At least three of them had that appearance—the fourth was the man in the tweed jacket, who was perhaps in his 70s. I was told that he had been a race car driver for the factory in the 1950s and '60s. I opted to ride with him.

He motioned us into a silver Milano, with one dealer in the front passenger seat while I shared the rear with a dealer from Alabama. We started off slowly onto the wet track and it quickly became obvious that this driver knew this track better than I knew my own driveway at home. With no effort he turned into the first corner with the car showing excellent grip and took us down the straightaway into the next series of curves, all the time making minute, very precise steering corrections. The Alabama dealer asked me if we weren't going too fast in the rain, and didn't seem comforted by my assurance that the driver was experienced and could control the car. After a few more turns and while flying down another straightaway at an indicated 130, I was deeply impressed with both driver and car, but my southern friend was in a near panic as he saw the speedometer reading. I explained—with a little white lie—that it was actually kilometers per hour, not miles per hour, and that we were really only going 80 mph, which calmed him somewhat.

We were all impressed with the Milano and pleased that we would finally have a sedan worthy of the name to go along with the GTV6 and the spiders; now all we wanted to know was what it would sell for and when it would arrive. We hoped we would find out soon, perhaps at Alfa Romeo headquarters in Arese on our visit the next day.

The factory itself was imposing and modern, with much more automation and robots doing work than I would have imagined. Fritz said it was very different than what he had seen a decade earlier, and we saw no evidence of labor/management issueds now. Fiat had pioneered the use of robots in assembly lines with the result of increased production quality on many of their cars, especially Alfas, and as we toured the production facilities we could see the Milanos being assembled with these strangely human-looking robots happily doing the difficult welding and assembly. It was borderline creepy yet futuristic.

That afternoon we went to the museum where we saw so many of the famous racing Alfas, including the really odd bi-motor car which had two engines, front

Alfa Romeo test track at Balocco. In a Milano at full speed in the rain, I was very impressed.

and rear (maybe Tesla has been channeling that model). With obvious pride in the company's racing history, members of the museum staff told us a wild story about a number of 1940 cars being hidden behind a false wall to keep them away from the Germans, against whom Alfa Romeo had competed fiercely in the late 1930s, particularly Auto Union. It seemed like just a story until I read later that it was perhaps true and that both Enzo Ferrari and Luigi Chinetti were somehow involved in the concealment of the cars until after the end of World War II.

We did find out about the pricing of the models which included three versions of the Milano and three versions of the spider, but much to our surprise the GTV6 was being discontinued. I guess its time was up. Once again the Italians made everyone feel comfortable and pleased to be handling the Alfa franchise.

Back at the dealership after a short but great trip, we were entering the strong selling season of late spring and early summer. BMW was selling well and we decided to employ a well known Boston advertising agency to create ads showcasing our history and association with BMW. I was driving one of the new M6 coupes as my new demo. With the factory sport modifications, it handled better than the 635CSi and although its acceleration was only marginally quicker, it felt faster because of the taut suspension and the sounds it made. Alice was driving a red Ferrari Mondial cabriolet that we had traded and she looked perfect in it with the top down, although I doubt the engine ever fully warmed up because she used it primarily to go back and forth to her home three miles away—a fun three miles, though.

A few weeks after we got back, one of the salesmen told me someone had come into the dealership looking for a BMW limousine to rent or buy and he had advised him to call back when I returned. A limousine? BMW did not make any such vehicle although in some countries the 7 series was called a limousine. A few days later the same person called and inquired about renting not one but *two* BMW limos, for a movie being filmed around Cohasset. They specifically wanted two BMWs and nothing else. I told him that no such car existed and that I regretfully couldn't help. After he hung up I realized I had broken one of my cardinal rules…always get the customer's name and phone number!

Well, two weeks later—you guessed it—into our dealership drives a BMW stretch limousine with a man wanting to know if we would be interested in buying the car! The car had been built in Poland from a regular BMW 7 series and had the look of a stretch Mercedes 220 or one of our Cadillac limos—but it was a BMW. Since the man had only one, I figured this wouldn't work even if I heard back from the interested party whose contact info I had neglected to get.

I have written about the house I had on the island in Marshfield and how beautiful and remote it was. It was those things and also a handful to take care of, so for the last few summers I had hired a high school student to mow the lawn, take care of the pool and watch over Bully, the Lab. It had worked out pretty well and allowed me more time at the office during the busy season, and the kids that worked there had been really reliable. About two weeks after the limo incident, Steve from the house called me and said there was some fellow there from a movie company that was interested in renting the house. The house? He must have misunderstood as I figured it was the same guy looking for the two BMWs—but how did he find my house, and me? So Steve put him on the phone, and yes he was from a movie company, and yes he wanted to rent the house, but no he didn't want to rent BMW limos, that was someone else, but yes it was the same movie company. Was I confused or what?

The guy on the phone was the location manager while the BMW fellow was the prop manager—same company, same movie, different managers. How odd was this! The location manager was asking if it might be possible to rent our house as a "star house" for a few of the movie's stars to have the use of, because the location of the house and especially the dirt road that went from it toward the ocean were perfect for one of the important shots in the film, but at the same time the road was too narrow for the stars' usual trailers to drive down. So they needed a place to change, relax, learn their lines, etc. He couldn't tell me what the film was or who the stars were as not everything was firmed up, and his inquiry was just that, an inquiry. After checking with Jack to make sure he wasn't planning something on the same dates, I told the location manager that we would entertain the idea once he could confirm their intent. In the same conversation I asked him about the prop manager and he told me that he had secured the two cars he was looking for. That I didn't believe, at least that he had found two BMW limousines, and indeed the cars turned out to be two Mercedes 600 sedans.

The first thing I did was to call my friend Jack DePalma in New York to tell him what was going on and to ask him for advice as to what to charge for the potential use of our humble cottage as a star house. He gave me some guidelines and then said he would try to find out what movie company and what movie and what stars were lurking around Cohasset. Two days later he called me all excited to tell me what movie it was, but I had already had a call from the location manager confirming their intent to rent the house and the details on the film and its cast. The film was titled *The Witches of Eastwick* and the stars who wanted to use the house were Cher and Jack Nicholson—and suddenly the whole South Shore was talking about it. Did that news get out fast or what!

So in the middle of July on one of those perfect Massachusetts days, the entourage arrived. The trailers were set up back on the mainland and the stars, production crew, director, assistants and just about everyone else that you see listed in those credits at the end of a film descended on Macomber's Island along with neighbors from all around the area. It seemed like time was standing still for this event. They were filming the scene in which Cher is riding her bike along a dirt road and first encounters Nicholson. The scene lasts maybe two or three minutes but took the whole long day to film, and in between the shots Cher and Jack were in the house, relaxing, eating and studying their lines while constantly being interrupted by their staff and my friends and family. For two world-famous stars they couldn't have been nicer. And then all hell broke loose—in the form of one very large black Labrador Retriever named Bully.

On about the third take of Cher riding her bike down the dirt road to meet up with Nicholson, the scene was being shot with just Cher on the bike while Nicholson would appear in the next shot showing her arriving. Nicholson was in the house and watching along with all of us from the screen porch. When the director said "Quiet

Witches of Eastwick **stars Cher and Jack Nicholson practicing their lines. Macomber's Island was never the same after their visit.**

Witches of Eastwick stars Jack Nicholson and Cher. Action!

on the set," there was total human silence. But that didn't include Bully, who must have seen something moving in the tall marsh grass and suddenly let out this series of loud barks while breaking himself loose from my taut grip and hurtling *through* the porch screen and into the marsh after this invisible critter. We all were startled when Nicholson started yelling at the top of his lungs—"Bully, get back in here"—which only got Bully to look around briefly before continuing into the marsh. After we rounded up Bully he was put in the shed in the back yard—no more cameos for him.

    The shooting went on for the entire day with Cher and Nicholson (who was still learning his lines) coming in and going out of the house constantly. Jon Peters, a producer, was cornered by my mother who was quizzing him on his life in show business and I'm sure telling him about her show business career. It was too much. Interestingly, all the California visitors were impressed and surprised by the beauty of the marshes with the ocean in the background, many of them never having seen this type of setting before. We were very proud of Marshfield.

    At lunchtime we were all invited to go to the food wagon on the mainland, where it was set up like a giant picnic; everyone partook and everything was delicious. After lunch as we were all walking back to the house, there was a muffled roar and down the dirt road came Alice in her red Mondial Cabriolet, with the top down, looking like an arriving movie star herself. She wasn't going to stay at the office while all this Hollywood activity was going on. She loved it, as did friend Archie's son Jay.

    At the end of the day everything miraculously returned to normal. The stars were gone—but not before they were invited to return any time—the trucks disappeared

Alice arriving on set with Jay in a Mondial Cabriolet, looking like a movie star.

and everything was cleaned and restored to the island's beauty. Hollywood could come again anytime, I thought.

That was a tough act to follow, as the show business saying goes, but the summer was a very good one for business, a happy surprise since mid-summer often was a slow time in showroom activity. In July we received our second Testarossa for the year—we were allocated four for 1986—with a price increase to $102,500, from $89,200 the year before. The price increases didn't seem to bother the Ferrari customers as they knew when they ordered the car it would probably bear a higher price when we actually delivered it. The year would end with us receiving only three Testarossas, not four, but we were happy with that.

In August my good customer Roland from New Hampshire was on the phone again asking about the new 328 and if he would like it more than his 308qv. On my recommendation that he probably would, he ordered one in red with beige, which we could get relatively quickly, on the sole condition that I again deliver it to him myself. In mid-August the car was ready for him, and after making arrangements with him I headed north to New Hampshire.

Normally my route would be to go around Boston via Route 128 and north to Route 3 north into New Hampshire, but for some reason I decided to go through Boston via the expressway, thinking that mid-morning traffic was bound to be moving swiftly with no backups. So with the roof off and my sunglasses on, I entered the Southeast Expressway in Quincy and was left-laning it at a steady 50 or so until traffic stopped as I approached the South Station tunnel.

Visible just a few hundred yards ahead was a breakdown in the passing lane, and police were directing traffic around the stalled car. As I was creeping forward there was a sudden crunching sound behind me and the Ferrari lurched ahead even with my foot fully on the brake pedal. I stopped a foot or so behind the car in front and when I looked in the rear view mirror all I could see was a massive bumper that was about two feet behind the glass rear window, *and my head!* I shut off the engine, applied the emergency brake while leaving the car in gear, and hopped out of the car. Had I been lucky! There, perched over the entire rear of the car, was the huge bumper and hood of a massive earth moving type truck, with a horrified driver staring ahead. As I was staring at the scene, the police officer who was directing traffic ran back to see why the cars weren't moving. "You can't stay here, you'll have to move your car right away," he told me. No way, I said, nothing was moving until I got some papers from the truck driver. And so with the policeman yelling, and the traffic backing up now in the two left lanes, I got the information from the driver. It turned out he was a trainee, learning how to handle this large rig in an urban traffic setting. He received his training, all right, but I'd say he failed the test. The other man in the truck was his teacher, and he too was dumbstruck, but I got the info, and we finally got off the expressway as the Ferrari was still running fine, it just didn't look too good.

I limped back to Cohasset and told the story to a surprised and yet amused Fritz and our Ferrari technician, and then I called New Hampshire to tell my customer that I wouldn't be coming today. He wanted a replacement 328 rather than that particular car even if it was well repaired, and was not in a hurry. After all the insurance people came and went, we ended up selling the car in the damaged condition it was in, to a dealer in New York who was happy to have a new 328 even if it needed body work. So much for using the expressway for deliveries from then on. Six weeks later when we got another GTS in red with beige leather, I drove it up to New Hampshire—via Route 128—and Roland couldn't have been more delighted.

We had received word earlier in the year of a semi-sponsored FNA meeting in Detroit in conjunction with this year's Detroit Grand Prix Formula 1 race there. I opted to go and brought along one of the newest salesmen, Richard Cyr, to show him some of the Ferrari camaraderie and excitement. Well, there was excitement there but Alboreto couldn't get past 4th place—which was hotly contested.

With racing so recently in our veins, it seemed like a natural segue to the biennial factory trip in September. We always looked forward to these trips with great enthusiasm as it was an opportunity not only to visit the factory but to visit friends and relatives—in Switzerland and Italy for Alice and Fritz, in Italy and France for me.

The new President of FNA, Emilio Anchisi, and his charming wife, Moya, gave us all a warm welcome to this third factory sponsored trip to Maranello. The factory meeting was informative and the tour of the factory added new sights and new areas that we hadn't seen before. It was a little like seeing a movie more than once where you notice different scenes and some new actors too. It was then that we learned that Ferrari was planning a successor to the 288GTO, tentatively named the F40, in honor of Ferrari's 40th year of automobile production; it sounded great to us. Ferrari was putting all its eggs in this basket, and if all came out as planned, this was going to be a road car capable of exceeding 200 mph—the first production car ever to make that claim. Take that, Porsche and Corvette. But first, they had to make it happen.

Detroit Grand Prix, 1986. Alboreto, piloting, came in fourth.

Although they admitted that it was going to be difficult to federalize the F40 for the States, they added that they didn't want to put dealers in the same position they had faced with the 288GTO, with prices and federalization processes varying greatly, adding to customers' confusion. The new cars would be fully federalized to both EPA and DOT specifications, be handled through the regular distribution channel, and have a standard Monroney label (a factory provided price and specification sticker) affixed to the window. We all hoped that would be the case. It was becoming apparent that a certain group of investors might be driving (no pun intended) the overzealous interest and pricing for these small production Ferraris, and that their ability to pay inflated prices might make normal marketing difficult. We'd have to wait and see. FNA also introduced a new allocation system for the cars, starting soon, and would be monitoring where we sold our vehicles and how our market area would be defined.

As before, it was an excellent trip with side excursions to sites that I hadn't visited before, and we got to meet the latest group of executives at Ferrari. They changed frequently, which made it difficult to form any type of long lasting connections with them, other than Piero Lardi who was always very friendly and talkative with me.

Back in Cohasset, BMW and Nissan sales were doing very well and even the new Alfa Milano was attracting quite a bit of attention. It was going to be at the auto show, so now we would have four lines of cars that we would have to provide salesmen for, and fortunately we now had five great full-time sales people.

Through the years we had to provide business cards for the salesmen plus myself and Fritz, plus the parts manager and also blank business cards for various other people if needed. The cards plus our stationery and envelopes were designed and printed

We thought better of this Ferrari ad after a few exposures.

by a fellow, Julius, whom I had known for quite a few years since I first advertised in *Panorama*, the Boston theater program. I had been introduced to him by my friend and customer Mac Thames, who was a born salesman and got all the ads for the magazine and seemed to know everyone in Boston. A very funny guy and a good customer, he had just bought his third BMW from us at the time, a bronze BMW 3.0Si, and he kept his cars in perfect condition—and I mean perfect.

ROBERT E. GUARINO

autohaus
——— Since 1967 ———
ROUTE 3A • COHASSET, MASSACHUSETTS 02025 • 617 383-0095

Autohaus business card, now a multicolored fine design by Julius.

Now we thought we could afford to have a more prestigious looking stationery, one that would include all four brands with their logos in full color at the top of the page and our name at the bottom. The envelope would feature the four logos on the front with our name and address on the back. The business cards would have the four logos at the top also. They all came out beautifully and people frequently commented on the attractiveness of both the stationery and the cards. Another reason I created that stationery was that I realized in the back of my head that having these four lines of cars together under one roof was not going to last forever, and it would be nice to memorialize that fact.

21

200 MPH!

Our advertising program was in high gear going into 1987 as our agency was producing current and clever copy. One BMW ad that we all thought was excellent was directed at the ever growing female market and showed the newly released 325i convertible with a woman driving it very fast, as indicated by her flowing hair and a blurred background. The copy read "For a Woman That Really Likes to Cook," intimating that she liked to drive fast as the word "cook" meant in automotive jargon. We ran the ad in *Boston Magazine* expecting a positive response. Instead we received letters and phone calls from irate women who accused us of sexist and chauvinistic advertising and demanded that we remove the ad from all publications as they found it offensive to all women. That was a quick learning curve for us, as we were soon discovering that women of the time did not want to be separated from male buyers in advertising copy; they wanted to be equal and they wanted the ad copy to be the same for men and women. We were really surprised, as was our agency, where one of the creators of the ad was a Sarah who was certainly a modern woman. We pulled the ad.

Other ads they did for us had Ferrari as the subject accompanied by clever copy, though in retrospect they were probably just a little too clever or cocky in tone. One we ran in *Harvard Magazine* and programs for squash tournaments and such showed a 328GTB at a three-quarter angle with the copy, "One test drive and I'm asking my sons to consider state schools." Just a bit much, we later decided. It was difficult to gauge if these ads were resulting directly in any sales, but at least they were getting our name out there. We always listed all the cars we were selling, hoping for some "halo" effect, meaning the attractiveness of the featured car would rub off onto the other lines and make them attractive at our dealership also.

We were also doing some innovative Nissan ads including our first TV commercial—actually a series of sketches that ran together so that they resembled a storyline in numerous cartoonlike boxes, under the title "Taking a Japanese Bath." We tried that only once as we got no response other than a couple of comments from existing customers who drove Nissans anyway.

Twenty years after opening Autohaus, we felt good about what we had accomplished. We had retained most of our original customers—if they were still driving imported cars—and were now even selling cars to their children who had first visited our showroom when they were just kids and would tell us stories about being awed by all the exotic cars they saw and, just as memorably, heard driving in and out of the dealership yard.

WHOEVER SAID YOU CAN'T BUY HAPPINESS, HAS OBVIOUSLY NEVER DRIVEN ONE OF THESE.

Ferrari 328 GTB

 **autohaus**
Since 1967
Route 3A, Cohasset, Massachusetts 02025
617 383-0095
Sales, Service and Leasing.

This Ferrari ad hit the mark.

    We had established ourselves as a reputable dealership in a small town but in fact had a national and international clientele. It had been our desire to be a different type of dealership where what we said was true. We stood behind whatever we sold, however difficult that may have been at times. Fritz and I frequently were at odds about whether a customer should have to pay for repairs that were done a second time to correct a problem and whether the "used car department" would have to absorb the costs. Sometimes Fritz was right and sometimes I was, but whatever the outcome, we quickly forgot any disagreements. In fact, over the twenty-year period we had had very few serious disagreements about anything pertaining to the business operations, and for that we were very fortunate.

It was still the time when local customers wanted to purchase just from us and were willing to pay our price (within reason) without shopping around at other dealerships, but we realized that this could not go on indefinitely. A very different sales atmosphere was developing in the business. Early on, a genuine respect had existed amongst some dealers for one another, so much so that often they would pass up sales to people who did not live in their geographic area, referring them to the dealership in their neighborhood. A few of these dealers really stood out, including Tom Mix at Foreign Motors in Boston, Ken Fullerton at Auto Engineering in Lexington, Guido Mondello at Foreign Engine Co. in Everett, John Adamonis at Transatlantic Foreign Cars in Hyannis and Don Guertin at Imported Cars of Worcester, to name a few. But now new dealerships were being appointed in the surrounding metro Boston area and being run by very aggressive organizations, and their arrival would start to hurt our new car sales unless we made some changes. Thus came our decision to open an exclusive Nissan showroom.

Because Nissans were really selling well, we decided to create a separate identity and location for the Nissan line under the name South Shore Nissan, placing the sales part of the franchise in the vacant restaurant building adjacent to Autohaus.

After consulting with Nissan and receiving their OK, we signed a lease with the restaurant owners (with whom we had always had excellent relations) and proceeded to modify the space for our automobiles. Nissan products would have their own space and the original Autohaus building would sell BMW, Ferrari and Alfa Romeo and service them as well as Nissan products.

BMW buyers were not as quick to start price shopping as they were ultimately concerned with the service department, and that's where Fritz was unbeatable. His friendliness and knowledge of the product—not to mention his Swiss accent which never seemed to falter—instilled in our customers a feeling of confidence in the dealership that no other BMW dealer could provide.

The same was true of Ferrari buyers, although typically they drove too few miles per year to be frequent visitors to the service department. Most of our buyers came from metropolitan Boston and eastern New England, including Rhode Island, and

South Shore Nissan rear window sticker. No more Datsun.

that was a good thing as Ferrari North America's new allocation policy took into consideration how many cars you sold *outside* of your market area.

While the service department did its job, the sales department was often the first exposure a customer had to the dealership, and the sales force that included Jim, Fred, Richard, Dwight and Mike was magnificent. They were led by Jim, who was not only experienced in sales but knew the products completely and projected such passion and professionalism that new customers knew they were dealing with a staff they could rely on and trust. The whole customer experience was almost magical, and customers often left with the feeling that they were not going to have that same positive reaction at any of the new larger dealerships that were being built around Boston.

Meanwhile we were still attempting to get town approval for the new dealership facility across the street, which meant seemingly endless meetings with the zoning boards and our local attorney, who was very attuned to the town's attitudes and demands for new construction, especially in the business zone. As of May 1987, however, we still had no approval or even an indication that they were thinking positively about our application. So we continued with a two-track strategy by inquiring about other properties on the South Shore that might be feasible and acceptable to BMW and Ferrari. None of this seem to make any difference to our customers; they had no problem seeing new cars for sale other than the brand that they came in to look at. In fact, many bought less expensive cars for family members realizing that they would get the same attention no matter which vehicle they purchased. Of course the factories didn't really want to hear about this as they just wanted things their way and they were willing to wait, at least for a time.

At about this time two of the BMW dealers with whom I was most friendly decided to sell their BMW franchises; one sold it back to the factory and the other to a dealer of another make in his area, and they both told me that they had received a good price. BMW was soliciting buybacks from dealerships in areas that they wanted to consolidate, or sometimes to reappoint someone willing to invest heavily in a stand-alone exclusive facility, which was actually their long range goal. Shortly thereafter a BMW district sales manager whom I had known for many years visited to inquire whether Fritz and I we wanted to sell. After much discussion and many numbers being thrown about, we told him that we were not about to give up the franchise after twenty years and that we would continue making the factory proud of our commitment to the product and to our customers. Now we just had to placate the factory with a new facility, which we were earnestly trying to provide.

The demand for new Ferraris—and used ones—remained extremely strong in 1987. Our total vehicle allocation was 16 cars, 4 of which were Testarossas. With orders for 10 TRs we could say that there was a 2½ year wait for a new vehicle, which was really outrageous. We told buyers at the outset that there could be a lengthy delay, but they never seemed to mind and would place an order with a sizeable deposit that was returnable if they changed their mind about the car or simply got tired of waiting. Our policy was to always return a customer's deposit even if the car was special ordered (which most were) with the provision that if the car ordered had unusual specifications—e.g., a color combination that would not normally be chosen such as *viola metallizzato* with green leather—it must first be retailed before the deposit would be returned. That policy turned out to be acceptable to everyone who placed their name on the waiting list. Remembering that all Ferrari orders were placed six months in advance with the factory, the time for delivery always was quicker than originally anticipated as customers often chose a red car that might suddenly become available due to a cancellation or to a change of mind. One reason we had so many orders was that we were still selling Testarossas at sticker price, which in spring of 1987 had climbed to $122,700 from the $89,200 in 1985. Many dealers were adding on to the sticker price with terms such as "availability surcharge," but we were staying with the philosophy of customer retention above short term profit. Concurrent with these price increases was factory notification that they were extending the warranty period to 24 months, unlimited mileage. The longer term was helpful, but the mileage factor was of course nil.

Being a Ferrari dealer also led to a great many strange requests, mostly from people wanting to be photographed in or near the cars, sometimes for their own keepsake and sometimes wanting to impress others. Often we obliged them, knowing that for most that would be the closest they would ever come to these beautiful machines

From time to time we would receive from Europe correspondence and solicitations for products that related to Ferrari automobiles. Often these were items that were not produced with authorization from Ferrari, meaning that they sometimes infringed on the Ferrari trademark, of which the factory was rightfully protective.

Sometimes, however, we would receive letters advising us of a collaboration between Ferrari and another manufacturer, including one for a bicycle and another for their association with Riva boats. Riva is the manufacturer of some of the most beautiful boats to be seen afloat, ranging from small runabouts such as the Riva Aquarama up to majestic custom built yachts, so it was not a surprise to learn that they were intending to produce the Riva 32 Offshore Runabout at their shipyards in Sarnico, Italy, in collaboration with Ferrari Engineering. The letter was advising us of their plans to produce these boats and to perhaps notify some of our Ferrari customers of their intent.

Another possible addition to our Ferrari line was the "Mondial Cabriolet Junior," a pint size version of the original that was powered by a 50 cc single cylinder, two stroke engine that could reach a top speed of 22 mph. Nothing like getting them hooked at an early age!

The annual Ferrari trip this year was a cruise to Alaska which Fritz and Alice attended while I remained in Cohasset to supervise the dealership. On this cruise a number of dealers brought up the idea of presenting a 90th birthday gift to Enzo Ferrari. Although there was much discussion about this and what to get for him, it was finally determined that he didn't want anything tangible. So with 100 percent participation of the North American Ferrari Dealers, in February of 1988 a group of dealers representing all of us went to Maranello and presented "Il Commendatore" with a check for 100,000,000 Lira (equal to about $85,000 at the time) payable to the Dino Ferrari Muscular Dystrophy Account. Dino, of course, was the son of Ferrari who died of the disease while in his early twenties.

The Frankfurt Auto Show that opened in September saw the debut of the long awaited Ferrari F40, named in honor of Ferrari's 40 years in business. Another great

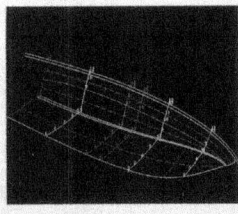 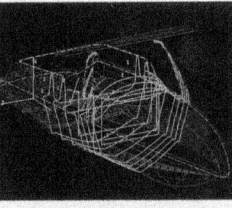 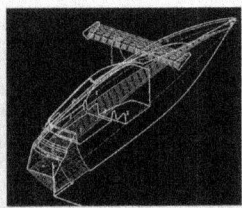

Riva boat ad in conjunction with Ferrari Engineering. Just the right boat for the Riviera.

Pininfarina execution, it was supposed to have almost 500 horsepower and a top speed in excess of 200 mph—and if that was true, it would be the first production car to have that performance capability. We had problems enough with the local gendarmes—how would this go over? It was going to be mind blowing.

Rumors were also swirling around Europe and the States about the replacement model for the 328, to be named the 348. To forestall any customer confusion, we received a letter in December from the factory stating that "the 348 would not be available for sale in any market including Italy, in the course of 1988," and that indeed was the case. In another unusual letter from the factory was a notice that they were ending the tradition of using odd numbered serial numbers for production cars and would henceforth use both even and odd numbers beginning with serial number 75,000. Maybe they were making too many cars.

But there could never be too many, as interest kept increasing. We did as much as we could to keep our name and the Ferrari name in the spotlight, including attending Ferrari meets and of course the auto shows. One meet was held late in the summer at the Larz Anderson Auto Museum, where we had introduced the 308GT4 some 13 years before, and it remained a perfect venue for anything automotive. We participated by providing cars to be displayed and a salesman (or myself or Fritz). One day of the weekend was so beautiful I had to ride my newest BMW bike, a K1000 which replaced my R100. This new bike was totally different, a lot more stable and a lot faster—did I need that? But it was top heavy and didn't seem quite as balanced although so responsive, it almost felt Japanese.

And then came Black Monday. On October 19, 1987, we were reviewing how good business had been over the weekend when one of our customers who had just arrived asked if I had heard what was going on with the stock market as it has dropped almost 500 points. That couldn't be too good. What was this going to do for business? There were different schools of thought on the effect of a plummeting market; one was that our customers would have lost substantial dollars and would be less likely to buy our medium price cars, but another was that they might decide to retreat from the market and invest in durable goods such as a classic foreign car or even a new one (or some other work of art) to hedge against any inflation or international currency increases. Whatever the case, we felt sure that we would not be impacted by this drop anytime soon.

The Autohaus showroom still held the 288GTO, of course, plus a new BMW and a new Alfa and sometimes a fourth car, normally another Ferrari such as a 328GTS. BMW seemed pleased that they no longer were beside Nissans but remained unhappy about our having Alfa Romeo. They couldn't have considered the Italian marque competition as it appealed to a very small group, but they still didn't like it and never missed an opportunity to say so. Ferraris they certainly didn't object to, and welcomed as an additional franchise in the facility.

Now that Nissan was in its own facility, the more accommodating showroom for BMW was just in time as they were introducing the new 7 series for 1988, which was to up the ante against Mercedes-Benz with attractive bodies and a choice of six cylinder power (still available with a standard shift) or, for the first time, a newly developed V-12 engine in a 7 series with an extended wheelbase. It was going to be both popular and potent and provide us with our best BMW sales year. Other dealers were surprised that we sold so many standard shifts, but we all liked driving them and the connection to the BMW driving experience was all the more exciting when you shifted.

As a result of new models, storage was becoming a problem, especially in winter.

New England winters could be a dealer's nightmare as snowstorms kept the cars parked outside covered with snow and the cars inside glad to be where they were. We didn't have enough space to keep the Ferrari inventory inside during the day (we parked them in the empty service department at night) so we used an offsite "annex" building which we were renting about a mile north on route 3A.

We used some of the annex building to operate our wholesale parts business, which was very busy with three delivery trucks that were always going and coming and going to body shops, other dealers and repair shops. Some deliveries were to shops north and west of Boston so that there were a lot of miles put on the vehicles, but it added to our bottom line and created a substantial cash flow which helped, especially during the winter months when accidents increased and sales slowed down.

Ferraris in the snow at Autohaus, winter 1981. The limited slip differential helped.

Members of the T&R continued to come to Autohaus to buy cars no matter how I tried to discourage them—not really but I never wanted to solicit their business. We also continued selling cars to other new car dealers that wanted either a Ferrari or a BMW, and it made us feel good that they came to us rather than to someone else in New England. I wondered how long that camaraderie would last, but the goodwill remained for years amongst the group of dealers that had started in the 1960s and 1970s as we had mostly been in on the ground floor of the imported car wave and had started with so little other than the passion for the cars themselves and the appreciation of our loyal customers. And now we were being rewarded.

In July Fritz and I went to a Ferrari meeting in New York City at Le Cirque, a well known restaurant that I had heard of but never visited. At the meeting we were introduced to Mario Clava, the new Director of Ferrari S.p.A., and had an opportunity to talk with him and ask him questions in an open forum. Most of the questions were about the F40 and how soon we would receive it, but he really couldn't answer as so much depended on the engineering aspect and how the car would be accepted by the EPA and DOT. They also announced another meeting at the factory in October and promised some surprises in store for us. We were already excited. The meal was really exceptional and for some reason the crème brûlée dessert stood out in my memory, and Le Cirque has always remained my standard for that dessert. The way Ferrari organized those events was always impressive; there was never a hitch and always they and the hosts of their choice of venue were gracious and solicitous.

The enjoyment of that meeting was followed on August 17, 1988, by sad news in a mailgram from FNA advising us of the death of Enzo Ferrari on August 14 at his home in Modena, at age 90. Everyone knew he was in poor health and very frail, but nevertheless it was a shock and a sad announcement. They added in the notice that the management, "in full agreement with Mr. Ferrari's wish, has confirmed that Ferrari S.p.A. is and will remain a totally independent company, run by independent management. The philosophy of the Company and its product will remain the same as it has been in the past. The guidance that Enzo Ferrari gave to all his men will continue to inspire their work." And they added that

Enzo Ferrari memorial photograph. August 14, 1988, was a sad day for all.

we should all should remember him as he was in life ...builder of cars that will carry his name, unmatched in quality, in performance, in image, for years to come. I think all the dealers agreed that it was the right thing to say at the right time.

And so that chapter had ended, and with it an automotive story that probably won't be repeated, for Enzo Ferrari represented not only the magnificent automobiles that wore his name, but also a way of living his life true to his passion and becoming a success at doing same. From the first time I saw that black 250 coupe, I knew that I loved these automobiles. When I was fortunate enough to be a salesman for the brand, and then a dealer too, it fulfilled a dream that culminated on the day that I met Enzo himself. And what was that dream, I asked myself—was it to be involved with Ferraris in a tangible way, by buying and selling them; was it to visit the factory and experience the thrills of driving on the world famous racetracks; or was it the meeting of and connection to the personalities that made the meetings so personal and enjoyable? I think it was a combination of all those thoughts, all intertwined, that made Autohaus and me a fitting conduit for the automobiles from Enzo through the factory to our customers, and our ability to convey that passion to them helped give owners the same appreciation for the automobiles that we had.

Those feelings were accentuated that summer as we stayed busy and I delivered a special order Testarossa to a really great customer and true Ferrari lover. We had ordered it for him in late 1986 as a 1988 model, and when it arrived it was stunning and stealthy at the same time. The exterior color was *marrone metallizzato* (dark brown metallic) with tobacco seating and with a special leather dashboard in *testa di moro* (dark brown), all in all one of the most beautiful Ferraris we had ever seen.

Ferrari customers were often lured by outside forces into thinking that they should just choose a red color, but it would be a shame to have them drive a car in a color that was not their first choice. The argument for red was based on the heritage of the cars, the *Magnum, P.I.* factor, and also the belief that red cars always were easier to sell as used cars. We certainly disagreed with that thinking. What sold a used—or pre-owned, as some like to say—Ferrari was its condition and its history; that was what buyers were most concerned with.

The 288GTO remained in our showroom except for occasional runs down the road to make sure that all was operating properly. These excursions were often made by Fritz, who would invite a preferred customer to go along for the ride. It was always interesting to see the expression on his passenger's face after even a short trip with Fritz, as it was either an expression of awe or one of terror. Well, it was one of the world's fastest, cars wasn't it?

Although it was a great showroom conversation piece, we thought it might be smart to have the 288GTO disappear from the showroom for a while—you know, absence makes the heart go fonder. But where could we transfer it to? Early in the summer I had attended a fund raiser in Boston for the Institute of Contemporary Art and met the woman who organized exhibitions, quite a responsible position. So I thought perhaps the Museum might entertain exhibiting the 288 as a work of art—which it certainly was, within the context of modern designs. I contacted the woman, who remembered me, and broached the subject. After a few seconds she responded, "We are a museum that shows fine art, and no automobile can be described as modern art." Wonder what the Guggenheim in New York City thinks about that? So the GTO kept gracing our showroom.

There was the small Art Center in Cohasset of which I was president for many years, including while they were raising money to build a new (modest) facility, and the director to whom I had told the Boston museum story suggested we could display the car in their new art center, and to accommodate a piece of sculpture of that size they would make one outside wall have two large doors through which they could drive the Ferrari. Although we never did put a car in their museum space, the doors were, and I believe still are, referred to as the "Ferrari Doors"!

It was somewhat of surprise in late August when we received notice from Dr. Anchisi, FNA President, that the plans for the October dealer meeting were still on but were being changed to a factory visit followed by a trip to Pompeii and then Positano. We were all delighted with that decision as we really wanted to be in Italy and to enjoy their hospitality and of course, the food.

In early October we went to JFK airport in New York and boarded an Alitalia flight to Milano. It was getting to be a cohesive group as we were largely the same American and Canadian dealers for the last eight years. With business going so well, everyone wanted things to stay the same, and they would for a while.

Although Fritz and Alice had been south of Naples on the east side before, I never had, and the beauty of the Amalfi coast was breathtaking. There are some places that get a real buildup in your mind and then disappoint when you actually visit them. Not so with the Amalfi drive, or with the island of Capri or the ruins of Pompeii or the majesty of Mount Vesuvius; they were all spectacular and worthy of their superlative description and eternal beauty, and we were going to visit them all.

After arriving in Milano we were shuttled to Modena for the night as the business meeting would be the next day and perhaps we would get an update on the F40. We could hardly wait. The meeting in Maranello was somewhat subdued, understandably in view of Ferrari's passing, but we carried on with visits to the assembly line and the engine testing area which was always exhilarating. I did get a chance to talk with Piero, Ferrari's son, and offered him my condolences and expressed my pride to have represented him in Boston, and he thanked me for my thoughts.

We heard pretty much the same story about the F40 and how it was going to be a while before the U.S. would give its seal of approval, so we were encouraged to think about today's product and not to tomorrow's. Easy to say but not easy to adhere to, we thought. They did tell us, however, that they were going to produce a total of 800 F40s including 180 to be sent to the States in federalized and legal form. As a comparison the total production of the 288GTO was 272 units. Seeing the car and not being able to drive it was almost too much for all of us as we had imagined going around Fiorano in it—but it wasn't going to happen, at least not on this trip. But we received all the technical information and specifications and the affirmation that the car in showroom trim would be capable of in excess of 200 mph. We wished them luck with the certification process and with the federalization—accomplishing that would be a real testimonial to Ferrari's engineering prowess.

The next day we were taken to the train station in Bologna where we boarded a special train to Naples, where we would board busses for Positano. The five-hour trip didn't seem that long as the accommodations were luxurious, including a delicious lunch.

I think my favorite part of the sightseeing on that trip was the climb up Mount Vesuvius. That volcano had been an image in my mind since I was a child, so I was excited when it was announced that if we were up for it, Dr. Anchisi would lead a not-so-difficult climb to the summit, where we could enjoy the view and look down into the caldera from which there were always wisps of smoke escaping. It was an easy ascent, passing by the ubiquitous T-shirt and souvenir kiosks and seeing an old gondola that once had brought visitors to the infrequently snow covered mountain, but at the top it was incredible as you could see the whole bay of Naples and Capri in the distance. Before descending I picked up a small rock of red pumice to place beside the grey pumice I had gathered at the top of Haleakala on Maui. It was really thrilling.

The trip ended on a bittersweet note as the passing of Enzo Ferrari had quieted the usual excitement, but the relationships between factory and dealers was highlighted by the respect we had for each other and the mutual appreciation of being associated with the most extraordinary cars.

We returned home to find that BMW had announced a replacement for the square looking 5 series. The new generation would come with two different engines, and to properly introduce the car to the American dealers they were planning a meeting in Munich later in October. When Fritz and Alice decided not to go, I invited my

Euro traveling partner, Jack, to attend as he had helped so much with unusual automotive requests.

It might seem to some that these trips were all too frequent and too much of a perk for dealers. In our case we just had three lines that gave us overseas trips, whereas some of the other dealers in the area were franchised for five or six makes, including English and Swedish brands, and therefore seemed to always be out of the country on some important meeting or mission. I guess it was all relative.

Oslo, the first stop on the way to Munich, was where I met my indefatigable traveling friend Jack. In Munich all the dealers would be picking a new 535i, all in white with black interior. It was an opportunity to purchase a new 535i, and most dealers wanted to do that so that they could (a) enjoy driving the car at top speed in Germany, and (b) have an extra allocated car to show back at their dealerships. Sounded great to us.

In Oslo we ate salmon and visited the fjords, then headed to Munich where the dealers were feted royally with a fascinating visit to the BMW factory and numerous dinners including the farewell feast at the Residence—a former royal palace. The morning after arriving, we went to the Olympic stadium—remembering the 524td rally a few years before—just across from BMW headquarters, where we saw arranged in a perfect semicircle some 100 new BMW 535is, all in white with black leather interiors and all with German export license plates. For variety there were also maybe 20 or so BMW motorcycles, also in white, arranged just in front of the

Waiting for the Olympic start. Jack, Author BMW 535i. Olympic Stadium, Munich, October 1988.

cars. What a scene! Especially when all 100 cars and the motorcycles tried to leave the stadium at the same time.

We headed to Zurich at high speed—remembering Fritz's maxim that "the faster you break the car in, the faster it will be later on"—on the now well known route going south through Bavaria and then through a little section of Austria and into Switzerland. In Zurich we met up with Fritz's brother, who happily took the 535 and arranged shipment to Boston.

I think these times in 1988 were about as good as they could get. We had an efficient and profitable business with excellent employees who were proud to be part of Autohaus, and we had four lines of cars that were in demand and well made. We had the right mix of models with neither too many nor too few of any particular make, so there were few customer problems in relation to availability. Things seemed almost too good, which was sort of a phobia I harbored, thinking that since business "couldn't be better" then it probably was going to get worse at some point. That would probably be true as the business was cyclical, being subject to the economy—read the stock market—currency fluctuations, foreign wars, etc.; but for now, at least, it was excellent.

22

Ciao, 328

What great news from Ferrari! The 1989 328GTS and GTB were now to be equipped with ABS (antilock braking system). Not long before, airbags and ABS brakes were not available on even the most expensive cars as the technology was not acknowledged or trusted by all manufacturers, but that would change soon. So the adoption of ABS was the good news, although, as with all new developments, there were two schools of thought on the merits of ABS. One group hailed the addition as another sign that Ferrari was catching up with modern times and adding a safety feature to their cars, while the old school lamented losing the driver's control over the braking system, feeling that ABS would determine for the driver how they should drive. If only that group could see automotive technology today!

A footnote to the announcement held some bad news, which was that this would most probably be the last year for the enduring Pininfarina creation that went back to the original 308GTB fiberglass coupe of 1976. Its design certainly was one of the most beautiful that ever came from Maranello and ranked up with the 250GT Lusso, at least in my mind.

It was with that information and with the knowledge of the new design that we were gleaning from spy photos that Fritz (read Alice) and I decided to purchase and keep one each of the new models. Alice wanted a *rosso corsa* (red) with beige leather GTS and I wanted a *verde scuro* (dark green of course) with tobacco (dark brown) leather seats and dashboard GTB. We ordered them with an estimated delivery time of about five months, and although it would take away from the total available cars for sale, we felt we deserved it. I had had the same color GTB as a demo from late 1988 and although I had planned on keeping that car, one of my overachieving salesmen, Jim, convinced a Lotus owner from the Cape that he couldn't pass up owning that car. It was hard to deprive a salesperson of a hard earned commission—but did it have to be on my car?

Alice's red GTS made a lot of sense as it was by far the most popular color and people reacted positively to its appearance no matter where it went, while the dark green I chose was one of the least chosen colors for Ferraris or in fact for most cars until recently. Dark green was always my favorite color—probably some British influence from the '60s that I didn't even know had touched me. Once we started our own business and were able to order new cars with color specificity, I always looked for green. The early Porsche 911 had a dark green—interestingly called Irish green—and the early Datsun 240Z had a color similar to the traditional British Racing Green.

Alice's Ferrari 328GTS in Rosso Corsa (red) with beige leather.

Ferrari sales surged on. The Testarossa was still in demand, now with a list price of $145,580, and once customers discovered that the 328 series was going out of production, the desirability factor increased for that model also. The only series that had sluggish sales was the Mondial T, the upgraded version of the series. That car packed more than just subtle design changes; there also was a substantial engine rearrangement in that the V8 was no longer placed transversely like in the 328 series, but was now longitudinal as in the 288GTO, which made the application of power more seamless and the overall feel of the car more neutral.

The rumor mill about the impending arrival of the F40 was the main Ferrari topic of conversation, reaching ridiculous heights, and to exacerbate the frenzy, FNA decided to show the car at the New York Auto Show in April—but to quell the frenzy they were going to describe the car as "for display only"! Fantastic—here's the car that you've been reading about for two years and that you really want and that you'd be willing to pay some outrageous price for—but you can't have it. What were they thinking? It was interesting to observe how few people in management of these imported car companies had actually ever been in automobile sales—probably none. Well at least we'd have something to keep the talk going as it would be another six months before the car was federalized and authorized for sale in the U.S.

Alfa Romeo was selling about the same as 1988 and Nissan too, but BMW was feeling a little pinched, especially from our "yuppie" base, as demand had softened since "Black Monday" in October of 1987. As a result of this slowdown, caused partially by the economics of the time, and partly by BMW's appointment of new dealer franchises in the Boston metropolitan area, sales dropped in 1989. It wasn't only the increase in the number of dealerships per se that impacted us, but also that the new dealerships tended to have what we then called "domestic brand merchandising"; in other words, they were heavily into discounting their products. The business was changing. Meanwhile with BMW's new models (and ignoring the downward sales trend) the factory was telling us it was all the more reason to construct a new facility, and we kept telling them that we were working on it. And we were. However, we were still stymied as to what direction to go; build on the land we already owned, or purchase land and build closer to the main north-south Route 3.

Nissan never bothered us about our facility, and what we did with the other brands was really never discussed. As long as our mechanics were up to date with their training and we had a good cross-section of models available for sale, they were fine. The new showroom helped, of course, but the monthly rent was getting more difficult to justify as the competition with other Nissan dealers, including a new one in nearby Quincy, resulted in lower profits per new car sold—it was becoming a more challenging business.

We often sold new cars to other automobile dealers for their own use—mostly Ferraris although we also sold some 7 series BMWs and even a few Datsun/Nissan 300ZX's—and once in a while we would also sell a car to a factory representative, including a Ferrari Testarossa we sold to someone from BMW. He was a frequent visitor to Autohaus, ostensibly checking up on our sales figures and making sure we had a car in the showroom, but I began to think his visitations were related more to his interest in Ferraris than maybe his regular duties, and I was right. He called me one day and ordered a black with red leather Testarossa (a beautiful combination) for delivery in December, and just before a certain price increase. We were still selling Testarossas at list price in 1988, but beginning in late 1989 Fritz and I relented to the crazy price structuring that was surrounding the entire Ferrari line and started to sell cars for more than the sticker price.

That decision really started because of an incident with a good customer from New Hampshire, to whom we had sold a 512BBi back in 1984. Being a Ferrari enthusiast, he ordered a new 1989 Testarossa, in red, that we delivered to him at his home. The Commonwealth of Massachusetts was getting suspicious of some of the very expensive cars being sold out of state—and therefore not subject to the Massachusetts sales tax—and wanted to insure that in fact the vehicles were being *actually delivered* to where the Bill of Sale stated. We of course, conformed to the letter of the law, and had several forms that we used to assure the state that we did in fact deliver the car out of state. We did know of several dealers that weren't so careful with their paperwork and had to pay sales taxes to the state even though the deliveries were in compliance.

About a week after the delivery I had a call from a man in New Hampshire who said he had just bought a new Testarossa and had a few questions about its operation. I naturally asked him where he purchased it, intending to advise him that the selling dealer should provide that information for him—although I would be happy to answer his questions. Well, he didn't buy it from a dealer at all, he said, but had just bought it from our customer, who had only had the car for one week. Whoa! What was going on here? So, I answered the gentleman's questions and even set up a service appointment for the first inspection and oil change with Fritz, and he seemed very pleased—who wouldn't be?

I called the original buyer, told him of my conversation with the new owner and asked if he had been unhappy with the Testarossa. He said, no, he wasn't unhappy at all, but he had the opportunity to make a handsome profit on his Ferrari in less than two weeks and thought he would be crazy not to sell it. Well, he wasn't the only crazy one—that's when we decided to change the pricing structure of the cars. And except for the BMW representative's purchase, all subsequent Testarossas were being sold at "market price." Had we been stupid in not selling them all along for higher prices? We still thought no.

To introduce us to the new 348TS, the replacement for the beloved 328GTS and GTB, Ferrari scheduled a meeting at the Riverside International Raceway in Riverside, California, where we would have an opportunity to see, drive and appreciate this new model on a very famous racetrack. So Fritz, Alice and I took a rare trip in the U.S. together and met up in sunny California with most of the 40 other North American Ferrari dealers to see this new car.

There it was. Certainly not an evolutionary design from the 328, the 348 looked kind of stubby and although also designed by Pininfarina, it was actually a visual disappointment. The engine, also mounted in the rear, was more powerful and had the same longitudinal setup as the new Mondial T, so it was going to be a better car, we hoped, to make up for the design setback. But the driving was what it was all about, wasn't it? So we all drove it on the track, slowly at first and then faster. At first I thought it was me having a problem with the car as it felt squirrelly, unpredictable. It had more power, but it was tough getting it to the road as the car seemed to slip and slide too easily—maybe it was the tires? Or maybe all that California sun was distorting our sensations. Other dealers had the same reaction to the handling. We were assured it was just a situation with the hot tarmac and the new tires and the suspension setup, etc., and all would be perfect when the car was released to the public. We certainly hoped so.

When we returned to Cohasset, we received the letter from Ferrari that we had been expecting, announcing that Dr. Anchisi would be leaving his position as President of FNA at the end of October. He exemplified Italian gentility and had been a perfect person to be in that post; knowledgeable, personable, easy to deal with and friendly—all that a dealer could ask for in his relationship with a factory. His replacement, Giuseppe Greco, was another person of similar qualities and we hoped the connections to FNA and Ferrari S.p.A. would continue amicably.

In fact, these last two presidents of Ferrari North America represented an end to the old ways of harmony and rapport between the manufacturer and the dealers. It was as though the era of personal feelings had been arrested starting with the death of Enzo Ferrari, and now with what would be the last two true representatives of his legacy and his affiliation with his dealer network, that era was coming to a close.

Finally in December of 1989 the factory announced with an "urgent" and exciting mailgram that the F40 had passed the U.S. EPA and DOT tests and would be available for sale here. They also announced a dinner and meeting to "celebrate this new Ferrari achievement of technological prowess," to be held in New York on December 11 and attended by two factory executives. It really was a success story considering that the F40 was a thinly disguised race car capable of exceeding 200 mph on the road. The factory's success in getting the car to pass all the (stringent) federalization tests with its outstanding performance intact was indeed incredible. Kudos to Maranello! Now we just had to wait to get one. And we would wait quite a while, but it was the perfect way to end the year.

How long until they arrived, we asked ourselves as we all couldn't wait—but we would have to as the cars were being delivered to the largest (not the oldest) dealers first. When I mention the oldest Ferrari dealers under the original ownership, that included us at place number two. The only continuously operating Ferrari dealer that preceded us was Ron Tonkin in Oregon as Chinetti Motors in Greenwich, Connecticut, was no longer a dealer, having been replaced by Miller in that town. But what did #2 get us—not much except some bragging rights, which were not really our thing, although we probably had more stories to tell at the dealer meetings and that was always fun.

In the meantime we started to get a few 348TS models, which were also very scarce, and for a short time they were selling at "market price" as the Testarossa and of course the F40 were. It was not long after the first dealer started receiving F40s that we saw advertisements offering the cars at prices exceeding $1,000,000, figures that were unheard of in the automotive world except for classic models such as the first Ferrari 250GTOs and later the 288GTOs. Whether the dealers were actually getting that much for F40s we never found out, but judging from FNA's displeasure with those ads it might have been close to seven figures.

Our other Italian line, Alfa Romeo, was threatening to bring out a new model, the 164, whose platform would be shared with Saab, Fiat and Lancia (which Fiat had purchased). What was that about, we wondered—well, it was about Fiat having also taken over Alfa from the Italian government. Having struggled financially for years, Alfa Romeo had been approached by Ford to buy it out, and after reaching a tentative agreement Alfa suddenly changed gears and was sold to Fiat instead. Shades of the Ferrari-Ford story of the 1960s, we thought. Also, distribution in the U.S. would be through a new company, ARDONA, which was a combination of Alfa and Chrysler Corporation. Interesting, as Alfa would have a national sales network through existing Chrysler dealers, if they wanted the franchise.

The 164 series was subsequently introduced to us at an event in Disney World in Orlando, Florida, at what was a very good time and where we met some of the Chrysler execs who intended to finally make Alfa a household name (it already was because of the film *The Graduate*). We also met some of the Chrysler dealers who had signed up for the franchise and who were full of questions about the reputation of Italian cars in general. They might have been successful Chrysler dealers, but dealing with Alfa Romeo was entirely different. Although they seemed a bit nervous, we generally tried to convince them that it would be a good addition to their dealership. We were concerned, however, that the delay between the 164's announcement and its actual introduction had somewhat stalled the momentum of the new model. We would see.

In the spring of 1990 we received our first 164 models, including the 164S, which

22. Ciao, 328

Alfa Romeo 164S factory brochure. This model took a while to get here.

had a different suspension than the standard sedans, plus Recaro type sport seats. With a standard shift it was a really nice car to drive—even with the front wheel drive setup. I took a black one as a demonstrator and liked it, as did the customers that had a chance to drive it, but although we were expecting great things saleswise, it was arriving one year later than it should have and was encountering the continuation of an economic downturn, meaning it was going to have a difficult time breaking into the existing sport sedan market of BMW, Audi, and even Saab. Too bad.

The summer did bring some new customers in on the new Alfa 164 series, and to highlight these new models we had a red 164S proudly displayed in our front row under our sign pole that at that time held the Ferrari, Alfa Romeo and BMW illuminated signs. It turned out to be a very unfortunate place to put the Alfa.

As I was walking through the showroom late in the morning on a clear July day, I heard the screech of tires and looked out the window to see a large, white van type truck approaching our driveway entrance in front of the showroom, kind of swaying. Suddenly it started to turn into our driveway heading for the showroom windows, and as it turned it started to tilt over. As if in a horror movie in slow motion, it continued to lean over until it fell completely on its side—and onto our front row of cars.

The few of us that had witnessed the scene ran out of the showroom to see if anyone had been hurt. Fortunately no one was, as the uninjured driver was the only person in the truck and no one on the street or in our parking area was in the way. Our proud red Alfa 164S had bravely stopped the truck from going any further and suffered the indignity of a white van loaded with ice now firmly lying on top of it. A new BMW 735iL and a 525i were also crunched. This did not look good. But better than if the truck had continued into our showroom, where it would have met the 288GTO and another Alfa 164—and us. Good grief, were we lucky or what!

The wayward ice truck that took out three cars.

The truck driver said another driver had cut him off and forced him to swerve, and as he did the load of ice shifted and caused him to lose control, resulting in the ungracious entrance into our lot. He couldn't have been more apologetic, having crushed the Alfa and the two BMWs, and was worried about his job. I guess I would have been also—but wasn't that what insurance was for? After we reported the accident to our insurance company, they quickly followed up with an inspection as did the insurer for the truck. Though it seemed like an easy situation to resolve, in fact it wasn't.

It was easy enough to get estimates on the damages of the cars—we had the 735iL towed to our master body shop in Somerville—but the problem arose with the salability of the repaired vehicles. How could you sell a $53,000 BMW as a new car for that price after it had $15,000 worth of repairs done to it? Clearly we couldn't, and so the fight began (fortunately between the insurance companies), dragging on until December, after it had gone to arbitration, when they came to an agreement and paid us as the cars were considered a total loss. I will say that over the years our relationship with our insurance companies was always more than satisfactory. We were paying the high premiums, but whenever a claim situation arose, they were quick to resolve it, and with compensation in line with other companies. No complaints there. Quite a scary moment in the life of a car dealer!

We were still looking for good used Ferraris, as just about any recent model was still very desirable. I can't remember how I learned about a 512BBi for sale in Houston, Texas, but I called the (used car) dealership and found out that it had all the DOT and EPA certifications and was in really perfect condition according to the

The heroic Alfa Romeo 164.

dealer. Well, who ever heard of a fishmonger crying "stinkin' fish for sale," went the aphorism from many years ago. So I checked with two fellow Ferrari dealers in Texas who actually knew the seller and said he was reputable—as far as they knew. That was good enough for us and so I made arrangements to fly to Houston and check the car out.

I had never been to Texas before—other than a stopover at the Dallas airport which didn't count—so I was excited to see what all the "deep in the heart" hoopla was about. It turned out to be a nice place with friendly people—at least at the Cadillac Bar—and the fellow who I had talked to on the phone was nice also, and had a Porsche 944S that he drove very well. The Ferrari was in beautiful shape and after a short drive I knew it was at least running on all 12 cylinders. The body seemed unblemished and so we made a deal, and I arranged to have it shipped to Cohasset. The only glitch was with the paperwork. Oh, the federal papers were OK, but the car itself had originally been sold in Mexico and had a Mexican title. Was there even an authorized Ferrari dealer in Mexico? We had dealt with many cars with European titles and certificates of origin, but this was the first Mexican one, so I was, let's say, hesitant to part with some $40,000-plus and not have a valid title. After some telephone calls to FNA we were able to find out that all was on the up and up, and so we bought the 512—which had previously been owned by the Mexican distributor of a very well known soft drink—and had it trucked to Autohaus.

It didn't last two weeks in our inventory as one of our newer salesmen already had someone lined up for just such a car that could be bought for less than a new 328 or Mondial. Were there any more around? We of course did trade Ferraris from time to time, mostly on newer models, although there was a Mondial Cabriolet that belonged to a man from Maine who wanted to buy a 300ZX turbo and had visited a number of Nissan dealers who were scared to death of the Ferrari. So he came down to see us—which he hadn't done when he bought the Mondial—and agreed on terms for the trade. We didn't have the Mondial for more than a week when a customer looking for a used 308 saw this and bought it instead. That was a difficult lesson to teach salespeople. A customer can tell us that he only wants this model in that color with that equipment, but if you show them something close that's been well cared for and suits their parameters, you very well may see them drive away in it. So much of sales was presentation, both with the vehicle itself and with the salesperson too.

Ferrari had advised us in the spring that they would have their biennial dealer meeting in Italy, so we were all warmed up about that. It would be in the beginning of September, so we hoped we might have our first F40 by that time though we doubted it, as just a few cars were trickling into dealers. The meeting would coincide with the Grand Prix of Italy, which this year would be held at Monza, and that was going to be a memorable trip.

The Grand Prix trip began as we flew into Milano and went from there by coach to Stresa on Lago Maggiore. The factory had scheduled a boat trip to the Borromeo Isole, but we were running late and could only see the islands from the boat without actually visiting them. We were really disappointed as the gardens on Isola Bella were famous for their design and uniqueness.

Instead we returned to a magnificent hotel on the shore of the lake, where we would have lunch. Next was Florence, where we were to attend the opening of a new exposition titled "L'Idea Ferrari." This show assembled some of Ferrari and Pininfarina's most sensational and exquisite designs inside plexiglass cubes and situated in the Parco Valentino, overlooking the city of Florence. Ferrari had a cocktail party there for the dealers, many factory executives and also the editors of the book *L'Idea Ferrari*.

The next day we traveled to the factory for our annual meeting, which really centered on the F40 and the question of how soon we should expect them, and also the new 348 series which was not receiving the attention that the factory thought it should. We were introduced to Luca Montezemolo, who would be the new president of Ferrari S.p.A. We had met him briefly in 1975 at Watkins Glen when he was the racing team manager; after varying roles at Fiat he was now in Maranello. The meeting also introduced a number of new programs—there must be a high powered consulting company involved, we thought—including customer satisfaction surveys, new facility guidelines with new signage, technician recognition levels, etc., etc. Well, new management often brings new ideas, many of which are just that, ideas, but we would go along with what they proposed as long as they kept on producing cars that we could sell in the States.

A new model that we got to see and drive was the Mondial T with the heralded Valeo clutchless transmission. This was really still a manual shift arrangement; what was different was there was no clutch pedal. By touching the gearshift lever, an electrical relay would disengage the clutch and the driver could shift to the next gear, either higher or lower, or into reverse, proper speed being the limiting factor. It was

Monza, Italy, September 9th, 1990.

All of us at Ferrari would like to welcome you to Monza and the Italian Grand Prix.

Today is the first day of what promises to be a very exciting week for all of us. We will have the unique opportunity to experience L'Idea Ferrari and get a first hand look at how the "myth" began.

Again, welcome to Monza and let's cheer the Ferrari Formula 1 Racing Team on to Victory.

Giuseppe Greco

L'Idea Ferrari welcoming program to Ferrari dealers, Monza, Italy, September 1990.

not at all difficult to operate, but you still had to shift if you wanted acceleration (or you could leave it in high gear and accelerate from a dead stop, but very slowly). That's what drivers of automatic cars didn't want to do: shift.

It was hard to believe that Ferrari was going for such a transmission, which in varying forms had been a disaster for so many other manufacturers including Mercedes, Saab, VW and even Porsche with their Sportomatic. I guess they thought they could widen their market appeal by saying they had some sort of automatic transmission, and that's what it was—"some sort of automatic transmission." When I asked the chief engineer why they were going halfway with this transmission rather than a full automatic like what had been available in the 400 and 412, he said that the V8 cars were not designed with an automatic in mind, so this was the only possible automatic transmission to put in the cars. It really felt just like the Porsche Sportomatic, and while some of the dealers said they could sell some, most of us saw it for what it was—a half hearted measure. But disregarding the Valeo aspect of the Mondial T, the car was exciting to drive and once again we were circling Fiorano. I realized I was becoming familiar with its turns and nuances—maybe I had a Formula One career in my future!

Following up the day at Fiorano we were going to the Italian Grand Prix at Monza. Fritz, Alice and I were all excited as Ferrari might have a chance at winning this, and if they did the whole country would go wild. Wasn't it wild enough? Ferrari's number one driver was Alain Prost and number two was Nigel Mansell, and they would be up against Senna in his very fast McLaren Honda. It was quite a race to watch as we had many vantage points across from the pits where we could see the teams doing their mechanical ballet as they switched tires on the cars and filled them with petrol in what seemed like a split second. Ferrari also had a VIP tent set up in an area behind the pits (an area that was hard to get to as it was a long walk around the track) where they had refreshments and light food along with TVs on which to watch the race if you didn't want to be part of the throbbing and yelling crowd. We ended up watching the end from the grandstands opposite the finish line where Senna won just six seconds ahead of a speeding Prost.

It was a big disappointment for (most) everyone there as we all thought that Prost would make a heroic effort on the last couple of laps to get into first, but it didn't happen. It was similar to other 1990 Formula One races with one-two finishes, and at the end of the season they were in the same sequence: Senna won the driver's title and Prost came in second, and that was just the same as the manufacturers' finish; McLaren-Honda in first and Scuderia Ferrari in second.

As exciting as the race was, we hadn't seen anything yet as we were about to experience the exodus of thousands of unhappy fans from the Autodrome at Monza. There seemed to be no exit organization—they needed some Disney World help—as everyone was wandering toward some exit that we couldn't see. Maybe we were the only ones that didn't know their way around but I doubted that, so we kind of headed to where we thought our coaches had parked. It was so crowded that you had to kind of go with the flow. We had heard about the possibility of pickpockets—a common enough problem in Italy—but with the crushing of everyone together it meant you

Ferrari F40 looking unbelievable outside Autohaus showroom, 1991.

22. Ciao, 328

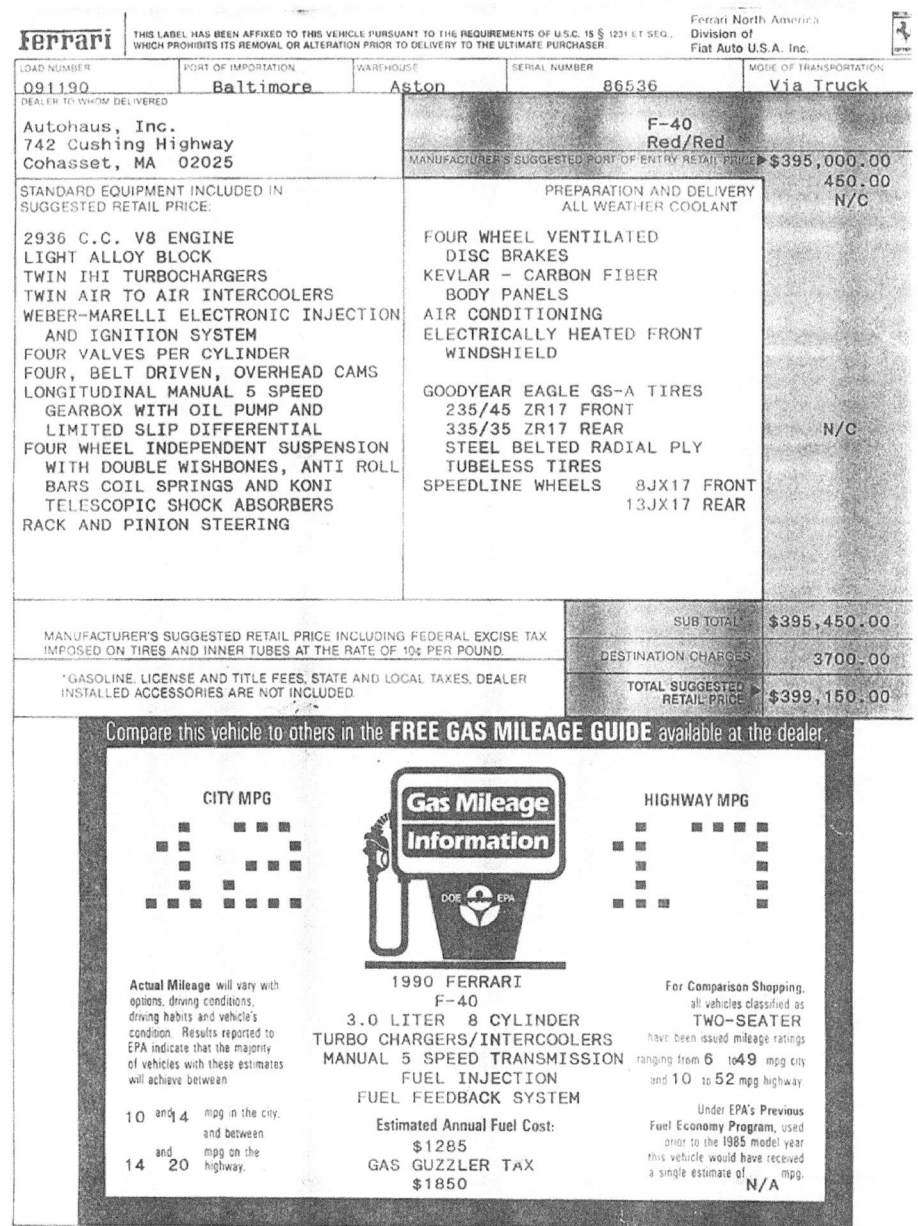

Ferrari F40 window sticker: $399,150, and no extras on this model.

had to hold on to your wallet all the time. At least one dealer lost his wallet but fortunately not his passport. Where was Ferrari? Fortunately they were waiting for us at the coaches, which we finally found, and they apologized for the lack of communication. At least we were unscathed, but for some also a little poorer. It really had been an unforgettable event.

Just as unforgettable was the phone call I received the week after returning from Italy advising us that our F40 was going to be delivered the first week in October.

Hoorah!! We had decided not to sell the car right away, instead waiting for a while to show it to the many people who had expressed an interest in seeing (and driving) it. Ferraris were now arriving in enclosed trucks, often with no signage on the exterior, so they could have been transporting refrigerators or building supplies; all very anonymous. When ours arrived it was quickly surrounded by admiring—and drooling—employees and some customers, and of course Fritz and I, who surveyed the car's physical condition.

We found a few little paint chips and scratches and one small crack in a marker light, but otherwise it was all there and ready to go. So let's go, we said, and with me in the driver's seat and Fritz beside me we took off—figuratively—down Route 3A, followed by so many admiring eyes. The sound, the sight, the seats—everything was superlative, and did it go or what. It was a racier race car than the 288GTO in just about every respect and it certainly looked racier too— now we had to see if its 200 mph plus top speed was attainable. Just kidding…but maybe later?

This Ferrari was a total sensation. As many as we had seen and driven, this was the car that we wanted to drive around Fiorano and push as much as we dared. But we were in Cohasset, not Italy, so we had to make do with what we could get away with, and Fritz was much better at that than I.

I remember one time Fritz was delivering a customer's 365GTB/4 Daytona to his house on the Cape when he was stopped by a state trooper on Route 3 just south of the Plymouth exit. Fritz pulled over and got out to speak with the trooper, and in no time Fritz had the hood open on the car showing the trooper the magnificent V12 engine with its six carburetors all neatly lined up in a row. What with his knowledge of the mechanics and his Swiss accent, Fritz left the trooper hardly any chance to write that ticket, and after some fifteen minutes talking about cars the trooper let him go and told Fritz if there was anything he could do for him or Autohaus, just let him know. With that Fritz said well, there was one thing—could he please radio ahead to any other troopers that might be on Route 3 and tell them that Fritz was heading south and just "road testing" the Daytona. The trooper laughed and said, "OK just be careful."

With all the interest in the F40 from old customers and potential new ones, we decided to keep the car through the winter—unless someone was willing to pay our price—in the showroom beside the 288GTO. It was certainly one of the most impressive automobile showroom scenes ever.

So that's the way we ended 1990. As impressive as our display was, the general trend of business was slowing down, and although Ferrari sales were still strong we could sense a downturn heading for that prestigious line also. BMW sales were also decreasing, but the factory's demand for a new facility would reach a head in 1991.

23

The Blue Prince

THE STREAM OF INTEREST IN THE F40 remained constant, although as of January 1991 we had received no offers on the car, which we were now offering for sale. Granted, we were asking well above the sticker price of $399,150 and maybe that was wishful thinking, but with sales activity in all the lines decreasing, we thought that maximizing profit on any vehicle should be the objective. The factory was enticing potential buyers with additional incentives by inviting the original purchaser of an F40 to visit the factory and be fitted for a custom designed seat that would then be installed in their own F40. The invitation included "business class" travel for two, hotel accommodations, and transportation within Italy for the F40 owner and spouse or guest, plus a visit and tour of the factory and (weather permitting) a demonstration of the F40's potential in the hands of a Ferrari S.p.A. test driver. Why weren't the dealers given these perks—we were buying the cars from FNA, didn't that count? It didn't, of course, but we fantasized about driving the F40 around Fiorano—maybe the next dealer meeting?

In March, we got our wish and sold our first F40. Although we didn't come near the price we were hoping for, it was a clear offer and one we accepted. The buyer never even drove the F40 but simply wired us the money and sent an enclosed van to pick it up and carry it away, never to be seen again by us.

This was a problem—philosophically, I mean—that now we weren't even meeting some of the buyers as they were not so much enthusiasts as investors, much like our customer from New Hampshire who resold his Testarossa after just a week. If the business was changing in this manner, we didn't like it. Granted, we could make a profit on these transactions, but the lack of interaction with the customers themselves made the experience less satisfying. Was this what we were in the business for? Ferrari buyers were becoming less involved in the actual purchase experience, and that went for the other lines as well. Often leasing companies called us for prices and availability on BMW models and Nissans as well, and of course it was the same with individual buyers as the phone was becoming more the method of purchase rather than the face-to-face experience.

Our BMW sales, in fact, were slowing down more than in the previous two years as the recession that had started in 1990 continued. Spending was decreasing and financial institutions were getting more difficult to deal with as the Gulf War and resulting spike in oil prices complicated what was a very slow recovery. The effects of Black Monday of 1987 were still being felt. As if to magnify the situation, it was at this

F40 and 288GTO in the showroom. Enough said.

time in early April that we received a letter from BMW demanding that we erect a new facility or give up the franchise. The timing could not have been worse.

We had suspected that eventually it would come to this, but we had no intention of giving up without a fight. Our protests were unsuccessful so by September BMW was no longer selling us cars or parts and we were no longer able to service cars under warranty—even ones we had sold—or provide factory authorized service. We had many connections in BMW over the years, but our reasonings went unheeded and so we realized that it was going to be life without BMW, at least under the umbrella of the factory.

We continued to sell new cars that we purchased from sympathetic dealers, mostly to our old customer base, but this eventually stopped as the factory was warning other dealers not to sell us cars, even though they all could use additional sales any way they could get them. Fritz and I were upset but realized we just had to soldier on with the other three lines, which would have to make do. We wondered what would have happened to us had we built that new million dollar plus facility with decreasing sales and profit. We might not have been in business at all for very long. Our service business continued very strong in all the lines; in the ideal dealership the profitability of the service and parts departments should be able to cover all the expenses of the dealership and the sales department should provide the net profit. Hopefully this would be the case with our new situation—and it was, in the short term at least.

The service department lived up to its reputation by increasing activity with the

Ferrari F40 and BMW M6. I had just come back from a test drive in the F40 in a jacket and tie!

addition of a new assistant service manager to help Fritz with the daily operation and to oversee directly the technicians, who now numbered eight in our very busy shop. It was a great addition, enabling Fritz to spend more time assisting the technicians with ever more complex problems with engines and transmissions. I went along with Fritz's lead and hired a sales manager to help with the day to day requirements of assessing trade-ins and interaction with the sales force. We were both reluctant to have these assistants as our history of being directly involved with most of our customers was what we both so enjoyed about the business.

The general economic decline plus the loss of the BMW franchise contributed to a poor year and the loss of several longtime sales people who had families to feed and needed to keep in the BMW loop. We actually lost some technicians too, and although we were unhappy about that I never felt that employees leaving for good reason should be considered disloyalty; after all we had done a similar thing in 1966. Granted, we had spent a great deal of money and time training them, but in return we had the reward of their skills and satisfied customers as a result of those combined efforts. Fritz, Alice and I didn't necessarily agree on the impact of these losses but there was little we could do to stop them, so we just accepted reality and looked for replacements, which was never an easy task.

We sold a few 348TS models, including a yellow one that looked very good and of course the red with tan and red with black combinations that always sold well, but keeping with our tradition of ordering unusual colors we received in the late spring a light blue metallic (*metallizzato azzuro*) 348TS with dark blue leather seats and blue dashboard. The sales staff didn't like it too much—knowing that it would be more difficult to sell than red or black—but this meant that they would have to test their skills even more and not just sit back and take a phone order for the cars.

It was just that scenario that unfolded in May as one of our new salesmen came into my office saying that he had just received a telephone inquiry about what Ferrari spyder we might have available to see, and when he mentioned the blue metallic, the caller said he would be down the next day. When I asked his name, as expected the salesman had not made note of it, being too excited over having a potential customer in what could be his first Ferrari sale. He was sure, however, that he had given the caller his name and that if he came down as promised, he would certainly ask for him.

The next day two young men arrived in a Jeep Wrangler and asked for Robert, who brought them over to the blue 348 that was on the showroom floor. I decided to go out and help, if I could, and while Bob was showing the car to the taller youth I was talking to his friend who told me that the interested party was a student at Northeastern University and having just arrived in the U.S. from the Middle East he needed a car—a Ferrari? That was only part of the story, as not only was this new student a resident of the Middle East but he was also a member of the royal family in his country; in fact he was a prince of the family. He loved the car—and the color—and said that it would be paid for by a wire transfer from a relative in Washington.

A few days later I had a call from the country's embassy in Washington and was connected to this student's uncle, who wanted to make sure that we were treating him fairly. I assured him that we were. I suspect that he had already researched us as he sounded satisfied that his nephew was being handled properly, and the following day full payment for the Ferrari arrived at our bank. It turned out that the friend who had driven him to Cohasset was actually along to protect the prince and had enrolled at NU to keep tabs on him at all times. Quite an arrangement, we thought. They were both very nice and after we arranged for registration, insurance and plates they picked up the car with very little fanfare, driving away in short order as they were late for a class. Ah, the student life.

A few weeks later the prince arrived back at Autohaus for the Ferrari's first service, and this time his friend was not driving the Wrangler but rather a new Mercedes-Benz SL in the same color as the Ferrari. He said the prince had just bought it as he needed another car for bad weather. Made sense to us.

In June FNA advised us of a replacement for the Testarossa, tentatively named the 512TR, which would carry some mechanical and cosmetic changes and be available early next year. Sales of the existing Testarossa were still OK but the inquiries about availability were decreasing, and the prices we heard through the dealer network were decreasing all the time. We hoped the new 512 release would excite the public again, but we would have to wait until 1992. We also received word that our second F40 was in the pipeline, and with that information we were happy that we had sold our first one back in March. We certainly didn't want two F40s in our inventory—and neither did our bank.

Although the F40 was in high demand and the Testarossas still could be sold, the Mondial T and the 348 were not creating the usual demand for Ferrari cars that we were so accustomed to. Some of the dealers wanted to set up a dealer council such as existed with other makes, but it seemed unnecessary to me and to others. The organizer of the council idea was a western dealer who outlined in a letter that there was indeed a crisis in our business and that more communication was needed between dealers and FNA and by extension, the factory. Well, they were right about a crisis but I had never experienced a lack of communication with Ferrari over the years; in fact they were the one manufacturer who would always talk with you and would remember who you were when you either spoke with them or met with them, so why confuse things with a dealer council? Plus the National Sales Manager, Hugh Steward, was a man of his word and could be trusted to give us all the relevant information that he could.

Ferrari 512TR factory brochure. Modest changes to the Testarossa resulted in this model.

FNA followed up with a letter that they were against adding another layer of communication between the dealers and Ferrari, and the matter seemed to disappear after all the dealers received the letter. Fine with me.

Interestingly, Ferrari seemed to be the only manufacturer that was directly addressing the slowdown in sales. The others acknowledged it by incentive discounts and other means but never really said that things were poor.

The second F40 arrived soon after FNA notified us that it was coming, and we were not the only ones happy with that news. One of our very best customers who had already bought three Ferraris from us had expressed keen interest in the car and was excited when we told him that we had a second one coming. Of course he wanted to drive the F40 before buying and arrived with his wife to try it out. We had no issue with certain trusted customers driving alone without one of us accompanying them. They were special in that they not only were passionate about Ferraris, but had a respect for the machines that made them appreciate them as much as we did, and we never questioned the care they would give to the cars; and so it was with this customer. So we watched as the couple went down Route 3A while cars around them

Ferrari F40 awaiting delivery. A perfect day to drive away, summer 1991.

pulled over to the side of the road as if an ambulance were coming by; it was amazing. They returned from the test drive all smiles and said they would love to have it.

Fritz had the F40 in perfect shape as it left for its new home a few days later, but shortly thereafter the customer called Fritz and said the car didn't seem fast enough. Fritz asked him to bring it back, and after testing it himself, Fritz agreed that it seem slower than he remembered. After checking with Ferrari he was told that there was an electronic glitch that sometimes occurred and how to remedy the problem. When the customer returned and drove the repaired car with Fritz, you could see the smile on both their faces. Problem corrected!

We were pleased with the Ferrari story but unhappy about the rest of the business slowdown, as were all the dealers we spoke with. Our wholesale parts business was also slowing down, and now that BMW would not sell us parts directly, we had to purchase new parts from accommodating dealers, with a decrease in our profit margin which was small enough. We decided to keep that part of the business but it didn't look promising when we calculated three delivery vehicles on the road and six employees in that department. Something was going to have to change.

So we decided to offer the 288GTO for sale. Although Fritz had wanted to keep that car forever, we both recognized that at some point we would have to sell it to realize some cash from that minimal investment back in 1985. We tried a few ads in the New York papers and some financial papers as well, but there was no response at all. What was going on with this car market? Most of the other Ferrari dealers had sold their GTOs a long time ago and were surprised that we still had ours and thought it was a good idea to sell it—who knew what next year's market might look like. It wasn't unlike the art market in that the demand and subsequent value were highly volatile at this time, so after getting no response from our ads we took the advice of another dealer and put the car in an international automobile auction in Indiana.

We had the GTO shipped to the auction house by our reliable transporter, Ralph Smith, but after some lively bidding the amount did not come near our reserve, so back to Autohaus came the 288—it did not want to leave us.

Maybe the F40's appearance had reduced the appeal of the 288, we began to speculate. But that proved untrue as we soon had an interested party from the North Shore of Boston who came down to see, not drive, the car. He seemed very interested but as he explained, he would have to rearrange his assets before he could discuss the price. I said we could wait for him to do that.

It was a tough year and just as I thought it couldn't be worse, old Bully died and it was sorrowful to me. His ashes were buried out in the lawn the next spring under the roots of a fruit tree that I planted; I hope it's still flowering.

I still drove the green 328GTB occasionally while Alice drove her red GTS more frequently. In the summer I kept the car in Marshfield, but with the dirt road and the occasional flooding of the road it was not the best environment for the car—or any car for that matter—so it mostly stayed in the showroom near the 288GTO—quite a nice pair!

As the year ended a letter from Luca Montezemolo, the new president of Ferrari S.p.A., announced a dealer meeting in Maranello early in 1992 to discuss the future of Ferrari products and business commitments. It was a meeting that all dealers looked forward to, including us.

January started with a positive phone call from the North Shore doctor who had expressed interest in the 288GTO. He visited us the second week of the year and wanted to talk about buying the car and at what price. He actually was interested in buying not only the GTO but also a 512 Boxer in our used car inventory, so we talked and talked and finally he decided on just the GTO, for which he would pay $575,000; he would give us a deposit of $25,000 and take delivery in the summer after rearranging his financing. There were parts of the arrangement that were agreeable to us, and other parts that weren't, such as waiting until summer for payment of the car.

As I've said before, if there's one thing that's a certainty in the automobile business, it is the second buyer syndrome. As soon as you have a buyer for a car that has been in your inventory much too long, you suddenly have a second buyer—and if you're not careful you end up with no buyer at all. We didn't want that to happen with the GTO. So after receiving another inquiry about the car from a person in California, we advised our buyer that he would have to agree to forfeit his deposit if he couldn't complete the transaction within the time agreed to in the purchase contract, unless he could provide us with additional surety. It was always interesting to me that an agreement to purchase a half million dollar vehicle could be written up on a single sheet of paper with a couple of signatures, while if you were buying a house for a similar price there would be all sorts of paperwork and side agreements, attorneys, etc., etc.

The buyer agreed to give us two deeds to property he owned out west to hold

Ferrari F40 ad from the Boston Open Squash Tournament program, February 1991.

until he could convert them into cash. After reluctantly involving an attorney, we settled on the time of delivery and the details of the transaction. Whew! Was this finally going to happen?

At about the same time Ferrari finally introduced the Testarossa replacement, the 512TR (a slightly modified and renamed Testarossa) at the Los Angeles Auto Show. Although the people out west got to see the new car, we still had no idea when we might see one—in fact we weren't really sure we wanted to see one, what with sales so slow. Maybe the meeting in Italy in February would bring information on sales promotions.

There was one car that really needed some promotion, and that was our white with white leather 1990 Mondial Cabriolet. This car had a tortured history beginning with the original special order for the car by one of our customers who had purchased a new 308GTS a few years before. He enjoyed the 308 and had traded it in 1988 for a white with white leather interior 328GTS which he also liked, but he really wanted a truer convertible. So when the Mondial Cabriolet came out, it piqued his interest and after a year or so he decided to order one, in the special combination of white with white. He actually had considered a Mondial coupe when they first arrived in 1982, but didn't like the way the car drove and bought the 308 instead.

Our customer had a very particular sense of color, and since it was what he

Ferrari 288GTO press release photograph.

wanted we agreed to order a Mondial Cabriolet for him after many discussions about how it would look, how long it would take to get, etc. About six months later the car arrived—and he hated it. Not the car itself, but just the look of it as the white leather did not seem to him the same as what he had seen on the leather samples and the combination with the white exterior just didn't match his vision. Actually, we all sort of agreed with him—the car just didn't look right. But since he wasn't going to take it, we'd have to find another buyer. That took a long time and the eventual buyer was not who we would have ever expected.

The car sat around for over a year with almost no one expressing interest. Since it was a convertible it was always inside, mostly in the showroom, where although being weather protected, it began to look "shopworn" with little nicks in the paint, little scuffs on the leather, etc. We were beginning to wonder what to do when an old Ferrari customer came in—he had purchased a 308 and also a Testarossa—and liked the look of the white exterior but not the white leather (we had expected that comment). He asked if we could change the interior to black leather, an idea we hadn't really considered. Here was a possible end to this white saga, we thought, and asked Ferrari if we could change the color and not void the warranty. They said it might be possible and incidentally the fading of the white leather might actually be covered under the new car warranty that wasn't even in effect yet. So after a lengthy discussion FNA they agreed to pay for new leather seating in black, which was great—and very accommodating of them. We ordered the new interior and after a surprisingly

Ferrari Mondial Cabriolet.

short wait received the black seating and had our best upholstery shop install them while keeping the white seats, which we sent back to FNA.

The car looked fantastic, just as it should have when new, so we called the customer to advise him that the project was finished. And guess what—he had changed his mind and was no longer interested in the car. Ouch! This car just wasn't going to leave. But then, just as in an overly long novel, there was a surprising twist in the story. We received a letter from FNA saying that they were aware we had a new two-year-old vehicle in our inventory and wanted to repurchase it from us—at a slightly lower price than what we had paid for it—just to get it out of our inventory. We never did find out what prompted them to do this, nor did we really try—we were just grateful to accept their offer and finally say goodbye to what I guess could be accurately called a "white elephant."

24

Mugello

AMIDST OUR ANXIETY ABOUT SALES, we hoped the trip to Maranello would offer something helpful for the slow U.S. market—or were we being summoned to help Ferrari? We would soon find out at this earlier than expected dealer meeting. It wasn't to be a traditional dealer meeting with spouses or guests invited, so it was decided that I would attend alone, and Fritz and Alice would stay home in Cohasset.

Just before I left, we received a letter from FNA concerning the "Advertising of Price," which surprised me and other dealers I spoke with. In fact, one of the things dealers—or factories for that matter—were *not* supposed to discuss was price. Yes, we could talk about MSRP (manufacturer's suggested retail price), but we couldn't discuss what discounted (or inflated) price we actually might be selling the vehicles for, as that would be considered price fixing, a definite no-no. The letter acknowledged the downturn in the economy—thanks for that—and objected to some dealers advertising what Ferrari termed "distressed prices," which they said was "counterproductive to the theme of advertising" used by the company over the past ten years. We agreed with that thinking as Ferrari buyers could purchase their car anywhere as they were so mobile and we were selling the product, not the price. They concluded by saying that they weren't trying to limit the final sale price, however, just the manner of advertising it. With that we also concurred.

We then received the agenda for the meeting in Italy and were advised that it was going to be a short four-day trip where we would get to talk business and racing with the new president of Ferrari, Montezemolo. It would be interesting to see how he compared with the past presidents, almost all of whom were very cordial and approachable. We were also going to visit the new Ferrari owned racing circuit of Mugello, which originally was a road racing course around Florence and the Tuscan countryside but was now a closed circuit owned by Scuderia Ferrari. As was always the case, this meeting did not disappoint.

We arrived at Maranello and had a short introduction to the newest group of Italian executives of the company (without Montezemolo), and that evening we socialized amongst ourselves and Ferrari personnel. I also met two Italians that were not with Ferrari but had been invited to join us for the next few days including the factory visit and the trip to Mugello. They were nice fellows with good English—I had pretty much given up with my Italian lessons at that point—but they were vague about why they were attending other than obviously knowing Montezemolo well enough to be here.

Ferrari's Mugello Circuit aerial view, from a factory brochure. Wringing out the revised 348TS on this course was challenging with the changes in elevation.

The next morning we went from our hotel to the factory where we were to congregate to take the bus to Mugello. I and two others had misread the itinerary and missed the bus so we called a taxi and caught up with the bus just as it was entering the race circuit. Great taxi drivers, those Italians. On the ride there we talked about things Ferrari and things Italian, but the two Italians still wouldn't say anything more as to why they were there. I didn't push the issue but it became clear they were more than just friends of Ferrari and Montezemolo. I guessed that we would find out at some point.

The track facility was absolutely beautiful; everything seemed brand new and state of the art. We were given a tour of everything from the control tower to the restrooms and all seemed spotless and unused. It was clear that Ferrari (and Fiat?) had spent a lot to make this a showcase and to impress not only us and other Ferrari dealers around the world, but racing fans and drivers as well. We could see just how serious they were in convincing us of their continuing investments in product advancements and testing.

There were a number of new cars in the pit area, and we were told that we were going to drive the 348s around the track after a lesson with one of the factory's test drivers, which we were all very eager to do. There were probably around 40 people there so it took a while for everyone to get their turn, which left me time to reminisce about my test drives on various tracks with different drivers, including my favorite drive with Piero Lardi many years before. When my turn came up I was introduced to Dario Benuzzi, the factory's top test driver, who spoke no English. The language of driving was international so I wasn't concerned, but I guess the question was—was he concerned?

We started out with him at the wheel, driving the 348 like an extension of himself—just what I hoped to accomplish. After a couple of turns around the track it was my turn. I was familiar with the 348 and its quirkiness, but this car had been revised and reengineered and its improvements were one of the reasons for this meeting. We dealers were not very excited about the car as originally presented, and if the dealers weren't excited, then their staffs were not excited and it followed that there wouldn't be much enthusiasm projected to potential customers, and there was the problem. So this car had to be better—and it was. But I was still having a difficult time becoming a grand prix driver, as I showed on my second time around when I lost it and almost did a 360 on an uphill curve to the right where I failed to listen to Dario's screaming—*freni, freni, freni!* or brakes, brakes, brakes! After I straightened things out I tried that turn again and made a much better job of it—and that was the part of my driving experience that I was going to remember. Everyone agreed that the revised 348 was a better car and now we all would see if those improvements enhanced its reputation and sales.

After a lot of driving and a lot of stories we had a beautiful lunch—with wine of course—and then went back to the hotel to get ready for a dinner meeting to be held at a well known restaurant in Bologna often frequented by Enzo Ferrari and many, many drivers. It was really a race driver's (and racing enthusiast's) restaurant, with pictures and posters adorning the walls, many of them signed by famous Formula 1 competitors.

Montezemolo chaired the meeting and talked about the future of Ferrari, their products and their plans for the dealer network. It was all very interesting but it was still under the economic umbrella of dismal sales and struggling products, and while he could give us hope with products he of course could not reassure us about the economy. He told us that a new model replacing the 412 series would debut at the fall Paris Auto Show, code named the F116 (marketed as the 456GT), and it would be designed for the U.S. market—at last. He said there would be a coupe initially and then a cabriolet the following year; we would see about that. This was our—at least

Ferrari 456GT factory brochure. In 1992 the 456 replaced the 412, whose basic design had existed since 1972.

most of the dealers'—first exposure to Montezemolo and he was definitely in charge of Ferrari, although his style was quite different in speaking and interaction with his audience. It would take a while to know how he effectively he would lead.

It was a pleasant enough meeting, the meal was exceptional, and Bologna lived up to its reputation as having the best food in Italy (aside from the Fini) in my opinion. Of the two Italians who were guests and somewhat anonymous, one had a last name that sounded familiar and in fact was the name of a well known international pasta company, Buitoni—what was this all about, I wondered. We would find out soon enough. So it was a short meeting with no lavish side trips—even Ferrari was economizing—but it introduced the dealers to the new regime, showed us the latest testing circuit, and gave us some optimism for the factory's determination to include the U.S. market in all their new products.

After the meeting I had arranged to meet my Euro travel friend Jack in Rome, where he was on a short vacation from business in Milano. I decided to rent a car and drive to Rome from Modena as it had been a while since I was behind the wheel of a car on the autostrada, having mostly been just a passenger on a huge autobus with my colleagues most of the time—except for test driving on Ferrari's tracks. So I decided to try out a Lancia Thema, their version of an Alfa 164 (also Saab 9000 and Fiat Croma) and I found one at a local Hertz dealer. At the same time one of my fellow dealers from Canada said he would love to accompany me as he had friends in Rome that he wanted to visit and could share the driving with me. OK, I said gladl,y as it could be a tiring trip and I didn't mind being a passenger for once in a high speed vehicle.

At dinner that last night in Modena, one of the other dealers came over and asked if it was true that I was driving to Rome with our Canadian colleague Ron, and I said yes, to which he replied, "What, are you crazy, Guarino? Have you ever driven with him?" I had not, but I was sure that I had seen him driving around the various tracks and he certainly seemed to know how to handle a car—and a Ferrari at that. My friend said that I hadn't been paying attention as he was known as the wildest of all the dealers behind the wheel of a car and it was craziness to bring him along for the ride. I thought that it was all a lot of hyperbole as I liked the guy and his quasi British love of cars and their handling capabilities, so I ignored his admonition and those of a few other dealers as well.

The next morning Ron and I got a cab to the Hertz dealer (an Agip gas station in the center of Modena) to pick up our Lancia, which was one of the rare V8 models that had a detuned Ferrari engine; this was going to be one hell of a drive. As an aside I always tried to gas up at Agip stations ever since my first trip to Italy while visiting my Uncle Chester in Milano who loved their high test brand of gasoline named *Supercortemaggiore*—it just had the beauty of long Italian words. I signed the papers and got in the car with Ron after stowing our luggage in the sizeable trunk, and turned the ignition key only to find that the car wouldn't start. What? This wasn't a very good beginning to our 200 mile plus journey, so I went and got a mechanic in the station who quickly diagnosed the problem as electrical and went under the hood to make a few adjustments, after which it started right up. Could he come with us? we asked.

24. Mugello

So off we went—talk about torque steer—with me driving and zoomed onto the autostrada, heading for Rome as fast as the Lancia could go, which wasn't very fast as there was a lot of traffic. We still could hog the left lane, and that we did. After about 30 minutes Ron asked if he could drive as he was interested in how this front wheel drive Ferrari-powered sedan would handle. I said sure and we switched sides at a restaurant stop, buckled up and headed back out, with voices in my head reminding me that he was crazy behind the wheel. Well, he definitely drove fast, but no faster and no crazier than myself; in fact he was a damn good driver. I began to think that all these warnings I got from other dealers were just an admission that they couldn't (or wouldn't) drive like him (or me). It felt really good to be a passenger in a relatively fast car on the autostrada, and after a while we switched back so that I could be at the wheel as we entered Rome. Ron was meeting up with some friends also, although he didn't know when they would be arriving, so as we got closer to the center he said I could let him off as soon as we saw a taxi stand, of which there were plenty. We crested a hill and there in front of us was a roadblock with a female policeman holding up her hand for us to stop, and as we approached her Ron said, "I'll get out here" and, grabbing his bag, virtually leapt out of the Lancia. What the heck was that about?

The policewoman must have seen him leaving, but as I pulled up beside her she just asked for my papers—and the Lancia's documents—and never mentioned my missing passenger. My Italian got me by and I took in enough information to understand that all main roads into the city were blocked so all traffic had to stop; it was just an occasional and normal police action and nothing to worry about, she said. OK, I said, and went off to find the Forum hotel that was adjacent to the Forum. Jack was already there. After I dropped my gear in my room we headed right for the bar, where I ordered a Cardinale. We'd see if this was a first class hotel or not. It was.

After too short a time in Rome I was back at Autohaus, where I found out that our GTO customer had provided all the documentation that was needed to go ahead with his purchase. Although it was still going to be a while before the purchase was finalized, we had good reason to believe that this sale was going to take place after all.

In April 1992 we received notice that FNA was going to have a new president, replacing G. Greco, and it was going to be none other than Gian Luigi Buitoni, the somewhat secretive Italian that I had met in February in Maranello. His friend would become a new dealer in Canada. Now we knew what it was all about—he was being given an introduction, although somewhat quietly, to the dealer network and to the operation of Ferrari S.p.A., and now was being awarded the post of leading FNA, not an easy job.

Meanwhile our local financing bank for Ferrari and Alfas (our Nissans were financed by Nissan's credit division) was beginning to signal that with the economic slowdown and the ever increasing costs of the cars, maybe we should begin to look for another lending institution—easier said than done. We were their only dealer that had cars priced above $30,000 or so (way above, and I often wondered how their board meetings were reacting to our request for financing cars that cost us over $300,000). So we began a search for a different bank or credit company but soon realized that it was going to take a long time to find someone, if we could at all.

And then the day came. We heard from our GTO customer that all the funds were available to him—and to us—and that he wanted to have the car delivered to his house on the North Shore as soon as we could arrange it. He wired the payment to our bank and we arranged a mutually agreeable time for delivery although we were not driving it up; no way. The last thing I needed was another incident like the one that had happened to me on the Southeast Expressway—there was not going to be a repeat of that catastrophe, I promised myself. So Fritz got the car in perfect running order, took it for its last test drive down Route 3A, and returned quickly to the waiting ramp truck that was going to take it north.

The driver was Ralph Smith, owner of the truck transport service that we had been using for some 20 years and in whom we had complete trust. I was going along with him, riding shotgun so to speak, and after loading the GTO onto his truck, away we went for my last ride with this incredible Ferrari. It had been almost seven years since first seeing the car in Maranello and it still thrilled me every time I walked by it in the showroom or, on rare occasions, drove it.

The new buyer was truly appreciative of what he was purchasing, as we could see in his face as we pulled into his driveway of his surprisingly modest home. We completed the paperwork in his kitchen, and after a brief overview of the car's operation he was ready to put it in his garage beside his Bentley. All the time his wife, who was very pleasant, could not be convinced to come out and look at the Ferrari. Staying out of that conversation, I said goodbye to both of them and got in the truck to head back to Autohaus and the empty spot in our showroom.

Now what?

At least we had a good financial cushion to help ride out this recession—but when were things going to improve? Needing to cut our costs, we decided to give up the Nissan showroom and put all the brands back into our one showroom—if Nissan would agree. And they did.

Ferrari continued with new ideas to generate sales, and in August announced their first ever sales contest for the period of August 1 to December 31. The prize (they were awarding four, to the eastern U.S., western U.S., Canada and the fourth to small volume dealers—maybe us) was a four-day trip Italy in June of 1993 with a visit to the factory and driving at Fiorano. That should work, we thought. But would it?

Later that month we received our first "Dealer Performance Report" for the one-year period July 1, 1991, to June 30, 1992, which was calculated with 14 customer survey returns. It was similar to what we had seen from other manufacturer surveys, and once again our service facility exceeded the national average by earning 100 percent satisfaction, and the sales department performance came close to that. One area where the sales department didn't meet the national average was in the category "introduction to service manager," which was a real surprise as Fritz always wanted to meet everyone. Maybe they had taken delivery when he was not at the dealership and they were disappointed by that. In any case we felt very good about the report.

We had discovered over the years, primarily through word of mouth, that many of our high profile customers preferred the intimacy of our dealership where most knew their name. So many of the newer dealerships were so large, almost resembling the "big box" stores of today, and had such high employee turnover that customers coming back for service or to buy another car very likely would not be able to find the contact that they had made just a few months before. We too suffered some attrition this year, as two of our longtime employees left—probably because they realized that without BMW their incomes might suffer, and they had families to support and their own future to think about. Those departures left a void in the dealership that we hoped we could fill, but it would prove difficult.

We showed the satisfaction report to our bank in an effort to keep them interested, but by the end of the year they advised us that they would no longer be able to give us a line of credit for any new vehicle purchases (although they would continue the credit line for vehicles we had already bought).

This was a big problem as the dealer agreements with Alfa Romeo and Ferrari required a dealership to have a line of credit to purchase vehicles at all times; we could not just buy cars for cash, although Ferrari allowed us to do that as we were looking for another source of credit. Lines of credit were becoming increasingly difficult to obtain, and we realized that 1993 would not be an easy year.

One of our best Ferrari customers at some point sensed that we were in some sort of financial bottleneck (he was a successful businessman and probably adept at recognizing the signs) and approached us about providing the necessary financial backing for us to have a line of credit. Fritz and I discussed his offer and thought it might be a good idea, but felt that first we had to exhaust conventional credit lines. The customer said he understood and would wait for the outcome.

In December Ferrari had a dealer meeting in New Jersey where I was able to speak with Buitoni and the Sales Director, Hugh Steward, and related to them our problem. They were sympathetic (especially Hugh) and promised to give us time to try to find another credit line, but not an infinite amount of time—and that was what we might need.

At the same meeting FNA announced the creation of a new 348tb model, the 348 Serie Speciale, with some cosmetic differences from the standard 348 and some mechanical modifications including Pirelli P Zero tires and a free flow exhaust system which should improve performance a bit. They also announced the replacement for the 412, the 456GT of which we had heard earlier, which looked much meatier and was a genuine 2 + 2. Anything to help sales was greatly appreciated, although at the same time there was the inevitable price increase, which was modest—but why do it? At least we had something new to talk about, and that was a good thing.

As 1992 ended we looked back on all things Ferrari and reflected on the extraordinary level of knowledge and connection to the factory and people associated with it that we had experienced. And the dealer trips—would they continue? And if so, could they ever be as inclusive and exciting? Who could know?

Epilogue

THE NEXT FOUR YEARS WERE BITTERSWEET. As a result of the outside pressures on financial institutions it proved impossible to arrange a line of credit for Ferrari, and the difficult realization came that we had to discontinue our relationship with FNA and also Ferrari S.p.A. But what a ride it had been!

A few years later Alfa Romeo withdrew from the American market, although we were still able to service their automobiles under warranty so as not to dishearten their customers.

So by 1997 we were a Nissan only dealer, and after much negotiation and internal discussion we decided to sell the dealership and to pursue other interests.

We sometimes wondered if it would be possible for young people starting off in business today to create a business model as we had with such a modest investment.

With my traveling partner Jack and my 328GTB on Cape Cod, 1996.

Autohaus pen and ink drawing.

Perhaps not, but with the passion to become involved with what you love to do there is always that possibility.

For our employees, the new owners were retaining the existing staff who wanted to remain—and for our long-term employees, retirement benefits that had been accruing would be transferred to them. Some would be pleasantly surprised to see what their loyalty was to provide them with—and they deserved it.

At the end we still had the Ferrari 328s. Alice was to keep the red spyder, and after some cajoling by Fritz I sold him the green coupe as I really had no place to store it and he thought it would be nice to have the pair. I agreed.

Fritz and Alice were going to get a long overdue retirement as now they could travel as they wished or just relax. For myself, I would be doing some writing, which had been in the back of my mind for many years.

Some twenty years later I still have friends and acquaintances asking me about automobiles, such as what I think about such and such model and whether a price they might pay for a car is a fair one, etc. I just recently had a call from a good friend who was traveling in Italy with his wife and had rented an Alfa Romeo to drive around in. He was inquiring as to why I thought the model he was driving had a six speed gearbox and I replied, "probably because 5 speeds would be too few, and 7 speeds would be too many." Made sense to me.

I guess I'll always think like an Italian.

Index

Numbers followed by an asterisk (*) indicate pages with photos

Adamonis, John 255
Aerosmith 145, 148
AGIP 292
Alboreto, Michele 249, 350*
Alfa Romeo 29, 85, 99, 137, 139*, 145, 166, 167, 174, 176, 186, 211, 220, 224, 230, 243, 244*, 255, 259, 267, 270, 295–297; **164** 270, 271, 273*, 292; **164S** 270, 271*; **2000** 42; **2000 Berlina** 138, 139*; **2000 GTV** 138, 139*; **2000 Spider Veloce** 139*; **2600** 42, 75; **Alfetta GT** 138; **Alfetta Sports Sedan** 138; **Giulia** 42; **Giulietta** 8*, 30, 40, 42; **GTV** 164, 186; **GTV6** 186, 187*, 211, 220, 243, 244; **Milano** 231, 242, 243*, 244, 250; **Montreal** 180, 181; **Sprint Speciale** 42, 48
Alfa Romeo Distributors of North America (ARDONA) 270
Algar Enterprises 111, 154
Amerispec 165, 248
Anchisi, Emilio 249, 262, 263, 269
Andrey, Gaston 57, 201, 220, 221*
Arese 242, 243
Arnoux, Rene 202*
ASA 1000 96*
Aston Martin 16, 30, 49; **AMV8 Volante** 200; **DB4** 43, 48, 51* (*see also* Aston Martin Shooting Brake); **DB4GT** 43, 50; **DB5** 43; **DB6** 50; **James Bond** 43; **Shooting Brake** 43 (*see also* Aston Martin DB4)
Athens 121, 122
Audi 80–83, 271
Austin Healey 13, 14, 47
Auto Engineering (A/E) 29, 30–45, 47, 49*, 51*, 55*, 57, 61, 63, 66, 67, 71, 72, 80, 102, 115, 116, 128, 153, 157, 158, 25
Autocross 15, 69, 70, 217
Autoshow 22, 25, 72, 84, 85, 92, 117, 126, 128, 133, 141*, 146*, 147*, 168*, 181, 182, 184, 210, 211, 250, 267, 286, 291

Baggenstoss, Ruedi 73, 152
Balocco 220, 242, 244*

Barrow, Dave 77
Bavaria (state) 213, 214, 265
Bentley 63, 75*, 294
Benuzzi, Dario 290
Berlin 19, 20*, 21, 209
Bertone 129, 132, 133, 187
Biagi, Elaine 9, 10, 11
Black Monday 259, 267, 279
BMW 42, 45, 65, 72, 76, 80, 86, 88, 89, 93, 99, 108, 117, 121, 151, 152, 166, 168, 176, 183, 184, 199, 212, 220, 230, 244, 245, 255, 256, 269, 268, 272, 278, 280, 281; **3 series** 144, 220; 3.**0CS** 123*, 151; **3.0Si** 251; **5 Series** 144, 185, 212, 263; **7 Series** 144, 220, 245, 259, 268; **320i** 169; **320iS** 169; **325e** 207, 220; **507** 42*; **524td** 212, 220, 232, 264; **525i** 271; **528e** 207; **533i** 212, 220; **535i** 264*; **630CSi** 144, 150–152, 157, 166, 177; **633CSi** 166; **635CSi** 244; **735iL** 271, 272; **1600** 65, 71, 114; **2000 CS** 64, 65; **2000 TISA** 65; **2002** 79, 106, 112, 144, 184; **2002Tii** 114, 129; **2500** 87, 99; **2800** 99; **2800 CS** 151; **318i** 220; **Bavaria** 99, 144; **K1000** 259; **M6** 244, 281*; **R100RS** 156
Bond, James 43
Bondurant, Bob 192
Borgward 6, 63
Boston 7, 8, 9, 16, 17, 23, 26, 28, 36, 51, 55, 59, 79, 89, 128, 154, 206
Boston Globe 79, 81*, 131*, 141, 194*, 218*
Boston Herald 72*, 77*, 79
Boston Magazine 253
Brazil 171, 172*
Bristol 18
Bugatti 179
Buick 86, 272
Buitoni, Gian Luigi 292, 293, 295
Burke, T. 69

Cadillac 38, 55, 56, 79, 212, 216, 217, 245
Caldwell, Sarah 41, 128
Canadian Grand Prix 173, 174*
Carrera Panamericana 193

Celli, Vinny 17*
Chalk Airlines 211
Charles Pozzi S.A. 191
Chase, Lanny 111, 112
Cher 129, 246*, 247*
Chinetti, Coco 71, 98
Chinetti, Luigi 85, 98, 244
Chinetti-Garthwaite 111, 145, 148, 149, 168, 170*, 172
Chinetti Motors 37, 84, 165, 194, 270
Chrysler 6, 25, 200, 270
Citroen 69, 115, 206
Class 197
Clava, Mario 260
Comacchio 23, 151, 154, 155*
Concorde 193, 201
Corvette 14, 21, 38, 40, 43, 75, 145, 249
Crusoe, Jack 29, 30, 32, 35–38, 40, 41, 44, 47, 50, 80, 128
Cusack, John 233
Cyr, Richard 249, 256

Daimler 18
Datsun 56, 64, 65, 77, 80, 84, 85, 89, 99, 105, 106*, 108, 114, 117, 130, 144, 166, 167, 176, 178, 184, 185, 211*, 212, 232, 240Z 85, 86*, 105, 106, 114, 234, 266; **260Z** 145, 169; **280Z** 145, 169; **280ZX** 169, 185; **300ZX** 232; **411** 59; **810** 184; **810 Maxima** 184; **1200 coupe** 114; **Patrol** 64, 70; **Pickup truck** 72; *see also* Nissan
Daugherty, Jimmy 61
DePalma, Jack 156, 197, 245
Department of Transportation (DOT) 250, 260, 269, 272
Dermanian, Serge 146*, 147, 168*, 211
De Tomaso 206
Detroit Grand Prix 249, 250
di Montezemolo, Luca Cordero 142*, 143, 274, 285, 286, 289, 291, 292
Display Data 189
DKW 56
Donahue, Liz 128

299

Index

Eastern Airlines 161–163
Edwards, Bob 35
England 86, 158, 206, 235
Enviromental Protection Agency (EPA) 165, 196, 250, 260, 269, 272

Facel Vega 25
federalization 161, 165*, 173, 196, 198, 240, 250, 263, 270
Ferrari, Alfredo (Dino) 109, 157
Ferrari, Enzo 71, 85, 109, 110, 138, 149, 195, 205, 222, 224, 226, 228, 244, 257, 261*, 263, 269, 291
Ferrari, Piero Lardi 201, 202, 250, 263, 290
Ferrari models: **126 C2B** 202*; **166 Barchetta** 107; **250 California spider** 23, 25*; **250 GT 2+2** 54* (*see also* 250 GTE); **250 GT Berlinetta** 224; **250 GT Berlinetta lusso** 30, 35–37, 85, 130, 140, 141, 196, 207, 266; **250 GT Cabriolet** 38; **250 GT Coupe** 3*, 4, 36; **250 GTE** 31, 36, 37; **250 GTO** 231*, 232, 237; **250 LM** 25; **275 GTB** 72, 126, 138, 154, 199; **275 GTB4** 68, 71, 168*, 211; **275 GTS** 37, 38, 185, 186*; **288 GTO** 215, 224, 231, 235–237*, 239, 249, 250, 259, 262, 263, 267, 271, 278, 280*, 284, 285, 287*; **308 GT4** 114, 131, 132*, 133*, 137, 141*, 142. 145, 147, 161, 166, 171, 173, 182, 182, 187, 231, 259 (*see also* Dino 308GT4); **308 GTB** 145, 146*, 148*, 150, 153, 158, 161, 166, 168, 173, 215, 217, 224, 266; **308 GTBi** 177*, 180*; **308 GTS** 55, 153, 166, 169, 171, 179, 181, 197, 200, 215, 233, 286; **308 GTSi** 177, 181, 188*, 189. 215, 216, 222; **312 B3** 143*; **312 T3** 171*; **328 GTB** 240, 253, 285, 296*; **328 GTS** 240, 259, 266, 267*, 269, 286; **330 America** 36, 37, 51, 68; **330 GT** 51, 54*, 59, 60, 65, 67, 68, 86, 103, 158; **330 GTC** 68; **330 GTS** 68, 71, 135; **335 S** 146*, 147, 211, 220; **340 Mexico** 64: **348** 259, 269, 274, 282, 291; **348 Serie Speciale** 295; **348 TB** 295; **348 TS** 269, 270, 281, 290; **365 BB** 129, 149; **365 California** 68, 115; **365 GT 2+2** 85, 86, 91, 92 (automatic 89, 91, 97*, 115, 175); **365 GT4 BB** 150 (*see also* 365 BB); **365 GTB4** 85, 92, 109, 112*, 113*, 116, 118*, 119, 120, 138, 145, 278 (*see also* Ferrari Daytona); **365 GTC4** 115, 116*, 117, 118*, 123, 126, 129, 133, 135, 136, 138, 140*, 168, 173, 197, 198, 200; **365 GTS4** 110, 129, 179, 183 (*see also* Ferrari Daytona); **365 P** 96; **400** 149, 275; **400 GT** *see* Ferrari 400, Ferrari 400i; **400i** 183, 188, 189, 191, 192, 194, 195*, 196–198, 199*, 200, 201, 208, 209*, 220, 240; **412** 275, 291, 295; **456 GT** 291*, 295; **500 TRC** 220; **512 BB** 149, 158, 161. 162*, 165*, 285; **512 BBi** 191, 196, 197, 198*, 216, 220, 222–234, 268, 272 (*see also* Ferrari Boxer); **512 TR** 282, 283*, 286; **Boxer** 129. 141, 149–160, 161, 162, 164–66, 181, 191, 197, 200, 222 (*see also* 365 BB; BB; Ferrari 512 BBi); **Daytona** 98, 99, 115, 117, 119, 123, 126*, 129, 133, 138, 140, 145, 165, 173, 180, 181, 183, 207, 238 (*see also* Ferrari 365 GTB4; Ferrari 365 GTS4); **Dino** 98, 99, 110, 112–117, 121, 123, 126–129, 133, 135, 136, 145, 165, 173; *see also* Ferrari Dino 246 GTS; **Dino 246 GT** 88, 109*, 110*, 111*, 116, 130*, 131*; **Dino 246 GTS** 130*, 133, 135, 145, 222, 231 (*see also* Ferrari Dino); **Dino 308GT4** 132*, 133* (*see also* 308GT4); **F 40** 249, 250, 257, 260, 263, 267, 269, 270, 274, 276*, 277*, 278, 279, 280*, 281*, 282, 283, 284*, 285, 286*; **F1/86** 250*; **Mondial** 183*, 188, 192*, 201, 202, 205, 215, 220, 244, 247, 248*, 268*, 273, 288; **Mondial 8** 182, 187, 192* (*see also* Ferrari Mondial); **Mondial T Cabriolet** 267, 269, 274, 275, 282, 287; **Testarossa** 222, 223*, 224, 225, 229, 231–235, 240, 248, 261, 268–270, 279, 282, 283, 286, 287
Ferrari North America (FNA) 173, 184, 212, 215, 240, 249, 250, 261, 262, 267, 269, 273, 279, 282, 283, 287, 288, 289, 293, 295, 296
Ferrari S.p.A. 191, 260, 261, 269, 274, 279, 285, 293, 296
Fia t 153, 242, 243, 270, 274, 290
Fiorano 201, 202, 263, 275, 278, 279, 294
Fioravanti, Leonardo 114, 145, 207
Floor Plan 59, 184
Ford 6, 16, 17, 30, 51, 66, 71, 93, 206, 212
Ford, Henry II 71
Foreign Engine Company 255
Foreign Motors 255
Formula 1 Grand Prix 93, 94, 142, 143, 171*, 173–175, 186, 249, 250*, 274, 275
France 25, 92, 101, 102, 177, 191, 194, 216, 227, 228, 232, 249
SS *France* 99
Frankfurt 22, 212
Frankfurt Auto Show 212, 257
Fritz, Dick 84, 85, 96, 98, 110, 165, 239
Fullerton, Ken 30, 31, 33, 36, 38, 40, 47, 48, 50, 51, 52*, 53, 57, 80, 255

Garthwaite, Al 111
Gaston Andrey Motors 8
Germany 6, 17, 19, 81, 82, 101, 176, 177, 178, 235, 264
Goldoni, Emilio 235–238
Gopen, Larry 13, 217–219
Gray, Pres 64
Greco, Giuseppe 269, 273, 275
Greene, Al 35
Greenwich, Conn. 37, 96, 110, 166, 270
Grimaldi, Frank 49, 50*
Guarino, Dick 28, 29*, 82*
Guarino, Doug 9*, 82*, 129, 135
Guarino, Gerry 82*, 121, 122*, 124*, 129, 169
Guarino, Jim 6, 8*, 10*, 11, 16, 17, 22, 26, 27, 28, 47, 135, 136* 169
Guertin, Don 255

Hangsen, Walt 30, 41
Hansen, Lindy 31, 32, 33, 47, 51, 56, 58–60, 63, 65, 68, 80, 81, 88
Harrah, Bill 107, 108*
Harriet 18
Harvard Magazine 126*, 253
Hawaii 169, 188*, 189, 233
Heidelberg 6, 22, 27
Higgins, George 238
Hoffman, Max 14, 39, 42, 64, 99, 144
Hoffman Motors 144, 152
Hollywood 197, 233, 247, 248
Hynes Memorial Auditorium 84, 117, 133, 182*

Ibarra, Madame 191, 194, 198
Ickx, Jackie 93
Imola 223*, 224, 228, 234
Imported Cars of Worcester 255
interest rates 184–186
Italian Grand Prix 174; *see also* Monza
Italy 9, 23, 89, 90, 92, 99, 113, 114, 121, 138, 149, 153, 155*, 158, 168, 173, 178, 194, 201, 205, 206, 221, 222, 224, 226, 232, 240, 242–252, 257, 259, 262, 274, 275*, 277–279, 286, 289, 292, 297

Jaguar 29, 38–40, 144, 158; **3.8S** 51, 53; **C Type** 40, 179; **D Type** 30, 41; **E Type** 41 (*see also* Jaguar XKE); **MK IX** 41, 42; **MK VIII** 41, 42; **MK X** 50, 51; **XK120** 7, 13, 14, 41, 49, 50*; **XK140** 13, 40; **XK150** 41; **XKE** 33, 35, 40, 41, 50, 51, 53, 54, 71, 75, 153, 158
Jarama Circuit 93, 94*
Jenner, Bruce 147
Jones, Alan 174, 175

Katayama, Yutaka 106*
Kay, Chuck 111, 112, 116, 212
Kelley, Pauline 222, 228
Kennedy, John F. 11, 27

Lada 21
Lamborghini 75, 205, 206; **350GT** 178; **Countach** 206; **Jalpa** 206;

Index

Jarama 168, 206; **LM** 206;
Miura 109, 206
Lancia 40, 41, 128, 138, 270, 292, 293
Land Rover 72
Larz Anderson Museum of Transportation 131, 132*, 133*, 209*, 259
Lauda, Niki 142*, 143*
leasing 169, 186, 279
Le Mans 68, 71, 85
Leonard, Jack 168, 177, 212–214, 235, 236, 237, 245, 264*, 292, 293, 296*
L'Idea Ferrari 274, 275*
Lime Rock Track 16, 17*, 30, 48, 75, 76, 144
Lincoln 11, 38, 112, 206, 212
Lloyd, Dick 47–51, 53, 57
Loring 79, 171
Lotus 78, 266
Lowe, Rob 197
Luigi Chinetti Motors 37, 84, 85, 92, 96, 165, 194, 270

SS *Maasdam* 18, 19*, 26, 27
MacPhee, John 21, 33
Magnum, P.I. 188*, 189, 266
Mansell, Nigel 275
Maranello 68, 87*, 89, 91, 92, 98, 99, 104*, 113, 127, 138, 149, 150, 153, 197–210, 224, 225*, 226*, 235*, 237, 238, 240, 249, 257, 263, 270, 274, 285, 289
Maratona 220
Marchal 127
Maserati 29, 30, 43, 75, 92, 205, 206; **3500GT** 88*, 128; **5000GT** 43; **A6G2000** 43; **Birdcage** 57; **BiTurbo** 206; **Bora** 206; **Ghibli** 129; **Kyalami** 206; **Merak** 206; **Mexico** 206; **Mistral** 51; **Sebring** 43
McLaren Honda 276
McNaughton, Bill 28
Mercedes Benz 1, 6, 8, 11, 12*, 17, 29, 30, 31, 39, 40, 50, 51, 55–57, 61, 63, 65, 92, 99, 144, 152, 195, 199, 212, 259, 282; **190D** 38; **190SL** 38; **220** 6, 7*, 21, 35, 38, 60, 245; **220SE** 30; **230SL** 22, 37, 38, 46, 47, 48*, 54, 105; **250** 51; **280 SL** 75; **300** 38, 42, 157; **300SL Gullwing** 22, 32, 33, 34*, 193; **300SL roadster** 35, 38, 52*, 53, 75; **600** 39, 245
MG 10*, 11, 13, 14, 16, 17*, 64
Michaels, Karl 35
Milano (city) 23, 91, 138, 169, 242, 262, 263, 274, 292
Milton, Mass. 10, 15, 18, 27, 42, 44, 47, 72, 82*, 157
Mix, Tom 255
Modern Classic Motors 111, 149, 168
Monaco 23, 173, 242
Mondello, Guido 255
Monroney Label 250

Monte Carlo 242
Monteverdi 175, 208
Montreal (city) 147, 173, 175*
Monza 173, 274, 275*, 276
Moore, Demi 233
Morgan 135, 136*
Muelhaupt, Alice 57, 61, 63, 66*, 73*, 88*, 89, 99, 103, 124, 133, 134, 142, 159, 162, 178, 202, 220, 224, 244, 248*, 266, 281, 285, 297
Muelhaupt, Fritz 35, 40, 55–57, 59, 61–63, 65, 66*, 68, 71, 73, 80–82, 89, 99, 113, 119, 130, 131, 136, 138, 159, 160, 165, 167*, 176, 180, 199–201, 211, 221*, 222, 239, 243, 254, 255, 262, 275, 278, 281, 284, 297
Munich 88, 99, 121, 122, 152, 163, 164, 177, 212, 213
Murphy, Dick 157, 158, 235

Nassau 26*, 211
National Highway Traffic Safety Administration (NHTSA) 165, 176, 196
National Maximum Speed Law (NMSL) 176
Nicholson, Eddy 200
Nicholson, Jack 246*. 247*
Nickerson, Linda 89, 211
Nissan 184, 211*, 212, 230, 250, 253, 255, 259, 267, 268, 274, 294, 296*; **300ZX** 268, 274; **Maxima** 185
Nissan Motor Corporation 106, 184
Northeastern University (NU) 7, 8, 13, 15, 41, 217, 282

Oktoberfest 212, 213, 215
Oldsmobile 28, 29*, 207, 212
One Crazy Summer 233
OPEC 126
Opera Company of Boston 41, 128, 148*
Orange, Mass. 69*, 70
Orient Express 226, 227*, 228
Overseas Delivery 38, 76, 89, 113, 129, 145, 151, 152

Panhard 6
Peggy 18, 26
Peter Fuller Cadillac Oldsmobile 55
Pinin 207
Pininfarina 114, 133, 145, 187
Piper Cherokee 135, 137, 193
Pirelli 10, 292
Pittsburgh 196, 197, 198, 200, 216
Porsche 30, 31, 32, 35, 39*, 40, 43, 44*, 48, 51, 54–57, 60*, 64, 65, 71, 72, 73*, 75, 77*, 80, 81*, 83, 88, 89, 99, 103, 123, 129, 144, 147, 249, 275; **356** 22, 25, 50, 51, 54, 70; **356A** 35, 44, 47*; **356B** 44*; **356C** 39*, 40, 43, 54, 79*, 187; **356SC** 187; **901** 22, 25, 40, 46; **904GTS** 40; **911** 25, 40, 46, 50,

52*, 54, 59, 60, 69*, 70, 73*, 75, 92, 238, 266 (Sportomatic 75, 76, 79, 144, 275); **911L** 75, 79; **911S** 75, 79; **911T** 79; **912** 48, 49, 51, 59, 65, 75, 79, 83; **924** 138; **1500** 15, 22, 35, 39, 44; **Carrera** 17, 39, 40, 49; **Speedster** 13, 14–29, 35, 44, 78, 217; **Speedster Replica** 179*; **Targa** 60, 73*, 75, 76*, 123, 206
Porsche Cars Northeast 47, 56, 79, 80
Porsche Club of America 43, 69
Port Newark 161, 162, 164, 165, 191
Posey, Sam 144
price list 77, 78*, 87*, 100*, 104*, 115*
Prost, Alain 275, 276

SS *Queen Elizabeth II* 155, 156, 157* 235
Quincy Patriot Ledger 60*, 64*, 101*

SS *Rafaello* 89, 93
Rapallo 23, 24*, 92
Reitshamer, Paul 35, 40, 46, 51, 52*
Remick, Ray 85, 96, 98
Reutemann, Carlos 171*
Riggs, Dave 109*, 269
Riley 18
Ristorante Cavallino 224, 225*
Riverside Raceway 192*, 269
robots 243
Rodrigues, Gary 173, 184
Rodriguez, Ray 221
Rolls-Royce 66, 67, 86
Rome 9, 23, 121, 158–160, 191, 201, 207, 292, 293
SS *Rotterdam* 26, 27

St. Onge, Roland 179, 181, 248, 249
St. Tropez 23, 92
Scheckter, Jody 173, 174
Shanahan, Jack 17, 18, 19*, 24, 26
Sigma Phi Alpha 11
Smith, Ralph 285, 294
South Shore (region), Mass. 55, 57, 62–64, 66, 103, 167, 168, 246, 256
South Shore News 62*, 110*, 196*
South Shore Nissan 255*
Spanish Grand Prix 93; *see also* Jarama Circuit
Spiech, John 184, 212
Sports Car Club of America (SCCA) 16, 40, 50, 144
Spring, Fred 158, 159*, 178, 197, 200, 256
Squazzini, Claudio 212, 226
Steingold, Charlie 67, 68, 75
Steward, Hugh 225, 283, 295
Stone, Carl 18, 19*, 20*, 24
Studebaker-Packard 39, 46
Stuttgart 21, 22, 24, 25
Sunbeam 6
Supercortemaggiore 292

Swartz, Fred 13, 17, 18, 19*, 20*, 24*, 26, 27, 156
Switzerland 23, 57, 62, 73, 82, 89, 90, 114, 130, 152, 161, 176, 200, 226, 228, 249, 265

Tambay, Patrick 202*
Tatra 21
Tennis & Racquet Club (T&R) 221, 240, 260
Thames, Mac 251
Theriault, Jim 111, 112, 123, 124, 127, 133, 134, 161, 163, 182, 200, 209*, 212, 233, 256, 266
thermal reactor 173
Thompson, Jonathan 182
Thompson Raceway 16, 30, 48, 49

Torino 92, 99, 121, 122*
Trans-Atlantic Motors 255
Triumph 13, 14
Turney, Bob 111

United States Grand Prix (Watkins Glen) 142*, 143*, 171*, 174, 274
Ustinov, Peter 16

Valeo 274, 275
vehicle identification number (VIN) 178
Venice 154, 201, 226, 238
Vespa 8, 9*, 10, 11
Villeneuve, Gilles 173, 175
Volkswagen 18, 21*, 28, 31, 32, 40, 43, 99, 172*

Volvo 11, 14, 29, 30, 36, 42, 55, 56
Von Kuenheim, Eberhard 297

Wartburg 21
Weinberger, John 217
Williams, Stan 11, 13, 15, 16, 17*, 18, 24, 27, 49, 54, 55
Williams F1 Team 174
The Witches of Eastwick 246*, 247*
Worcester Polytechnic Institute 7, 11, 13

Zurich 23, 73, 89, 90, 99, 100, 113, 151, 152, 159, 160, 177, 191, 198, 265

www.ingramcontent.com/pod-product-compliance
Lightning Source LLC
Chambersburg PA
CBHW060336010526
44117CB00017B/2845